Android™
Programming

Pushing the Limits

Erik Hellman

WILEY

Dedication

This book is dedicated to my amazing dad, Ingemar Hellman, who taught me programming when I was nine years old. None of this would have been possible if it weren't for all the amazing things he taught me.

Erik Hellman,
Second generation software developer

Publisher's Acknowledgements

Some of the people who helped bring this book to market include the following:

Editorial and Production

VP Consumer and Technology Publishing Director: Michelle Leete
Associate Director–Book Content Management: Martin Tribe
Associate Publisher: Chris Webb
Project Editor: M. Faunette Johnston
Copy Editor: Melba Hopper
Technical Editor: Erik Westenius
Editorial Manager: Jodi Jensen
Senior Project Editor: Sara Shlaer
Editorial Assistant: Annie Sullivan

Marketing

Associate Marketing Director: Louise Breinholt
Marketing Manager: Lorna Mein
Senior Marketing Executive: Kate Parrett
Marketing Assistant: Polly Thomas

Composition Services

Compositor: Jennifer Goldsmith, Andrea Hornberger
Proofreader: Wordsmith Editorial
Indexer: Potomac Indexing, LLC

About the Author

Erik Hellman grew up in the small town of Borlänge in the middle of Sweden and currently lives in the city of Malmö with his wife. From an early age he showed a great interest in all kinds of technology, much thanks to his father. This interest has carried on over the years and he likes to spend time tinkering with all kinds of technology, be it hardware or software.

Erik currently works as a developer consultant at Factor10. He previously worked for Sony Mobile as one of the lead architects for their Android development and later as a research engineer where he participated in the development of the next generation of mobile solutions from Sony.

Erik has a lifetime of experience with software development and programming. His father taught him how to write code in Turbo Pascal at the age of nine, as well as how to design relational databases in Oracle 3 on his old IBM AT 286. Much later, Erik studied Software Engineering at Blekinge Institute of Technology where he also worked as an assistant teacher in various software engineering courses.

Erik can often be found at various developer conferences where he likes to speak about cutting-edge software technologies. You can also find out more about Erik and his other hobbies at his blog (http://blog.hellsoft.se) or follow him on Google+ (http://gplus.to/ErikHellman) or Facebook (https://www.facebook.com/ErikHellman).

Acknowledgements

First of all, I'd like to thank my wife Kaisa-Leena. Without her love, support, and infinite patience with me during the writing of this book, this book would never have been finished.

A big thank you goes out to all my friends and former colleagues at Sony Mobile. Almost everything I've learned about Android and mobile technologies came from my years working with all of you. I'm extremely proud to have been part of the team that built the Xperia series of devices. A special thank you to my former boss, Henrik Bengtsson, and his team at the Sony Mobile Research in Lund.

Finally, I'd like to thank my editors; Faunette, Melba, Erik, and all the people working at Wiley for helping me write this book. A big thanks goes to my technical editor Erik Westenius for his eye for details and making sure that my code and examples are understandable. Also, a thank you to Kristoffer Åberg at Sony Mobile for giving me valuable input on the UI design sections.

Contents

Introduction

If you're reading this book, you're probably familiar with the Android platform, smartphones, and application development. You're well aware of the tremendous growth of Android devices over the last few years and the potential that the platform holds for application developers. I could give you specific numbers and statistics about Android, but that wouldn't serve much purpose because those numbers most likely would be invalid by the time you read this book. It's enough to say that the Android platform is here to stay, and you can expect its growth to continue for the foreseeable future.

All of this is great news to people like you and me. Those of us who are aiming to becoming experts at Android development face a bright future. The demand *for* skilled application developers for Android is growing every day, and at the same time, the demand *on* developers is growing because the features that users want and the possibilities provided by the new technologies require us to constantly think ahead.

Although Google provides a great set of tools and APIs to help you perform your magic, you still need to push yourself on what you can now do with Android. That is the goal of this book: to push the limits of the Android platform and build ever more advanced applications.

Who This Book Is For

You've probably written a few Android applications already and are eager to learn more advanced APIs and tricks. Perhaps you generally program using Java, but you don't have any problems learning a new language. As a developer, you're not afraid to try out new things, be it a new IDE or a brand new API. You like to test all the latest features, and you don't' become discouraged when things initially fail.

While you can find plenty of introductory books on Android development, this is not such a book. Instead, this book is targeted toward developers who have previous experience with application development for Android. You know all the basics and how to create an app using the `Activity`, `Service`, `BroadcastReceiver`, and `ContentProvider` classes. You're familiar with the core concept of the application manifest and the different types of application resources for Android. If you can build a simple Android application in a matter of minutes, you're well prepared for the contents of this book.

My goal for this book is just what the title says: *pushing the limits.* In each chapter, I try to push the limits on what typical Android developers know and use in their daily work. Even though you may be familiar with some of this book's topics, I provide an in-depth discussion on each topic; so, trust me, there's something new for all Android developers in this book.

What This Book Covers

The Android platforms have developed at an amazing pace. Even while writing this book, I had to change my original plans because Google kept coming out with new APIs, tools, and technologies for Android developers! While many of the examples in this book require a later version of Android, my assumption is that you are familiar with the different API levels and understand which Android version is required in each case.

My goal is to discuss those aspects of Android that I believe are of value for developers. Some technologies were excluded, either because they aren't "pushing the limits" or they wouldn't add real value to the book. So, rather than being a collection of "recipes" for Android applications or an extensive walkthrough of all the features, each chapter goes into the deep technical details of their respective topic. Thus, rather than provide complete applications, I provide numerous pieces of substantial code that you can use to enhance your own applications.

Depending on your experience, you might encounter some unfamiliar technologies. For example, Chapter 12 covers security issues and assumes a basic understanding of encryption and private/public keys, and Chapter 18 covers technologies such as USB communication, Bluetooth Low Energy, and WiFi Direct. But don't worry. In such cases, I direct you to sources where you can find additional information. Each chapter has a Further Resources section where I've listed additional resources such as books and websites where you can find more information on the topics covered in each chapter.

How This Book Is Structured

This book is divided into three parts. The first part covers tools available to Android developers and the specifics on the Java programming language for Android. The second part focuses on core Android components and how to use them in an optimal way. The third and final part focuses on the latest and most advanced technologies, including both the Android platform and the services that can be used with an Android device.

Part I: Building a Better Foundation

Chapter 1: Fine-Tuning Your Development Environment deals with the Android development tools. You'll find an introduction to the new IDE for Android called Android Studio. There is also a brief introduction to Gradle, which is now used as the standard build system for Android applications.

Chapter 2: Efficient Java Code for Android focuses on the Java programming language and the specifics for Android. I discuss some tricks that can help you reduce the load on memory and on the Dalvik garbage collector. You'll also find some examples showing the pros and cons of the different methods for multi-threading.

Part II: Getting the Most Out of Components

Chapter 3: Components, Manifests, and Resources gives a general overview of the components and goes on to describe some of the less frequently used parts of the application manifest. You'll also find examples of advanced use of Android resources.

Chapter 4: Android User Experience and Interface Design focuses on the theory behind the design of user interfaces. I describe how you should work when designing your user interfaces, starting with user stories, personas, and the design-process for the different screens in your application. I explain how people think about, react to, and interpret the various aspects of user interfaces. I describe details about fonts and what makes one font more readable than another. This chapter gives a better understanding of the theories behind good design that you can apply while designing your own interfaces.

Chapter 5: Advanced User Interface Operations focuses on the technical aspects of the Android UI. I show how to use the new APIs with multiple screens in an application. A complete example of how to build a custom `View` is covered followed by a section on advanced multi-touch handling.

Chapter 6: Services and Background Tasks focuses on how to use the `Service` component for optimal background operations in your application. This chapter focuses on `Services` that aren't published to other applications.

Chapter 7: Android IPC covers Android IPC and how you can communicate between two separate Android applications running on the same device. I explain the details of the Binder and how you can use it to build applications that support plug-in functionality.

Chapter 8: Mastering BroadcastReceivers and Configuration Changes focuses on the use of `BroadcastReceivers` and how to use them optimally to listen for system-wide events and configuration changes. I describe the different types of broadcasts and how to use them, and I give some guidelines on how to use the receiver component in a way that reduces the load on the device.

Chapter 9: Data Storage and Serialization Techniques focuses on data persistence and on the `ContentProvider` component. I show how to use the `SharedPreferences` and how to create a Settings UI using the ready-made Android components. High-performance providers are covered as well as different methods for serializing data where the standard SQLite-based solution isn't sufficient. Also, the serialization methods explained here are useful when communicating with `Services` online. I conclude this chapter with some details on how to use the Android backup agent in your application.

Chapter 10: Writing Automated Tests is dedicated to building automated tests for your Android application. I give thorough examples of everything from simple unit tests to complete integration tests for the four different components. I highly recommend that all readers go through this chapter thoroughly because writing tests for your application will greatly improve your development cycle and the quality of your code.

Part III: Pushing the Limits

Chapter 11: Advanced Audio, Video, and Camera Applications deals with advanced graphics, audio, and video. I explain the use of the different audio APIs, including the use of Open SL ES for any high-performance and low-latency requirements you might have regarding audio. I explain the use of both Text-To-Speech and the Speech Recognition API for Android. The use of OpenGL ES for high-performance processing of camera input and video is demonstrated as well. Finally, I discuss a feature introduced in Android 4.3 for using an OpenGL ES surface as an encoding source, which you can employ to record a video of your OpenGL ES scene.

Chapter 12: Secure Android Applications looks at the different security aspects in Android with a focus on how to use the cryptographic APIs. I explain how to use key management in android in a secure way and how to encrypt data on a device. I conclude this chapter with a section covering the Device Management API.

Chapter 13: Maps, Location, and Activity APIs focuses on the new maps and location API for Android. You find out about the new fused Location Provider and how to use features such as geofencing and activity recognition in order to build advanced location-based applications.

Chapter 14: Native Code and JNI delves into native development for Android using the C programming language. I explain the use of the Android NDK (Native Development Kit) and how you can combine native code with Java code through the use of JNI.

Chapter 15: The Hidden Android APIs looks at how the hidden APIs in Android work, how you can find them, and how you can safely invoke them in your application. You also find out how to search the Android source code in order to discover the hidden APIs.

Chapter 16: Hacking the Android Platform describes how to work with the Android Open Source Project (AOSP), build your own custom firmware, and extend the Android platform. I explain how the AOSP is designed and to work when modifying the Android platform. You'll also find an introduction on the process of contributing your changes to the AOSP so that they can become a standard part of the Android platform.

Chapter 17: Networking, Web Services, and Remote APIs looks at integrating online web services in an Android application and how to optimize network operations. I cover the use of recommended third-party libraries for working with network operations, from standard HTTP to Web Sockets and SPDY, and I explain how to invoke three different types of web services. I explain the concept of authenticating toward third-party web services, including how to use OAuth2 in your Android application as well as how to integrate the Facebook SDK for Android.

Chapter 18: Communicating with Remote Devices delves into the different methods for communicating with remote devices using the various connectivity technologies available on Android. I explain how to talk to USB devices using the built-in APIs in Android. I describe the APIs for communicating with Bluetooth Low Energy devices (also called Bluetooth Smart). You'll find an introduction on utilizing the network discovery API for Android, and I show how you can implement ad hoc peer-to-peer communication using the WiFi Direct standard. You'll also find a section on implementing on-device services supporting both RESTful web services and asynchronous communication using Web Sockets.

Chapter 19: Google Play Services covers the use of some of the APIs from Google Play Services. You'll find out how to get authorization for any of the online Google APIs and an example of using the Application Data feature for Google Drive to store your application's data across multiple devices. You'll also find a guide to building Google Cloud Endpoints using the built-in feature in Android Studio, and I show how you can extend this with your own services. This chapter also includes a guide on implementing Google Cloud Messaging. Also, I demonstrate how you can use the real-time multiplayer API that is part of the Google Play Game Services to build advanced multiplayer games.

Chapter 20: Distributing Applications on Google Play Store, the final chapter, focuses on aspects of distributing your application on the Google Play Store and how to include the different monetization options. I explain how to add In-app Billing and ads in your application as well as the use of the licensing service for verifying the license of your application on the user's device. The chapter ends with a guide to utilizing the APK Expansion Files feature to distribute application data that exceeds your application's 50MB limit.

What You Need to Use This Book

Although you can run many of the examples in this book on an emulator, I strongly recommend that you acquire a device with the latest version of Android because many examples in the book use hardware that isn't available on the emulator. Although any Google-certified Android device is sufficient (that is, an Android device with the Google Play Store) for the examples in this book, given that it has the correct Android version, I always recommend purchasing a Google Nexus device so that you can try all the latest platform features as early as possible.

You also need a computer running Linux, OS X, or Windows for your development environment, as well as an Internet connection to access the online resources needed in some chapters. You need to have Java SDK version 6 installed on your computer. (You can download it at `http://java.oracle.com`) in order to run the IDE and other tools.

In Chapter 18, you'll need additional hardware to implement the examples. You'll need a device with Bluetooth Low Energy support, such as an activity tracker or a heartbeat monitor. For the samples on USB communication, you'll need an Android device that supports USB On-The-Go, a USB OTG cable, and a USB-connected device that you can connect to. The easiest approach to testing USB is to use an Arduino Uno board.

Source Code

Most of the source code samples in this book aren't complete implementations; rather they are snippets of code I use to demonstrate the most important parts of the topic being covered. My assumption is that you are familiar enough with Android development to understand where to fit these snippets of code into your own project.

Some of the samples and source code snippets in the book are available on my GitHub site (`https://github.com/ErikHellman/appt1`). However, I strongly recommend that you manually type the code you find in the book instead of simply copying a file. Doing so will give you a better understanding of how the code works.

You can also download the code files from the book's companion website at `http://www.wiley.com/go/ptl/androidprogramming`.

Errata

I've tried to review and verify everything in the book as much as possible, but sometimes mistakes happen. It could be a typo in the text or the source code, but it could also be something that is missing or simply mistaken. I'll update any errors in the sample code in the GitHub repository at `https://github.com/ErikHellman/appt1` with proper bug fixes.

Part I

Building a Better Foundation

Chapter 1

Fine-Tuning Your Development Environment

Depending on what you're developing, you have different choices when it comes to the tools you can use. Your requirements on the development environment differs if you're writing an HTML5 application or if you're developing a server-side application in Java. Some platforms offer more choice than others, and as I describe next, developing Android applications gives you a lot of choice for your development environment.

I begin this chapter with some more advanced internals of the Android SDK and how you can use them in your daily development and how they can assist you in improving the quality of your application. I continue by describing how to structure your code projects in an optimal way for reuse by using library projects. You also learn how to take version control to a new level by integrating Git with a code-review tool called Gerrit. As a developer, you will spend most of your time using the IDE tool. While the Eclipse IDE is still supported by Google, they are now pushing developers to use their new Android Studio IDE for all Android projects. So, I give an introduction to Android Studio as well as to the new build system called Gradle. Finally, I go through the developer settings that are available on Android devices.

Operating Systems for Android Development

This is probably the one topic you don't have to worry about. Either you can pick the operating system on your computer used for development, or it is limited by the IT-policies of your employer. For most Android developers, any of the officially supported operating systems works fine. However, there are situations where the choice will matter.

Google supports Windows, Linux, and OS X for developing Android applications. Although Windows is officially supported by the Android SDK, you'll have problems if you decide to do advanced development, especially when it comes to writing native applications or building your own custom ROM. The best choice is either Linux or OS X. If possible, try to have one of these as your primary operating system, and you'll run into far fewer problems. Another reason for avoiding Windows on your Android development environment is that you won't need to install new USB drivers for every Android device you work on.

Advanced Android SDK Tools

After you have your operating system and the required (and recommended) tools installed on your computer, you can focus on the Android SDK. You will find the download for your operating system and the latest installation instructions at `http://developer.android.com/sdk`. Android Studio comes with an SDK bundle that is completely managed from within the IDE, but if you prefer to have a standalone version you can download that as well.

Make sure that you always keep the SDK up to date and that you download the APIs for all the Android versions that you're developing for. The easiest way to update your standalone Android SDK is to run the update tool from the command prompt:

```
$ android update sdk --no-ui
```

Inside the Android SDK folder, you will find a number of subfolders. From a tools perspective, only the `platform-tools` and `tools` folders are of interest for now. I will introduce some of these tools and explain how to use them, starting with the adb (Android Debug Bridge) tool. If you are frequently using the command line tools in the Android SDK I recommend that you add the path to these folders in your local PATH variable.

> **You can find the official documentation for most of the tools in the Android SDK at** `http://developer.android.com/tools/help/index.html`.

The adb Tool

In the `platform-tools` folder, you will find the adb tool that is used to communicate with your device to install and start apps during development. In earlier versions of the Android SDK, this tool was found in the `tools` directory, but it has since been moved. Besides being used for installing, starting, and debugging applications from your IDE, the adb tool enables you to manually call many of the low-level operations on your Android device for debugging purposes. To list all the commands available, simply type `adb help all` in your terminal (Linux or Mac OS X) or command prompt (Windows).

Some common adb commands are

- `adb devices`—List all connected Android devices and Emulators.
- `adb push <local> <remote>`—Copy a file from your computer to a device (usually on the SD card).
- `adb pull <remote> <local>`—Copy a file from the device to your computer.

adb and Multiple Devices

If you ever need to develop and debug an application for two or more devices simultaneously, such as for a multiplayer game or an instant-message application, adb needs an additional argument to know which device you want to address. You do so by adding `-s <serial number>` as the first parameter to adb. You can see the serial number for your connected devices by executing the `adb devices` command. To run the `logcat` command on a specific device, run the following:

```
$ adb devices
List of devices attached
0070015947d30e4b      device
015d2856b8300a10      device

$ adb -s 015d2856b8300a10 logcat
```

When you have multiple devices connected or emulators started a dialog box will appear when you launch your application in your IDE.

Mastering Logcat Filtering

Logging is an important part of Android application development. Although using breakpoints and a debugger from your IDE is extremely powerful when you want to follow the execution flow and inspect the values and state of different variables, simply reading the output from logcat can sometimes be more efficient. Android logging is handled by the `logcat` function, which is usually integrated in your IDE but can also be called via the `adb` command.

Because Android outputs all system and application log messages to the same stream, it can become quite complicated to find the messages that relate to your application. Luckily, there are some easy ways to filter the logs, as I show in the following code.

Android log messages are prepended with a tag and a priority. Usually, you declare a separate log tag for each class in your application like this:

```
private static final String TAG = "MyActivity";
```

You can then use this tag when printing a log message somewhere in the code for that class:

```
Log.d(TAG, "Current value of moderation: " + moderation);
```

To filter out all log messages except those that have `MyActivity` as the value for the tag, you can execute logcat as follows.

```
$ adb logcat MyActivity:* *:S
```

The parameters after logcat are the filters you want to apply. They are formatted as `<tag>:<priority>` where an asterisk (*) indicates all possible values. One important thing that can easily be missed is that you must include the special filter `*:S`, which tells logcat to silence all messages. In combination with your own filters, you can easily control logcat to print only the messages you want to see.

If you use filters when viewing the logcat output, I also recommend adding `AndroidRuntime:*`. This will show you relevant information from the Android system as well as exceptions that are generated by your application but caught by the platform.

Connecting adb over Wi-Fi

Usually, you connect to your Android device using a USB cable plugged into your computer. However, you can also connect to an Android device over Wi-Fi using a standard TCP/IP connection. This can be very useful when developing applications that are listening for events related to USB (since then the normal connection to your computer will interfere), like connected/disconnected or when you simply don't want to bother with USB cables during development.

In order to enable adb connection over Wi-Fi, you first need to plug your device into your computer using USB as you normally do. Also, make sure your computer and your Android device are connected to the same Wi-Fi. You also need to know the IP address of your Android device, which you can find on your device by choosing Settings⇨ Wi-Fi⇨Advanced. In the bottom of the list that appears you will find your device IP address for the current Wi-Fi.

After you have this set up correctly, run the following commands from your terminal:

```
$ adb devices
List of devices attached
0070015947d30e4b                device
$ adb tcpip 5555
$ adb connect 192.168.1.104
$ adb devices
List of devices attached
192.168.1.104:5555     device
```

The first command is just to verify that your device is connected in debugging mode. The second command tells the device to restart the adb daemon on the device in TCP/IP mode and listen on port 5555 (the default port for adb). The third command tells the adb Service on your computer to connect to the IP address (using default port 5555) of the device. Finally, the fourth command verifies that the computer is connected to the device over TCP/IP. You can now unplug the USB cable from your device and start developing with your IDE as usual.

The device will keep the adb daemon in TCP/IP mode until it is restarted or until you run the command adb usb, which restarts the adb daemon in USB mode.

Connecting adb over WiFi is not guaranteed to work on all devices. Also, the communication performance with the device is much worse, which can be annoying when you need to deploy a large application.

Executing Commands on an Android Device

Because an Android system is basically a custom Linux distribution, you can interact with it in much the same way as you can with Linux on your PC. By running a special adb command, you can start a standard Linux-shell on your Android device that lets you perform command-line operations in the same way as you do on your other Linux installations as shown here.

```
$ adb shell
```

When running a shell on your Android device, two useful commands are am and pm. These commands aren't related to the time of day; instead, they enable you to interact with the Application and Package Managers, respectively, which can be useful during early development and testing. For instance, if you're implementing a Service that will be started by some externally triggered Intent, you can manually send this Intent using the am command.

To start a Service using an Intent action, simply type the following on the command line:

```
$ adb shell am startservice –a <intent action>
```

You can add parameters for extras and even specify a certain component name. In addition to `startservice`, you can launch an `Activity` or send a broadcast `Intent`. Calling `adb shell am` without additional parameters will display a full list of possible commands. You will find that this command is especially useful when you start developing an Android application and need to test a `Service` before you create the `Activity` that will launch it. Also, it's useful for simulating `Intents` that will be launched by other applications, such as `ACTION_VIEW` or `ACTION_SEND`.

The Package Manager is a central Android component that manages the installed applications on a device. You can control use of the `pm` command in a similar way to how you work with the Application Manager. The Package Manager lets you interact with the installed applications (packages), allowing you to list, install, uninstall, and inspect the features and permissions on the device. Although the `pm` command isn't as useful during development as the `am` command, it can sometimes be helpful if you want to find out details about the device that are otherwise a bit complicated to discover. For instance, if you want to list all the installed packages (that is, installed apps), you can type the following:

```
$ adb shell pm list packages
```

In addition to the adb commands just covered, there are many others you need to be familiar with. If you haven't done so already, take some time to experiment with the adb commands.

You can find a list of `adb` **commands and their uses at** `http://developer.android.com/tools/help/adb.html`.

Stress-Testing an Application's UI with Monkey

Most developers often consider testing a tedious and boring task, and Android developers are probably no exception. A good developer handles testing by writing automated tests that verify parts of the code in the application when running on the device. You can also find code inspection tools that search for common coding mistakes (you'll look at one of these in the section "Static Code Analysis with Lint," later in this chapter). However, as much as you might wish, writing automated tests and performing static code analysis is never 100% foolproof. A user doesn't behave according to a certain pattern all the time. Users can click a button at an unexpected moment or accidentally click the wrong button, which can cause your application to crash. You basically need something that behaves like a user would, or better yet, like a monkey would!

The Android SDK comes with a powerful tool called the Application Exerciser Monkey, or simply, Monkey. This is a command-line tool that allows you to generate pseudo-random user events like touches or system events on a device. The purpose is to stress test your application by simulating what a user could do. Although Monkey doesn't simulate a typical use-case scenario for your application, it provides valuable feedback on how your application will work if the user interacts with your user interface in an unpredictable way.

The following command executes the Monkey tool on an application with the specific `<package name>` and injects as many random events as specified by `<event count>`.

```
$ adb shell monkey –p <package name> <event count>
```

The default behavior for Monkey is to stop when an unhandled exception occurs and to report the error. This behavior is useful for finding things like unexpected `NullPointerExceptions` or similar issues in your code. You can fine-tune the behavior through various parameters and tell Monkey to halt only if, for instance, a security exception occurs.

Scripting Monkey with Monkeyrunner

A more advanced way of executing Monkey on your application is by writing a Python script that uses the Monkeyrunner API. This can be very useful in a continuous development environment where you want to run the Monkey tool and perform other actions as well. It also allows you to provide input values for keystrokes and capture screen shots programmatically that can be compared (also using the Monkeyrunner API) to a set of screen shots known to be correct.

For a team of Android developers, this can prove to be a huge advantage because it provides a robust regression-testing solution with very little effort. Even small changes to your code can sometimes provide unexpected results that can be very difficult to detect when you're the only person testing the application before release. Using the Monkey tool, and preferably building Monkeyrunner scripts for regression testing, is highly recommended before publishing your application.

You can find the API for the Monkeyrunner at `http://developer.android.com/tools/help/monkeyrunner_concepts.html#APIClasses`.

The Gradle Build System for Android

With the release of Android Studio, Google also introduced a new modular build system that replaces the old Ant scripts that were generated by the older versions of the SDK. When you create a new project in Android Studio, it will also create all the Gradle scripts for your project.

Gradle is a modular build system similar to Ivy and Maven. It combines the flexibility of Ant with the dependency management from Maven. Instead of writing build-scripts in complex XML-files, Gradle has its own Groovy DSL (Domain-Specific Language) that allows you to express more clearly your build configuration.

The following code is the default `build.gradle` file that is generated for new projects. The first block tells gradle which repository to download plug-ins and dependencies for the build. (This is not the same as the dependencies for your project, which is defined in a later block.) The next part tells Gradle to *apply* a plug-in, in this case the Android plug-in, which enables the specifics for Android development. Next come the dependencies for your project, in this case only the support library that is located in the `libs` directory of your project. The final block, starting with android, specifies the configuration for your project.

```
buildscript {
    repositories {
        maven { url 'http://repo1.maven.org/maven2' }
    }
    dependencies {
        classpath 'com.android.tools.build:gradle:0.5+'
    }
```

```
}
apply plugin: 'android'

dependencies {
    compile files('libs/android-support-v4.jar')
}

android {
    compileSdkVersion 18
    buildToolsVersion "18.0.0"

    defaultConfig {
        minSdkVersion 18
        targetSdkVersion 18
    }
}
```

> **The user guide for the new Gradle build system can be found at** http://tools.android.com/tech-docs/new-build-system/user-guide.

The default directory structure for an Android project using the new build system is slightly different from what you may be used to. Instead of having a flat structure, there are two main source sets: source code and test sources. They are in the following directories:

src/main/

src/instrumentTest/

Under the main directory the Java source code is placed in the java and resources are placed in the res directory. The AndroidManifest.xml file is located directly in the main directory (see Figure 1-1).

The other directories for project files are assets (for binary assets), aidl (for Android IDLs), rs (RenderScript sources) and jni (native C/C++ code).

While building and running your project is supported directly in the Android Studio IDE, you can interact with the build system through the command line as well. Gradle defines a number of tasks and to list all available tasks, simply type the following from the root of your Android project.

```
$ ./gradlew tasks
```

If you, for instance, want to build the application from scratch you would run the following.

```
$ ./gradlew clean build
```

This will execute first the clean task, followed by the build task.

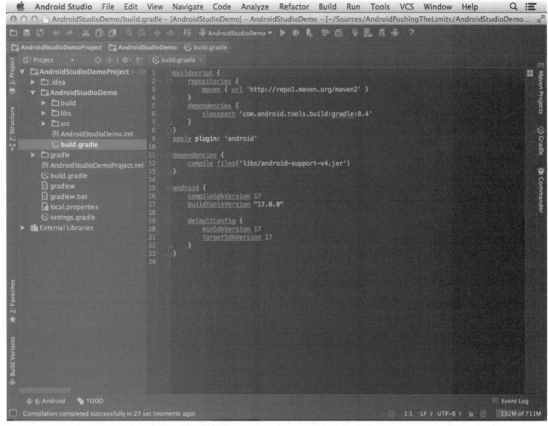

Figure 1-1: The directory structure and Gradle build file shown in the Android Studio IDE

Migrating Existing Projects to Gradle

Since most existing Android projects are not using the Gradle build system, a migration guide might be in order. The easiest way to migrate is to create a new Android project using Android Studio. Then, copy your own project to a sub-folder in the new project.

Next, take the `build.gradle` file for the application created by Android studio and copy it to the root of your own application.

```
android {
    sourceSets {
        main {
            manifest.srcFile 'AndroidManifest.xml'
            java.srcDirs = ['src']
            resources.srcDirs = ['src']
            aidl.srcDirs = ['src']
            renderscript.srcDirs = ['src']
            res.srcDirs = ['res']
            assets.srcDirs = ['assets']
        }
    }
}
```

Edit the `android` section of the file so that it looks like the previous example. This should work well for all existing Android projects that follow the old standard directory structure. If your project has a different structure, simply change the paths from the previous example. (Note that all paths are relative.)

Optimize and Obfuscate with ProGuard

An Android application is the compiled result from your Java, XML, and other resource files. The Java code is compiled into a binary format called dex, which is what the Dalvik virtual machine on Android reads when executing your code. This format is not designed to be human-readable, tools are available for decompiling a dex file back to a human-readable format.

In some cases, decompiling the code can be a security issue—for instance, when your code contains keys or other values that should not be easily accessible (such as integration with Licensing Server). Although it isn't possible to completely prevent decompilation of your code, you can make it much more difficult by obfuscating it before you publish it. This method will make reverse engineering much more time-consuming and hopefully discourage hacking attempts on your application.

You obfuscate your code for Android by using the ProGuard tool that's integrated in the Android SDK. The tool is supported by the Gradle build system, and all you need to do is to add the following to the android section in `build.gradle`.

```
buildTypes {
    release {
        runProguard true
        proguardFile getDefaultProguardFile('proguard-android.txt')
    }
}
```

This will enable ProGuard to be applied to the release-build of your application. During normal development this step is excluded.

Another reason to obfuscate your code is that doing so performs some additional optimizations, as well as shrinking the resulting dex binary by removing unused code. This is especially useful when you've included a large third-party library, because it can significantly reduce the final file size and memory usage during runtime.

Android Library Projects and Third-Party Libraries

Developers tend to write the same code over and over for new applications, which is why we create code *libraries* that can be reused in the next project. The result is a faster development cycle because there's less code to write and test.

Android offers you two ways to reuse code among your application projects: by using either a precompiled JAR file or a library project. The first method is preferable when you're dealing with third-party code that you don't control or when you have a stable and complete set of library functions that won't change during the current project. The second method, using a library project, is useful if you're developing multiple applications in the same project that will share some code—for example, when you've decided to create one application for smartphones and one for tablets, or when you have two different applications that will communicate (for example, client and server).

Precompiled JAR Libraries

Using a precompiled JAR file in your Android project is very simple. Simply copy the file to the `libs` directory in your project folder and then add it as a library within your IDE. The code in the JAR file will be available directly, and when you build the application, the Android tool chain will automatically include and package the included classes. If you're obfuscating your application code with ProGuard, all included JAR files will be processed as well. This is especially useful when you're including large third-party libraries where you use only part of the classes it provides. To include a local JAR file as a dependency to your project, simply add it to the dependency section in `build.gradle` like this:

```
dependencies {
    compile files('libs/android-support-v4.jar')
}
```

Another way of doing this is by using a remote dependency repository, such as the central Maven repository. To enable this and include a third-party library found in that repository, you update your `build.gradle` as follows:

```
repositories {
    mavenCentral()
}

dependencies {
    compile 'com.google.code.gson:gson:2.2.4'
}
```

The string in the `dependencies` section is an identifier for a specific version of a library. The call to `mavenCentral()` will configure your build environment with the correct Maven settings.

To search for third-party libraries you can use the Maven search site at `http://search.maven.org/`. Once you've found the right library, simply click on the version and copy the identifier string from the *Grails* section. Note that not all libraries found on the central Maven repository are supported on Android. Refer to the documentation first.

Setting Up a Library Project

An Android library project is basically a standard Android project that doesn't declare any components that can be started (`Activities`, `Services`, `BroadcastReceivers`, or `ContentProviders`) and that won't generate an APK when compiled or exported. The library's sole purpose is to be shared by multiple application projects so that you don't have to copy the same code between them, which is very useful for sharing constants, utility functions, common custom views, and other components. Because you're dealing with the actual code and not a precompiled JAR file, the code can be changed, which will affect all the applications that include this library.

Because Android development uses the Java programming language, using a library project to share code between an Android application and a server-side component written in Java (for instance, a Java Enterprise application) can be especially useful. Common code to share in such a setup is the class representation of the shared data and how to serialize and deserialize objects of these classes.

The Android SDK comes with a number of ready-to-use library projects that can be found under `extras/google` in the SDK folder. More specifically, you can find library projects for the Play Services, APK extensions, In-app Billing and Licensing features. To use these, you simply have to import them into your IDE and add a dependency to your own project. *Note:* You can refer to multiple library projects in one application project.

You can set up a library project from the Android Studio IDE. Simply create a new module and choose Android Library as the module type. A `gradle.build` will be generated for the new library project as shown next.

```
buildscript {
    repositories {
        maven { url 'http://repo1.maven.org/maven2' }
    }
    dependencies {
        classpath 'com.android.tools.build:gradle:0.4'
    }
}
apply plugin: 'android-library'

dependencies {
    compile files('libs/android-support-v4.jar')
}

android {
    compileSdkVersion 17
    buildToolsVersion "17.0.0"

    defaultConfig {
        minSdkVersion 7
        targetSdkVersion 16
    }
}
```

Note that the only difference from the default build file for Android project is the use of the plug-in `android-library` instead of `android`.

To include a library project in your application's build configuration, you simply refer to it as a dependency as shown in the following.

```
dependencies {
    compile project(':libraries:MyLibrary')
}
```

Version Control and Source Code Management

Chances are that most development projects you'll work on will involve other developers. A development team usually comprises four to eight people, all working on the same code in parallel. Although the team could decide who will make the changes for every file, it's much more practical to apply a *version control system* to the project files that supports a parallel method for development. Another benefit of a version control system is that you can track changes back in time (who made what changes and when in a specific part of a file) and then merge changes from different developers into the same file.

One of the most common version control systems used today is *Git,* and it's also the system used to manage the source code of both the Android Open Source Project and the Linux kernel. Git is a distributed version control system that allows a developer to work independently from other developers. After the developer completes the changes to the source code for a certain feature, he can push the changes to a server where the other developers can retrieve it.

You can read more about Git and download it for various platforms at `http://git-scm.com`. For a deeper introduction to Git and version control, I recommend the book, *Version Control with Git* (see the "Further Resources" section at the end of this chapter).

A great feature with Git is that you don't need a server in order to use it, which makes it suitable for all types of projects, from projects where you're the only developer to projects consisting of multiple teams. I recommend that you always initiate a new Git repository for every new Android application you start developing. Although you can perform all Git operations from your IDE, it's always good to be able to use the command-line tool as well. The example that follows shows how to initialize a new Git repository:

```
$ git init <path to project directory>
Initialized empty Git repository in <path to project directory>./git
```

After you set up a Git repository for your project, you can start to add and commit changes. Usually, you perform these operations through your IDE, but if you want, you can also perform the `add` and `commit` commands from the command line. If you're new to Git, I recommend that you take a tutorial before you start using it.

Git becomes really powerful when a team of developers needs to work together on the same source code. The team should set up a remote Git repository to which all the team members can synchronize their changes. The easiest way to do so is either to set up a *gitolite* server, which is dedicated server software that provides remote access to Git repositories, or to use a ready-made hosting solution like GitHub for remote Git repositories.

Gitolite allows you to set up your own server for hosting Git repositories, as well as define fine-grained access control. If you need full control of your source code management or aren't able to store your source code outside the company network, gitolite is your best choice.

You can find the documentation and download for gitolite at `http://gitolite.com/gitolite`. An excellent quick installation guide can be found at `http://gitolite.com/gitolite/qi.html`.

GitHub is a web-based hosting service for development projects that use Git. This online service provides both a free and a paid service for individuals and businesses. The great thing about GitHub is that it provides an easy way to share code with anyone on the Internet. If you want to be able to access your central repository when outside the office or share your code as open source, then GitHub is a good choice.

Read more about GitHub at `http://github.com.`

Regardless of the size of your project, version control is very important. Even if you're making only a small prototype or test app, it's good practice to always set up a Git repository. When you can track the history of your code, you not only have the ability to track your changes efficiently but also the ability to understand why a change occurred, because each commit will contain a message describing it. Take the little extra time required to set up version control every time you start a project. Doing so will pay off.

Many developers working with software code will find one more very useful "tool" related to version control: namely, two pairs of eyes inspecting the work, rather than just one, because developers working alone can easily miss their own mistakes. This is why code reviewing is such a powerful technique when it comes to improving the quality of your code. The problem with code reviewing is that it has often taken a lot of effort. Fortunately, there are now excellent tools to support code review, and one of the best is *Gerrit*.

Gerrit's two main advantages are that it integrates with Git perfectly and it's completely web-based. Gerrit is also the same code-review tool used for the Android Open Source Project. The basic idea with Gerrit is that a developer pushes a change up the main repository. Before the change gets merged to the main branch, Gerrit sends a notification to all project members that have "subscribed" for these changes, letting them know that there is something new to review. Each reviewer can then compare the change with the previous commit and give the change a ranking and a comment, indicating if something should be fixed or if it looks okay. If something needs to be fixed, the original developer can push up another update that gets tracked by Gerrit. When everything looks okay and is verified, the change can be pushed to the main branch and be available to all developers.

You can find out more about Gerrit and download the server at `https://code.google.com/p/gerrit.`

When you're working on a team with many developers, code reviewing with Gerrit is a great tool because it supports a distributed review method. The reviewer doesn't need to be located near the developer to ask questions or give feedback but can do so directly in the tool. It might seem at first that this extra tool will add unnecessary overhead to a project, but anyone who has been doing code reviewing on a regular basis knows how much it improves the quality of the code. For an example of what the Gerrit tool looks like, see Figure 1-2.

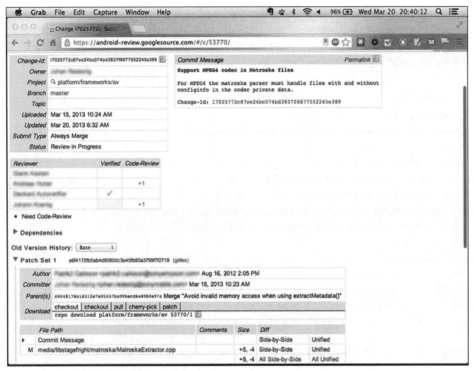

Figure 1-2 The web interface for the Gerrit code-review tool

Mastering Your IDE

In May 2013 at the Google IO conference, Google announced a new IDE for Android named Android Studio. This IDE is based on the open-source version of IntelliJ IDEA (Community Edition). The reason for switching from Eclipse, which was the previously supported IDE, to IntelliJ IDEA was due to the complexity involved in developing the Android plug-in for Eclipse. IntelliJ IDEA provided a far more superior platform for development and allowed the Android tools team at Google to take the development experience to a new level as they could integrate the Android tools into the IDE instead of simply providing a plug-in.

In this section, I cover three useful features that are supported by Android Studio: debugging, static code analysis, and refactoring. Although these features have been available from both IntelliJ IDEA and Eclipse for some time, I keep seeing many developers, both beginners and experienced developers, not using them to their full extent. A developer who fully masters these features in his IDE will notice that he becomes much more efficient in producing high-quality code.

Debugging Android Applications

Debugging capabilities give you fine-grained control over the execution of an application. You can set breakpoints where execution will pause and inspect every aspect of the application state. This feature becomes most useful when it comes to discovering the source of a bug or when you need to carefully inspect exactly what happens during execution. The capability to debug Android applications is built into the IDEs, providing a simple user interface for stepping through the code, inspecting variables, and even changing their values.

You can debug Android applications on your device through the Android SDK. Your IDE will connect to the debugging `Service` (adb) running on your device, which in turn connects to the Dalvik virtual machine (VM) that your application is running. The procedure is basically the same one you follow when you run an application from your IDE.

Figure 1-3 shows one of the sample applications from the Android SDK opened in Android Studio. As you can see, I set a break point in the code and started the debugging from my IDE. The figure shows how the IDE looks once the execution hits the breakpoint.

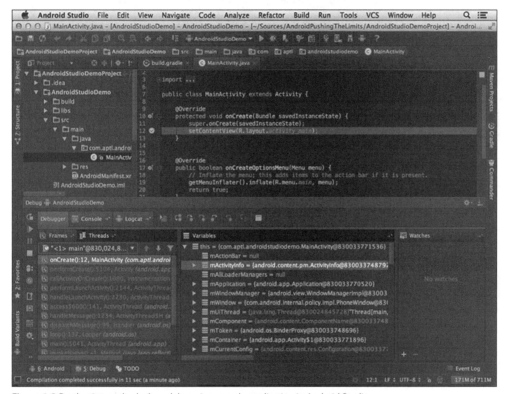

Figure 1-3 Breakpoint reached when debugging sample application in Android Studio

When a breakpoint is reached, you can inspect the state of the application at that specific point. All variables accessible in that scope are listed in the debugger UI in the IDE. While debugging applications, you can change the value of a variable in the current scope without having to restart the application and change the assignment in the code, which is useful for testing how an application works depending on different input values. For instance, if your application reads input from a sensor and you are unable to control the values from this sensor, setting a breakpoint after data from the sensor has been read can be a powerful tool during development.

Android Studio contains a very powerful debugger tool that not only allows you to change the value of variables but also to execute arbitrary code at the current scope, as shown in Figure 1-4. This capability is especially helpful when you're performing more advanced inspections that require the temporary injection of several lines of code at the breakpoint.

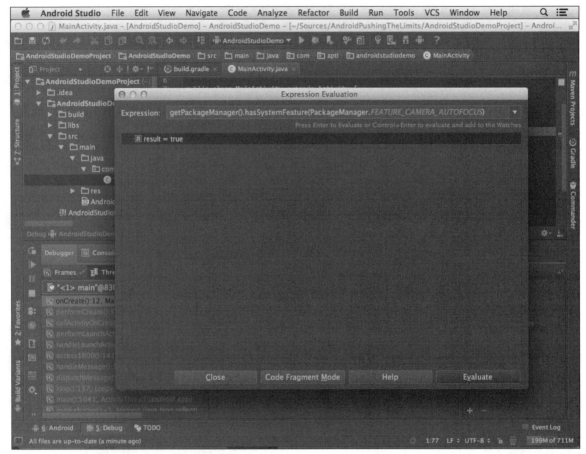

Figure 1-4 Executing the code evaluation tool in Android Studio

Remember that using the debugger is not a substitute for writing tests for your application.

Static Code Analysis with lint

Even the best developers make mistakes in their code, and over the years different ways of dealing with this fact have been developed. Writing unit tests has proven to be very effective and is something I highly recommend to all developers. However, even with carefully written unit tests, it's hard to cover all possible situations that might occur in the code, which is why it's important to complement unit testing with other methods@mdfor instance, static code analysis. Fortunately, Google has added such a tool, called *lint*, to the Android SDK.

The lint tool performs checks on your project's source files, both XML and Java, and searches for missing elements, poorly structured code, unused variables, and more. In your IDE, the results appear as highlighted areas (see Figure 1-5) indicating that something needs to be fixed. Hovering the cursor over these highlights shows you more details and in some cases allows you to perform the "quick fix" command in order to correct the problem.

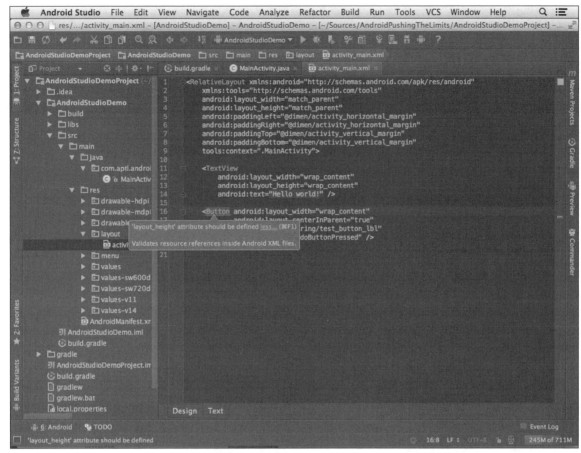

Figure 1-5 Android Studio showing missing attributes highlighted in a XML layout file

Although it's a very powerful tool, sometimes lint can indicate a warning in code that may be correct. A warning could be about an unused method declaration or a missing recommended attribute in the manifest. In these cases, the lint warnings may become irritating, especially if several developers are involved in a project. In that case, it may be a good idea to actively suppress a warning for a specific part of the code to indicate that things are okay, despite what lint thinks.

Suppressing lint warnings can be done for both Java and XML source files. For Java, you use the annotation @ `SuppressLint` with the warning you want to suppress as an argument, as shown in Figure 1-6.

In XML files, you include the lint namespace and add `tools:ignore="WarningName"` (where `WarningName` is the warning you want to suppress; see Figure 1-7) to the part where you want to suppress the warning.

Remember that lint warnings are there for a purpose. They indicate areas that are potential bugs, so always carefully consider whether you really want to suppress the warning. It's often better to leave the warning in place rather than remove it, as a reminder that it should be dealt with later.

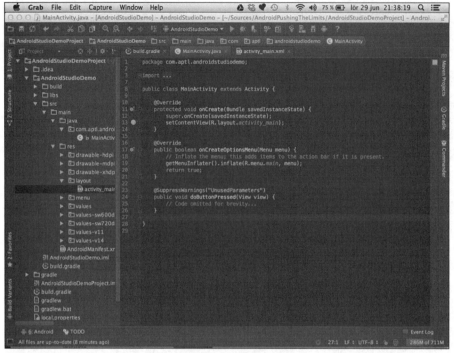

Figure 1-6 Warning suppressed in Java source

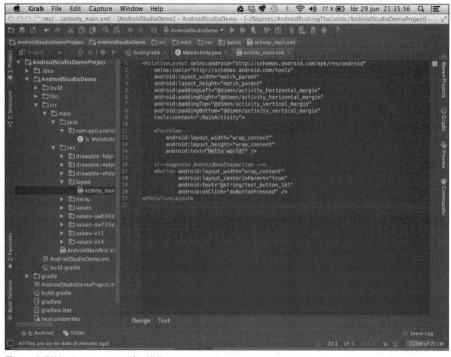

Figure 1-7 Warning suppressed in XML source

Refactoring Your Code

When you write code, you rarely get it perfect on the first try. You tend to change the structure and names of methods, variables, and classes. When the number of classes grows in a project, you might move them into a separate package. As you write more and more code, you suddenly realize that you have code that does the same thing written in several different places with just minor differences.

Making changes in existing code can become a complicated process when that code is referenced in many places. If you want to add another parameter to a method, you need to find all the places where the method is used and update those. This can become a very complicated and error-prone process if done manually. Fortunately, your IDE has a built-in function called `Refactoring` that makes this task simple and eliminates the risk of introducing any bugs.

Many refactoring tasks are available in your IDEs. Refactoring involves simple things like renaming and moving variables, methods, classes, and packages, as well as more complex operations such as changing the signature of methods, encapsulating fields, replacing code duplicates, and replacing inheritance with delegation. I cover some of the most common tasks in the following sections.

To use refactoring in Android Studio, place the cursor at the position in the code where you want to change something and then select the refactoring task from the Refactor menu.

Extracting Constants

When you write code it is easy to ignore some best practices that we all know would benefit us in the long run. A common example is when writing constant values in the code (that is, using the actual value instead of a variable) instead of declaring a constant variable (a variable declared as `public static final`). The problem is that once you decide to change the value, you need to find all the occurrences of that value and replace it with the constant's name. This is where the *Extract Constant* refactoring task comes in. As shown in Figure 1-8, this task allows you to quickly and correctly replace all occurrences of that value with a newly declared constant.

Changing the Method Signature

The method signature defines the access modifier (`private, protected, package local` or `public`), return type, name, and parameters for a method. If you have a commonly used method where you want to add an extra parameter, making the correct change in all places where the method is used in your project can become complicated. Figure 1-9 shows how you can change all the parts of a method signature as well as all the places where it's used in your code.

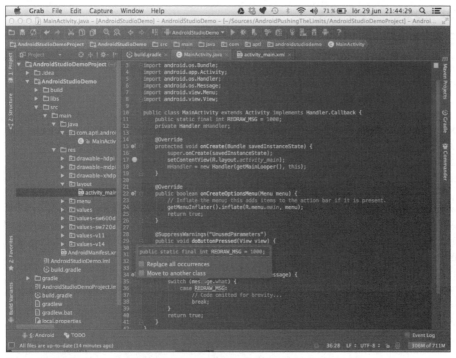

Figure 1-8 Extracting a repeated value to a constant in Android Studio

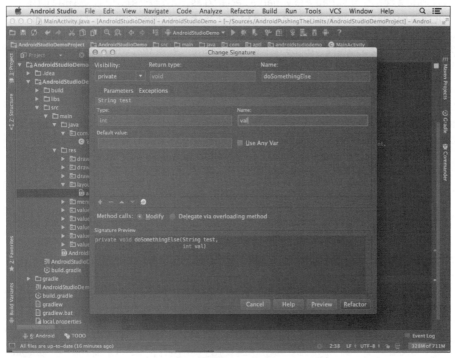

Figure 1-9 Changing a method signature in Android Studio

Extracting the Method from Code Block

It's good practice to keep methods small to make code more readable and allow for more efficient reuse of the code. When you see that a method is growing out of proportion, you can mark off a block in the code and perform an *Extract Method* task as shown in Figure 1-10. After that, you can also perform the *Change Method Signature* task to make the method more generic and reusable if needed.

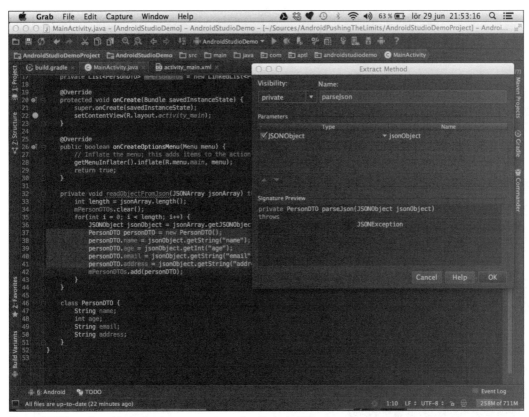

Figure 1-10 Extracting a block of code to a separate method in Android Studio

There are many more refactoring options available in the IDE. I recommend that you become familiar with all of these as they will make you a more productive developer. For more refactoring options in Android Studio, which is based on IntelliJ IDEA, users can find a comprehensive guide to most of the refactoring tools at http://www.jetbrains.com/idea/features/refactoring.html.

Developer Options on Android Devices

In the Settings application on your Android device, you can find the Developer Menu. Depending on which version of Android you're running, this can present different options. Also, some device manufacturers may add their own settings in the Developer menu. In this section, I cover the most important details of the Developer menu in Android 4.2 on a Nexus device.

Starting with Android 4.2, Google hides the Developer menu by default, purely for security reasons: Showing the Developer menu could create some serious security issues if it's enabled by mistake. Here's how you enable the Developer options on an Android device with version 4.2 or later:

1. Go to the Settings application.

2. Scroll down the list of options and tap the About Phone option, located at the bottom of the list.

3. Locate the row with the label Build Number and tap the Build Number option seven times.

   A notification saying "You're Now a Developer" appears, and the Developer Options menu now appears in the Settings list.

Understanding Developer Settings

In the Developer Options menu (see Figure 1-11), you will find many choices that may be confusing at first. Although they're all useful in certain situations, I cover those that I believe are most useful for application developers.

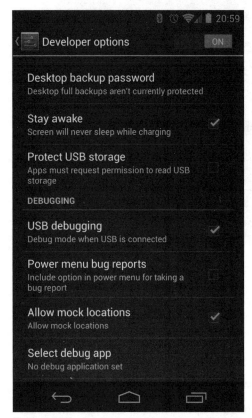

Figure 1-11 The Developer Options menu on a Nexus 4 device running Android 4.2

The first option you want to enable is Stay Awake, which causes your device to keep the screen on while it's charging—of course, the USB cable needs to be connected to your laptop. This way, you don't have to unlock your device whenever you want to deploy and run the application you're developing, which saves a lot of frustration.

A bit further down the list is the Debugging option, which contains a number of useful options that you need to understand. The first option you want to enable is USB Debugging. Without this option, you won't be able to connect the device to your development environment using the adb tool. If you'll be working with Google Maps or the Location API, enable Allow Mock Locations too, so that you can test different location parameters without having to travel all over the world.

Under Input are two settings (Show Touches and Pointer Location) that you'll find useful when writing applications that rely on advanced touch input, such as gestures and multi-touch interfaces.

The Drawing option contains several settings options that allow you to get visual feedback on how the user interface is laid out and how fast and often a redraw occurs. You can also set scaling parameters for animations and transitions as well as disable them completely for debugging purposes. One setting that is new with Android 4.2 is the possibility to simulate a secondary screen. With the introduction of multiple displays in Android 4.2, this feature makes it easy to develop multi-screen applications without having to connect your device to a real secondary screen. Instead, the Android system will draw an overlay on top of the standard user interface that simulates this second display.

Under Monitoring, you find some options that can prove invaluable for ensuring that your device runs smoothly. Most developers are usually equipped with the latest version of high-end smartphones. Normal users, however, may use older devices with less powerful CPUs and memory. An application that runs fine on your high-end device can become sluggish and even encounter the dreaded Application Not Responding (ANR) message if you're not careful. The options under Monitoring in the Development Options menu can help you spot these problems early on. By checking Strict Mode Enabled, the screen on your device will flash when you're performing a long operation on the main thread. Show CPU Usage is useful for tracking how much more the CPU is working when your application is running, which you can use for comparison with other applications on the same device to see if you're doing better or worse than they are. Comparing the performance of your application with other similar and popular apps is a good practice.

In the final section, named Apps, there are three options that are also useful for simulating the behavior of devices with less CPU and memory. The Don't Keep Activities option makes sure that your Activities are restarted from scratch every time they're launched. Normal behavior for Android is to keep Activities alive for as long as possible so that they can be launched faster. The system will completely remove (that is, destroy) Activities only when the device runs low on memory. By checking this option, you can simulate how your app will behave on a device with much less available memory. You can further simulate this kind of behavior by changing the Background Process Limit option, which forces background operations to stop much earlier.

Finally, checking Show All ANRs is recommended for all developers, because it will become much more obvious when an application crashes in the background. Normally, ANRs aren't shown unless the current foreground application causes it to show.

Summary

In this chapter, I covered the details of the Android SDK, some of the hidden features of the adb tool, how to stress test your application with the Monkey tool, how to use the ProGuard tool for obfuscating your code, and how the new build system based on Gradle works. I continued with more details on how to setup an Android Library Project or how to integrate a third-party library for your Android application.

Because the use of Git as a Source Code Management system for software development is quite widespread today, I also described how you can combine Git with various `Services` in order to make it easier for a team to work together.

The new IDE for developing Android applications, called Android Studio, contains a number of advanced features that many developers have rarely used. By understanding and mastering the refactoring features in this IDE, you can simplify complex tasks when you need to re-structure your code. It also helps to simplify existing code without the risk of introducing new bugs.

Finally, I outlined some of the more important details about the developer options settings in Android. It's important to have a full understanding of how these work and how they can assist in development, debugging, and testing. Just remember to switch them all off and test your application without them to ensure that everything works as intended on a normal user's device.

Developing software is more than simply writing code, regardless what kind of application or service you're developing. For Android, mastering the tools is as important as the quality of your code, because when the tools are used to their fullest extent, the writing of the code becomes much easier and less error prone.

Further Resources

Books

Loeliger, Jon, and Matthew McCullough. *Version Control with Git*. O'Reilly Media, Inc., 2012.

Websites

Android development resources from the official Android Developer site: `http://developer.android.com`

The Gradle build system: `http://www.gradle.org`

Chapter 2

Efficient Java Code for Android

Today there are three versions of the Java platform, Java ME (Micro Edition, for certain mobile phones), Java SE (Standard Edition, for desktops), and Java EE (Enterprise Edition, for server-side applications). When talking about Java in general, I am usually referring to Java SE because this is the version that contains a virtual machine and a compiler.

Java code is compiled to an intermediate format called *byte-code*. This byte-code is then parsed by a virtual machine on the target computer that can quickly translate it to the native format required for that particular hardware and operating system.

Besides providing a "Write Once, Run Anywhere" advantage for developers, Java has automatic memory management through a garbage collector (GC), reducing the need for you, as a developer, to de-allocate memory from unused objects in your code. Although this feature is very useful and greatly reduces the risk of introducing memory bugs in your code, because the garbage collection process needs to execute continuously, it adds an overhead when running.

I start this chapter by doing a high-level comparison of the differences between Java SE and the Java used for Android development. I focus on the Java SE language construct that you may be used to and how it works on Android. Then I focus on how to optimize Java code for Android, how to optimize memory allocations, and how to handle multithreading properly.

Comparing Android's Dalvik Java to Java SE

Although developers were able to write applications for mobile devices using the Java programming language long before Android, it was a severely limited version of Java called Java ME (Micro Edition). Java ME also differed among different device manufacturers, making it almost impossible to write an application that would work on any phone supporting Java ME. Also, the distribution of apps was very complicated because no well-supported online stores existed at that time.

The launch of Android gave developers the option to build very capable applications for smartphones by writing code using the Java programming language and using the same API they were used to in the standard Java domain. However, although Android developers still use the compiler from Java SE to compile their applications, you can find many differences between the Java that James Gosling developed and the way Java works on your Android device.

The VM (virtual machine) that runs on an Android device is called Dalvik. It was originally developed by Dan Bornstein at Google and provided a virtual machine suitable for CPU and memory-constrained devices. There are several differences between Java SE and Dalvik Java, mostly regarding the virtual machine. Although Java SE uses a stack machine design, Dalvik was designed as a register-based machine. The Android SDK has a tool called dx that converts the Java SE stack machine byte-code to Dalvik register-based machine byte-code. The conversion step is done automatically by your IDE so that you don't need to bother about it.

The exact definition and technical difference between a stack-based machine and a register-based machine is beyond the scope of this book. Android uses a register-based machine for historical reasons. Although a register-based machine can be up to 32% faster than a stack-based machine, this is true only for virtual machines that are interpreting the byte-code at execution (that is, interpreted virtual machines). Up until Android version 2.2 (also known as Froyo), the Dalvik VM was purely interpreted. With the Froyo version of Android came the introduction of a *JIT* compiler (Just In Time), something that Java SE had benefitted from for a long time.

JIT compilation, also known as *dynamic translation,* takes the byte-code and translates it into native code prior to execution (see Figure 2-1), which has two major benefits. First, it eliminates much of the overhead associated with pure interpreted VMs; second, it can perform optimizations to the native code that wouldn't be possible with statically compiled code. For instance, the JIT compiler may choose the most appropriate optimizations for the CPU it is currently running. It's also possible for a JIT compiler to analyze how the code is running to perform further optimizations based on the application's input.

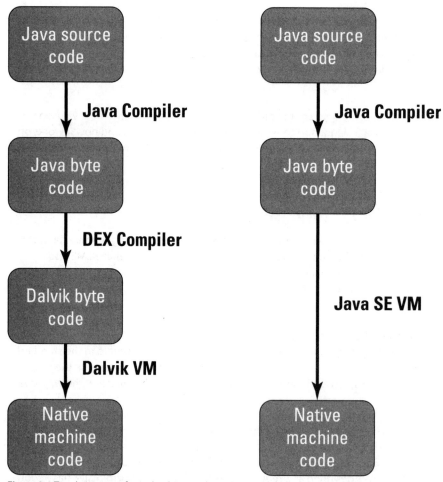

Figure 2-1 Translation steps for Android Java and Java SE

As promising as this sounds, Android's Dalvik JIT compiler has a long journey ahead before it reaches the same level of maturity as the JIT compiler in Java SE. Still, the presence of a JIT in Dalvik provides great performance benefits for Android, and it's continuously being improved.

Another difference between the Java SE VM and the Dalvik VM is that the latter is optimized for running in multiple instances on the same machine. This is handled by a process started at boot called *zygote* that creates the first Dalvik instance that will be the parent of all other instances. Once an application starts, the zygote process receives a request for a new VM instance and forks a new process that is assigned to the newly started application, as shown in Figure 2-2. This design may seem impractical if you're used to working with Java SE, but it has a major advantage because it protects you from multiple application crashes in cases where one application has a runtime failure that will crash the Dalvik VM.

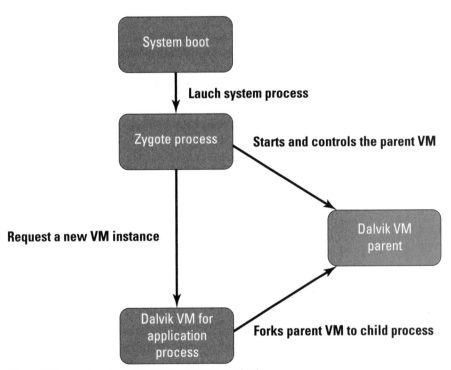

Figure 2-2 Launching of new Dalvik VM instances in Android

In addition to running with a different virtual machine than the one Java SE uses, Android has a different implementation of the APIs. All the APIs in Android that belong to the `java` or `javax` packages come from Apache Harmony, an open-source project aiming for reimplementation of the Java SE stack. (The Apache Harmony project has been retired since November 2011 and is no longer being actively developed.) In terms of developing, these APIs are identical to the ones that are found in Java SE, but some differences do exist. (For instance, Google has made major upgrades to the `HttpUrlConnection` class that is not present in the Java SE version.)

Also, not all of the Java SE APIs are available on Android because they're irrelevant for this platform. For instance, the Swing/AWT packages have been completely removed because Android uses a different UI framework. Other APIs that have been removed are RMI, CORBA, ImageIO, and JMX. These have either been replaced by an Android specific version (in the `android` package space) or simply don't have an equivalent in Android for practical reasons.

Optimizing Java Code for Android

Java SE has evolved over the years with new features that simplify writing complicated code structures. Many of the features make it easier for developers, and you need to understand when and how to use them properly. Also, because Java SE has been used mostly for server-side development (using the Java Enterprise Edition APIs), Java code has been optimized to meet server-side requirements. Annotations and support for scripting languages in the Java SE virtual machine are examples of optimizations focused on server-side development. Although powerful tools when building your back end, these kinds of features serve little purpose and can even be fatal when writing client-side code as done in an Android application. Java developers have gotten used to unlimited amounts of RAM and CPU, whereas Android development requires close attention to performance and allocations. Simply put, you need a slightly different approach when writing code for Android as compared to developing back end solutions in Java.

However, some recommendations have changed since Android was first released. Some modern Java constructs once avoided on Android are now recommended, mostly because of the modern JIT compiler for Android that removes many of the performance bottlenecks these constructs used to cause.

This section deals with the aspects of Java code that you need to understand when writing Android applications. While the details of the Java programming language are outside the scope of this book; instead, I focus on what is important for Android development. Still, it's important to understand that most of the rules and recommendations that apply to Java SE apply to Android and the Dalvik VM.

Type-Safe Enum on Android

With Java SE 5.0 came many new features in the Java programming language that made life easier for Java developers. One of the most anticipated features was the introduction of *type-safe enumerations*. Enumerations are used to represent a number of choices in code that belong to a common group. In earlier versions of Java, multiple integer constants were used to solve this. Although this works technically, it suffers from being quite error-prone. Take a look at the following code:

```java
public class Machine {
    public static final int STOPPED = 10;
    public static final int INITIALIZING = 20;
    public static final int STARTING = 30;
    public static final int RUNNING = 40;
    public static final int STOPPING = 50;
    public static final int CRASHED = 60;
    private int mState;

    public Machine() {
        mState = STOPPED;
    }

    public int getState() {
        return mState;
    }

    public void setState(int state) {
        mState = state;
    }
}
```

The problem is that although the constants are the values you expect in the setter, nothing is preventing the method `setState()` from receiving a different value. If you add a check in the setter, you need to handle the error in case you get an unexpected value. What you want is a compile-time check that prevents you from ever assigning an illegal value. Type-safe Java enum solves this problem, as shown here:

```
public class Machine {
    public enum State {
        STOPPED, INITIALIZING, STARTING, RUNNING, STOPPING, CRASHED
    }
    private State mState;

    public Machine() {
        mState = State.STOPPED;
    }

    public State getState() {
        return mState;
    }

    public void setState(State state) {
        mState = state;
    }
}
```

Notice the new inner enum class added where you declare different states as type-safe values. This solves the problem with unexpected values at compile time, so the code will be much less error-prone.

Before the Dalvik VM had a JIT compiler that optimized the code, using type-safe enum was discouraged on Android because the memory and performance penalties associated with this design were greater than when using integer constants. This is why so many integer constants are in the older parts of the Android APIs. These days, with a capable JIT compiler and an ever-improving Dalvik VM, you don't have to worry about that issue and are encouraged to use type-safe enum in your application code.

However, there are still situations where integer constants are preferable. With basic types like the Java int, you won't increase the amount of work for the GC. Also, many existing APIs in the Android SDK still rely on basic types as parameters—for example, the `Handler` class described in the "Multithreading on Android" section later in this chapter—in these cases, you don't have much choice.

Enhanced For-Loop on Android

Java SE 5.0 also introduced the enhanced for-loop that provides a generic an abbreviated expression for looping over collections and arrays. First, compare the following five methods:

```
void loopOne(String[] names) {
    int size = names.length;
    for (int i = 0; i < size; i++) {
        printName(names[i]);
    }
}
```

```
void loopTwo(String[] names) {
    for (String name : names) {
        printName(name);
    }
}

void loopThree(Collection<String> names) {
    for (String name : names) {
        printName(name);
    }
}

void loopFour(Collection<String> names) {
    Iterator<String> iterator = names.iterator();
    while (iterator.hasNext()) {
        printName(iterator.next());
    }
}

// Avoid using enhanced for-loops for ArrayList
void loopFive(ArrayList<String> names) {
    int size = names.size();
    for (int i = 0; i < size; i++) {
        printName(names.get(i));
    }
}
```

These methods show four different ways of looping through collections and arrays. The first two methods have the same performance, so it's safe to use the enhanced for-loop on arrays if you're just going to read the entries. For Collection objects, you get the same performance when using the enhanced for-loop as when you manually retrieve an Iterator for traversal. The only time you should do a manual for-loop is when you have an ArrayList object.

In the cases where you not only need the value of each entry but also the position, be sure to use either an array or an ArrayList because all other Collection classes are much slower in these situations.

In general, if you need high-quality performance when reading sets of data that rarely change, use a regular array. However, arrays have a fixed size and will affect performance when adding data, so consider all factors when writing your code.

Queues, Synchronization, and Locks

Frequently, an application will produce data in one thread and consume them in another. A common example is when you're reading data from the network on one thread and want to display the data to the user on a different thread (the main thread where UI operations occur). This pattern is usually called the *consumer/ producer* pattern, and in their object-oriented programming courses, programmers may spend several hours implementing this in their algorithm. In this section, I'll show some of the ready-made classes that make it easier to implement this behavior.

Smarter Queues

Many Java developers still choose to implement queues in their code using `LinkedList` and
`synchronized` blocks, although there are ready-made classes that do so and require much less code. You
can find the classes for performing concurrent programming in the `java.util.concurrent` package. In
addition, you can find classes for semaphores, locks, and atomic operations on single variables. Consider the
following code where a thread-safe queue using a standard `LinkedList` is implemented:

```java
public class ThreadSafeQueue {
    private LinkedList<String> mList = new LinkedList<String>();
    private final Object mLock = new Object();

    public void offer(String value) {
        synchronized (mLock) {
            mList.offer(value);
            mLock.notifyAll();
        }
    }

    public synchronized String poll() {
        synchronized (mLock) {
            while(mList.isEmpty()) {
                try {
                    mLock.wait();
                } catch (InterruptedException e) {
                    // Ignore for brevity
                }
            }
            return mList.poll();
        }
    }
}
```

Although this code is correct and would probably merit a full score on an exam, it's simply a waste of your time
to implement and test it. Instead, you can replace all the preceding code with the following line:

```java
LinkedBlockingQueue<String> blockingQueue =
        new LinkedBlockingQueue<String>();
```

This one line gives you the same type of blocking queue as the previous example and even provides additional
thread-safe operations. The `java.util.concurrent` package has a number of alternative queues and
deuce classes as well as concurrent map classes, so in general, I suggest using them rather than using lengthier
code similar to my earlier example.

Smarter Locks

The `synchronized` keyword in Java provides a powerful feature that allows you to make a method
or call-block thread safe. Although easy to use, it is also easy to apply it too widely, which can have very
negative impact on performance. When you need to differentiate between reading and writing data, the
`synchronized` keyword is not the most efficient. Luckily, a utility class in the `java.util.concurrent.`
`locks` package provides exactly that support.

```java
public class ReadWriteLockDemo {
    private final ReentrantReadWriteLock mLock;
    private String mName;
    private int mAge;
    private String mAddress;

    public ReadWriteLockDemo() {
        mLock = new ReentrantReadWriteLock();
    }

    public void setPersonData(String name, int age, String address) {
        ReentrantReadWriteLock.WriteLock writeLock = mLock.writeLock();
        try {
            writeLock.lock();
            mName = name;
            mAge = age;
            mAddress = address;
        } finally {
            writeLock.unlock();
        }
    }

    public String getName() {
        ReentrantReadWriteLock.ReadLock readLock = mLock.readLock();
        try {
            readLock.lock();
            return mName;
        } finally {
            readLock.unlock();
        }
    }

    // Repeated for mAge and mAddress…
}
```

The preceding code exemplifies where to use a `ReentrantReadWriteLock` that allows read-only access from multiple concurrent threads while making sure that only one thread at a time can write to the same data.

Using `synchronized` in your code is still a valid way of handling locks, but always consider whether a `ReentrantReadWriteLock` could be a more efficient solution.

Memory Management and Allocations

The automatic memory management in Java has effectively eliminated many of the most common bugs in software development. When you no longer have to remember to release every allocation of a new object in your code, you save time that you can use to improve the features and overall quality of software.

But this feature doesn't come for free because you now have an automatic garbage collector that runs in parallel with your application. The GC will run continuously and check whether any memory allocations can be reclaimed. This behavior means that the threads in your application will compete for CPU time with the GC, so it's crucial to make sure that GC calls don't take too long whenever it is running.

Also, automatic memory management does not remove the possibility for memory leaks. If you keep references to objects that are no longer needed, the GC will not collect them, and they will waste memory. If objects are being allocated continuously but are never being released, you'll eventually run into an `OutOfMemory` exception, and your application will crash. So, try to avoid keeping references to objects in the main Android components; otherwise, they may never be "garbage collected" during the application's lifetime.

Reducing Object Allocations

On Java and Android, the most common problem with automatic memory management is when you are allocating unnecessary objects that keep the GC working more than it should. Consider a case in which a simple class represents a pair of integers:

```
public final class Pair {
    public int firstValue;
    public int secondValue;

    public Pair(int firstValue, int secondValue) {
        this.firstValue = firstValue;
        this.secondValue = secondValue;
    }
}
```

Now, say that you receive an array of integers in your application that you divide into pairs and then send to the method `sendPair`. Here is an example of when memory allocation is done badly:

```
public void badObjectAllocationExample(int[] pairs) {
    if(pairs.length % 2 != 0) {
        throw new IllegalArgumentException("Bad array size!");
    }
    for(int i = 0; i < pairs.length; i+=2) {
        Pair pair = new Pair(pairs[i], pairs[i+1]);
        sendPair(pair);
    }
}
```

Although this is a very crude example of how to generate `Pair` objects (and potentially cause a crash if the length of the array is not an even size), it demonstrates a surprisingly common mistake: allocating objects inside a loop. The GC will have a lot of work to do inside the previous loop above and will most likely cause the application UI to stutter from CPU exhaustion. If you know that the `sendPair` method won't keep a reference to the `Pair` object after it returns, your solution is simply to move the creation of the `Pair` object outside the loop and reuse the object, as shown as follows:

```
public void betterObjectAllocationExample(int[] pairs) {
    if(pairs.length % 2 != 0) {
        throw new IllegalArgumentException ("Bad array size!");
    }
    Point thePair = new Point(0,0);
    for (int i = 0; i < pairs.length; i+=2) {
        thePair.set(pairs [i], pairs [i+1]);
        sendPair(thePair);
    }
}
```

In this new version of the method, you ensure that the object is reused during the entire run of the method. There will be only one GC call once the method returns. Remember, when allocating objects, avoid doing so inside a loop when possible.

Sometimes, however, you can't avoid creating objects inside a loop, so you also need a way of handling those situations. The solution here is to allocate objects on demand using a *static factory method*. (Joshua Bloch describes this method in detail in Item 1 of his book *Effective Java*.)

This approach is commonly used in the Android framework and APIs and allows you to use a behind-the-scenes object cache that is populated on demand. The only drawback is that you need to manually recycle the objects, or the cache will always be empty.

Based on your previous example, you start by refactoring the `Pair` class so that you have a simple pool for reusing objects.

```java
public final class Pair {
    public int firstValue;
    public int secondValue;

    // Reference to next object in the pool
    private Pair next;

    // The lock used for synchronization
    private static final Object sPoolSync = new Object();
    // The first available object in the pool
    private static Pair sPool;

    private static int sPoolSize = 0;
    private static final int MAX_POOL_SIZE = 50;

    /**
     * Only allow new objects from obtain()
     */
    private Pair() { }

    /**
     * Return recycled object or new if pool is empty
     */
    public static Pair obtain() {
        synchronized (sPoolSync) {
            if (sPool != null) {
                Pair m = sPool;
                sPool = m.next;
                m.next = null;
                sPoolSize--;
                return m;
            }
        }
        return new Pair();
    }
```

```
/**
 * Recycle this object. You must release all references to
 * this instance after calling this method.
 */
public void recycle() {
    synchronized (sPoolSync) {
        if (sPoolSize < MAX_POOL_SIZE) {
            next = sPool;
            sPool = this;
            sPoolSize++;
        }
    }
}
```

Note that a number of fields are added, both static and non-static. You use these fields to implement a traditional linked list of `Pair` objects. Objects of this class are created only through the `obtain` method. You prevent new objects from outside this class by making the constructor private. The `obtain` method first checks whether the pool contains any existing objects and removes the first element in the list and returns it. If the pool is empty, it simply creates a new object. To put the object back into the pool, you call `recycle` once you're done. At that point, it is very important that you don't touch that object again.

With this modification of the `Pair` class, your previous method with the loop also needs some changes.

```
public void bestObjectAllocationExample(int[] pairs) {
    if(pairs.length % 2 != 0) throw new IllegalArgumentException ("Bad
array size!");

    for (int i = 0; i < pairs.length; i+=2) {
        Pair pair = Pair.obtain();
        pair.firstValue = pairs[i];
        pair.secondValue = pairs[i+1];
        sendPair(pair);
        pair.recycle();
    }
}
```

The first time this method runs, you create a new instance of `Pair`, which will then be reused for every new iteration. However, the next time you run this method, no new object is created. Also, because the `obtain` and `recycle` methods are thread-safe, this method is safe to execute in multiple concurrent threads. The only drawback is that you have to remember to call `recycle` manually, but this is a small price to pay considering you've postponed all GC calls for the `Pair` class until the application exits.

The example with the `Pair` class is very trivial, but it illustrates a pattern that is highly encouraging if you have a class that would otherwise be created frequently in your code. This design may look familiar because it's in several places in the Android source code and APIs. Commonly used classes such as `Message`, `MotionEvent`, and `Parcel` all implement this pattern in order to reduce unnecessary GC calls. The example with the preceding `Pair` class is basically a copy of the `Message` class implementation. When using this approach, remember to call `recycle` once you're done with an object that implements this, or the pool will be empty all the time.

Multithreading on Android

One of the most difficult parts of programming is when you have to write code that executes on multiple threads. It's a requirement for modern applications because you can't have everything executing in a serial order on one single thread. An Android application starts with a thread called *main,* also known as the UI thread (in this book, I use main and UI thread interchangeably). Unless you start another thread or implicitly call a function that starts a new thread, everything you do in an Android application will execute on the main thread. This means that if your code performs an operation on the main thread (say, running code in the `onResume` method) that will take a significant amount of time, all drawing and input events will be blocked until that operation is completed. So, the first thing to remember when you start writing your application code: Make sure that any code you execute won't ever block the main thread.

But how do you know if a method is executing on the main thread? The official Android documentation states: *"By default, all components of the same application run in the same process and thread (called the 'main' thread)."* More specifically, all the callbacks (basically, all the `onX` methods) in the Android components (`Activity`, `BroadcastReceiver`, `Service`, and `Application`) are executed on the same thread. The `onStartCommand` method of a `Service` is thus running on the same thread as the `onResume` of your `Activity`. Remember this when you design your code because blocking one of these methods will cause the system to "kill" your application.

The main thread in Android will run as long as your application's process is alive. It is kept alive during the application life cycle by the `Looper` class. This class creates a loop inside the current thread that queries a message queue (using the `MessageQueue` class). The query to this queue will block until a new message has arrived, which ensures that the thread sleeps when there's nothing to do. All execution on the main thread is done by sending messages to this queue, either directly through a `Handler` object or indirectly through some part of the Android API (for instance, the `runOnUiThread` method). You can retrieve the `Looper` for the main thread of your application through `Context.getMainLooper()`.

What is safe to execute on the main thread and what should be moved to a different thread? To be very strict, only the methods that must be executed on the main thread should be executed there. Everything else should go on a separate thread. For practical reasons, you can bend this rule in some cases where the operation you perform will never take a long time. If you make sure that any file, database, or network operations are performed on a separate thread, you are usually safe. Also, for certain applications and games, you will perform calculations at regular intervals that don't directly have anything to do with the UI, and these should also execute on a separate thread. However, it's also important to ensure that you don't have too many threads running at the same time because a performance penalty is involved when the CPU switches from one thread to another. In later chapters in this book, I give more specifics on when and when not to put your code on a separate thread.

How do you declare and manage your threads when writing Android code? In the following section I show you several ways to spawn new threads, and I explain each of these methods in detail, including their pros and cons.

Thread

This is the base class for all threads in Android. It is the same class as found in Java SE, and it behaves the same way. If you want to execute something inside a thread, you can either make a specialization (that is, a new class that extends `Thread`) or create a class implementing the `Runnable` interface that you pass to the constructor of `Thread`. This example uses the latter option.

In this example, you need to iterate over an array of `Objects` in order to "upload" data to a server (the actual code for uploading is not part of this example). You need to execute this operation on a separate thread; otherwise, it will block the user interface. Also, the operation needs to update its progress by increasing a `ProgressBar`. The following code shows an implementation of `Runnable` that resolves this issue:

```java
public class MyThread implements Runnable {
    private Object[] mInput;
    private Activity mActivity;
    private int mProgress = 0;

    public MyThread(Activity activity, Object ... input) {
        mActivity = activity;
        mInput = input;
    }

    @Override
    public void run() {
        mProgress = 0;
        Runnable runnable = new Runnable() {
            public void run() {
                mActivity.findViewById(R.id.progressBar).
                        setVisibility(View.VISIBLE);
                ((ProgressBar) mActivity.
                    findViewById(R.id.progressBar)).setProgress(0);
            }
        };
        mActivity.runOnUiThread(runnable);

        // Loop through and process mInput
        for (Object input : mInput) {
            // Post the input to a server (fake it with a sleep)
            SystemClock.sleep(50);

            runnable = new Runnable() {
                public void run() {
                    ((ProgressBar) mActivity.
                        findViewById(R.id.progressBar)).
                            setMax(++mProgress);
                    ((ProgressBar) mActivity.
                        findViewById(R.id.progressBar)).
                            setProgress(mInput.length);
                }
            };
            mActivity.runOnUiThread(runnable);
        }


        runnable = new Runnable() {
            public void run() {
                mActivity.findViewById(R.id.progressBar).
                        setVisibility(View.INVISIBLE);
            }
        )
```

```
    };
    mActivity.runOnUiThread(runnable);

    }
}
```

As you can see in the preceding example, you need to create a new `Runnable` every time you want to update the UI. This makes the code messy and will also cause unnecessary object allocations that need to be garbage collected, which is always a bad thing. The `Runnable` is needed in order to post UI updates back to the main thread through the `runOnUiThread` method.

There's another problem with this solution: Because you can call `start` on an instance of `Thread` only once, you must create a new `Thread` object every time you need to perform this operation. A new thread is an expensive thing to create again and again, so there is definitively room for improvement here. All together, this is not a very flexible method, and I discourage the direct use of the `Thread` class.

AsyncTask

This class is probably one of the more popular classes in Android because it is so simple to use. It allows you to define a task that will run on its own thread and provide callbacks for the different stages of the task. The callbacks are also designed to remove the need for using the `runOnUiThread` method to update the UI while it's running, which makes it very appropriate for indicating the progress of a long-running operation. Here is an `AsyncTask` that does the same thing as in the `Thread` example:

```java
public class MyAsyncTask extends AsyncTask<String, Integer, Integer> {
    private Activity mActivity;

    public MyAsyncTask(Activity activity) {
        mActivity = activity;
    }

    @Override
    protected void onPreExecute() {
        super.onPreExecute();
        // This will run on the main thread
        mActivity.findViewById(R.id.progressBar).
                setVisibility(View.VISIBLE);
        ((ProgressBar) mActivity.findViewById(R.id.progressBar)).
                setProgress(0);
    }

    @Override
    protected Integer doInBackground(String... inputs) {
        // This will run NOT run on the main thread
        int progress = 0;

        for (String input : inputs) {
            // Post the input to a server (fake it with a sleep)
            SystemClock.sleep(50);
            publishProgress(++progress, inputs.length);
        }
```

```
            return progress;
        }

        @Override
        protected void onProgressUpdate(Integer... values) {
            // This will run on the main thread
            ((ProgressBar) mActivity.findViewById(R.id.progressBar)).
                    setMax(values[1]);
            ((ProgressBar) mActivity.findViewById(R.id.progressBar)).
                    setProgress(values[0]);
        }

        @Override
        protected void onPostExecute(Integer i) {
            super.onPostExecute(i);
            // This will run on the main thread
            mActivity.findViewById(R.id.progressBar).
                    setVisibility(View.INVISIBLE);
        }
    }
}
```

In the preceding example, you see the implementation of four callbacks with a comment regarding which thread they will execute on. As you can see, onPreExecute, onProgressUpdate, and onPostExecute are all executed on the main thread, so it is safe to update the UI from these. publishProgress is also called for each input to trigger the onProgressUpdate callback so that you can update a progress bar.

This class makes it much easier to perform long-running operations on a different thread and still be able to communicate easily with the main thread when needed. The only problem with AsyncTask is that you can use each instance of this class only once, which means that you have to call new MyAsyncTask() every time you want to perform this operation. Although this class is not a heavyweight—the actual thread is managed by an ExecutorService behind the scenes—it is not suitable for operations that you perform frequently because you would quickly gather up objects that need to be garbage collected and eventually cause your application's UI to stutter.

In addition, you cannot schedule the time for the execution of this operation or perform the operation at a certain interval. The AsyncTask class is suitable for things like file downloads or similar situations that will happen relatively infrequently or by user interaction. Nevertheless, because it's so easy to implement, this is likely to be the class you will use at first in your application.

Handler

When you need a more fine-grained control for executing operations on a separate thread, you have a great utility at your disposal in the Handler class. This class allows you to schedule operations with exact precision, and you can reuse it as many times as you want. The thread that executes the operations loops until you explicitly terminate it; the class Looper takes care of this behind the scenes. You will rarely need to set up your own Looper; instead, you can create it through the wrapper called HandlerThread. The following example shows how to create a new Handler in your Activity.

```java
public class SampleActivity extends Activity implements Handler.Callback
{
    private Handler mHandler;

    @Override
    public void onCreate(Bundle savedInstanceState) {
        super.onCreate(savedInstanceState);
        setContentView(R.layout.main);
        // Start a new thread with a Looper
        HandlerThread handlerThread
            = new HandlerThread("BackgroundThread");
        handlerThread.start();
    // Create your new Handler
        mHandler = new Handler(handlerThread.getLooper(), this);
    }

    @Override
    protected void onDestroy() {
        super.onDestroy();
        // Shut down the Looper thread
        mHandler.getLooper().quit();
    }

    @Override
    public boolean handleMessage(Message message) {
        // Process incoming messages here...

        // Recycle your message object
        message.recycle();
        return true;
    }
}
```

With your new `Handler` object, you can now safely schedule operations with exact precision. The usual way of working with a `Handler` is by sending `Message` objects, which are simple, cheap, and reusable objects for passing data and arguments to your background thread. A `Message` object is usually defined by its public integer field name `what` that works as a flag that can be used in a switch-case statement in the callback `handleMessage`. There are also two integer fields named `arg1` and `arg2` that are suitable for low-cost arguments, as well as a field name `obj` for storing a single arbitrary object reference. If needed, you can also add a set of more complex data using the `setData` method with a standard `Bundle` object. You can send your messages to the handler using a number of methods. The three most common ones are demonstrated here:

```java
public void sendMessageDemo(Object data) {
    // Create a new Message with data as a parameter
    // and send it for execution on the handler immediately
    Message.obtain(mHandler, SYNC_DATA, data).sendToTarget();

    // Send a simple empty message on your handler immediately
    mHandler.sendEmptyMessage(SYNC_DATA);

    // Send a simple empty message to be executed 30 seconds from now
    mHandler.sendEmptyMessageAtTime(SYNC_DATA,
            THIRTY_SECONDS_IN_MILLISECONDS);
```

```
        // Send a message with both arguments fields and
        // the obj set to be executed in two minutes.
        int recipient = getRecipientId();
        int priority = 5;
        Message msg = mHandler.obtainMessage(SYNC_DATA, recipient,
                priority, data);
        mHandler.sendMessageDelayed(msg, TWO_MINUTES_IN_MILLISECONDS);
    }
```

The first two examples show that you can create and send messages through both the `Message` class and the `Handler` object. In the third and fourth example, you see how to schedule the message for processing with millisecond precision.

When the `Message` is processed from the message queue, it will be sent, on the looping thread, to the callback you've implemented. You can use the same callback for multiple `Handler` objects, which makes it useful as a proxy-like method for dealing with the messages in your application. You can even share the callback between `Activities` and `Services`. The most optimal way of implementing your callback is by keeping all the constants representing the `what` value of a `Message` in the same class that implements the callback and then use a standard switch-case statement to handle each message type. In the preceding example, I implemented the callback on the `Activity`, but it can often be useful to have a separate class for this that you pass your application's `Context` to so that it can be used in all parts of your application. Here is an example of a typical callback:

```
    // Constants used for the what field in a Message
    public static final int SYNC_DATA = 10;
    public static final int PING_SERVER = 20;

    @Override
    public boolean handleMessage(Message message) {
        switch (message.what) {
            case SYNC_DATA:
                // Perform long-running network I/O operation
                syncDataWithServer(message.obj);
                break;
            case PING_SERVER:
      // Ping your server. This should be called at regular intervals
                pingServer();
                break;
        }

        // Recycle your message object to save memory
        message.recycle();
        return true;
    }
```

The `handleMessage` callback in this example has only two operations implemented, `SYNC_DATA` and `PING_SERVER`. The first one will probably be triggered by a user event—for example, when a file is saved or new data is ready to be posted to a server. The second one is supposed to execute at regular intervals. However, there is no method on the `Handler` class for sending messages at an interval, so you need to implement that behavior.

Scheduling Operations at Recurring Intervals

Say that as soon as your `Activity` starts, you want to start pinging the server every minute. When the user exits the `Activity`, you should stop pinging.

In the following example, I add calls to the `Handler` in `onResume()` and `onPause()` (see the earlier examples in this section for the setup of the `Handler` instance), effectively making these happen when the `Activity` is shown and dismissed. In `onResume`, I set the boolean for pinging the server to `true` and sent a `PING_SERVER` message to be executed immediately (the first ping should happen as soon as possible). The message arrives in your callback message shown in the previous example, which calls your `pingServer()` method.

```
public class SampleActivity extends Activity implements Handler.Callback {
    private static final String PING_URL = "http://www.server.com/ping";
    private static final int SIXTY_SECONDS_IN_MILLISECONDS = 60 * 1000;
    public static final int SYNC_DATA = 10;
    public static final int PING_SERVER = 20;
    private Handler mHandler;
    private boolean mPingServer = false;
    private int mFailedPings = 0;

  ... code from previous examples omitted for brevity


    @Override
    protected void onResume() {
        super.onResume();
        mPingServer = true;
        mHandler.sendEmptyMessage(PING_SERVER);
    }

    @Override
    protected void onPause() {
        super.onPause();
        mPingServer = false;
        mHandler.removeMessages(PING_SERVER);
    }

    private void pingServer() {
        HttpURLConnection urlConnection
        try {
            URL pingUrl = new URL(PING_URL);
            urlConnection = (HttpURLConnection) pingUrl.openConnection();
            urlConnection.setRequestMethod("GET");
            urlConnection.connect();
                if(urlConnection.getResponseCode() == 200) {
                mFailedPings = 0;
        } // Here you should also handle network failures...
            } catch (IOException e) {
                // Network error should be handled here as well...
            } finally {
                if(urlConnection != null) urlConnection.disconnect();
            }
```

```
        if(mPingServer) {
            mHandler.sendEmptyMessageDelayed(PING_SERVER,
                    SIXTY_SECONDS_IN_MILLISECONDS);
        }
    }
}
```

In `pingServer()`, you make a simple HTTP call to see if your server is alive. Once your call is completed, you check whether you should keep pinging the server, and if so, you schedule a new message to be processed in 60 seconds. In the `onPause()` method, you change the boolean to `false` and then remove any pending messages with the `what` field set to `PING_SERVER`.

Using the MainLooper with a Handler

Because you assign a thread to a `Handler` by giving it a `Looper` object in the constructor, you can create a `Handler` that processes messages on the main thread. Doing so is especially useful when you want to avoid using the `runOnUiThread()` method, which tends to result in rather ugly and less optimal code if used often. I use this pattern frequently in my applications so that I can simply send messages between the main thread and the thread used for background operations.

```
@Override
public boolean handleMessage(Message message) {
    switch (message.what) {
        case SYNC_DATA:
            syncDataWithServer(message.obj);
            break;
        case SET_PROGRESS:
            ProgressBar progressBar =
                    (ProgressBar) findViewById(R.id.progressBar);
            progressBar.setProgress(message.arg1);
            progressBar.setMax(message.arg2);
            break;
    }

    message.recycle();
    return true;
}
```

In the preceding `handleMessage` example, you can receive two types of messages, SYNC_DATA and SET_PROGRESS. The first one needs to run on a separate thread, whereas the second one must run on the main thread because it will update the UI. To do this, you create an additional `Handler` object that will be used to send messages that are processed on the main thread.

```
@Override
public void onCreate(Bundle savedInstanceState) {
    super.onCreate(savedInstanceState);
    setContentView(R.layout.main);
    mMainHandler = new Handler(getMainLooper(), this);
    HandlerThread handlerThread = new HandlerThread("BackgroundThread");
    handlerThread.start();
    mHandler = new Handler(handlerThread.getLooper(), this);
}
```

Notice that this is basically the same `onCreate` method as shown earlier. The exception is the line where you create `mMainHandler`. Instead of starting a new `HandlerThread`, you simply retrieve the `Looper` for the main thread. This doesn't affect how the main thread is running; you just connect an additional `Handler` and callback to the main thread. Messages posted to this `Handler` are processed by the same callback as the second `Handler` you create for background operations. When you want to update the `ProgressBar`, you send a simple message, as shown here:

```
Message.obtain(mMainHandler, SET_PROGRESS, progress, maxValue).
sendToTarget();
```

You can use this approach for any operation that must be executed on the main thread. You can either send simple `Message` objects as just shown or pass along more complex data in the `obj` field or as a `Bundle` in `setData`. You just need to make sure that you post messages to the correct `Handler`.

Picking the Right Solution for Threads

I've now shown three different methods for creating and using threads on Android. There are other utilities in the API for doing this as well, such as the `ExecutorService` and the `Loader`. The `ExecutorService` is useful if you need to have multiple operations running in parallel, which is usually the situation when writing server-side applications responding to multiple clients. This `Service` is also used behind the scenes in `AsyncTask`, and if you want to be able to execute multiple `AsyncTasks` in parallel, you can do so using the right `ExecutorService`.

The three preceding examples are the ones to start with when you need a dedicated thread for an operation. Using the `Thread` class directly is discouraged unless you need full control of the entire execution of the thread. `AsyncTask` and `Handler` are recommended in most cases, and which one you choose depends on your needs. If the operation isn't performed frequently, like more than once every minute, `AsyncTask` is probably a good choice. If you need to schedule operations or need to do something at a fast, recurring interval, `Handler` is a better choice. Working with the `Handler` tends to generate less code in the long run, whereas `AsyncTask` is easier to use.

Summary

In this chapter, I covered some of the advanced Java features in Java SE 5.0 that with the modern JIT-enabled Dalvik VM are now safe to use on Android. Understanding and using these features will likely simplify your code, which makes the code easier to test and maintain. I also showed how to use the concurrency API from `java.util.concurrent`, instead of implementing your own queues or locks. Whenever you reinvent the wheel by implementing your own version of a basic class, you're making a common but big mistake: You'll have more code to test, more code that can cause bugs, and more code to maintain.

I also explained how to avoid many pitfalls when it comes to memory allocations. If your code creates a lot of temporary and short-lived objects, your application will most likely perform badly in the user interface. Understanding how to efficiently and safely reuse objects allows for a much smoother user experience.

To conclude the chapter, I covered three methods for using threads on Android but recommended using only two of them (`AsyncTask` and `Handler`). Multithreading is a complex topic and often the cause of many bugs that are hard to find. Always try to use the ready-made utility classes for threads because they will make things simpler and allow you to focus on the functions of your own code.

Java is a powerful language that makes it easier for developers to express what they want to achieve and learning how to use the language most efficiently will make you a better developer and help you create high-quality code.

Further Resources

Documentation

I recommend reading the performance tips chapter at: `http://developer.android.com/training/best-performance.html`

Books

Bloch, Joshua. *Effective Java,* 2nd Edition. Addison-Wesley, 2008.

Online Sources

Google IO video sessions on YouTube at: `www.youtube.com/user/GoogleDevelopers`

Part II

Getting the Most Out of Components

Chapter 3

Components, Manifests, and Resources

So far I've covered the more general aspects of development, much of which you can apply to generic Java development as well. In this chapter, I start going through some more Android-specific information. (*Note:* I'm assuming that you're familiar with the basic concepts of Android and have already written applications for this platform.)

The three core concepts of any Android application are the components, the manifest, and the resources. Every Android application uses all of these, so you need to fully understand them. Although your IDE will most likely assist you in setting up the basics, you can do a lot more by optimizing them yourself.

I start with an overview of the Android components and how to use them optimally for the software architecture of your applications. Next, I cover some of the details of the Android manifest and explain how you can fine-tune the parameters to suit your application. Finally, I cover some advanced details of the resources and assets and how you can work with these.

Android Components

When you write an Android application, you usually start by defining a main `Activity`. In fact, your IDE will probably ask you for the name of the main `Activity` and create it for you. You continue by setting up `Services`, `BroadcastReceivers`, and `ContentProviders` and then tie them all together using the `Intents`. The common name for these parts is *components*.

These four types of components (`Activity`, `Services`, `BroadcastReceivers`, and `ContentProviders`) are the ones most frequently used. `Activities` are responsible for the user interface, `Services` implement operations running in the background, `BroadcastReceivers` listen for system events, and `ContentProviders` store application data.

They all come with a base class that you extend and a section in the application manifest XML file that exposes them to the Android system. There is also a fifth type of component with the name `Application` that, though rarely utilized, is useful in some situations.

Allow me to walk you through these five components and put them into context before moving on to the software architecture for a standard Android application. (I cover each component in more detail in later chapters, as indicated in the following sections.)

The Activity Component

User interfaces for an Android application are managed by extensions of the `Activity` class. Your application can have several `Activities` for different functions, but only one `Activity` can be displayed at any given time. As with all other components, a number of lifecycle callbacks will notify you of the current state.

The general guide regarding `Activities` is that they handle only UI-related operations. Although you can use `AsyncTask` or `Handler` (as I describe in Chapter 2) to execute things off the main thread, the preferred practice is to always delegate long-running operations to a `Service` and execute them on a separate thread there—because the state of an `Activity` is very much controlled by the user, and it becomes a bit complicated if you need to cancel a running operation because the user happens to press the Home button. Instead, let a `Service` handle these operations and focus on the user interface in your `Activities`.

Starting with Android 3.0 (Honeycomb), the Fragments API became available for building dynamic user interfaces. This API was specifically designed to allow application developers to implement user interfaces that will adapt to the size of the devices they'll be running on. Instead of simply scaling the entire application when running on a 10-inch tablet, you can use Fragments to show more details than when running the same application on a 4-inch device.

The Service Component

The second most-common component is the `Service`. Basically, anything that doesn't involve normal user-interface operations goes into a `Service`. Remember that all components run on the same main thread, so you still have to make sure that your potentially long-running operations are executed on a separate thread using either a `Handler` or an `AsyncTask`. You want to move these operations to a `Service`, and not simply keep them in a background thread inside your `Activity`, because you want to complete the operation even if the user presses the Back or Home button during the `Activity`. By allowing a `Service` to control long-running operations, you can more easily keep track of the state of these operations.

I recommend that each task have a dedicated `Service`. You can use one `Service` for storing data and another one for communicating with an online web `Service`. For instance, if you're building a music player, create one `Service` for the playback and another `Service` for tasks that aren't related to music. You want different `Services` for different operations so that `Services` can be started and restarted differently; it's easier to have multiple `Services` than to try to build one `Service` that handles everything.

You learn more about `Services` and background operations on Android in Chapter 6.

The BroadcastReceiver Component

`BroadcastReceivers` are special components because they are stateless, which means that the `BroadcastReceiver` object is valid only during the `onReceive()` call. Therefore, you can't keep a reference to the `BroadcastReceiver` instance that's declared in the manifest anywhere in your code. Also, you can't add the instance as a listener or callback to an asynchronous operation. Basically, the only thing you can and should do in the `onReceive()` method of a `BroadcastReceiver` is to delegate the call to another component, either through the `Context.startActivity()` or the `Context.startService()` method.

This limitation makes `BroadcastReceivers` useful for one thing only: listening to system events. Many `BroadcastIntents` are defined in the Android SDK, and they're spread out in different classes in the API. All you can do is check the part of the API you're interested in to see if a `BroadcastIntent` is there that provides what you're looking for.

The `BroadcastReceiver` component is also a bit special because it can also be programmatically declared inside a `Service` or an `Activity`. These instances are manually registered and unregistered from the system in your code. *Always* unregister a programmatically defined `BroadcastReceiver` or you will leak a reference and waste memory.

A programmatically defined `BroadcastReceiver` is sometimes the only way you can listen for a certain broadcast. Some `BroadcastIntents` don't allow you to register them through the manifest. For instance, the broadcast defined by `Intent.ACTION_BATTERY_CHANGED` can be received only from a `BroadcastReceiver` registered with `Context.registerReceiver()`.

You find out more about `BroadcastReceivers` in Chapter 8.

The ContentProvider Component

You don't need to define a `ContentProvider` in order to store data for your Android application. In many cases, a simple key/value storage using `SharedPreferences` is sufficient, and you can store data in an SQLite database using the SQLite API directly from your `Services` and `Activities`. Storing files inside your application's data folder is another way of persisting application data.

However, if the application data you're going to store is suitable for SQL, it's usually easier to implement a `ContentProvider` even if you won't be sharing the data with other applications. Doing so becomes especially useful when you want to display the application data using an `AdapterView` (like a list or a grid) because the Loader API provides readymade implementations for loading data from a `ContentProvider`.

I go into the details of different data storage techniques for Android in Chapter 9.

The Application Component

There is also a fifth component, simply called `Application`, that is rarely used but can come in handy sometimes. You can consider the `Application` component as a top-level component that's created before `Activities`, `Services`, and `BroadcastReceivers`.

Your Android app will always have an `Application` component, and unless you define one, a default one will be created for you. You can always retrieve a reference to the `Application` component through the method `Context.getApplication()`. Because all Android apps will have one and only one instance of this component, you can use it to share variables and communicate across the other components within your app. Although sharing a global state can be solved using a singleton class as well, using the `Application` component has the advantage that it also implements application lifecycle callbacks.

The following code exemplifies code for a custom `Application` component. This example also shows how to use this component for sharing global variables and notifying listeners whenever these variables are added, changed, or removed. Although simplistic, this example demonstrates how you can utilize an already-existing Android component to solve a problem that would otherwise require a singleton class.

```java
public class MyApplication extends Application {
    private ConcurrentHashMap<String, String> mGlobalVariables;
    private Set<AppStateListener> mAppStateListeners;

    @Override
    public void onCreate() {
        super.onCreate();
        // Called before any other component is created
        mGlobalVariables = new ConcurrentHashMap<String, String>();
        mAppStateListeners = Collections.synchronizedSet(new
HashSet<AppStateListener>());
    }

    public String getGlobalVariable(String key) {
        return mGlobalVariables.get(key);
    }

    public String removeGlobalVariable(String key) {
        String value = mGlobalVariables.remove(key);
        notifyListeners(key, null);
        return value;
    }

    public void putGlobalVariable(String key, String value) {
        mGlobalVariables.put(key, value);
        notifyListeners(key, value);
    }

    public void addAppStateListener(AppStateListener appStateListener) {
        mAppStateListeners.add(appStateListener);
    }

    public void removeAppStateListener(AppStateListener appStateListener)
{
        mAppStateListeners.remove(appStateListener);
    }

    private void notifyListeners(String key, String value) {
        for (AppStateListener appStateListener : mAppStateListeners) {
            appStateListener.onStateChanged(key, value);
        }
    }

    public interface AppStateListener {
        void onStateChanged(String key, String value);
    }
}
```

The manifest file (`AndroidManifest.xml`) will always have an application element. However, in order for Android to recognize that your custom `Application` component is to be used, instead of the default, you need to declare the custom `Application` component in a `android:name` attribute (see the bold text in the following example).

```xml
<application android:label="@string/app_name"
             android:icon="@drawable/app_icon"
             android:name=".MyApplication">
    <!-- All other components are declared here -->
</application>
```

As just shown, you declare your custom `Application` component much as you declare an `Activity` or a `Service`. Simply add the class name in the `android:name` attribute, and you're set to go.

```java
public class MyActivity extends Activity
        implements MyApplication.AppStateListener {

    @Override
    protected void onResume() {
        super.onResume();
        MyApplication myApplication = (MyApplication) getApplication();
        myApplication.addAppStateListener(this);
    }

    @Override
    protected void onPause() {
        super.onPause();
        MyApplication myApplication = (MyApplication) getApplication();
        myApplication.removeAppStateListener(this);
    }

    @Override
    public void onStateChanged(String key, String value) {
        // Handle state change...
    }
}
```

When you need to access your custom `Application` component from somewhere in your code, you simply call `Context.getApplication()` and cast it to your custom class, as shown in the preceding example. Because you're using a listener pattern in this example, make sure that you register and unregister the listener correctly in the `onResume()` and `onPause()` methods.

Application Architecture

Generally, Android developers start a new project by creating an `Activity` and designing the user interface. Although this approach is okay, my suggestion is that you first consider the overall application architecture from a broader perspective. If you plan to do network calls, moving them to a separate `Service` is a good approach. If you need to be notified about certain system broadcasts, it's probably wise to set up a `BroadcastReceiver` and decide where to delegate those events. If your application needs to store data beyond simple key/value pairs, I suggest making a `ContentProvider` responsible for that scenario. Finally, if you have a complicated application, it may be worth your time to add a custom `Application` component as well to track global states and communicate between the other components.

I usually sketch an overall architecture using the components as a base. I ask myself what `Activities` and `Services` are needed at first and then move on to consider broadcast events and `ContentProviders`. This architecture doesn't need to reflect the actual user interface of your application because `Activities` can have a dynamic user interface with the help of Fragments. I tend to rely on the readymade extensions of the basic components as much as possible. For instance, the `PreferenceActivity` class is great for building the user interface for the settings part of your application.

Figure 3-1 shows a simple diagram that exemplifies how you can combine the components in Android to create a well-designed architecture. By always making sure that each component handles only the operations it's designed for, you'll have a stable foundation for the development of your application.

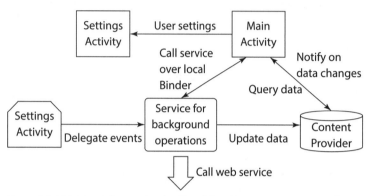

Figure 3-1 A high-level diagram showing the relationships among components in a typical Android application

You now have a general understanding of the components in Android, but along with the Java code that you write to implement your own versions of these components, you also need to know how to add them to the application manifest, which is the topic of the next section.

The Android Application Manifest

The manifest is an XML file where you define each component and declare everything else about your application. The manifest is the core of any Android application, so it's important to fully understand how to structure such files. Small mistakes in manifests can cause performance issues with your application (which could affect the entire system), unnecessary power consumption (which could cause the battery to drain), and security issues (which could leak sensitive information to other applications), and under certain conditions, they can cause your application to crash.

Fortunately, the lint tool (refer to Chapter 1) in the Android SDK provides inspections for the manifest file, so your IDE will let you know about areas in the file that need to be fixed. In this section, I provide some tips that you can use to optimize your application and that will be useful when you start doing more advanced development.

The Manifest Element

The top-level element in the `AndroidManifest.xml` file is named *manifest*. This is where the package name, the unique identifier for your application, is defined. You can also define the Linux user ID and name that your application will be running under, the version information about your application, and where the APK file should be installed.

The following example shows the `manifest` tag with all the possible attributes set. The first attribute, `package`, defines the unique identifier for you application in the Android system, the name of the application process, and the name of the default task affinity for `Activities`. Be sure to choose the package name well because it cannot be changed after the application is released.

```xml
<?xml version="1.0" encoding="utf-8"?>
<manifest xmlns:android="http://schemas.android.com/apk/res/android"
          package="com.aapt1.pushingthelimits.sample"
          android:sharedUserId="com.apptl.userid"
          android:sharedUserLabel="@string/userLabel"
          android:installLocation="auto"
          android:versionCode="1"
          android:versionName="1.0">

</manifest>
```

> When deciding on the package name, it's best to use the domain name of the company or organization that publishes the application and append a shortened, lowercase version of the name the application will have on Google Play. If you're working as a consultant or a freelance developer, be sure to use a name based on your customer's domain name, and not your own.

The `android:sharedUserId` and `android:sharedUserLabel` are the Linux user ID and name that your application will run on. By default, these are assigned by the system, but if you set them to the same value for all the applications you publish using the certificate, you can access the same data and even share the process of these applications. If you're building a suite of applications or if you have a free and a paid version, this can be very helpful.

> In regard to free and paid versions of your game, when people try your free version and decide to purchase the paid version, they don't want to lose all the progress they achieved before the purchase. To solve this issue, make sure that both your versions share the same user ID and simply synchronize the data from the free to the paid version on startup.

When multiple applications share the same process, you can save the total amount of RAM your applications use. However, all the applications that share the same process will also crash if one of the applications experiences a runtime error.

You can use the `android:installLocation` attribute to control where the application is installed. You can install it either on the device's internal storage (the *data partition*) or the external storage (for instance, the SD card). *Note:* You control only the location of the APK file through this attribute. The application data is still stored safely on the internal storage.

The version information is important when you publish your application on Google Play. `android:versionCode` is the value that is read by the Google Play Store, whereas `android:versionName` is what is presented to the user. My recommendation is to use a version code that makes it easy for you. The simplest solution is to start at 1 and simply increment it with 1 with every new version. You can set up your build script on your continuous integration system to increment this for each nightly build (highly recommended!), or you can increase it manually before you commit new code to your repository. Either way, increment the value before trying to publish a new version to Google Play.

Google Play Filters and Permissions

The next part of your manifest should contain the details about how it is made visible in Google Play and the features in the platform you're using. Here, you also declare the permissions you use as well as the new permissions that your application requires when providing interfaces for other applications.

You can find more about permissions in Chapters 12. At this point, just remember to declare the permissions you need, or you'll get a nasty error when your application tries to access a restricted API. If your application will provide an interface (through a `Service`, content provider, or custom `BroadcastIntent`), be sure to define your own permissions in the manifest.

One of the most important parts of your `AndroidManifest.xml` file, but which is also often forgotten, is the `uses-features` element. This is what Google Play uses when it filters which applications will be visible on each device. For example, if your application needs the capability to send SMS, you probably want to exclude the devices that lack support for this (Wi-Fi–only tablets), and add an element saying that you need telephony support.

Also, with new types of Android devices appearing, some features we've come to expect on an Android device aren't always there. For instance, although most Android devices have a touch screen, you won't find one on a device that runs on TV. If your application requires a touch screen and cannot work via a mouse pointer, be sure to declare this in your manifest. The following example shows how to specify that your application needs telephony support and a touchscreen supporting full "Jazz Hands" multi-touch.

```
<uses-feature android:name="android.hardware.microphone" />
<uses-feature android:name="android.hardware.telephony" />
<uses-feature android:name="android.hardware.touchscreen.multitouch.
jazzhand" />
```

You can find a complete list of all the standard features in Android at `http://developer.android.com/guide/topics/manifest/uses-feature-element.html#features-reference`.

Android supports many different screen sizes by default, but you won't always want your application to be available for all of them. For instance, if you're developing an application that's intended for tablets, you may want to limit it to only devices with that screen size. You can do so by using the `supports-screens` element, which allows you to specify which screen sizes your application works on as well as the smallest width required for a device screen. The following is an example of what to use for a tablet-only application.

```
<supports-screens android:smallScreens="false"
                  android:normalScreens="false"
                  android:largeScreens="false"
                  android:xlargeScreens="true" />
```

Another important function of the manifest is determining the API levels your application supports. You can define minimum, target and maximum levels: Minimum defines the lowest Android version you support, whereas maximum defines the highest. The latter is useful when you have multiple APKs for different Android versions for a single application or if you want to delay publishing an application for new versions of Android until you've had time to verify your application. My recommendation is to avoid the `android:maxSdkVersion` attribute if possible.

The interesting attribute in the `uses-sdk` element is the `android:targetSdkVersion`. This attribute tells a device which API level you're targeting. Although `android:minSdkVersion` lets you limit the lowest Android version you support, it tells Android not to enable any compatibility behaviors with the target version. More specifically, this combination allows you to gracefully degrade feature support in your application for older versions while still maintaining an up-to-date user interface and functionality for later versions.

```
<uses-sdk android:minSdkVersion="11" android:targetSdkVersion="16"/>
```

My recommendation is to always specify `android:minSdkVersion` and `android:targetSdkVersion`, as shown in the preceding example. Unless you specify `android:minSdkVersion`, it will default to 1 (that is, Android version 1), which you probably want to avoid. By specifying `android:targetSdkVersion`, you can easily increase your support for new versions.

You can find a complete list of all API levels and which Android version they represent at `http://developer.android.com/guide/topics/manifest/uses-sdk-element.html`.

The Application Element

As I described earlier, there is a fifth, rarely used, type of component named `Application`. This component is represented by the application element in the manifest file. Unless you provide your custom `Application` class using the `android:name` attribute, the system default will be used.

A number of other important attributes are on the application element. Some of these attributes provide additional functions to your application and others are only for information. I'll go through those I consider most important, as shown here:

```
<application
        android:label="@string/app_name"
        android:description="@string/app_description"
        android:icon="@drawable/app_icon"
        android:name=".MyApplication"
        android:backupAgent=".MyBackupAgent"
        android:largeHeap="false"
        android:process="com.aaptl.sharedProcess">

    <!-- activities, services, receivers and providers go here. -->

</application>
```

Because users may have hundreds of different applications installed, it helps if you provide as much information about your application as possible to the system. I recommend that you set both the `android:label` and the `android:description` attributes to values that are localized (that is, with translations in different languages). The description attribute should also contain detailed text about what your application does so that when the user looks at your app in the settings, he immediately can tell what the app does.

Eventually, users will change their smartphones, and they'll want to be able to move all their applications, including the data, to their new device. Fortunately, Google provides a backup `Service` that helps to solve this issue, but you have to declare this in your application and implement your own backup agent. You do so using the `android:backupAgent` attribute, which points to the class that implements this. I go through the details of the backup agent in Chapter 9, but it's a good idea to always provide this from the start so that you don't forget it.

If you're building an application that requires a large amount of memory, you'll soon run into a problem with the default limit of the heap size of the Dalvik VM. You can solve this issue by adding the `android:largeHeap` attribute to your application manifest to let the system know you require more memory. However, never add this unless you really need to; doing so will waste resources, and also the system will terminate your application much sooner. For most applications this attribute is not necessary and should be avoided.

If you have a suite of applications sharing the same user ID (as described earlier for the `manifest` element), you can also force them to share the same process by setting the same value to the `android:process` attribute. This helps to reduce the use of your applications' resources but also leaves them all vulnerable if one of them crashes; the most likely situation is when you have one application that supports plug-ins that can be installed from Google Play. *Note:* All applications must share the same user ID and be signed with the same certificate in order for this to work.

Finally, you have the `android:theme` attribute that can be set either for the entire application (in the applications element) or on individual `Activities`.

Component Elements and Attributes

Each of the standard components (`Activity`, `Service`, `BroadcastReceiver`, and `ContentProvider`) has its own elements in the manifest. While the default attributes created by Android Studio is usually good enough for most situations, you should always review them in order to ensure you have the optimal values.

Every component you define is enabled by default. You can change this by setting `android:enabled="false"`, which will prevent them from receiving `Intents`. Disabled `Activities` won't show up in the application launcher, `Services` won't respond to `startService()` calls, `BroadcastReceivers` won't listen to `BroadcastIntents`, and `ContentProviders` won't respond to the `ContentResolver`. You can change this setting in your code, which is especially efficient if you want to make sure that parts of your application remain disabled until the user completes certain configuration steps.

In the following XML, you see two `Activities` declared where the second one is disabled by default. You want the user to start and complete the setup process before you show the main `Activity`. You also want to hide the setup `Activity` once it's completed.

```
<activity
        android:name=".SetupActivity"
        android:label="@string/app_name_setup"
        android:icon="@drawable/app_setup_icon"
        android:enabled="true">
    <intent-filter>
        <action android:name="android.intent.action.MAIN"/>
        <category android:name="android.intent.category.LAUNCHER"/>
    </intent-filter>
</activity>
<activity
        android:name=".MainActivity"
        android:label="@string/app_name"
        android:icon="@string/app_icon"
        android:enabled="false">
    <intent-filter>
        <action android:name="android.intent.action.MAIN"/>
        <category android:name="android.intent.category.LAUNCHER"/>
    </intent-filter>
</activity>
```

The following code is a simple example of where you use the PackageManager API to toggle the enabled state for the `Activities`. This way, you can change which `Activity` is shown in the launcher as well.

```
private void toggleActivities() {
    PackageManager packageManager = getPackageManager();
    // Enable the main activity
    packageManager.setComponentEnabledSetting(new ComponentName(this,
MainActivity.class),
            PackageManager.COMPONENT_ENABLED_STATE_ENABLED,
PackageManager.DONT_KILL_APP);
    // Disable the setup activity
    packageManager.setComponentEnabledSetting(new ComponentName(this,
SetupActivity.class),
            PackageManager.COMPONENT_ENABLED_STATE_DISABLED,
PackageManager.DONT_KILL_APP);
}
```

Sometimes you have a component, usually a `Service`, that you don't want to expose to the rest of the system for security purposes. To do this, you can set the `android:exported` attribute to `false`, which will effectively hide that component from the rest of the system.

If you want a component to be available for other applications but want to provide a level of security, you can provide a permission that the calling application needs to specify in its own manifest (by using `uses-permission`). Usually, you define your own permission (using a permission element under the manifest element) and then apply it to the components that require it. You apply a permission requirement to a component through the `android:permission` attribute.

Intent Filtering

All components in Android are accessed using `Intents`. An `Intent` is an abstract description of an operation that you want to perform. `Intents` are either sent to an `Activity`, a `Service`, or a `BroadcastReceiver`. Once sent, Android's `Intent` resolution kicks in to decide where the `Intent` should be delivered.

The first thing during `Intent` resolution is to determine if it is an explicit or implicit `Intent`. Explicit `Intents` contain information about the package and the name of the component, and these can be delivered immediately because there can be only one match. This method is generally used for application-internal communication. Implicit `Intent` resolution depends on three factors: the action of the `Intent`, the data URI and type, and the category. Extras and flags on `Intents` carry no meaning when it comes to deciding where they should be delivered.

Action is the most important test and usually the one you should focus on. Android has a number of predefined actions, and you can define your own actions as well. When defining your own actions, it's customary to prepend the string with your package name so that you don't end up with conflicting action strings between applications.

Data doesn't really carry actual data but contains a URI and a MIME-type, which is useful when you want to use an `Activity` to open only certain file types.

The category is mostly relevant for `Activities`. All implicit `Intents` sent by `startActivity()` will always have at least one category defined (`android.intent.category.DEFAULT`), so unless the `intent-filter` for your `Activity` also this category, it won't pass the `Intent` resolution test. The only exception here is for `intent-filters` for the launcher.

The following XML shows an `Activity` with two `intent-filters`, one for the launcher and one for opening files with the MIME type starting with `video`.

```
<activity
        android:name=".VideoPlayer"
        android:label="@string/app_name_setup"
        android:icon="@drawable/app_setup_icon"
        android:enabled="true">
    <intent-filter>
        <action android:name="android.intent.action.MAIN"/>
        <category android:name="android.intent.category.LAUNCHER"/>
    </intent-filter>
    <intent-filter>
        <action android:name="android.intent.action.VIEW" />
        <category android:name="android.intent.category.DEFAULT" />
        <data android:mimeType="video/*" />
    </intent-filter>
</activity>
```

The first `intent-filter` doesn't need a category `android.intent.category.DEFAULT` because it will be managed by the launcher application. The second `intent-filter` will match when the user triggers a `VIEW` action on a video file. The file can be stored on the local storage or on a web server as long as the MIME type starts with `video`.

You can read more about `Intents` **and** `Intent` **resolution for Android at** `http://developer.android.com/guide/components/intents-filters.html`.

Resources and Assets

Although most of your development work for an application will go into the source code, there is also the embedded content like XML layouts, icons, and text values, to name a few. This static content is either stored as resources or assets in your application's APK file. All resources belong to a certain type (such as layout, drawable, and so on), whereas assets are simply generic files stored inside your application. Most of your application's content that is not code will be represented as resources because they are tightly integrated into the Android APIs.

The resource feature in Android is one of the most powerful features of the platform from a developer's standpoint. It allows you to provide multiple versions of each resource depending on screen size, localization parameters, device capabilities, and so on. The most common solution is to use the resource feature to support multiple languages by having several versions of the text strings in different files and to support various screen sizes through different layouts and icons of varying sizes.

When you start to define your resources in an application, you need to keep a few rules in mind. First, always have a default resource for every resource type in your application, which means that you need to keep default images and icons, text strings, and layouts in a resource directory without any qualifiers. Doing so ensures that your application won't crash if it runs on a device with a resource qualifier that doesn't match those you've provided. The easiest way to ensure this is to start with the default resources and create the alternate versions once you know which variations you need.

Also, use resources whenever possible and avoid hard-coded strings and values. Don't keep strings in your application's code that will be printed in the user interface; instead, externalize them by putting them in the `strings.xml` file. Values that can be placed in a resource file should be moved there. Doing so may require some extra effort, but once you get used to always defining strings and other values in the resources, you'll see that other more complicated tasks become easier. Localization, adding support for more languages, becomes easier if everything is defined as resources from the start. Changing sizes on fonts, margins, paddings, and other properties becomes easier if they're all defined in one place.

Resources are filtered using a number of qualifiers that you specify. For instance, if you want to provide a high-resolution set of icons for devices with very high-density pixel displays, you can do so by storing a separate set of them in a directory named `drawable-xhdpi`. The most common qualifiers are for screen rotation and size, language, and region. It's important to name the directory with the resource qualifiers in the correct order; otherwise, Android will ignore that directory. For instance, language and region should always come before screen size.

You can find a list of all the resource qualifiers, their order of precedence, and their meaning at `http://developer.android.com/guide/topics/resources/providing-resources.html#table2`.

You can access resources in two ways: in XML or in Java code. When accessing the resources, you don't need to specify qualifiers; the system handles this automatically.

Now, it's time to take a look at some more advanced examples of using resources. I cover user-interface resources, such as drawables, in Chapter 4 and focus on the more generic types here.

Advanced String Resources

Basically, every string in your application should be externalized into a string resource. As you can see in the following example, several options provide an advantage over Java's `String` handling and eliminate many of the problems, especially when it comes to formatting and localization.

```xml
<?xml version="1.0" encoding="utf-8"?>
<resources>
    <string name="personal_welcome_message">Welcome %s!</string>
    <plurals name="inbox_message_count">
        <item quantity="zero">Your inbox is completely empty!</item>
        <item quantity="one">You one message in your inbox!</item>
        <item quantity="two">You two messages waiting to be read!</item>
        <item quantity="few">You have %d messages waiting!</item>
        <item quantity="many">%1$d messages in your inbox! %2$s, you
should really login here more often!</item>
        <item quantity="other">%1$d messages in your inbox! %2$s, you
should really login here more often!</item>
    </plurals>
    <string-array name="default_categories">
        <item>Work</item>
        <item>Personal</item>
        <item>Private</item>
        <item>Spam</item>
        <item>Trash</item>
        <item>Draft</item>
    </string-array>
</resources>
```

This example defines three different types of string resources. The file should be named `strings.xml` (although the name doesn't matter as long as it ends with `.xml`) and placed in the resources directory named `values`. You then duplicate this file for each language you support and put the file in a `values-<language qualifier>` directory.

The preceding example is a simple string that takes one string parameter as its input and inserts it where the `%s` is placed. The following code snippet shows how you can use the `getString` method to retrieve the resource and pass a `String` variable as input.

```java
public void showWelcomeMessage(String name) {
    ((TextView) findViewById(R.id.welcome_message_field)).
            setText(getString(R.string.personal_welcome_message, name));
}
```

> **You can find detailed rules on formatting resource strings in the JavaDoc for the** `java.util.` `Formatter` **class at** `http://developer.android.com/reference/java/util/` `Formatter.html.`

The preceding code snippet is a plurals resource that allows you to define different strings depending on the amount of input. This is especially useful because the grammar for a language can be very hard to manage using normal string operations. The following example shows how you first retrieve the `Resources` object and then call `getQuantityString` to get the right string value depending on the input. This method can also take formatting parameters if one of the choices requires that.

```
public void showInboxCountMessage(int inboxCount, String name) {
    Resources res = getResources();
    String inboxCountMessage = res.
            getQuantityString(R.plurals.inbox_message_count, inboxCount,
name);
    ((TextView) findViewById(R.id.inbox_count_field)).
            setText(inboxCountMessage);
}
```

The preceding example shows how to provide an array of strings. These are useful when you want to provide an array of constant string values. In the following code, you see an example where you populate a `ListView` using an `ArrayAdapter` with the string array declared earlier.

```
public void displayCategories() {
    ListView listView = (ListView) findViewById(R.id.category_list);
    Resources res = getResources();
    String[] categories = res.getStringArray(R.array.default_categories);
    ArrayAdapter<String> categoriesadapter = new
ArrayAdapter<String>(this,
            android.R.layout.simple_list_item_1, android.R.id.text1,
            categories);
    listView.setAdapter(categoriesadapter);
}
```

Localization

As I described earlier, resources in Android can be efficiently used for providing localization support. To do so, you copy the default string resources into a new directory with the appropriate language and region qualifier and then start translating the text.

Although no tool is available in the Android SDK to help you with the actual translation of one language to another, the built-in lint tool (described in Chapter 1) shows whether you have a resource directory for a language without a translation.

Because you probably don't know all the languages you want to support (if you do, please let me know so we can be friends!), you will need some help translating your resources. Your first choice, especially if you're on a tight budget, is to use Google Translator Toolkit (see Figure 3-2). This is a `Service` from Google that allows you to upload an Android resource XML and have it automatically translate your strings to a new language. The result might not be perfect, but the `Service` is getting better all the time, thanks to the efforts of Google.

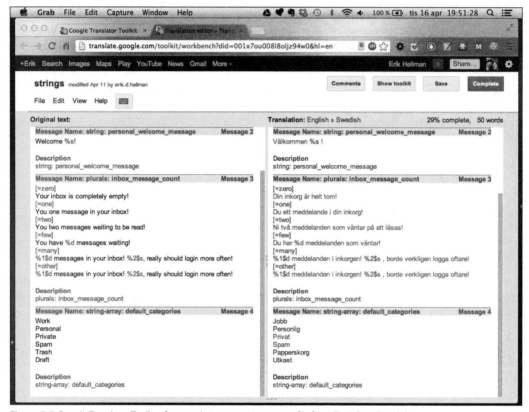

Figure 3-2 Google Translator Toolkit after translating a `string.xml` file from English to Swedish

---

You can access the Google Translator Toolkit at `http://translate.google.com/toolkit`.

You can also hire a professional translation service to do the work. Although the quality will most likely be much better than when using an automatic tool, a professional service will also cost quite a bit if you have many different languages. Also, if you update your application and add new strings in your default resources, you'll need to submit the new strings, further increasing the cost of developing your application.

Using Resource Qualifiers

Providing alternative resources for different screen sizes and locales (language and region) is fairly straightforward, so I won't cover that topic much more in this chapter. There are, however, other things you can use the resource qualifiers for.

You can use Android resources in your application to control the application logic based on things that can be expressed as resource qualifiers.

Consider the following example: You have a very popular game that you provide for free on Google Play. The game is financed through in-game advertisement that the user can disable by doing a simple in-game purchase. However, a major carrier has offered to buy an ad-free version of your game for all its customers.

One way to approach this issue is to build a duplicate version of the game and publish that version on Google Play for a specific region and carrier. Although this will work technically, you'll have to do more work because you'll have to publish two distinct versions of the game. Also, customers who suddenly find two versions of the game on Google Play might become confused. A possible solution is to turn ads on or off in the game depending on which carrier the game belongs to. You can do this programmatically in Java, but a smoother way is to use a Boolean resource.

A great site for finding the mobile country codes (MCC) and mobile network code (MNC) values for various carriers and countries is www.mcc-mnc.com**.**

The following code shows the default resource file containing the Boolean expression. Put this file in the default values directory (that is, `res/values`) and then create a new resource directory with the correct qualifier. For instance, if the carrier is Vodafone UK, the resource directory is named `values-mcc234-mnc15`. Then you simply copy this resource file and change the value to `true`.

```xml
<?xml version="1.0" encoding="utf-8"?>
<resources>
    <bool name="disable_ads_by_default">false</bool>
</resources>
```

Whenever the application is opened on a device with a SIM-card belonging to Vodafone UK, the following code example returns `true`.

```java
public boolean disableAdsByDefault() {
    return getResources().getBoolean(R.bool.disable_ads_by_default);
}
```

The preceding code shows how to retrieve the resource in Java code. Although trivial, it serves as a useful example of how powerful Android's resource feature is. The preceding example using Boolean could be replaced with an integer resource telling how much in-game cash a player should start with or by providing higher-quality icons and images (using drawables with qualifiers) for customers on a certain carrier.

Using a resource with a MCC and MNC qualifier to control application logic isn't actually secure. A technically skilled user could bypass this check with relative ease. However, for the most part, you can consider this safe enough. Remember, though, that filtering on MCC and MNC requires that the device have telephony support.

Although the qualifiers are mostly used to provide localization and various screen size support, you can use them in many other ways as well. Don't be afraid to experiment with resource qualifiers, as long as you always provide a default version as a fallback.

Using Assets

Until Android 2.3, the maximum limit of a resource file was 1MB, which caused problems if you used resources that were larger—which is why you also had the option of storing arbitrary files in your project's assets directory. This limitation is no longer a problem, so you can now safely store arbitrary files in the `raw` resource directory. However, because the assets directory supports subfolders, in some situations, you may still want to use assets instead of resources.

Consider an example where you have a game and you have a number of sound effects that you want to put in the game. You start by creating a directory in the assets folder named `soundfx` and place all your audio files for the effect there.

The following code shows how to use the `SoundPool` API and the `AssetManager` to load the audio files contained in the `soundfx` directory of your assets. Remember that you need to close the files that you open from the `AssetManager`, or your application could leak memory.

```
public HashMap<String, Integer> loadSoundEffects(SoundPool soundPool)
throws IOException {
    AssetManager assetManager = getAssets();
    String[] soundEffectFiles = assetManager.list("soundfx");
    HashMap<String, Integer> soundEffectMap = new HashMap<String,
Integer>();
    for (String soundEffectFile : soundEffectFiles) {
        AssetFileDescriptor fileDescriptor = assetManager.
openFd("soundfx/" + soundEffectFile);
        int id = soundPool.load(fileDescriptor, 1);
        soundEffectMap.put(soundEffectFile, id);
        fileDescriptor.close();
    }
    return soundEffectMap;
}
```

The preceding example could, of course, be changed to use `raw` resources as well, but I'm leaving that as an exercise for you to explore.

Summary

I've now covered the three central elements that are part of any Android application: the components, the manifest, and its resources. Understanding how these work and how to use the features they provide will take you a long way toward becoming a master Android developer.

Try to design your application around your components because they provide lifecycle callbacks that are managed by the system, allowing you to focus on what is important in your application. By always making the components a first priority, you'll find it easier to build an application without ending up with tons of boilerplate code, something I've encountered far too often.

The manifest is the actual definition of your application, and you need to take extra care in structuring it and the attributes you use for each element. Remember to declare all the features that your application requires, even the ones that may be obvious, such as a touchscreen or camera. A common error that I've seen during development is missing permissions. Be sure you always add a `uses-permission` element for the permissions your application requires.

By using the `android:enabled` and `android:exported` attributes on selected components, you have access to a powerful control for dynamically changing the behavior and protecting your components. You should, at the very least, make sure none of your `Services` and content providers are exported, unless they need to be accessed from other applications.

Make sure you are fully aware of how `Intent` resolution works. A small mistake here could cause your app to respond in unexpected ways (or not respond at all).

When it comes to the static content in your application, move as much as possible into the resources. Make sure every constant text string that is printed somewhere comes from the string resources, and not a constant value in your code. Remember to define the resource in the default resource directory (that is, a directory without any qualifiers appended to the name) and copy it to the new qualifier when needed.

Google Translator Toolkit can help you with localization of your string resources. Also consider using resources for application logic where qualifiers like network carrier or region can be part of the factors.

Further Resources
Documentation

```
http://developer.android.com/guide/components/fundamentals.html

http://developer.android.com/guide/topics/manifest/manifest-intro.html

http://developer.android.com/guide/topics/resources/index.html
```

Chapter 4

Android User Experience and Interface Design

Android's user interface has changed quite a bit over the years. One of the biggest changes came with Android 3.0 (Honeycomb) where the new Holo theme was introduced. Since then, we've seen Android's UI become a polished and sleek experience that easily appeals to users of all backgrounds.

The team at Google behind the Android UI design has done some great work at explaining how to apply the same design into your own applications. This is covered in great detail at `http://developer.android.com/design/index.html`. I strongly recommend all Android developers to go through these guidelines to fully understand how to work with the different aspects of Android UI design.

In this chapter I'm going to cover UI design for Android applications at a more theoretical level. While the Android design site I just recommended does cover many things a developer and UI designer need to know, there are still things I believe you need to have a better understanding of when designing state-of-the-art user interfaces.

I start this chapter with a description of a process for identifying the different parts of your application UI and how they work together. I then move on to describe Android specific UI concepts like navigation, sizes and colors. I've also written a section covering usability and what you should consider when you do the detailed design of your user interface. The final part of this chapter covers the concept of gamification and explains how you can use this to increase the use of your application.

User Stories

The first thing you should do when you start to design your application is to write down the *user stories* that describe what a user can do with your application. A user story is commonly used in agile software development as the basis for defining product requirements. Typically, a user story uses the following form (sometimes with a slight variation):

As a <role>, I want <goal/desire> so that <benefit>.

For instance, if you're designing a sketching application, one of the user stories could be:

As a user, I want to change the color used by the current drawing tool so that it only affects the next use of that tool.

The final part that describes the *benefit* can sometimes be left out when it is obvious.

Your user stories should be brief and concrete. Each story should focus on one thing. It is better to use two similar stories than a long and complicated one. Start with the obvious user stories, split them up, and add more as you see fit. You will probably end up with a lot of stories once you're done. But this process will help you when you start to design your user interface as each story should be easily mapped to an action in the user interface. Although not every user story might start with a user interaction, they will most certainly affect the user interface in some way. For instance, a user story about an alarm is one such example:

As a user, I want the screen to display the current time when a preset alarm goes off.

User stories can then also be used to track the progress of your development work. Try to focus on completing one story at a time and once the entire story is implemented and tested, you can move that story to a "completed" state.

There are a few things to keep in mind when writing user stories. First of all, different stories can be implemented using a common software component. However, this might not be obvious when you first write a user story, but becomes apparent when you start writing your code. For instance, if your application will list items in different categories and provide a search interface, the list of items for categories and search result can probably use the same `Activity` and `View` layout. This is why it is a good idea to categorize your user stories early in the process, so that you can more easily identify the places where a common `Activity` or `View` can be used for different stories.

Understanding the User with Personas

When you're writing the user stories, it is easy to make assumptions of how things should work based on your own experiences and perspective. The problem is that real users lack the same knowledge about your application that you do. The way to deal with this is to create *personas* which are made-up users who each represent a typical user. For instance, if you're designing a newsreader you can make up a number of personas that represent who you believe are the most common users.

A persona should have a full name, description, age, sex, education and other relevant information. Also, you should list a number of goals that the user has when using your application (for instance, catching up on the news while commuting). Finally, you should define a priority for each persona based on their relative importance compared to every other persona. The following is an example of a persona that you can define when designing a newsreader application:

Name: John Smith

Sex: Male

Age: 31

Description:

- Commutes to work by bus where he reads news
- Works in an office
- Uses his smartphone as his primary source for reading news

Priority: High

You should define a number of personas that define the users you want to target. Try to imagine how each persona would use your application and what their needs are.

When you have the personas for your most important users, it's easier to define the user stories that fulfill the most important requirements for your application. You can now easily prioritize each user story for your project.

Android UI Design

When planning and designing the user interface for your Android application, there are a few basic principles you should follow. First, you should think in terms of *screens* when you plan the user interface. Model your applications so that you have multiple screens, each focusing on a small set of actions that the user can perform. For instance, a typical newsreader application would have one screen for listing news items, one for adding news sources, one for reading news, and probably one for searching.

When defining the different screens you don't need to focus on the details of the user interface. Simply try to figure out what kind of information you want to display on each screen and leave the details about how to display them for later.

Navigation

Once you have the different screens figured out you should start to think about how navigation works between them. The navigation should be simple and straightforward so that the user will never be lost. Android provides a number of navigational concepts that makes this process easier. When you start designing the navigational structure you might also add additional screens to your application as needed.

Navigation in Android applications can be divided into four different categories: temporal, ancestral, descendant, and lateral.

Temporal navigation is usually done with the Android back button, moving to the previous screen. This navigation is usually handled automatically by the Android framework and doesn't require any special code by a developer. However, there can be situations where you wish to override the default handling of the back button. For instance, when embedding a `WebView` for displaying web pages, you might wish to use the back button in Android as a back navigation for the web pages.

Ancestral navigation refers to the navigation where the user moves up through the hierarchy to a parent screen, like moving back to the start screen for the application. Ancestral navigation is solved in Android 4.1 and later through the use of the `android:parentActivityName` attribute for each `Activity` in the application manifest. For earlier versions of Android you need to use the Android support library together with a `meta-data` tag (see `http://developer.android.com/training/implementing-navigation/ancestral.html`).

Descendant navigation is when the user navigates down through a hierarchy, for instance clicking on an item in a list. Descendant navigation is the most common form in Android applications. It is typically handled through a combination of `Fragments` and `Activity` instances where the user triggers actions that change the screen. This kind of navigation will usually move down through the information hierarchy, but can also be used to display additional information about the current object.

Lateral navigation is when the user moves to a sibling screen, for instance moving from one tab to another sideways. This type of navigation is useful when your application will contain multiple lists of similar types, but divided into different categories. One of the most common examples of this is the list of different types of applications in the Google Play Store application.

Prototyping User Interfaces

When you get your screens and navigation completed, you can start prototyping the user interfaces. The best way to start prototyping is with a paper and pencil. It is cheap, fast, and since users will interact with the application using their fingers, it is easy to get a feel for how easy it is to use. Make a paper sketch for each screen and add notes to clarify the UI. You can now "navigate" between your prototype screens in a way that's similar to how a real user would navigate in your application on a real device.

The paper prototype can start out simple with very little detail and evolve into a complete sketch of what the user interface will look like. The important thing is to try several designs and not just stick to the first that comes to mind. You should compare all your sketches to each other to find the best approach for each screen.

Once you feel you've got a good paper prototype, you can move on to create a more advanced prototype of the user interface using Android Studio, as described in the next section.

Android Studio UI Designer

One of the best UI prototyping tools for Android applications is probably something that you've already installed. Android Studio comes with a great UI designer toolkit that lets you work directly with XML layouts for different screen sizes (see Figure 4-1). You can easily create a quick mockup that you can try out on your device or an emulator.

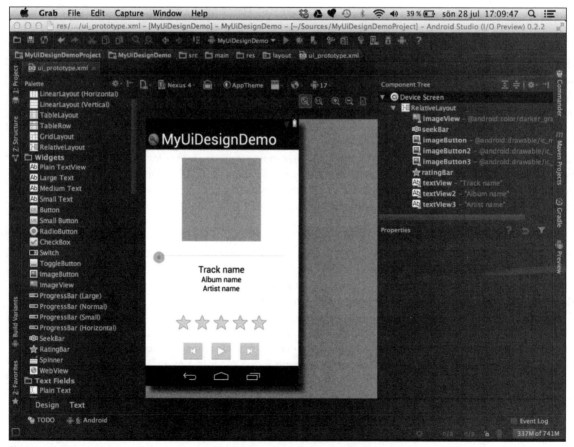

Figure 4-1 Android Studio as a UI prototyping tool

One advantage with Android Studio UI designer is the tight integration with your code. You can easily switch between different screen sizes, locale settings, and screen orientations and see the result immediately on the screen.

By using Android Studio and its UI Designer tool you can create a working mockup of your user interface that you can try out on a real device. You might have to add a minimal amount of code to fill the mockup with fake data, but with only minor effort you can have a working mockup of your application in no time.

Android UI Elements

When developing Android applications you have a large set of ready-made UI elements, called widgets, in the Android SDK that you can use. These widgets can be found in the `android.widget` package of the Android APIs. You should try to use the existing widgets as much as possible. However, if your `View` hierarchy gets very complicated you should consider creating a custom `View`, as described in Chapter 5, instead.

The main reason why you should use existing widgets as much as possible is because they are easily recognizable by the user. In many cases, you want to create an application that will be distributed on multiple platforms. When doing so, it can be tempting to re-use the same user interface design for all platforms. While the concept of designing once and running the app "everywhere" might seem tempting at first, you will likely create inconsistent user experiences that will have a very negative impact and alienate users.

This is also the reason why you should avoid creating your own look and feel for existing widgets. A user can become confused if buttons suddenly change their appearance when they start your application. This concept of "Pure Android" is described in further detail here: `http://developer.android.com/design/patterns/pure-android.html`.

Text in Android Applications

One of the most important aspects of any application is the text. While placement of UI components are important, it is the text together with images that is used to relay information to the user. Badly written text, the wrong font or a text size that is too small can lead to an overall bad user experience.

Also, how you express your message in text matters, which is described in detail in the Writing Style section found here: `http://developer.android.com/design/style/writing.html`.

Font Matters

There's been a lot of debate over the years about fonts, particularly about whether using serif or sans serif is better, even though studies have shown that neither appreciably affects how easy or fast people can read text.

What *does* matter is how easily a font can be recognized. The human brain uses pattern recognition to identify letters in a text, so logic says that you should use an easily recognizable font. So, limit your use of highly decorative fonts and use them only for logos and such.

Google has designed a default font for Android called Roboto (see Figure 4-2), which I recommend you use unless you have a well-designed font that is part of your brand. This font was designed with all the modern aspects of Android devices in mind, such as high-resolution screens.

The quick brown fox jumps over the lazy dog

Figure 4-2 Example of the Roboto font for Android

Text Layout

Another interesting aspect of readability is the fact that people read faster when lines are long but they prefer to read short lines, which is one reason newspapers often use narrow columns for articles. So, consider what's of the most importance in the text you present. Use longer lines only if reading speed is important, although text in applications is usually short, so this shouldn't be much of a problem. The point is to keep lines of text between 45 and 72 characters.

Length is less of a concern when you're writing applications that will run on phones in portrait mode. The lines will rarely be too long in those cases. However, when building applications for tablets or for landscape mode on smartphones, keep this issue in mind. When the UI is wide, try to limit text to columns with between 45 to 72 characters within a given line. Figure 4-3 shows two examples of using long and short text lines.

Figure 4-3 Two layouts showing the differences between long and short text lines

Dimensions and Sizes

If you've already written Android applications, you know that you're supposed to specify the sizes of your UI elements using the dp (density-independent pixel) unit. The basic reason is to allow an Android application to scale across different screen sizes, resolutions, and pixel densities without losing quality. When using dp, the goal is to draw a `View` so that it has the same physical size on all screens. One dp is roughly equal to one physical pixel on a 160 dpi screen.

You should specify all dimensions in your UI using the dp unit, with one exception: When specifying font sizes, use the unit sp, which is based on the dp unit but also scaled according to the users' preferences for font sizes. Thus, by using sp for fonts, you can be sure that the text is printed with the size chosen by the user.

The other dimension units supported by Android are pt (points), px (pixel), mm (millimeter), and in (inches). You should use these only in very specific cases and, as far as possible, provide all the default sizes in dp or sp.

Recommended Dimensions

How large does a button need to be in an Android application? How much margin and padding do I need to apply? How big should my icons be? If not for the dp unit, this question would have a very complicated answer. The short answer is "the 48-dp rhythm." Basically, 48 dp translates to about 9 mm on the screen, which is within the suitable range for objects on a touchscreen that users need to interact with using their fingers.

This doesn't mean that everything should be 48 dp, but that the UI components the user will interact with should be at least that size. If a UI component needs to be larger than 48 dp, try to make it an even multiplier of 48 dp if possible to keep your UI layout consistent. (See Figure 4-4; from `http://developer.android.com/design/style/metrics-grids.html`.)

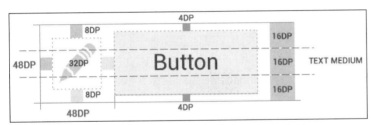

Figure 4-4 An illustration of the 48 dp rhythm for UI objects on Android

Icon Sizes

Outside the world of Android, the dp unit doesn't exist, and you have to create a version of each icon for every resolution you need to support. Android Studio will help you create the launcher icon for your application, and you can use these sizes as a template for the other icons in your application. The resolutions you need are 48 pixels for MDPI, 72 pixels for HDPI, 96 pixels for XHDPI, and 144 pixels for XXHDPI—this is called the *2:3:4:6 ratio*, and you can use it as a guideline for other pixel sizes as well. You can see an example of the relative icon sizes in Figure 4-5 (from `http://developer.android.com/design/style/iconography.html`).

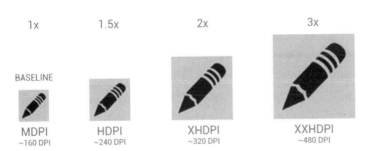

Figure 4-5: The relative sizes of icons in Android for different screen sizes

When you display a bitmap as an icon in Android, don't use px as the size for the `View`. Instead, use dp. A regular icon, like the launcher icon on the Home screen, should be 48 dp by 48 dp, whereas icons in the action bar should be 32 dp by 32 dp. Icons in the notification bar should be 24 dp by 24 dp. Smaller icons should use the size 16 dp by 16 dp. Avoid icon sizes below 16 dp because some users may have trouble distinguishing them.

Text Size

Google created the font Roboto, which is used in all the standard Android applications. Although you can use a different font in your application, using Roboto is recommended in order to be consistent with the standard UI paradigm.

The size of a font is very important when it comes to ease of reading. Figure 4-6 shows how the size of a font is measured. Different fonts with the same point size can seem to have different visual sizes. This comes from the measurement called x-height, which is literally the size of the lowercase letter x in the font. A large X-height makes a font look bigger and is easier to read. Other fonts that have large X-heights that we commonly use are Arial and Verdana.

Figure 4-6 An illustration with the Roboto font showing how a font size is measured

Google has also defined four standard font sizes for Android. These are micro (12 sp), small (14 sp), medium (18 sp), and large (22 sp). By using the same size in your application, you'll stay consistent with the rest of the Android framework. Note that the sizes should be in the unit sp, not dp, to allow users to apply the scaling factor they prefer in the Settings application.

Colors

I am actually the last person who should write about colors, given that I'm severely colorblind and need my wife to help me whenever I buy clothes. Choosing colors for a UI is very difficult for people with normal color sight, and being colorblind makes things even more complicated. Luckily, there are some general guidelines that even I can understand and follow.

First of all, black and white are great colors. They have very good contrast, especially on the screens of Android devices. If you're uncertain about which colors to choose, start with these two and add other colors later only to emphasize certain details.

When it comes to the color to use for text and its background, there are some governing rules. The LCD screens usually found on Android devices are very different from paper. First, they emit light, which can cause eye strain and make reading for a long time more difficult. Second, because the screen is refreshed continuously, the image on the screen is not stable, even if the device is still. The refresh rate for most LCD screens is usually 60 Hz, but some devices have a higher frequency.

Studies have shown that when reading text on a LCD screen, you should have as much contrast between the text and the background as possible. This is why black and white are great colors to use when displaying text. The best choice is to use black for the text color and white as the background—the opposite has proven to be harder to read (see Figure 4-7).

This text is the easiest to read. Black text on white background makes for a good contrast and should be used as much as possible.

This text is a little bit harder to read but still acceptable. Use this only when necessary and never for longer texts.

This text is really hard to read due to the low contrast. Be careful when using different colors together with text, as the contrast might be affected negatively.

Figure 4-7 An example of how contrast affects readability.

How the user may interpret a color is another reason to avoid using too many colors in your application. Colors have different cultural meanings all over the world. For instance, the color green represents luck in Western Europe, North America, and many Muslim countries, whereas Africa, Eastern Europe, and China use the color red instead. Picking the wrong color could affect a significant part of your user-base in a negative way. A great resource for interpreting what different colors mean in different cultures is the color wheel by David McCandles, which you can find at `http://www.informationisbeautiful.net/visualizations/colours-in-cultures`.

Google recommends that you use primary colors for emphasis. The Android Design Guidelines (see `http://developer.android.com/design/style/color.html`) contain a number of standard color swatches to use in your application. Pick the color scheme that matches your brand.

Color Blindness

There are different types of color blindness, and in most cases they all refer to an inability to distinguish the difference between certain colors. The most common type of color blindness involves the inability to distinguish between red and green, which can actually be difficult to do even when you're not color blind. About 9% of the male population and 1% of the female population are color blind.

A great tool for checking how your image looks to someone who is color blind is Vischeck, which you can find at `http://www.vischeck.com`. This tool also lets you correct an image with regard to color blindness.

Images and Icons

All applications will contain at least one image; the image used as the launcher icon for your application. Your application will most likely contain many other icons and images as well, and the way you design these can have a big impact on how users perceive your application.

An icon consisting of many different and complex objects can have a negative impact on the perception of your application. You should carefully design the launcher icon for your application so that it is easily recognized and can be shown on both light and dark backgrounds, as you cannot be sure what kind of background the user will have on her device.

Canonical Perspective

When told to draw an object from memory, most people will draw it as though looking at it from above at a slight angle. This is called the *canonical perspective,* and it is also how we remember objects. For example, take a piece of paper and draw a cup. Chances are it will look very much like Figure 4-8.

Figure 4-8 A teacup drawn from the canonical perspective

If you're going to provide an icon of a real-world object, do users a big favor by designing it from a canonical perspective; they'll be able to quickly recognize and match the icon to the real-world object it represents.

Geons

Another interesting thing about objects is how we construct them in our memory. Studies have shown that we are able to recognize objects by separating them into their component parts, or geons, and then using those parts to build up more complex shapes. In Figure 4-9, you can see some geons and how our memories can reconstruct them as real-world objects.

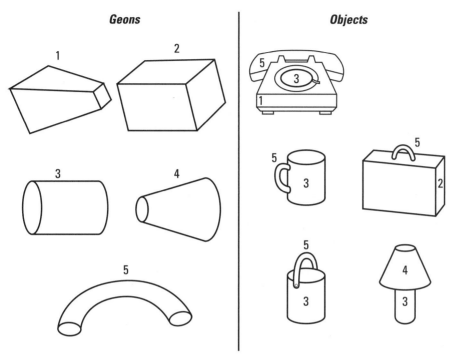

Figure 4-9 Objects and the geons they are constructed of

When you design an icon for your application, it is a good idea to construct it from simple geometric figures, and keep in mind that the fewer geons you use for your icon, the faster the user will recognize what it represents.

Recognizing Faces

As humans, we are very good at recognizing faces. Most people can easily pick out a friend's face in a crowd of people. We are actually faster at recognizing faces than other objects. Also, we are much slower at understanding text that we read than recognizing a person's face. By using this knowledge you can greatly improve the user interface of your application.

If your application will integrate with a social network such as Twitter or Facebook, use this to your advantage. Instead of having a long list of names with all the user's friends, show a grid of profile photos. This way you can fit more information on the screen at once, while making it easier to find the person the user is looking for.

Usability

According to Steve Krug in his book *Don't Make Me Think,* the first law of usability is simply that: "Don't make me think!" A user shouldn't have to spend a significant amount of time trying to figure out how to use your application. Steve argues that users seeing your application's UI for the first time shouldn't have to question what to do next; rather, the next step should be obvious.

This principle applies from overall UI navigation all the way down to single UI components. For example, users can immediately recognize standard buttons; on the other hand, buttons with unfamiliar designs will require conscious processing. Although you may favor a particular design over the standard button in Android, your best bet is to use the standard button—because that's what users will expect to see on their devices.

So, it's important to follow the Android design principles. Of course, you can provide your own unique look and feel to the user interface, but if you do so, make sure that you still provide a user-friendly interface that is obvious to any user. Basically, break the rules *only* if you know how to break them effectively.

Visual Cues

In order to make your application user friendly, you should consider the *visual cues* of the UI elements that a user will interact with. Visual cues are the "message" that an object signals to a user about how it is supposed to be interacted with. A visual cue that is hard to understand, because it is unclear or complicated, might cause the user to make mistakes or use the object in the wrong way.

An Android application is full of visual cues. The Home and Back buttons on Android devices are easily recognizable and have clear visual cues on what they do and how to use them. The same goes for many of the common actions, like the "share" action which is built-in in many Android applications.

Because people understand text slower than they understand a simple icon, you can make things much easier for the user by providing a suitable icon for all buttons in your application. If your buttons will only contain text, the visual cue that signals the action the button represents is harder to interpret and will require more time for the user to understand.

For instance, consider a typical file browser application. When listing files, you provide two buttons, *Send* and *Delete*. If the buttons will only contain text, it is much easier for the user to press the wrong button by mistake than it would be if you also added an icon to each button. If you can't fit both an icon and text, you should first provide an icon.

The Android Design site contains a set of freely available icons that you can use in your application. You can find these icons here: `http://developer.android.com/design/style/iconography.html`. By using these you will provide the same easily recognizable icons that many other applications use. This will reduce the time required for a user to understand your application, as well as minimize the risk of a user performing the wrong action.

Rewarding the User

Whatever the purpose of your application, the user will expect some sort of outcome. You can consider the outcome as a kind of reward for the work they perform. Studies in this area have given us a number of tools that we can apply when designing an application. In the world of Internet-connected apps and websites, the term *gamification* has emerged as a way of describing how to apply rewards in an efficient way.

Gamification

The term gamification was coined in 2002 by a British computer programmer named Nick Pelling, but although it was applied successfully at the time, the term didn't gain popularity until around 2010.

The theory behind gamification is that game elements and mechanics outside the world of games (real-world or computer-based) can improve the user's engagement. People will naturally strive to compete, reach new achievements, and achieve higher status. For example, when users are rewarded for using your application frequently, they will feel and become more deeply engaged. If you provide some sort of immediate satisfaction reward for every task completed, the users will respond at a faster rate than they would have without this element of gamification. If you also introduce a concept of competing with other users, such as a high-score list showing the "best players," you can further increase their engagement. This in turn improves learning, increases usage (and thus the profit), and provides you with more data for further improvements. When applied to websites or applications, gamification can be a very powerful tool.

One of the best-known examples of gamification in the world of mobile applications is Foursquare, the location-based social network service that lets users "check in" to locations. Foursquare badges are awarded to users when they check in to new locations, when they have frequently checked in to the same location over a period of time or when they manage to score the most number of check ins for a certain location. The result is that Foursquare gained an immense database of places of interest around the world. The use of the application shows Foursquare the places that are of most interest and how people move between these venues. This data can then be licensed to third-party services that want to provide information about relevant locations.

Virtually any application can use gamification to increase the use and engagement of its users. I once used the example of a notebook application for this purpose. If you want users to use your notebook application as much as possible, you can introduce the achievements that are rewarded after they've written a certain number of words, notes, or pages (see Figure 4-10). If you also provide a public high-score list that the users can see, you will further improve the engagement.

Using a gamification element in your application can certainly drive user engagement and quickly increase your user base. However, there are also risks involved. If it gets too easy, people will stop using it because there's no challenge. If it's too hard, you'll lose users who simply give up. Also, you have to be aware that some users might turn to cheating, and if it's easy to cheat, you'll end up with a ruined game element.

Avoid building the entire user experience around the game element. For instance, Foursquare lets users compete according to the amount of times they check in to a certain place and how many places they visit, but the app also provides a very good set of features for finding points of interest and giving reviews.

You can also use the element of gamification to teach the user how to use your application. This can be especially useful if you have a complicated app that requires some training.

Figure 4-10 An example of adding gamification elements to a notebook application

Summary

In this chapter, I focused on the theory behind some of the concepts of interface design. You can learn much more about this topic than I could ever cover by going through all the guidelines and tips on the Android Design site. Also, I strongly recommend the books and other references found in the upcoming "Further Resources" section.

Being a great developer doesn't automatically mean that you're also a great UI designer. But by understanding the basics of how and why people react as they do to your user interface, you can avoid most design pitfalls.

That said, nothing beats a good professional interaction and UI designer. If possible, make sure that you have one on your team and that she has an understanding of the Android Design guidelines.

Further Resources

Books

Weinschenk, Susan M., Ph.D. *100 Things Every Designer Needs to Know About People.* New Riders, 2012.

Krug, Steve. *Don't Make Me Think: A Common Sense Approach to Web Usability,* 2nd Edition. New Riders, 2005.

Lehtimäki, Juhani. Juhani Lehtimäki. *Smashing Android UI.* Wiley, 2012

Websites

Android Design at `http://developer.android.com/design/index.html`

The Easy Way to Writing Good User Stories at `http://codesqueeze.com/the-easy-way-to-writing-good-user-stories/`

Susan M. Weinschenks blog on how people think and behave: `http://www.blog.theteamw.com`

The Android Developers YouTube channel, specifically the Android Design in Action episodes: `http://www.youtube.com/user/androiddevelopers`

Chapter 5

Android User Interface Operations

In Chapter 4, I discuss how to design a good user interface, but that's only half the work. Equally important is knowing how to implement the interface using the Android APIs. Although the tutorials and guidelines available on the Android Developers site are useful for more general cases, writing custom `Views` or detecting advanced multi-touch gestures that aren't directly available from the standard APIs is more complicated.

This chapter begins with a brief discussion about the `Activity` component and `Fragments`, followed by an explanation of how you can use the new Presentation API to display a UI on a secondary screen.

`Activities` and `Fragments` are central to the user interfaces on Android. However, I cover them only very briefly because they are covered to a great extent on the Android developer site and in other tutorials. Also, because they're such a crucial component for Android applications, I assume that most readers are familiar with them.

Then comes an overview of how the `View` system works on Android, including the crucial issues involved in implementing a custom `View` and how to manage the drawing across different screen sizes.

Next, I explain how to implement advanced multi-touch features in your application. Android has built-in support for some multi-touch gestures, but for more advanced situations you need to build your own gesture detection components.

Activities and Fragments

If you're familiar with the lifecycle diagram for the `Activity` and `Fragment` classes shown in Figure 5-1, you probably won't have any problems with this part of Android UI. What is important with the lifecycles shown in these diagrams is that you should try to perform cleanup operations (stopping and unbinding a `Service`, closing connections etc.) in the callback method that matches the callback method where you performed the initialization. For instance, if you bind to a `Service` in `Activity.onResume()`, you should always perform the unbind operation in `Activity.onPause()`. This way, you reduce the chance that your application will leak resources accidentally.

You'll find `Fragments` beneficial when you need to reuse a part of your UI for different screen sizes. You aren't required to use `Fragments`, but doing so is recommended if your application will have one UI for handsets and another UI for tablets.

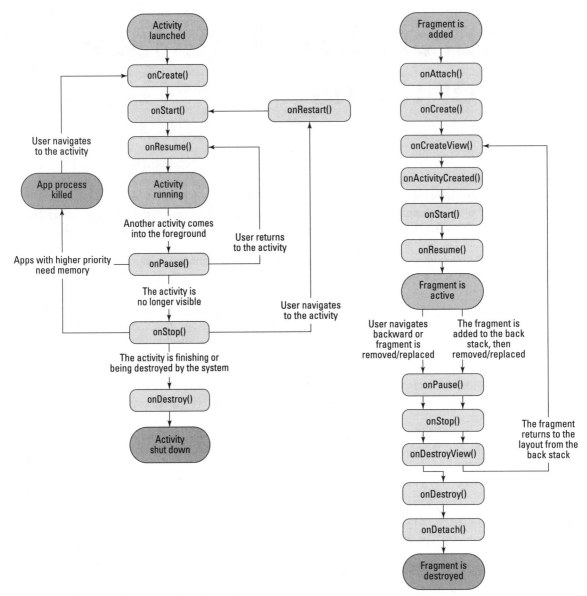

Figure 5-1 The lifecycle diagrams for `Activity` and `Fragment`

Android Studio provides a great template for building a *master/detail flow* UI. This UI presents two `Fragments` side by side on tablets (see Figure 5-2) and uses two separate `Activities` on handsets with smaller screens. I recommend using this UI when you need to build an Android application that must support multiple screen sizes in the same Android application package file (APK).

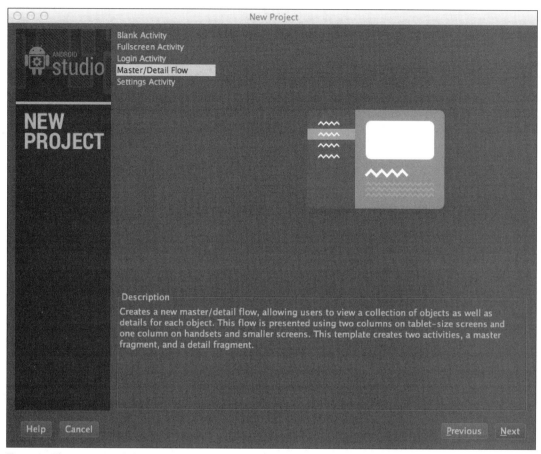

Figure 5-2 The Master/Detail Flow template set up in Android Studio

Using Multiple Screens

With the release of Android 4.2 came the ability to use multiple screens to display a UI from an `Activity`. This action is managed through the Presentation API that enables you to enumerate the available `Displays` and assign a separate `View` to each.

Android defines a secondary screen as an abstract `Presentation` output where you add a `View`. The actual physical display could be something connected by HDMI or a wireless display like a Miracast receiver. As a developer, you don't need to be concerned about the different types of displays, and you can work easily using the `Display` class.

The following example shows how to use the `DisplayManager` to enumerate all the available `Displays`:

```
public class SecondDisplayDemo extends Activity {
    private Presentation mPresentation;

    @Override
    protected void onCreate(Bundle savedInstanceState) {
```

```
        super.onCreate(savedInstanceState);
        setContentView(R.layout.device_screen);
    }

    @Override
    protected void onResume() {
        super.onResume();
        setupSecondDisplay();
    }

    @Override
    protected void onPause() {
        super.onPause();
        if (mPresentation != null) {
            mPresentation.cancel();
        }
    }

    private void setupSecondDisplay() {
        DisplayManager displayManager = (DisplayManager)
                getSystemService(Context.DISPLAY_SERVICE);
        Display defaultDisplay = displayManager.
                getDisplay(Display.DEFAULT_DISPLAY);
        Display[] presentationDisplays = displayManager.
                getDisplays(DisplayManager.DISPLAY_CATEGORY_PRESENTATION);
        if (presentationDisplays.length > 0) {
            for (Display presentationDisplay : presentationDisplays) {
                if (presentationDisplay.getDisplayId()
                        != defaultDisplay.getDisplayId()) {
                    Presentation presentation =
                            new MyPresentation(this, presentationDisplay);
                    presentation.show();
                    mPresentation = presentation;
                    return;
                }
            }
        }
        Toast.makeText(this, "No second display found!",
                Toast.LENGTH_SHORT).show();
    }

    private class MyPresentation extends Presentation {
        public MyPresentation(Context context, Display display) {
            super(context, display);
            // The View for the second screen
            setContentView(R.layout.second_screen);
        }
    }
}
```

In executing this example, you pick the first `Display` that isn't the default (that is, the physical screen on the device). You extend the `Presentation` class with your own implementation and add a different `View` as its content view. The `Presentation` instance is bound to the same lifecycle as your `Activity`, so when the user leaves the app, the default behavior for the second screen will kick in (usually cloning the default screen).

It may be a bit tricky to test the use of multiple screens during development, but you can find a developer setting using the Settings⇨Developer Options⇨Simulate Secondary Displays commands. The simulated screen appears where you can create a simulated display to use during development.

Designing Custom Views

Although the Android APIs provide a number of UI widgets that can be combined to form more complicated components, sometimes it's necessary to design your own custom `View` from scratch. Before you start implementing a custom `View` there are a few details that you should be aware of, which I will explain next.

By following the example in this section, you'll be constructing a custom `View` for a piano keyboard. This `View` will display the keyboard and also play the right tone and change the look of the key when it's pressed. Before I show the code for this `View`, allow me to first take you through its lifecycle.

View Life Cycle

Just as a `Fragment` or an `Activity` has a lifecycle, so to do `Views` have their version of a lifecycle. This cycle is not directly connected to the `Fragment` or `Activity` that displays the `View`; instead, the cycle is connected to the state of the window it's shown in and the rendering loop.

The first thing that happens when a `View` is added to the `View` hierarchy is that it gets a call to `View.onAttachedToWindow()`, which signals to the `View` that it can now load things that it needs to work properly. When building a custom `View`, you should override this method where you perform the loading of all the resources and initiate any dependencies that the `View` needs. Basically, this is where you need to perform any time-consuming initialization.

There is also a matching callback named `View.onDetachedFromWindow()`, which is called when the `View` is removed from the `View` hierarchy. Here, you need to take care of all resources loaded, `Services` started, or other dependencies that need explicit cleanup.

When the `View` is added to a `View` hierarchy, it will go through a loop where animations are calculated, followed by `View.onMeasure()`, `View.onLayout()`, and finally `View.onDraw()`, as shown in Figure 5-3. The system guarantees that these methods will be called in exactly that order every time.

View added

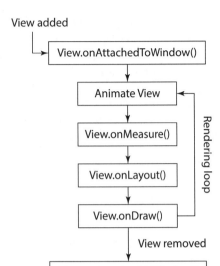

Figure 5-3 A diagram of the View lifecycle

Piano Keyboard Widget

The View described in this section (see Figure 5-4) allows a user to tap a key that will then play a note. Everything is managed by the View, so it needs to load all the audio clips for playback as well as manage the different states. Finally, the user should be able to play with more than one finger, which requires properly using the multi-touch features of the Android APIs.

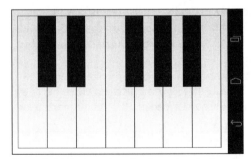

Figure 5-4 A custom View showing a piano keyboard

The following is the first part of the new custom View:

```
public class PianoKeyboard extends View {
    public static final String TAG = "PianoKeyboard";
    public static final int MAX_FINGERS = 5;
    public static final int WHITE_KEYS_COUNT = 7;
    public static final int BLACK_KEYS_COUNT = 5;
    public static final float BLACK_TO_WHITE_WIDTH_RATIO = 0.625f;
    public static final float BLACK_TO_WHITE_HEIGHT_RATIO = 0.54f;
    private Paint mWhiteKeyPaint, mBlackKeyPaint,
```

```
                    mBlackKeyHitPaint, mWhiteKeyHitPaint;
// Support up to five fingers
private Point[] mFingerPoints = new Point[MAX_FINGERS];
private int[] mFingerTones = new int[MAX_FINGERS];
private SoundPool mSoundPool;
private SparseIntArray mToneToIndexMap = new SparseIntArray();
private Paint mCKeyPaint, mCSharpKeyPaint, mDKeyPaint,
        mDSharpKeyPaint, mEKeyPaint, mFKeyPaint,
        mFSharpKeyPaint, mGKeyPaint, mGSharpKeyPaint,
        mAKeyPaint, mASharpKeyPaint, mBKeyPaint;
private Rect mCKey = new Rect(), mCSharpKey = new Rect(),
        mDKey = new Rect(), mDSharpKey = new Rect(),
        mEKey = new Rect(), mFKey = new Rect(),
        mFSharpKey = new Rect(), mGKey = new Rect(),
        mGSharpKey = new Rect(), mAKey = new Rect(),
        mASharpKey = new Rect(), mBKey = new Rect();
private MotionEvent.PointerCoords mPointerCoords;

public PianoKeyboard(Context context) {
    super(context);
}

public PianoKeyboard(Context context, AttributeSet attrs) {
    super(context, attrs);
}

public PianoKeyboard(Context context, AttributeSet attrs,
                     int defStyle) {
    super(context, attrs, defStyle);
}

@Override
protected void onAttachedToWindow() {
    super.onAttachedToWindow();
    mPointerCoords = new MotionEvent.PointerCoords();
    Arrays.fill(mFingerPoints, null);
    Arrays.fill(mFingerTones, -1);
    loadKeySamples(getContext());
    setupPaints();
}

@Override
protected void onDetachedFromWindow() {
    super.onDetachedFromWindow();
    releaseKeySamples();
}

private void setupPaints() {
    ... omitted for brevity
}

private void loadKeySamples(Context context) {
    mSoundPool = new SoundPool(5, AudioManager.STREAM_MUSIC, 0);
```

```
        mToneToIndexMap.put(R.raw.c, mSoundPool.load(context, R.raw.c,
1));

        ... omitted for brevity
    }

    public void releaseKeySamples() {
        mToneToIndexMap.clear();
        mSoundPool.release();
    }
```

This code shows the member variables needed for the `PianoKeyboard` class as well as the constructors and the attached/detached callbacks. Following this example, in `onAttachedToWindows()`, you reset the member variables and load the audio clips. You create the different `Paint` objects, one for each possible state for each key. The `SoundPool` is also populated with the audio clips stored in the `raw` resources.

Also, note that you create the `Rect` objects for each key as member variables with a default initialization. Although you can create these objects on-the-fly in the `onDraw()` method, the method shown in the preceding example will reduce the number of garbage collection (GC) calls which might impact the performance negatively.

The next part is the `onLayout()` and `onDraw()` methods:

```
    @Override
    protected void onLayout(boolean changed, int left, int top,
                            int right, int bottom) {
        super.onLayout(changed, left, top, right, bottom);
        // Calculate the sizes for the keys.
        int width = getWidth();
        int height = getHeight();
        int whiteKeyWidth = width / WHITE_KEYS_COUNT;
        int blackKeyWidth = (int) (whiteKeyWidth *
                            BLACK_TO_WHITE_WIDTH_RATIO);
        int blackKeyHeight = (int) (height * BLACK_TO_WHITE_HEIGHT_RATIO);

        // Define the rectangles for each key
        mCKey.set(0, 0, whiteKeyWidth, height);
        mCSharpKey.set(whiteKeyWidth - (blackKeyWidth / 2), 0,
                whiteKeyWidth + (blackKeyWidth / 2), blackKeyHeight);

        //... Remaining keys omitted for brevity
    }

    @Override
    protected void onDraw(Canvas canvas) {
        super.onDraw(canvas);

        // Start by drawing the white keys
        canvas.drawRect(mCKey, mCKeyPaint);
        canvas.drawRect(mDKey, mDKeyPaint);
        canvas.drawRect(mEKey, mEKeyPaint);
        canvas.drawRect(mFKey, mFKeyPaint);
```

```
            canvas.drawRect(mGKey, mGKeyPaint);
            canvas.drawRect(mAKey, mAKeyPaint);
            canvas.drawRect(mBKey, mBKeyPaint);

            // Draw black keys last since they will "cover" the white keys
            canvas.drawRect(mCSharpKey, mCSharpKeyPaint);
            canvas.drawRect(mDSharpKey, mDSharpKeyPaint);
            canvas.drawRect(mFSharpKey, mFSharpKeyPaint);
            canvas.drawRect(mGSharpKey, mGSharpKeyPaint);
            canvas.drawRect(mASharpKey, mASharpKeyPaint);
        }
```

In the `onLayout()` method, which is called during the layout pass, you calculate the size and position for each key. In the `onDraw()` method you should avoid performing any heavy calculations and focus on the actual drawing, which avoids potential drops in performance. *Note:* A custom `onMeasure()` method isn't implemented; that's because the default measuring is sufficient in this case.

The final part is the `onTouchEvent()` callback that performs the actual playback of the audio clips and changes the drawing state of the keys.

```
        @Override
        public boolean onTouchEvent(MotionEvent event) {
            int pointerCount = event.getPointerCount();
            int cappedPointerCount = pointerCount > MAX_FINGERS ?
                                                   MAX_FINGERS :
                                                   pointerCount;
            int actionIndex = event.getActionIndex();
            int action = event.getActionMasked();
            int id = event.getPointerId(actionIndex);

            // Check if we received a down or up action for a finger
            if ((action == MotionEvent.ACTION_DOWN ||
                action == MotionEvent.ACTION_POINTER_DOWN) &&
                id < MAX_FINGERS) {
              mFingerPoints[id] = new Point((int) event.getX(actionIndex),
                                            (int) event.getY(actionIndex));
            } else if ((action == MotionEvent.ACTION_POINTER_UP ||
                    action == MotionEvent.ACTION_UP)
                    && id < MAX_FINGERS) {
              mFingerPoints[id] = null;
              invalidateKey(mFingerTones[id]);
              mFingerTones[id] = -1;
            }

            for (int i = 0; i < cappedPointerCount; i++) {
                int index = event.findPointerIndex(i);
                if (mFingerPoints[i] != null && index != -1) {
                    mFingerPoints[i].set((int) event.getX(index),
                                    (int) event.getY(index));
                    int tone = getToneForPoint(mFingerPoints[i]);
                    if (tone != mFingerTones[i] && tone != -1) {
```

```
                        invalidateKey(mFingerTones[i]);
                        mFingerTones[i] = tone;
                        invalidateKey(mFingerTones[i]);
                        if (!isKeyDown(i)) {
                            int poolIndex =
                                    mToneToIndexMap.get(mFingerTones[i]);
                            event.getPointerCoords(index, mPointerCoords);
                            float volume = mPointerCoords.
                                    getAxisValue(MotionEvent.AXIS_PRESSURE);
                            volume = volume > 1f ? 1f : volume;
                            mSoundPool.play(poolIndex, volume, volume,
                                    0, 0, 1f);
                        }
                    }
                }
            }

        updatePaints();

        return true;
    }

    // Check if the key touch by this finger is
    // already pressed by another finger
    private boolean isKeyDown(int finger) {
        int key = getToneForPoint(mFingerPoints[finger]);

        for (int i = 0; i < mFingerPoints.length; i++) {
            if (i != finger) {
                Point fingerPoint = mFingerPoints[i];
                if (fingerPoint != null) {
                    int otherKey = getToneForPoint(fingerPoint);
                    if (otherKey == key) {
                        return true;
                    }
                }
            }
        }

        return false;
    }

    private void invalidateKey(int tone) {
        switch (tone) {
            case R.raw.c:
                invalidate(mCKey);
                break;
            // Remaining cases omitted for brevity...
        }
    }

    private void updatePaints() {
        // Start by clearing all keys
```

```
        mCKeyPaint = mWhiteKeyPaint;
        ... remaining keys omitted for brevity

        // Set "hit" paint on all keys touched by a finger
        // starting with black keys
        for (Point fingerPoint : mFingerPoints) {
            if (fingerPoint != null) {
                if (mCSharpKey.contains(fingerPoint.x, fingerPoint.y)) {
                    mCSharpKeyPaint = mBlackKeyHitPaint;
                } else if (mDSharpKey.contains(fingerPoint.x,
                                                fingerPoint.y)) {
                    ... Remaining keys omitted for brevity
                }
            }
        }
    }

    private int getToneForPoint(Point point) {
        // Start by checking the black keys
        if (mCSharpKey.contains(point.x, point.y))
            return R.raw.c_sharp;

        ... remaining keys omitted for brevity

        return -1;
    }
}
```

For each `MotionEvent`, you check to see whether a new finger (pointer) has touched the screen. If so, you create a new `Point` and store it in the array for tracking the user's fingers. If an up event occurred, you remove the `Point` for that finger instead.

Next, you go through all the pointers that are tracked by this `MotionEvent` and check whether they've moved since the last call to this method. If so, you play the tone for the key currently being pressed. There is also a check to ensure you don't play a tone for a key that's already being pressed when a second finger just moves over the key.

Whenever a `MotionEvent` occurs, you also check which parts of the `View` need to be invalidated using the `invalidateKey()` method. This check takes the ID for a key as a parameter and invalidates only that rectangle. Whenever you need to invalidate your `View` in order to redraw it, call this method with only the affected region. Doing so will significantly speed up the rendering of your `View`.

Multi-Touching

Ever since Android first achieved support for multi-touch technology, users have become accustomed to doing some of the more advanced navigation in Android applications using two or more fingers. Most prominent in this area is probably the Google Maps application. It combines most of the touch gestures—for example, pinch-zoom, tilting, and rotating. Games requiring more than one finger for control is another area in which multi-touch has become popular, and as shown in the `PianoKeyboard` example in the previous section, multi-touch interaction is also useful in other areas.

The challenge when working with multi-touch is to keep track of the individual fingers. Android's `MotionEvent` class is the core for all pointer-related interactions, which means fingers, a stylus, a regular computer mouse, or an external touchpad.

Take a look at another example for multi-touch. In this example, you create a custom `View` for finger painting. You use the `Path` class from the `android.graphics` package to keep track of what the user's fingers are drawing. The same principle (that is, the methods involved in a custom `View`) that applied to the earlier piano example is used here, but in this case there's much less code to keep track of.

Specifically, the following code is a very simple example for creating a multi-touch–enabled finger painting application.

```
public class PaintView extends View {
    public static final int MAX_FINGERS = 5;
    private Path[] mFingerPaths = new Path[MAX_FINGERS];
    private Paint mFingerPaint;
    private ArrayList<Path> mCompletedPaths;
    private RectF mPathBounds = new RectF();

    public PaintView(Context context) {
        super(context);
    }

    public PaintView(Context context, AttributeSet attrs) {
        super(context, attrs);
    }

    public PaintView(Context context, AttributeSet attrs, int defStyle) {
        super(context, attrs, defStyle);
    }

    @Override
    protected void onAttachedToWindow() {
        super.onAttachedToWindow();
        mCompletedPaths = new ArrayList<Path>();
        mFingerPaint = new Paint();
        mFingerPaint.setAntiAlias(true);
        mFingerPaint.setColor(Color.BLACK);
        mFingerPaint.setStyle(Paint.Style.STROKE);
        mFingerPaint.setStrokeWidth(6);
        mFingerPaint.setStrokeCap(Paint.Cap.BUTT);
    }

    @Override
    protected void onDraw(Canvas canvas) {
        super.onDraw(canvas);

        for (Path completedPath : mCompletedPaths) {
            canvas.drawPath(completedPath, mFingerPaint);
        }

        for (Path fingerPath : mFingerPaths) {
```

```
                    if (fingerPath != null) {
                        canvas.drawPath(fingerPath, mFingerPaint);
                    }
                }
            }

            @Override
            public boolean onTouchEvent(MotionEvent event) {
                int pointerCount = event.getPointerCount();
                int cappedPointerCount = pointerCount > MAX_FINGERS ?
                                             MAX_FINGERS :
                                             pointerCount;
                int actionIndex = event.getActionIndex();
                int action = event.getActionMasked();
                int id = event.getPointerId(actionIndex);

                if ((action == MotionEvent.ACTION_DOWN ||
                    action == MotionEvent.ACTION_POINTER_DOWN) &&
                    id < MAX_FINGERS) {
                    mFingerPaths[id] = new Path();
                    mFingerPaths[id].moveTo(event.getX(actionIndex),
                                         event.getY(actionIndex));
                } else if ((action == MotionEvent.ACTION_POINTER_UP ||
                            action == MotionEvent.ACTION_UP)
                            && id < MAX_FINGERS) {
                    mFingerPaths[id].setLastPoint(event.getX(actionIndex),
                                             event.getY(actionIndex));
                    mCompletedPaths.add(mFingerPaths[id]);
                    mFingerPaths[id].computeBounds(mPathBounds, true);
                    invalidate((int) mPathBounds.left, (int) mPathBounds.top,
                            (int) mPathBounds.right, (int) mPathBounds.bottom);
                    mFingerPaths[id] = null;
                }

                for(int i = 0; i < cappedPointerCount; i++) {
                    if(mFingerPaths[i] != null) {
                        int index = event.findPointerIndex(i);
                        mFingerPaths[i].lineTo(event.getX(index),
                                             event.getY(index));
                        mFingerPaths[i].computeBounds(mPathBounds, true);
                        invalidate((int) mPathBounds.left, (int) mPathBounds.top,
                                (int) mPathBounds.right,
                                (int) mPathBounds.bottom);
                    }
                }

                return true;
            }
        }
```

Note how you use the Path class to add a new line for each new event. Although this class isn't completely accurate (you should check that a pointer has actually moved before adding a new line), it illustrates how to create a more complex drawing application.

PointerCoordinates

Each `MotionEvent` contains all the information about each pointer. Because a pointer can be the result of many different types of input devices (such as a finger, a stylus, or a mouse), it can also contain more information than the *x, y* coordinates. The APIs in Android support all the input devices defined by the Linux kernel. Because the parameters for an input can vary between devices, the design is such that each pointer has a number of axes. The two most commonly used axes are the *x, y* coordinates for the pointer, but there is also axis information for pressure, distance, and orientation. Also, because the `MotionEvent` class can be used for inputs other than those for generating pointer coordinates, this class also has support for axis information related to gaming controllers and other ways of doing input, such as throttle, rudder, tilt, or scroll wheel. Use this class when you want to support external inputs such as game controllers.

The following code is a snippet from the previous `PianoKeyboard` example:

```
event.getPointerCoords(index, mPointerCoords);
float volume = mPointerCoords.getAxisValue(MotionEvent.AXIS_PRESSURE);
volume = volume > 1f ? 1f : volume;
mSoundPool.play(poolIndex, volume, volume, 0, 0, 1f);
```

This code shows how to populate a `PointerCoords` object with the data for a specific pointer. In this case, you use the pressure axis to set the volume for the audio clip playback.

The pressure axis (`AXIS_PRESSURE`) in the preceding example is usually a virtual value that's calculated by determining the surface covered by a finger. Normally, the capacitive touchscreens on modern smartphones don't support a real touch pressure value.

Rotate Gesture

In the Android APIs, you can find two utility classes that help you detect a number of touch gestures: the `GestureDetector` and `ScaleGestureDetector` classes. The first class supports a number of simple single-touch gestures, such a long press, double tap, and fling. The second class provides a way to detect the pinch-zoom gesture used in Google Maps and when zooming in on images. However, one gesture that lacks support in the Android APIs is rotation.

The following class exemplifies how to implement a rotation gesture detector for a `View`. The relevant code is marked in bold.

```
public class RotateView extends View {
    public static final String TAG = "RotateView";
    private static final double MAX_ANGLE = 1e-1;
    private Paint mPaint;
    private float mRotation;
    private Float mPreviousAngle;

    public RotateView(Context context) {
        super(context);
```

```
    }

    public RotateView(Context context, AttributeSet attrs) {
        super(context, attrs);
    }

    public RotateView(Context context, AttributeSet attrs, int defStyle) {
        super(context, attrs, defStyle);
    }

    @Override
    protected void onAttachedToWindow() {
        super.onAttachedToWindow();

        mPaint = new Paint();
        mPaint.setColor(Color.BLACK);
        mPaint.setStyle(Paint.Style.STROKE);
        mPaint.setStrokeWidth(10);
        mPaint.setAntiAlias(true);

        mPreviousAngle = null;
    }

    @Override
    protected void onDraw(Canvas canvas) {
        super.onDraw(canvas);
        int width = getWidth();
        int height = getHeight();
        int radius = (int) (width > height ?
                            height * 0.666f : width * 0.666f) / 2;

        canvas.drawCircle(width / 2, height / 2, radius, mPaint);
        canvas.save();
        canvas.rotate(mRotation, width / 2, height / 2);
        canvas.drawLine(width / 2, height * 0.1f,
                    width / 2, height * 0.9f, mPaint);
        canvas.restore();
    }

    @Override
    public boolean onTouchEvent(MotionEvent event) {

        if(event.getPointerCount() == 2) {
            float currentAngle = (float) angle(event);
            if(mPreviousAngle != null) {
                mRotation -= Math.toDegrees(clamp(mPreviousAngle -
                                            currentAngle,
                                            -MAX_ANGLE, MAX_ANGLE));
                invalidate();
            }
            mPreviousAngle = currentAngle;
        } else {
            mPreviousAngle = null;
```

```
        }

        return true;
    }

    private static double angle(MotionEvent event) {
        double deltaX = (event.getX(0) - event.getX(1));
        double deltaY = (event.getY(0) - event.getY(1));
        return Math.atan2(deltaY, deltaX);
    }

    private static double clamp(double value, double min, double max) {
        if (value < min) {
            return min;
        }
        if (value > max) {
            return max;
        }
        return value;
    }
}
```

The trick comes from using `Math.atan2()` to calculate the current angle. This method implements the two argument arctangent function, which is used for calculating the angle between the positive x-axis on a plane and the coordinates defined by the two parameters. Next, you subtract the previously calculated angle from the current one and clamp the result between a maximum and a minimum for each event. Finally, because the rotation operations on the `Canvas` use degrees, you convert the result using `Math.toDegrees()`.

OpenGL ES

Although most Android applications can be built using the widgets provided by the SDK or through a custom `View`, at times you may need a more low-level and high-performance API for graphics, most often for games. The API you will use in this case is OpenGL ES (Embedded Subsystem) and Android supports all versions up to 3.0 (depending on the hardware and Android version). The latest OpenGL ES standard, version 3.0, was added to Android version 4.3. This is the first mobile platform to support OpenGL ES, and it's expected to allow developers to create more advanced graphics for their games.

Android is already using OpenGL ES 2.0 for its standard UI framework to enable hardware-accelerated graphics, but it's hidden from developers. In this section, I introduce you to OpenGL ES 2.0 and 3.0. The 3.0 version is fully backward-compatible with 2.0, so you can build applications that do a graceful degradation to version 2.0 if the device doesn't support the later API.

For an introduction to OpenGL ES on Android, I recommend the guide from the Android Developers site (`http://developer.android.com/guide/topics/graphics/opengl.html`). However, when you need to use OpenGL ES in your application or game, you will most likely not write all the OpenGL ES code described in this guide. Instead, you should use a scene graph framework or game engine, which hides most of the complex details involved with OpenGL ES in an easy-to-use API.

Scene Graphs and Graphics Engines

The easiest way to work with OpenGL ES is to use a scene graph, which is basically a graph where each node contains information about something being rendered in your scene. You could write your own scene graph, but using one of the many that exist online is usually better. Some of the different options are free and open source licensed and some are commercial. Scene graphs are also called 3D, graphics, or game engines because they also contain functionality specific for advanced graphics and games.

One of the better and most active open source 3D engines is Rajawali, developed by Dennis Ippel. You can find all of the information, including a number of great tutorials, for Rajawali at `https://github.com/MasDennis/Rajawali`.

One of the better commercial alternatives you can find is Unity3D from Unity Technology. This is much more than a game engine and contains a complete development studio for game developers. You can find more information about Unity3D at `http://unity3d.com`.

Always consider the needs of your application or game before you pick a 3D engine because changing it later can be very difficult. One of the most important things to consider is whether you want to be able to easily port your game to a different platform (for instance, iOS). In that case, choose one that supports all the platforms you intend to target (Unity3D has very good multi-platform support).

Summary

With the advanced UI operations covered in this chapter, you have a set of tools that can help you enhance your application's performance. For example, perhaps your app would benefit by supporting a secondary screen using HDMI or Miracast, which is when the new `Presentation` API will be useful.

Eventually, all Android developers create custom `View` classes for their applications. When you do so, be sure to follow the lifecycle for a `View` and use the different callbacks correctly.

When you need to support advanced multi-touch interactions, you must distinguish between different pointers and track them individually. As I've shown in this chapter, all `MotionEvents` contain the current information about all the pointers.

When you create advanced and high-performance graphics, you'll probably need to use OpenGL ES. At the very least, use OpenGL ES 2.0; and for even more advanced graphics, consider using OpenGL ES 3.0 when it is available on the user's device. Also, I strongly recommend utilizing a complete 3D or game engine when developing games; doing so will make your work much easier.

The Android UI is probably the biggest single area of the entire platform. You can find numerous tutorials, guidelines, samples, and books online on this topic; I mention some of my favorites in the following "Further Resources" section. The important thing to remember when you implement your UI is to stick with what you can manage.

Further Resources

Books

Lehtimäki, Juhani. *Smashing Android UI.* Wiley, 2012.

Websites

The OpenGL ES guide from the Android Developers site: `http://developer.android.com/guide/topics/graphics/opengl.html`

Training on working with the `Fragments` API: `http://developer.android.com/training/basics/fragments/index.html`

How to write a custom `View`: `https://developers.google.com/events/io/sessions/325615129`

Chapter 6

Services and Background Tasks

An important part of any Android application is making sure that long-running and blocking operations are executed in the background so that the main thread is left alone as much as possible. Although you can simply start a new thread in your `Activities`, a better approach is to move many of the background operations to a separate `Service`. The `Service` component in Android provides an efficient way of separating application logic for background tasks from the code that handles the user interface.

In this chapter, I cover the use of a `Service` component when performing background operations. I start with explaining when it's appropriate to use a `Service` and how to design and configure the component in an optimal way. I also give a detailed description of the lifecycles that a `Service` runs through. I explain communication with a `Service` from the other components in detail and finish this chapter with some best practices for how to move the work on a `Service` to a background thread.

When and How to Use a Service

The Android documentation for `Service` components starts by describing a `Service` as follows (I suggest keeping this in mind when developing your Android application):

> *A Service is an application component representing either an application's desire to perform a longer-running operation while not interacting with the user or to supply functionality for other applications to use.*

In this chapter, I focus on performing long-running operations and cover the second part of the quotation in Chapter 7, where I describe how to communicate between two applications.

Because all Android components are running on the main thread of the application process, it might seem unnecessary to use a `Service` as you still need to use some thread mechanism to move the operation off the main thread. The reason for using a `Service` is based on the difference in how the lifecycle works in `Services` and in `Activities`. I go into the details of the `Service` lifecycle in the section "Understanding the Service Lifecycle" later in this chapter, but basically, the `Service` is better adapted to act as the component for managing long-running operations in Android than an `Activity`.

Other questions to consider: Should an operation be long-running? When should you move an operation to a background thread? Is it ever okay to use a background thread like an `AsyncTask` from within the `Activity`, instead of moving it to a `Service`?

I recommend moving any operation that doesn't focus on the user interface to a background thread and making sure that this thread is started and controlled by a `Service`. That said, I tend to bend that rule depending on the situation. For instance, I always, with no exception, perform network operations from a `Service`. However, it's usually okay to write data to local storage, such as a content provider or a preferences file, within the `Activity` if the data being written is also generated from the user interface, as in editing a contact's information.

Another example is when you're playing audio in your app. A `Service` typically controls a music player's `MediaPlayer` or `AudioTrack` object, whereas an `Activity` handles the sound effects in games and applications. If in doubt, it is usually safe to move the operation to a background thread in a `Service`.

Service Types

I like to divide `Services` into two different types. First is the one that performs work for the application independent of the user's input. For instance, a music player is able to play music, even if the user doesn't have the app in the foreground. When playback of the current track is complete, a `Service` in the music player app starts playing the next track in the playlist. Another example is a messaging application that needs to receive incoming messages at all times and needs to remain running until the user explicitly logs out.

The other type of `Service` is one that's directly triggered by an action from the user—for example, a photo-sharing application. The user takes a photo, and the application sends it (or rather, a `Uri` to the locally stored photo) to a `Service` using an `Intent`. The `Service` starts, parses the data in the `Intent`, and spawns a background thread that uploads the photo. When the operation is complete, the `Service` is stopped automatically by the system.

Understanding the Service Lifecycle

`Services` in Android have a slightly different lifecycle than `Activities` do. First of all, the `Service` lifecycle isn't directly affected by user interactions. In an `Activity`, when the user taps the Home button, the `onPause()` callback is always called. For a `Service`, no callbacks are directly triggered in the same way by the user's actions. Instead, there are only two callbacks that will *always* be called for a `Service`: `onCreate()` and `onDestroy()`.

(There are also other callbacks that *may be* called depending on the interaction with the `Service` or at system and device changes such as, when the screen orientation changes from landscape to portrait mode.)

Simplified, a `Service` is either started or stopped, which makes it much easier to handle than the more complicated lifecycle of an `Activity`. All you really need to remember is to create expensive objects in `onCreate()` and do all cleanup in `onDestroy()`.

Service Creation and Destruction

Because you have only two lifecycle callbacks for a `Service`, this is where you should do most of the initialization and cleanup. In the `onCreate()` method, you initialize new `Handler` objects, retrieve system `Services`, register new `BroadcastReceivers`, and perform other initializations that are required for the `Service` operations. Remember that this method is executed on the main thread, so you should still delegate any long-running and potentially blocking operations to a background thread using an `AsyncTask`, `Handler` or one of the other methods described in Chapter 2.

You do all the cleanup for your `Service` in the `onDestroy()` method. You especially need to stop any `HandlerThreads` that you started and unregister `BroadcastReceivers` that you registered earlier in the `Service`. Again, it's important to remember that what you do here is executed on the main thread, so any cleanup that takes a long time may require you to launch a new thread where you perform that work. For instance, you may need an `AsyncTask` to gracefully shut down a network server.

The `onDestory()` method is called when the system determines that the `Service` is ready to be shut down and removed. This usually happens when the application of the `Service` is no longer in the foreground.

Starting Services

A `Service` can be started in two ways: Either it receives an `Intent` through the `Context.startService()` method, or a client (either local or remote) binds to it using the `Context.bindService()` method. Both of these methods will result in the `Service` moving to the "started" state.

When calling `Context.startService()`, an `Intent` is sent that must match the `intent filter` for the `Service`. (It's also possible to use an explicit `Intent` with the `ComponentName` of the `Service` without having to define an `intent filter`.) This method doesn't provide any reference to the `Service` for normal synchronized method calls but it is useful for performing message-based triggering of an operation. This is normally something you do as a result of a user interaction that could take an arbitrary amount of time, such as uploading a photo or sending a status update to a server. It's also a useful way of providing a simple interface for other applications, as I describe in more detail in Chapter 7.

When you start a `Service` using `Context.startService()`, the `onStartCommand()` callback is triggered on your `Service`. In this method, you receive the `Intent` that was sent to your `Service`, and you return a constant telling the Android system how your `Service` should react if the system shuts it down. This is one of the most complicated parts of how `Services` work and is easy to get wrong. You need to remember three return values (there's also a fourth value for compatibility reasons that I won't cover in this book): START_ STICKY, START_NOT_STICKY, and START_REDELIVER_INTENT.

When you return START_STICKY, it signals that you want your `Service` to be restarted if the system shuts it down for some reason (usually when running low on memory). However, when the system restarts the `Service`, the `onStartCommand()` is called with the `Intent` parameters set to `null`, so you have to take care of this in your code. A typical example of this return value is a music player where the `Service` is always started in the same way. This means that you need to store the internal state of you `Service` when `onDestroy()` is called.

When you return START_NOT_STICKY, your `Service` won't restart after the system shuts it down. This is probably useful when you send an `Intent` to the `Service` to perform a one-shot operation, such as uploading something to a server. If the `Service` is shut down before completing its task, it shouldn't try to repeat the operation.

The third return constant, START_REDELIVER_INTENT, works like START_STICKY, except that the original `Intent` is redelivered when the system restarts your `Service`.

Regardless of what you choose to return from `onStartCommand()` in your `Service`, consider not only how the `Service` is started but also how it will be stopped. Choosing `START_REDELIVER_INTENT` or `START_STICKY` could have unforeseen consequences if you're not careful.

When you receive a call to the `onStartCommand()` in your `Service`, you have three parameters to deal with. The first is the `Intent`, which can be `null` depending on what you returned in previous calls to `onStartCommand()`. The second parameter is a flag indicating what this call represents. It can be either `0`, `START_FLAG_RETRY`, or `START_FLAG_REDELIVERY`. The third parameter, named `startId`, can sometimes be useful when you need to safely stop the `Service` and you have received multiple calls to `onStartCommand()` during the lifecycle.

Because using `Context.startService()` can be considered as asynchronous (see Figure 6-1), you may also need a way to signal back to the `Activity` that your operation is complete. One way of doing so is to use a programmatic `BroadcastReceiver` (see the section "Asynchronous Messaging with Intents" later in this chapter, where I briefly discuss this topic; see also Chapter 8, where I go into more detail).

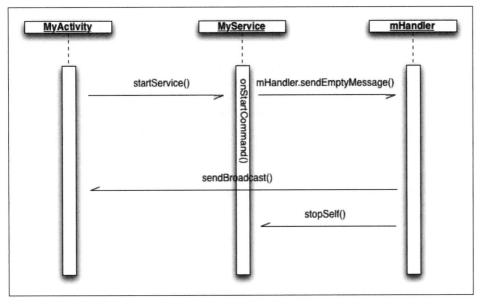

Figure 6-1 Sequence diagram over an asynchronous `Service` interaction

Binding Services

The second way to start a `Service` is through `Context.bindService()`. When you bind to a `Service`, it will continue operating until the last client disconnects. Binding to a `Service` in the same application process is a simple way to access a reference to the `Service` object from another component and call methods directly on it. This is called a *local binder* and is illustrated in Figure 6-2.

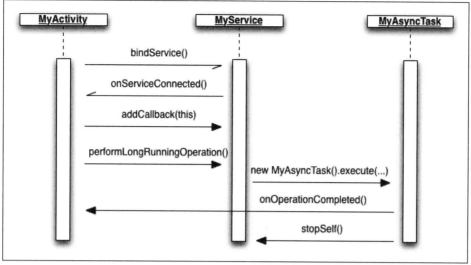

Figure 6-2 Sequence diagram illustrating the use of the local binder pattern

The following code shows how to implement a local `Binder` for your `Service` that you use when it is accessed only within your application. This approach doesn't work if your `Service` will be accessed from other applications. In those cases, you need to use an AIDL, Android's method for serializing method calls across process, which I describe in detail in Chapter 7.

```
public class MyLocalService extends Service {
    private LocalBinder mLocalBinder = new LocalBinder();

    public IBinder onBind(Intent intent) {
        return mLocalBinder;
    }

    public void doLongRunningOperation() {
        // TODO Start new thread for long running operation...
    }

    public class LocalBinder extends Binder {
        public MyLocalService getService() {
            return MyLocalService.this;
        }
    }
}
```

When your `Service` returns only `null` in the method `onBind()`, you can bind to it from another component. When doing so in an `Activity`, you usually implement the binding and unbinding in the `onResume()` and `onPause()` methods, as shown here:

```
public class MyActivity extends Activity implements ServiceConnection {
    private MyLocalService mService;

    @Override
```

```
public void onCreate(Bundle savedInstanceState) {
    super.onCreate(savedInstanceState);
    setContentView(R.layout.main);
}


@Override
protected void onResume() {
    super.onResume();
    Intent bindIntent = new Intent(this, MyLocalService.class);
    bindService(bindIntent, this, BIND_AUTO_CREATE);
}

@Override
protected void onPause() {
    super.onPause();
    if (mService != null) {
        unbindService(this);
    }
}

@Override
public void onServiceConnected(ComponentName componentName,
                               IBinder iBinder) {
    mService = ((MyLocalService.LocalBinder) iBinder).getService();
}

@Override
public void onServiceDisconnected(ComponentName componentName) {
    mService = null;
}
}
```

In this `Activity` example, the call to `bindService()` is asynchronous, and the actual `IBinder` interface that you return on `onBind()` is passed to the callback `onServiceConnected()`. The second callback, `onServiceDisconnected()`, is triggered from the call to `unbindService()` in the `onPause()` method. This design provides an efficient binding and unbinding to the `Service`, for when the `Activity` is active and dismissed, respectively. You can also use the callback where you receive the actual reference to the `Service`, `onServiceConnected()`, to update the UI and enable buttons or other components that require the `Service` to be available. Once you have a reference to the actual `Service` object, you can treat it as any other Java object. However, it's important to always release any references between an `Activity` and a `Service` in `onPause()`.

Staying Alive

When your `Service` starts and the application is running in the foreground (that is, when an `Activity` of the application is shown) your `Service` will be the last one shut down by the system. However, as soon as the user leaves your application, the `Service` will no longer be running in the foreground and may be targeted for shutdown by the system. If you need to keep your `Service` in the foreground even if your application is not the active one, you can do so by calling the method `Service.startForeground()`

The system tries to keep `Services` **alive and running for as long as possible. Only when it is running out of resources, usually free RAM, does it start to stop** `Services`**. However, you should always assume that the system may stop your** `Services` **at any given point.**

In the following code, you see an example of the `onStartCommand()` method for a `Service` that uploads a photo to an online server. In this method, also make sure that you're running in the foreground and that you provide the user with a notification that you have a background operation running.

```java
@Override
public int onStartCommand(Intent intent, int flags, int startId) {
    if (intent != null) {
        String action = intent.getAction();

        if (ACTION_SHARE_PHOTO.equals(action)) {
            // Build the notification to be shown
            Notification.Builder builder = new Notification.Builder(this);
            builder.setSmallIcon(R.drawable.notification_icon);
            builder.setContentTitle(getString(R.string.notification_title));
            builder.setContentText(getString(R.string.notification_text));
            Notification notification = builder.build();
            // Start the service in the foreground
            startForeground(NOTIFICATION_ID, notification);

            // Perform out background operation…
            String photoText = intent.getStringExtra(EXTRA_PHOTO_TEXT);
            Bitmap photoBitmap =
                    intent.getParcelableExtra(EXTRA_PHOTO_BITMAP);
            uploadPhotoWithText(photoBitmap, photoText);
        }
    }
    return START_NOT_STICKY;
}
```

First, you create a notification that you will use for your background operation. Next, you call `startForeground()` together with a unique ID and the notification you just created. The result is a new notification that appears in the status bar until the `Service` is either stopped (see the next section) or you call `stopForeground()` with the parameter `true`.

Although this is the recommended way of making sure your `Service` remains operating even though your application is running in the background, don't do so unless you really need to—because you could easily end up wasting system resources. Also, when the operation is complete, make sure you exit everything properly so that, again, you won't waste system resources.

Stopping Services

Once your `Service` starts, it will remain running for as long as possible. Depending on how it was started, the system will restart the `Service` if it's shut down due to lack of resources.

Some unexpected results can occur when a `Service` suddenly restarts, even though the user didn't launch the application. So, it's important to properly stop your `Services` once the user's work is complete.

If your `Service` started from `Context.bindService()`, it will be automatically stopped when the last client disconnects (that is, called `Context.unbindService()`). The exception is if you also call `Service.startForeground()` in your `Service` to keep it alive after the last client disconnects, which is why it's important to call `Service.stopForeground()` properly.

If you start your `Service` by using `Context.startService()`, then the only way to ensure that your `Service` is stopped is by calling either `Service.stopSelf()` or `Context.stopService()`. This signals to the system that it should stop and remove the `Service`. The only way to restart the `Service` is with an explicit call to `Context.startService()` or `Context.bindService()`. Also, calling `Service.stopSelf()` or `Context.stopService()` on a `Service` that was started with `Context.startService()` will always stop it, regardless of how many times `onStartCommand()` was executed (that is, calls to `Context.startService()` don't stack).

The code example that follows shows a (very) simple `Service` for a music player. Its only feature is adding tracks to a play queue. If the queue is empty when a new track arrives, it will start playing the track immediately; otherwise, it will place the track at the end of the queue. Once a track is finished, the callback `onCompletion()` is called, and a check is made to determine whether the queue is empty. If there are more tracks, the `MediaPlayer` is prepared with the next track, and playback starts again; if the queue is empty, you call `Service.stopSelf()`, which causes the `Service` to shut down and release the `MediaPlayer`.

```
public class MyMusicPlayer extends Service
            implements MediaPlayer.OnCompletionListener {
    public static final String ACTION_ADD_TO_QUEUE =
                            "com.aptl.services.ADD_TO_QUEUE";
    private ConcurrentLinkedQueue<Uri> mTrackQueue;
    private MediaPlayer mMediaPlayer;

    public IBinder onBind(Intent intent) {
        return null;
    }

    @Override
    public void onCreate() {
        super.onCreate();
        mTrackQueue = new ConcurrentLinkedQueue<Uri>();
    }

    @Override
    public int onStartCommand(Intent intent, int flags, int startId) {
        String action = intent.getAction();
        if (ACTION_ADD_TO_QUEUE.equals(action)) {
            Uri trackUri = intent.getData();
            addTrackToQueue(trackUri);
        }
```

```
            return START_NOT_STICKY;
        }

        @Override
        public void onDestroy() {
            super.onDestroy();
            if(mMediaPlayer != null) {
                mMediaPlayer.release();
                mMediaPlayer = null;
            }
        }

        /**
         * Add track to end of queue if already playing,
         * otherwise create a new MediaPlayer and start playing.
         */
        private synchronized void addTrackToQueue(Uri trackUri) {
            if(mMediaPlayer == null) {
                try {
                    mMediaPlayer = MediaPlayer.create(this, trackUri);
                    mMediaPlayer.setOnCompletionListener(this);
                    mMediaPlayer.prepare();
                    mMediaPlayer.start();
                } catch (IOException e) {
                    stopSelf();
                }
            } else {
                mTrackQueue.offer(trackUri);
            }
        }

        // Track completed, start playing next or stop service...
        @Override
        public void onCompletion(MediaPlayer mediaPlayer) {
            mediaPlayer.reset();
            Uri nextTrackUri = mTrackQueue.poll();
            if(nextTrackUri != null) {
                try {
                    mMediaPlayer.setDataSource(this, nextTrackUri);
                    mMediaPlayer.prepare();
                    mMediaPlayer.start();
                } catch (IOException e) {
                    stopSelf();
                }
            } else {
                stopSelf();
            }
        }
    }
}
```

This example illustrates how to use `Service.stopSelf()` to ensure that your `Service` doesn't use any more resources than necessary. A good Android application needs to always release as many resources as possible, as soon as possible.

Running in the Background

A `Service` can be running when your application isn't in the foreground, but this doesn't mean that it won't be executing any work on the main thread. Because all components' lifecycle callbacks are executed on the application's main thread, you need to make sure that any long-running operation you perform in your `Service` is moved to a new thread. (Refer to Chapter 2, where I explain how you can use a `Handler` or an `AsyncTask` to launch an operation on the main thread. In this section, I cover two additional methods for executing things on the main thread.)

IntentService

Using a `Handler` together with a `Service` has proven so efficient that Google implemented a utility class named `IntentService` that wraps the background thread handling of a `Handler` in a `Service`. All you need to do is extend the class, implement the `onHandleIntent()` method, and add the actions you want the `Service` to be able to receive, as illustrated here:

```java
public class MyIntentService extends IntentService {
    private static final String NAME = "MyIntentService";
    public static final String ACTION_UPLOAD_PHOTO =
                                "com.aptl.services.UPLOAD_PHOTO";
    public static final String EXTRA_PHOTO = "bitmapPhoto";
    public static final String ACTION_SEND_MESSAGE =
                                "com.aptl.services.SEND_MESSAGE";
    public static final String EXTRA_MESSAGE = "messageText";
    public static final String EXTRA_RECIPIENT = "messageRecipient";

    public MyIntentService() {
        super(NAME);
        // We don't want intents redelivered
        // in case we're shut down unexpectedly
        setIntentRedelivery(false);
    }

    /**
     * This method is executed on its own thread, one intent at a time...
     */
    @Override
    protected void onHandleIntent(Intent intent) {
        String action = intent.getAction();

        if(ACTION_SEND_MESSAGE.equals(action)) {
            String messageText = intent.getStringExtra(EXTRA_MESSAGE);
            String messageRecipient =
                intent.getStringExtra(EXTRA_RECIPIENT);
            sendMessage(messageRecipient, messageText);
        } else if(ACTION_UPLOAD_PHOTO.equals(action)) {
            Bitmap photo = intent.getParcelableExtra(EXTRA_PHOTO);
            uploadPhoto(photo);
        }
    }

    private void sendMessage(String messageRecipient,
                             String messageText) {
```

```
        // TODO Make network call...

        // TODO Send a broadcast that operation is completed
    }

    private void uploadPhoto(Bitmap photo) {
        // TODO Make network call...

        // TODO Send a broadcast that operation is completed
    }
}
```

The preceding example shows a class extending `IntentService` that handles two different actions, one for uploading a photo and one for sending a message. Each action needs to be added to the `intent filter` for the `Service` in the manifest as well. If you want to trigger an action, you simply call `Context.startService()` with an `Intent` carrying the specific action and extras. Multiple calls will result in them being queued up by the internal handler, so this class ensures that only one `Intent` is processed at any given time. A `Service` based on the `IntentService` will be kept in started state until no more operations are queued for processing.

Parallel Execution

The specialized `Service` class just described is very useful for most situations in which you simply want to spawn a background operation and don't care too much about when it starts. If you send five `Intents` to an `IntentService`, they will be executed in sequential order, one at a time. This is usually a good practice but can sometimes cause problems. To ensure that each background operation you spawn is executed as soon as possible, you need some kind of parallel execution. Because the `IntentService` is built around a `Handler` that has only one thread, you need to use some other thread mechanism to handle this kind of situation.

As I describe in Chapter 2, you can set up an `AsyncTask` to use an `Executor` for spawning instances in parallel. However, because `AsyncTask` is designed for operations running only a few seconds at most, you may need to do some more work if your operations are running for a significant amount of time.

The following example shows the stub for a `Service` used for transcoding media to a new format (for instance, WAV to MP3). I left out the actual transcoding step here and focused on the use of the `ExecutorService` API for setting up parallel execution. In order to ensure that the `Service` is kept alive even if the application is not in the foreground, you call `Service.startForeground()` on the `Service`. Because `Service.startForeground()` and `Service.stopForeground()` don't stack, you need to maintain an internal counter of how many active jobs you have and call `Service.stopForeground()` once the counter reaches 0 again.

```
public class MediaTranscoder extends Service {
    private static final int NOTIFICATION_ID = 1001;
    public static final String ACTION_TRANSCODE_MEDIA =
                            "com.aptl.services.TRANSCODE_MEDIA";
    public static final String EXTRA_OUTPUT_TYPE = "outputType";
    private ExecutorService mExecutorService;
    private int mRunningJobs = 0;
    private final Object mLock = new Object();
```

```java
    private boolean mIsForeground = false;

    public IBinder onBind(Intent intent) {
        return null;
    }

    @Override
    public void onCreate() {
        super.onCreate();
        mExecutorService = Executors.newCachedThreadPool();
    }

    @Override
    public int onStartCommand(Intent intent, int flags, int startId) {
        String action = intent.getAction();
        if(ACTION_TRANSCODE_MEDIA.equals(action)) {
            String outputType = intent.getStringExtra(EXTRA_OUTPUT_TYPE);

            // Start new job and increase the running job counter
            synchronized (mLock) {
                TranscodeRunnable transcodeRunnable =
                    new TranscodeRunnable(intent.getData(), outputType);
                mExecutorService.execute(transcodeRunnable);
                mRunningJobs++;
                startForegroundIfNeeded();
            }
        }
        return START_NOT_STICKY;
    }

    @Override
    public void onDestroy() {
        super.onDestroy();
        mExecutorService.shutdownNow();
        synchronized (mLock) {
            mRunningJobs = 0;
            stopForegroundIfAllDone();
        }
    }

    public void startForegroundIfNeeded() {
        if(!mIsForeground) {
            Notification notification = buildNotification();
            startForeground(NOTIFICATION_ID, notification);
            mIsForeGround = true;
        }
    }

    private Notification buildNotification() {
        Notification notification = null;
        // TODO Build the notification here...
        return notification;
    }
```

```
        private void stopForegroundIfAllDone() {
            if(mRunningJobs == 0 && mIsForeground) {
                stopForeground(true);
                mIsForeground = false;
            }
        }

        private class TranscodeRunnable implements Runnable {
            private Uri mInData;
            private String mOutputType;

            private TranscodeRunnable(Uri inData, String outputType) {
                mInData = inData;
                mOutputType = outputType;
            }

            @Override
            public void run() {
                // TODO Perform transcoding here...

                // Decrease counter when we're done...
                synchronized (mLock) {
                    mRunningJobs--;
                    stopForegroundIfAllDone();
                }
            }
        }
    }
}
```

Because most of the boilerplate code for dealing with threads is done in the `ExecutorService` API, this method for implementing parallel execution is recommended. Also, the `ExecutorService` shown in this example won't consume resources when not in use and will keep a cache of threads to minimize the creation of new threads.

Communicating with Services

Once you know when to use a `Service` and how it's executing, you need some way of communicating with it from your other component. You can communicate with a `Service` in two ways: by using the method `Context.startService()` or by using the `Context.bindService()` method. `Context.startService()` delivers the `Intent` to the method `Service.onStartCommand()` where you can trigger the background operation and later deliver the result back to the calling component through a broadcast or some other means. `Context.bindService()` is a way to retrieve a `Binder` that can be used to make synchronous method calls directly to the `Service` object. I start by describing how to communicate with a `Service` through `Intents`.

Asynchronous Messaging with Intents

The `IntentService` example shown earlier in this chapter provides an easy-to-use one-way communication between a component (usually an `Activity`) and the `Service`. But usually you want know the result of the operation you start, so you need some way for the `Service` to report back once it completes its task. You can do so several ways, but if you want to maintain the asynchronous behavior of the `IntentService`, the best approach is to send a broadcast, which is just as simple as starting an operation in your `IntentService`. You just need to implement a `BroadcastReceiver` that listens for the response. Figure 6-3 shows a simple diagram of this sort of communication.

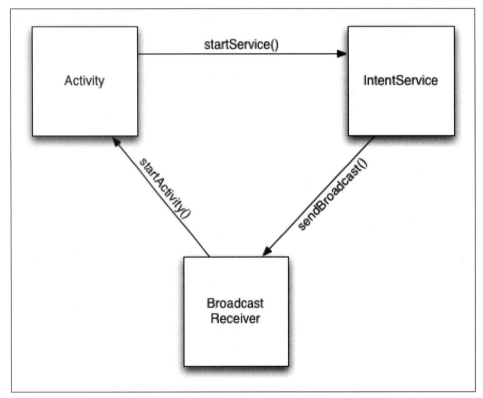

Figure 6-3 Diagram of asynchronous communication between an `Activity`, a `Service`, and a `BroadcastReceiver`

The following code is the modified version of the `uploadPhoto()` method from the earlier example. Here you send only a simple broadcast without any extras, but you're free to use this method to send back a more complex response as long as it can fit into an `Intent`.

```
private void uploadPhoto(Bitmap photo) {
    // TODO Make network call...

    sendBroadcast(new Intent(BROADCAST_UPLOAD_COMPLETED));
}
```

The advantage of this approach is that you have everything you need in Android and don't need to build some complex message handling system between your components. You just declare the actions that represent the asynchronous messages and register them appropriately for each component. This approach works even if your `Service` resides in a different application or runs in a separate process.

The drawback to this solution is that you're limited to what an `Intent` can carry. Also, you cannot use this solution for multiple, fast updates between the `IntentService` and your `Activity`, such as progress updates, because doing so will choke the system. If you need to do something like that, look at using a bound `Service` instead (see the next section).

I go into the details of declaring and setting up `BroadcastReceivers` in Chapter 8.

Locally Bound Services

In an earlier example in this chapter, I showed how to bind to a `Service` in the same application using the local binder pattern. This solution is very useful when your `Service` provides interfaces that are too complicated to solve using only `Intent` messaging and where normal Java methods are easy to implement.

Another reason for binding to a local `Service` is that you can provide a more complex way of doing callback from the `Service` back to the `Activity`. Because long-running operations still must be moved to a background thread in the `Service`, most of the calls to the `Service` should be asynchronous in their design. The actual call triggers a background operation and returns immediately. Once the operation is complete, the `Service` uses a callback interface to notify the `Activity` about the result.

In the following example, I've modified the earlier example with a local `Binder`. I've added a callback interface and a class implementing `AsyncTask` for performing the hypothetical background operation. The `Service` returns a `LocalBinder` object in the `onBind()` method, from which the client can retrieve an object reference to the `Service` object and call the method `doLongRunningOperation()`. This method creates a new `AsyncTask` and executes it with the parameters sent from the client. During the run on the operation, the callback instance is called to notify the client of the progress and eventually of the result.

```java
public class MyLocalService extends Service {
    private static final int NOTIFICATION_ID = 1001;
    private LocalBinder mLocalBinder = new LocalBinder();
    private Callback mCallback;

    public IBinder onBind(Intent intent) {
        return mLocalBinder;
    }

    public void doLongRunningOperation(MyComplexDataObject dataObject) {
        new MyAsyncTask().execute(dataObject);
    }

    public void setCallback(Callback callback) {
        mCallback = callback;
    }

    public class LocalBinder extends Binder {
        public MyLocalService getService() {
            return MyLocalService.this;
        }
    }
}
```

```java
    public interface Callback {
        void onOperationProgress(int progress);
        void onOperationCompleted(MyComplexResult complexResult);
    }

    private final class MyAsyncTask
                extends AsyncTask<MyComplexDataObject, Integer,
                MyComplexResult> {

        @Override
        protected void onPreExecute() {
            super.onPreExecute();
            startForeground(NOTIFICATION_ID, buildNotification());
        }

        @Override
        protected void onProgressUpdate(Integer... values) {
            if(mCallback != null && values.length > 0) {
                for (Integer value : values) {
                    mCallback.onOperationProgress(value);
                }
            }
        }

        @Override
        protected MyComplexResult doInBackground(MyComplexDataObject...
myComplexDataObjects) {
            MyComplexResult complexResult = new MyComplexResult();
            // Actual operation left out for brevity...
            return complexResult;
        }

        @Override
        protected void onPostExecute(MyComplexResult myComplexResult) {
            if(mCallback != null ) {
                mCallback.onOperationCompleted(myComplexResult);
            }
            stopForeground(true);
        }

        @Override
        protected void onCancelled(MyComplexResult complexResult) {
            super.onCancelled(complexResult);
            stopForeground(true);
        }
    }

    private Notification buildNotification() {
        // Create a notification for the service..
        return notification;
    }
}
```

Also, the `AsyncTask` implemented will call `startForeground()` and `stopForeground()`, respectively to make sure the `Service` is kept alive until the long-running operation is finished, even if no clients are bound to the `Service`. (It's outside the scope of this example to keep a count of how many times the method is called, as shown in the earlier example with parallel execution.)

The following code shows how the updated `Activity` looks. The noticeable change comes from implementing the `MyLocalService.Callback` interface on the `Activity`. When you receive a reference to the `Service` in `onServiceConnected()`, you can set the callback to the `Service` object so that you receive notifications when a long-running operation is running. Here it becomes very important to remove the callback (that is, set it to `null`) when the user leaves the `Activity` and `onPause()` is called, or you will leak memory.

```
public class MyActivity extends Activity
        implements ServiceConnection, MyLocalService.Callback {
    private MyLocalService mService;

    @Override
    public void onCreate(Bundle savedInstanceState) {
        super.onCreate(savedInstanceState);
        setContentView(R.layout.main);
    }

    @Override
    protected void onResume() {
        super.onResume();
        Intent bindIntent = new Intent(this, MyLocalService.class);
        bindService(bindIntent, this, BIND_AUTO_CREATE);
    }

    @Override
    protected void onPause() {
        super.onPause();
        if (mService != null) {
            mService.setCallback(null); // Important to avoid memory leaks
            unbindService(this);
        }
    }

    // Callback method assigned to onClick for the button in the UI
    public void onTriggerLongRunningOperation(View view) {
        if(mService != null) {
            mService.doLongRunningOperation(new MyComplexDataObject());
        }
    }

    @Override
    public void onOperationProgress(int progress) {
        // TODO Update user interface with progress..
    }
```

```
    @Override
    public void onOperationCompleted(MyComplexResult complexResult) {
        // TODO Show result to user...
    }

    @Override
    public void onServiceConnected(ComponentName componentName,
                                    IBinder iBinder) {
        mService = ((MyLocalService.LocalBinder) iBinder).getService();
        mService.setCallback(this);

        // Once we have a reference to the service, we can update the UI
        // enable buttons that should otherwise be disabled.
        findViewById(R.id.trigger_operation_button).setEnabled(true);
    }

    @Override
    public void onServiceDisconnected(ComponentName componentName) {
        // Disable the button as we are losing the
        // reference to the service.
        findViewById(R.id.trigger_operation_button).setEnabled(false);
        mService = null;
    }
}
```

and

Also, in the `onServiceConnected()` and `onServiceDisconnected()` methods, you can update the parts of the user interface that depend on the `Service`. In this case, you enable and disable the button that is used to trigger the long-running operation.

If the user leaves the `Activity` (that is, presses Home or Back) before the operation is completed, the `Service` still keeps running because `startForeground()` was called. If the `Activity` resumes before a previously started operation is finished, it will receive the callbacks about the progress as soon as it is successfully bound to the `Service`. This behavior makes it easy to separate a long-running task from the user interface while still allowing your `Activity` to retrieve the current state once it resumes.

If your `Service` maintains some kind of internal state, it's a good practice to allow clients (like `Activities`) to retrieve the current state as well as subscribe (using a callback as just shown) to changes in the state because the state may have changed when an `Activity` resumes and binds to the `Service`.

Summary

The `Service` class is a powerful component that can easily become very complicated to use. You discovered two ways to start a `Service` and how the lifecycle is affected by the chosen method. You saw a few examples of how to implement and control your `Service` to make sure that it can be safely disconnected and reconnected with the user interface.

When it comes to `Services` in Android, my best advice is to have one `Service` for each type of operation you want to perform that's not related to the user interface. At times, you may start by implementing everything within an `Activity` and then later discover that doing so was a mistake that now requires a lot of work to move all the operations to a `Service` in a less optimal way. I strongly recommend that you create `Services` from the start in your project to avoid this problem. It's easier to move operations from a `Service` to an `Activity` than to do the opposite.

Also, remember to be careful about how you start your `Services`. When using `Context.startService()`, you need to return the appropriate value from `onStartCommand()`. Returning the wrong value can have unforeseen consequences when the system eventually shuts down your `Service` because of lack of resources. Explicitly stopping your `Service` when it no longer has any operations to execute is a good practice.

If you need bidirectional communication between your `Service` and an `Activity`, I recommend using the local binder pattern and using a callback interface that your `Activity` can implement. Another way is to use `Intent` messaging and let the `Service` send broadcasts when operations are done. The first approach is more powerful and will allow you to do frequent progress updates from the `Service` to your `Activity`, whereas the second method requires less code but isn't as powerful.

Finally, remember that the lifecycle callbacks, like `onCreate()`, `onStartCommand()` and `onDestroy()`, are all executing on the main thread of your application. This is the same main thread that your `Activities` and other components use. Whenever you perform something that could potentially block the thread for more than a few milliseconds, you should move it to a `Handler` or an `AsyncTask`.

Further Resources

Blogs

Google's changes to the Service API at `http://android-developers.blogspot.se/2010/02/service-api-changes-starting-with.html`

Dianne Hackborn at `http://android-developers.blogspot.se/2010/04/multitasking-android-way.html`

Chapter 7
Android IPC

Android has a powerful feature that's capable of communicating between two different applications. You can set up this communication in many ways in your code, but there is one central mechanism behind the scenes that handles all inter-process communication, the Binder IPC (*Inter-Process Communication*).

The Binder in Android has a long history. It was originally developed as the OpenBinder at Be Inc. for the Be Operating System (BeOS) under the leadership of Dianne Hackborn. It was ported and later rewritten for Android in order to support IPC for applications. Basically, the Binder provides the features for binding functions and data between one execution environment and another. Because each Android application runs in its own Dalvik VM, which is an isolated execution environment, the Binder is very suitable for this purpose.

> **Back in 2009, there was a long debate in the Linux community about why Google chose to use the Binder for IPC rather than the existing solution in the Linux kernel named dbus. The simplest explanation is likely that Dianne Hackborn, one of the lead Android framework engineers, was also the one leading the development of the OpenBinder at Be Inc. When Android was first developed, this was their best choice for IPC, and today it's an integral part of the Android system. The dbus mechanism from Linux is also used on many Android devices, specifically for communication with the Radio Interface Layer (RIL) and for Bluetooth up until Android 4.3. However, most IPC calls on Android go through the Binder.**

In addition to being used for communication between Android applications, the Binder is actually essential in order for an application to communicate with the Android system. When you retrieve a system `Service` using the `Context.getSystemService()` method, the Binder is working behind the scenes to provide your application with a wrapper for a `Service` object. The Binder isn't just used by `Services`, it also handles all communication between Android components and the Android system.

Normally, an Android application doesn't have to contend with the low-level details of the Binder because the Android APIs provide nice wrappers that make it easy to perform IPC. In this chapter, I describe how the Binder works and provide a few examples that show you how to build remote APIs for other applications.

The Binder Explained

As I mentioned in the introduction, the Binder in Android was originally designed under the name "OpenBinder for BeOS" and not Linux, which is the kernel Android runs on. In earlier versions of Android, essentially the same code used for OpenBinder was used for the Linux kernel driver that implemented the Binder for Android. This was less than optimal because the architecture from BeOS is very different from the architecture found in Linux. In later versions of Android, Google rewrote the implementation so that now it's better suited for the Linux kernel architecture.

When two applications communicate using the Binder IPC, they're using this kernel driver to relay messages (see Figure 7-1) between them. Besides the messaging function, the Binder provides additional functions such as identifying the remote caller (process ID and user ID) and notifying when a remote process dies (called *link to death*).

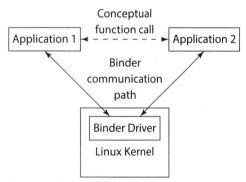

Figure 7-1 Simple diagram illustrating communication using the Binder IPC

For example, the system uses these additional functions in the Binder when the system `Service`, which manages all windows in Android through the `WindowManager`, keeps a `Binder` reference to every application and is notified through a link-to-death notification when an application's window closes.

Communication using the Binder follows the client-server model. Clients use a client-side proxy to handle the communication with the kernel driver. On the server-side, the Binder framework maintains a number of Binder threads. The kernel driver delivers the messages from the client-side proxy to the receiving object using one of the Binder threads on the server-side. This is important to remember because when you receive calls to a `Service` through the Binder, they will not be executed on the main thread of your application. That way, a client to a remote `Service` cannot block the `Service` application's main thread.

You implement the Binder in Android by using the base class `Binder` and the interface `IBinder`. As I show in Chapter 6, a `Service` can return a class implementing the `IBinder` interface in the method `Service.onBind()`. When the `Service` publishes a remote API, you generally use an AIDL file to generate this `IBinder` class, but as I describe next, other methods are available as well.

Binder Address

Communicating over the Binder requires that the client know the address of the remote `Binder` object. However, the design of the Binder is such that only the implementation, like the `Service` you want to call, knows its address. You address on the Android API level by using `Intent` resolution. The client constructs an `Intent` object, using either an action `String` or a `ComponentName` and then uses that to initiate communication with the remote application. However, an `Intent` is only an abstraction of the actual Binder address and needs to be translated in order to set up the communication.

A special `Binder` node called `ServiceManager` that is running inside the Android system server manages all address resolution in Android. This is the only `Binder` node that has a globally known address. Because all components in Android use the Binder for communication, they need to register using the `ServiceManager`, which they reach through the well-known address (see Figure 7-2).

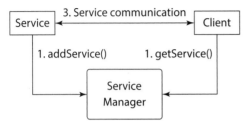

Figure 7-2 Diagram showing service registration and lookup through the `ServiceManager`

Clients that want to communicate with a `Service` or other component query the `ServiceManager`, implicitly through the `Intent` resolution, to receive the Binder address.

Binder Transactions

When one process sends data to another in Android, it's called a *transaction*. You start transactions on the Binder by calling `IBinder.transact()` on the client, and the `Service` receives the call on the method `Binder.onTransact()`, as shown here:

```java
public String performCustomBinderTransaction(IBinder binder, String arg0,
                                             int arg1, float arg2)
        throws RemoteException {
    Parcel request = Parcel.obtain();
    Parcel response = Parcel.obtain();

    // Populate request data...
    request.writeString(arg0);
    request.writeInt(arg1);
    request.writeFloat(arg2);

    // Perform transaction
    binder.transact(IBinder.FIRST_CALL_TRANSACTION, request, response, 0);

    // Read the result from the response...
    String result = response.readString();

    // Recycle the objects
    request.recycle();
    response.recycle();

    return result;
}
```

The method in the preceding example illustrates how from the client-side, once you have a valid IBinder reference, you can perform a custom Binder transaction toward the Service. I explain the Parcel objects in detail in the following example. They are used as simple data containers for the data you want to include in the transaction.

```
public class CustomBinder extends Binder {

    @Override
    protected boolean onTransact(int code, Parcel request,
                                 Parcel response, int flags)
            throws RemoteException {
        // Read the data in the request
        String arg0 = request.readString();
        int arg1 = request.readInt();
        float arg2 = request.readFloat();

        String result = buildResult(arg0, arg1, arg2);

        // Write the result to the response Parcel
        response.writeString(result);

        // Return true on success
        return true;
    }

    private String buildResult(String arg0, int arg1, float arg2) {
        String result = null;
        // TODO Build the result
        return result;
    }
}
```

If you implement a custom Binder object in your Service without using an AIDL, you need to implement the method Binder.onTransact() as just shown. Here you simply respond to the incoming transaction by populating the second Parcel object with the relevant data.

The result is a synchronized two-way call through the Binder IPC. You can also perform a one-way call from the client by setting the flag in the IBinder.transact() call to FLAG_ONEWAY, in which case, you can leave the second Parcel argument as null. Doing so provides better performance for this call because it needs to marshal and unmarshal only one Parcel object.

Using this low-level way of performing transactions between two applications is not recommended if you intend to publish an API for other developers to use. However, when you need fine-grained control of how data is sent between two applications, this can be an efficient method to use. I share it here to illustrate how the Binder works on its basic level. Most of the time, you'll use either AIDL or a Messenger as described in the "Messenger" section, later in this chapter.

Parcel

A Binder transaction will usually carry some transaction data, as shown in the previous example. This data is called a *parcel,* and there is an API for developers, which allows you to create a parcel for most Java objects.

You can compare parcels in Android with serializable objects in Java SE. The difference is that you need to implement the marshaling and unmarshaling of objects yourself using the `Parcelable` interface. This interface defines two methods you need to implement for writing an object to a `Parcel` and also a `static final Creator` object that implements the code for reading the object from a `Parcel`, as shown here:

```java
public class CustomData implements Parcelable {
    public static final Parcelable.Creator<CustomData> CREATOR
            = new Parcelable.Creator<CustomData>() {

        @Override
        public CustomData createFromParcel(Parcel parcel) {
            CustomData customData = new CustomData();
            customData.mName = parcel.readString();
            customData.mReferences = new ArrayList<String>();
            parcel.readStringList(customData.mReferences);
            customData.mCreated = new Date(parcel.readLong());
            return customData;
        }

        @Override
        public CustomData[] newArray(int size) {
            return new CustomData[size];
        }
    };
    private String mName;
    private List<String> mReferences;
    private Date mCreated;

    public CustomData() {
        mName = ""; // Defaults to empty string
        mReferences = new ArrayList<String>();
        mCreated = new Date(); // Defaults to now
    }

    @Override
    public int describeContents() {
        return 0;

    }

    @Override
    public void writeToParcel(Parcel parcel, int flags) {
        parcel.writeString(mName);
        parcel.writeStringList(mReferences);
        parcel.writeLong(mCreated.getTime());
    }

    @Override
    public boolean equals(Object o) {
        if (this == o) return true;
        if (o == null || getClass() != o.getClass()) return false;
```

```
            CustomData that = (CustomData) o;
            return mCreated.equals(that.mCreated) && mName.equals(that.mName);
        }

        @Override
        public int hashCode() {
            int result = mName.hashCode();
            result = 31 * result + mCreated.hashCode();
            return result;
        }
    }
```

The preceding code shows an object that implements the `Parcelable` interface. Note the implementation of the `CREATOR` field and how the `createFromParcel()` method uses the `Parcel.readStringList()` method to read the entire `List` object without having to specify how long the list is (this is handled internally by the `Parcel` object).

After you implement this interface, you can send objects of this class between applications through the Binder IPC.

Link to Death

Another feature of the Binder in Android is that it allows clients to be notified when a `Service` is terminated. As I mentioned earlier, this is called *link to death,* and it's implemented through the Binder method `IBinder.linkToDeath()`. When a client receives an `IBinder` object in the `onServiceConnected()` method, the client can call `linkToDeath()` with a callback implementing the interface `IBinder.DeathRecipient`. Because Android applications can be killed by the system when it's running low on resources (available RAM, and so on), it can be useful to register for these notifications in a client in case it wants to be notified when the remote side is terminated. The following code shows how to register for link to death once you receive a valid `IBinder` reference:

```
    public class LinkToDeathSample extends Service {
        private static final String TAG = "LinkToDeathSample";
        // Service methods exclude for brevity...

        private void notifyRemoteServiceDeath(IBinder iBinder) {
            try {
                iBinder.linkToDeath(new MyLinkToDeathCallback(), 0);
            } catch (RemoteException e) {
                Log.e(TAG, "Error registering for link to death.", e);
            }
        }

        class MyLinkToDeathCallback implements IBinder.DeathRecipient {
            @Override
            public void binderDied() {
                // TODO Handle death of remote binder...
            }
        }
    }
```

You can also check whether the process for the remote `Binder` is still alive by calling `IBinder.pingBinder()`. If that call returns `true`, the process is alive and ready.

If you're binding to a `Service`, this method is not necessary because you'll always have the `ServiceConnection.onServiceDisconnected()` callback to notify you when you lose your connection. However, if you received a `Binder` object some other way, this method can be useful.

Designing APIs

Most applications will rarely need to implement an API for third-party applications because doing so is outside the scope of their features. However, it does become relevant with the types of applications that provide a plug-in mechanism. If you search for "plugin" at the Google Play Store, you'll find tons of examples of these types of applications. If your application fits this category, you'll probably benefit from preparing an API for third-party applications.

An API for third-party applications can be either implemented as a `Service` or as a `ContentProvider`. In this section, I describe how to do so using a `Service`; I show how to use a `ContentProvider` in Chapter 9. When implementing an API, you need to consider a number of things. Do you need to handle concurrent requests, or is it enough to process one client request at a time? Will you publish only one or very few operations, or is it a more complex set of API methods that clients can use? The answer to these questions will determine the most appropriate method for implementing your remote API.

Another detail to consider is whether you'll be sharing this API with other developers or if it will be used only by your own applications (that is, only you will be publishing plug-ins). In the first case, consider building a library project that wraps the client-side implementation in an easy-to-use Java API. If you're the only user of the API, it is probably safe to use either the AIDL or the Messenger directly as described in the next two sections.

If it's enough that your API is one-way, you're probably fine with using an `IntentService` as I describe in Chapter 6. In that case, you just add the necessary permissions and make sure that the API is exported in the manifest.

AIDL

In software engineering, the term Interface Definition Language (IDL) has become the generic term for a specification language that describes the interface for a software component. In Android, the IDL is called Android Interface Definition Language (AIDL) and is written in text files with a Java-like syntax. However, you need to consider a number of differences between writing AIDL files and writing a Java interface.

First, for all non-primitive parameters, you need to specify one of three directional types: `in`, `out`, or `inout`. The `in` type indicates that they are used only for input and that your client won't see any changes that the `Service` does to this object. The `out` type indicates that the input object contains no relevant data but will be populated with data by the `Service` that's relevant in the response from the method. The `inout` type is a combination of both types. It's very important to use only the type that's needed because there's a cost associated with each type.

Another thing to remember is that for all custom classes used in communication, you need to create an AIDL file that declares your class as a `Parcelable`.

The following code snippet is an example of an AIDL file with the name `CustomData.aidl`. It should be placed in the same package as the Java class source file.

```
package com.aptl.sampleapi;

parcelable CustomData;
```

Finally, all custom classes you need for your API must be imported in the AIDL file for the API, as shown here:

```
package com.aptl.sampleapi;

import com.aptl.sampleapi.CustomData;

interface ApiInterfaceV1 {
    /**
     * Simple remote method for checking if a number is a prime.
     */
    boolean isPrime(long value);

    /**
     * Retrieve all CustomData objects since timestamp.
     * Will get at most result.length objects.
     */
    void getAllDataSince(long timestamp, out CustomData[] result);

    /**
     * Stores the CustomData object.
     */
    void storeData(in CustomData data);
}
```

This is an example of an AIDL file with three methods. *Note:* Primitives don't need a directional tag (they're always called by value).

Remember, after you've implemented a client, you cannot change or remove any methods that you've put in an AIDL. You can add new methods *at the end of the file,* but because of the way the AIDL compiler generates the identifier for each method, you cannot change any of the existing methods without breaking backward compatibility. When handling new versions of the API, the recommended way is to create a new AIDL file with the new or changed methods. Doing so allows you to maintain backward compatibility with older clients. As you can see by the name of the preceding AIDL file, you handle versioning of AIDL by appending V1 for the first version of the file. When you add new methods to the API, you create a file by ending with V2, and so on.

This method for versioning is one of the drawbacks with using AIDL files. One way to manage this issue is to provide a Java wrapper around the AIDL and you publish this either as a library project or as a JAR file that developers can use. This way, a client won't have to implement multiple AIDLs but can always download the latest version of your wrapper and be sure that it's compatible. I show an example of how to create such a wrapper in section "Wrapping APIs with Library Projects," later in this chapter.

When you have an AIDL file ready, you need to implement it on both the service-side and the client-side, as shown here:

```
public class AidlService extends Service {
    private ArrayList<CustomData> mCustomDataCollection;

    @Override
    public void onCreate() {
        super.onCreate();
        mCustomDataCollection = new ArrayList<CustomData>();
        // TODO Populate the list with stored values...
    }


    public IBinder onBind(Intent intent) {
        return mBinder;
    }

    public static boolean isPrimeImpl(long number) {
        // Implementation left out for brevity...
        return false;
    }

    private void getDataSinceImpl(CustomData[] result, Date since) {
        int size = mCustomDataCollection.size();
        int pos = 0;
        for(int i = 0; i < size && pos < result.length; i++) {
            CustomData storedValue = mCustomDataCollection.get(i);
            if(since.after(storedValue.getCreated())) {
                result[pos++] = storedValue;
            }
        }
    }

    private void storeDataImpl(CustomData data) {
        int size = mCustomDataCollection.size();
        for (int i = 0; i < size; i++) {
            CustomData customData = mCustomDataCollection.get(i);
            if(customData.equals(data)) {
                mCustomDataCollection.set(i, data);
                return;
            }
        }
        mCustomDataCollection.add(data);
    }

    private final ApiInterfaceV1.Stub mBinder
            = new ApiInterfaceV1.Stub() {

        @Override
        public boolean isPrime(long value) throws RemoteException {
            return isPrimeImpl(value);
        }
```

```java
    @Override
    public void getAllDataSince(long timestamp, CustomData[] result)
                            throws RemoteException {
        getDataSinceImpl(result, new Date(timestamp));
    }

    @Override
    public void storeData(CustomData data) throws RemoteException {
        storeDataImpl(data);
    }
    };
}
```

The preceding example shows the implementation of the AIDL stub in the end on the Service. This object is also what is returned to clients that bind to the Service in the onBind() method. Note that each call to the API in the Service will be running on its own thread because the Binder provides a pool of threads on which it executes calls from clients. This means that a client cannot block the main thread of the Service it is calling when you're using this method.

The following Activity shows how to bind to a remote Service and retrieve the interface for ApiInterfaceV1. This is the preferred solution if you're the sole user of the remote API and can manage the versioning on both sides (or on the same development team).

```java
public class MyApiClient extends Activity implements ServiceConnection {
    private ApiInterfaceV1 mService;

    @Override
    public void onCreate(Bundle savedInstanceState) {
        super.onCreate(savedInstanceState);
        setContentView(R.layout.main);
    }

    @Override
    protected void onResume() {
        super.onResume();
        bindService(new Intent("com.aptl.sampleapi.AIDL_SERVICE"),
                    this, BIND_AUTO_CREATE);
    }

    public void onCheckForPrime(View view) {
        EditText numberToCheck = (EditText) findViewById(R.id.number_
    input);
        long number = Long.valueOf(numberToCheck.getText().toString());
        boolean isPrime = mService.isPrime(number);
        String message = isPrime ?
                getString(R.string.number_is_prime, number)
                : getString(R.string.number_not_prime, number);
        Toast.makeText(this, message, Toast.LENGTH_SHORT).show();
    }
```

```
    @Override
    protected void onPause() {
        super.onPause();
        unbindService(this);
    }

    @Override
    public void onServiceConnected(ComponentName componentName,
                                   IBinder iBinder) {
        mService = ApiInterfaceV1.Stub.asInterface(iBinder);
    }

    @Override
    public void onServiceDisconnected(ComponentName componentName) {
        mService = null;
    }
}
```

Callbacks with AIDL

Clients can also implement an AIDL that can be used as a callback interface by the Service, which is useful if you want to register clients to receive callbacks when something happens on the Service—for instance, when data is updated from an online server that the Service is communicating with.

In the following example, you can see the new AIDL file for the callback interface, note the keyword oneway that tells the AIDL compiler that this interface is only a one-way communication. No response back to the caller, in this case the Service, is needed. This will give you a slight performance boost.

```
package com.aptl.sampleapi;

import com.aptl.sampleapi.CustomData;

oneway interface AidlCallback {
    void onDataUpdated(in CustomData[] data);
}
```

Next, you create an instance of this interface in your client, shown as follows. In this case, you simply show a Toast when you receive a callback from the Service:

```
private AidlCallback.Stub mAidlCallback = new AidlCallback.Stub() {
    @Override
    public void onDataUpdated(CustomData[] data) throws RemoteException {
        Toast.makeText(MyApiClient.this, "Data was updated!",
                       Toast.LENGTH_SHORT).show();
    }
};
```

In the AIDL for the Service shown earlier, you add one more line for registering the callback:

```
void addCallback(in AidlCallback callback);
```

Finally, you implement the `addCallback()` method on the `Service`. Here, you also use the `linkToDeath()` method to receive a notification in case the client Binder died.

```
@Override
public void addCallback(final AidlCallback callback) throws
RemoteException {
    mCallbacks.add(callback);
    callback.asBinder().linkToDeath(new DeathRecipient() {
        @Override
        public void binderDied() {
            mCallbacks.remove(callback);
        }
    }, 0);
}
```

Normally, you should have both an `addCallback()` and a `removeCallback()` method, but I'm leaving that as an exercise for you to explore.

The previous example shows how to create callback interfaces between applications. It also shows how you can transfer a `Binder` object between two applications without having to register it through the `ServiceManager`. Because only the client and the `Service` know the address for this Binder, it can effectively be used as a security mechanism when doing IPC.

Messenger

Another way of providing a remote interface is through the `Messenger` class. This class is useful when you have a `Service` where you don't need to support concurrent operations to clients. The `Messenger` class uses a `Handler` to execute each incoming message, so all client calls will run on the same thread in serial order. You also get rid of the problems with AIDL files and can more easily provide an asynchronous message-based API for clients. Although not as powerful, this class can be more efficient at times because you'll get much easier implementation, both for clients and `Services`.

The following example shows how to use the `Messenger` class to provide an asynchronous API. The `onBind()` method returns the `Binder` object from the `Messenger` created in `onCreate()`. When the `Messenger` receives a message, it can reply to the client using a `Messenger` object stored in the `replyTo` field.

```
public class MessengerService extends Service {
    private Handler mMessageHandler;
    private Messenger mMessenger;

    @Override
    public void onCreate() {
        super.onCreate();
        HandlerThread handlerThread = new HandlerThread("MessengerService");
```

```
        handlerThread.start();
        mMessageHandler = new Handler(handlerThread.getLooper(),
                                        new MyHandlerCallback());
        mMessenger = new Messenger(mMessageHandler);
    }

    public IBinder onBind(Intent intent) {
        return mMessenger.getBinder();
    }

    @Override
    public void onDestroy() {
        super.onDestroy();
        mMessageHandler.getLooper().quit();
    }

    private class MyHandlerCallback implements Handler.Callback {

        @Override
        public boolean handleMessage(Message message) {
            boolean delivered = false;
            switch (message.what) {
                case MessageAPI.SEND_TEXT_MSG:
                    delivered = sendTextMessage((String) message.obj);
                    break;
                case MessageAPI.SEND_PHOTO_MSG:
                    delivered = sendPhotoMessage((Bitmap) message.obj);
                    break;
            }
            Message reply = Message.obtain(null,
                                MessageAPI.MESSAGE_DELIVERED_MSG,
                                delivered);
            try {
                message.replyTo.send(reply);
            } catch (RemoteException e) {
                Log.e("MessengerService",
                        "Error sending message reply!", e);
            }
            return true;
        }
    }

    // Return true when delivered
    private boolean sendPhotoMessage(Bitmap photo) {
        // Implementation left out for brevity
        return true;
    }

    // Return true when delivered
    private boolean sendTextMessage(String textMessage) {
        // Implementation left out for brevity
        return true;
    }
}
```

The following example shows a client that first binds to the Service and then constructs a new Messenger object with the IBinder as a parameter. This now acts as a proxy for the Messenger running in the remote Service. When you send a message to the Service, you can also set the replyTo field of the Message object.

```java
public class MyMessengerClient extends Activity
                                implements ServiceConnection {
    private ApiInterfaceV1 mService;
    private Messenger mRemoteMessenger;
    private Messenger mReplyMessenger;
    private Handler mReplyHandler;

    @Override
    public void onCreate(Bundle savedInstanceState) {
        super.onCreate(savedInstanceState);
        setContentView(R.layout.main);
        HandlerThread handlerThread = new HandlerThread("ReplyMessenger");
        handlerThread.start();
        mReplyHandler = new Handler(handlerThread.getLooper(),
                                    new ReplyHandlerCallback())
        mReplyMessenger = new Messenger(mReplyHandler);
    }

    @Override
    protected void onResume() {
        super.onResume();
        bindService(new Intent("com.apt1.sampleapi.MESSENGER_SERVICE"),
                    this, BIND_AUTO_CREATE);
    }

    public void onSendTextPressed(View view) {
        String textMessage = ((EditText) findViewById(R.id.message_input))
                                .getText().toString();
        Message message = Message.obtain();
        message.what = MessageAPI.SEND_TEXT_MSG;
        message.obj = textMessage;
        message.replyTo = mReplyMessenger;
        try {
            mRemoteMessenger.send(message);
        } catch (RemoteException e) {
            // Remote service is dead...
        }
    }

    @Override
    protected void onPause() {
        super.onPause();
        unbindService(this);
    }

    @Override
    protected void onDestroy() {
        super.onDestroy();
```

```
            mReplyHandler.getLooper().quit();
    }

    @Override
    public void onServiceConnected(ComponentName componentName,
                                   IBinder iBinder) {
        mRemoteMessenger = new Messenger(iBinder);
    }

    @Override
    public void onServiceDisconnected(ComponentName componentName) {
        mRemoteMessenger = null;
    }

    private class ReplyHandlerCallback implements Handler.Callback {
        @Override
        public boolean handleMessage(Message message) {
            switch (message.what) {
                case MessageAPI.MESSAGE_DELIVERED_MSG:
                    // TODO Handle async reply from service
                    break;
            }
            return true;
        }
    }
}
```

This method is very similar to using the `IntentService` as I describe in Chapter 6, but instead of working with `Intent` objects, here you're utilizing the `Message` class used for triggering operations on a `Handler`, as I describe in Chapter 2. Also, using a `Messenger` provides a convenient way of implementing asynchronous communication without having to use `BroadcastReceivers`.

Wrapping APIs with Library Projects

Regardless of whether you use AIDL or the `Messenger` class to implement your remote API, it's a good idea to extract all the API-specific classes and interfaces to a library project and create a pure Java wrapper for clients to use. Because you probably want to support your complex objects in your API, providing only an AIDL file for your API is usually not enough. You also need to provide these custom classes to clients. As I describe in Chapter 1, when it comes to distribution and versioning, setting up an Android library project for your API is a simple and efficient way of handling all the problems related to remote APIs. You can also package the compiled wrapper code into a JAR file that is easily distributed as a third-party library. I recommend using an Android library project, uploading it to an online version control service like GitHub, and letting other developers simply use that code to integrate with your application.

The easiest way to set up a library project for your remote API is to move all AIDL files and `Parcelable` classes to a library project that you reference in the application that implements your remote API. However, if you have several AIDLs (new versions, client callbacks, and so on), it can easily become quite complicated, so it's also a good practice to wrap everything in a more easy-to-use Java class, as shown here:

```java
public class ApiWrapper {
    private Context mContext;
    private ApiCallback mCallback;
    private MyServiceConnectionV1 mServiceConnection =
                                    new MyServiceConnectionV1();
    private ApiInterfaceV1 mServiceV1;

    public void release() {
        mContext.unbindService(mServiceConnection);
    }

    public ApiWrapper(Context context, ApiCallback callback) {
        mContext = context;
        mCallback = callback;
        mContext.bindService(new Intent("com.aptl.sampleapi.AIDL_
SERVICE"),
                mServiceConnection, Context.BIND_AUTO_CREATE);
    }

    public void getAllDataSince(long timestamp, CustomData[] result) {
        if (mServiceV1 != null) {
            try {
                mServiceV1.getAllDataSince(timestamp, result);
            } catch (RemoteException e) {
                // TODO Handle service error
            }
        }
    }

    void storeData(CustomData data) {
        if (mServiceV1 != null) {
            try {
                mServiceV1.storeData(data);
            } catch (RemoteException e) {
                // Handle service error
            }
        }
    }

    private class MyServiceConnectionV1 implements ServiceConnection {
        @Override
        public void onServiceConnected(ComponentName componentName,
                                        IBinder iBinder) {
            mServiceV1 = ApiInterfaceV1.Stub.asInterface(iBinder);
            try {
                mServiceV1.setCallback(mAidlCallback);
            } catch (RemoteException e) {
                // Handle service error...
            }

            mCallback.onApiReady(ApiWrapper.this);
        }
}
```

```
        @Override
        public void onServiceDisconnected(ComponentName componentName) {
            mServiceV1 = null;
            if(mCallback != null) {
                mCallback.onApiLost();
            }
        }
    }

    private AidlCallback.Stub mAidlCallback = new AidlCallback.Stub() {
        @Override
        public void onDataUpdated(CustomData[] data)
                    throws RemoteException {
            if(mCallback != null) {
                mCallback.onDataUpdated(data);
            }
        }
    };

    public interface ApiCallback {
        void onApiReady(ApiWrapper apiWrapper);
        void onApiLost();
        void onDataUpdated(CustomData[] data);
    }
}
```

The preceding code shows how to create a wrapper for the AIDL examples shown earlier in this chapter. This method creates a much easier interface for your Service to the client. You can even manage AIDL callbacks by wrapping them in ordinary Java interfaces as shown with the preceding ApiCallback.

This method lets you use the standard Java approach for version-controlling your API. You can add the @ deprecated tag to methods, and you can add new methods to your wrapper that handle the versioning of the API behind the scenes. Clients will not have to worry about these details, and you can easily maintain backward compatibility.

You can implement different versions of your API on the Service by returning different IBinder objects depending on the contents of the Intent used in Context.bindService(), as shown here:

```
public IBinder onBind(Intent intent) {
    int apiVersionRequested = intent.getIntExtra(EXTRA_VERSION_TAG, 1);
    switch (apiVersionRequested) {
        case 1:
            return mBinderV1;
        case 2:
            return mBinderV2;
        case 3:
            return mBinderV3;
        default:
            return null;
    }
}
```

The preceding example shows how you can retrieve an `int` from the `Intent` to decide which version of the API to return. This method allows you to create new AIDL files for updates to your API. Your wrapper will now bind to each version and keep one local reference for every binding.

Securing Remote APIs

Security should always be a priority when you're designing Android applications, regardless of what you're doing. When providing APIs between applications security becomes even more important. (I go into security for Android applications in more detail in Chapter 12.) Luckily, securing your published `Services`, and other components, is quite easy, as shown here:

```xml
<?xml version="1.0" encoding="utf-8"?>
<manifest xmlns:android="http://schemas.android.com/apk/res/android"
          package="com.apt1.sampleapi">

    <permission android:name="com.apt1.sampleapi.CALL_SERVICE"
                android:protectionLevel="normal"/>

    <uses-sdk
            android:minSdkVersion="17"
            android:targetSdkVersion="17"/>
    <application
            android:icon="@drawable/icon"
            android:label="@string/app_name">
        <service
                android:name=".AidlService"
                android:exported="true"
                android:permission="com.apt1.sampleapi.CALL_SERVICE">
            <intent-filter>
                <action android:name="com.apt1.sampleapi.AIDL_SERVICE"/>
            </intent-filter>
        </service>
    </application>
</manifest>
```

This XML is an example of how the `AndroidManifest.xml` file might appear for a `Service` that you publish. The important areas are shown in bold. First, you need to set the attribute `android:exported` to `true`. The default value for this attribute depends on how you define the `intent-filter` for the `Service`. If you don't include an `intent-filter`, the `Service` is only for internal use (addressed through its component name), and it won't be exported. If you define an `intent-filter`, the `Service` is exported by default. I highly recommend that you always define this attribute and set the value according to your needs, whether or not it's an exported `Service`.

If you're exporting a `Service`, the most important part is to set up permissions. I go into detail about defining permissions in Chapter 12, but the previous example shows the simplest form. You define the permission above the application tag and give it a `protectionLevel`. Next, you set the `android:permission` attribute for the `Service` to declare that clients for this `Service` must declare this permission in their manifest.

It's usually enough to declare permissions as shown in the previous code block, but sometimes you need to go beyond Android's permission management. In Chapter 12, I discuss more advanced methods for securing your application that also apply to APIs that you'll publish.

Summary

In this chapter, you discovered how to use the `Service` component in Android to provide a remote API for other applications to use. You are now familiar with how the Binder IPC works in Android and the choices you have when it comes to implementing a remote API.

As I discussed, AIDL is a powerful but complicated method that requires more consideration when designing. It allows you to do normal synchronous Java method calls across applications in different processes, but you need to carefully consider how to design your API and think about versioning.

Also, using the `Messenger` class is an easy way to create an asynchronous remote API, but it's also limited because all client calls will be running on a single thread, as opposed to the AIDL approach where you have one thread for every client. That said, the message-based approach will usually perform better than AIDL, so many times this approach is preferable.

In addition, I recommended that you provide an Android library project that wraps your remote API in a more easy-to-use set of Java classes, especially if you will use the AIDL approach. Doing so also makes it easier for you to handle new versions of the API while maintaining backward-compatibility with older clients.

Finally, pay extra attention to securing your remote API. Declare permissions properly and make sure that only the components that should be published have the `android:exported` flag set to `true` in the manifest.

Further Resources

Websites

"Android Interprocess Communication" by Thorsten Schreiber at `www.nds.rub.de/media/attachments/files/2012/03/binder.pdf`

"Android IPC Mechanism" by Jim Huang at `http://0xlab.org/~jserv/android-binder-ipc.pdf`

"Deep Dive into Android IPC/Binder Framework" by Aleksandar Gargenta at `http://marakana.com/s/post/1340/Deep_Dive_Into_Binder_Presentation.htm`

Android Developers Blog. "Service API Changes Starting with Android 2.0" by Dianne Hackborn at `http://android-developers.blogspot.se/2010/02/service-api-changes-starting-with.html`

A summary of using Binder by Dianne Hackborn at `https://lkml.org/lkml/2009/6/25/3`

Chapter 8

Mastering BroadcastReceivers and Configuration Changes

An Android-based smartphone is a very powerful device with lots of different hardware components. Many of these components affect the state of the smartphone in different ways. The accelerometer detects the current physical orientation of the device (portrait or landscape), the Wi-Fi discovers new available networks and notifies the system when its connection to a network changes, the light-sensor controls the brightness of the screen, and the hardware buttons on the device trigger interrupts that generate some event in the system.

At the same time, the Android system always tries to consume as little power as possible in order to make the battery last as long as possible. However, because Android applications have a relatively high degree of freedom as to how much they can control the device, it's very important for you, as a developer, to react to the different events and changes to the device; otherwise, they could cause unnecessary power drain. By mastering the different system events and device changes, you can make your application more robust and work more smoothly with the overall system. A badly written application that eats up a user's batteries will receive bad reviews, and ultimately users will seek better alternatives.

Also, most of these events are not directly related to battery consumption or performance. However, you need to be aware of them in order to anticipate changes that will affect how your device is working. For instance, if the device loses its Wi-Fi connection and switches to the much slower EDGE connection, you may want to reduce the number of network calls or pick a smaller version of pictures you're downloading. By watching for events indicating if the screen changes from on to off (or vice versa), you can make additional assumptions about a user's activity and take appropriate actions based on that (for instance, screen off would probably mean that the user isn't actively looking at the device).

As an application developer, you can also send broadcast, either defined by the application as a new `Intent` action or by using some action defined by the Android APIs or third-party application. Doing so can be very useful when you want to dispatch events in the background, either within your own application or between two different applications.

Although an application can listen to numerous events, I cover only a few of them in this chapter because there are so many defined by the Android platform. For more information about broadcast events, go to the official Android documentation site: `http://d.android.com`, and check out the relevant APIs. For instance, events related to telephony features are usually found in the `android.telephony` package.

There are also different ways to listen for these events. Some are sent as broadcast `Intents` and received by `BroadcastReceivers`; others require you to implement some Java callback. In this chapter, I provide examples of these methods and how you can efficiently implement them.

BroadcastReceivers

The most common way that events are broadcast on Android is through `Intent` objects sent to `BroadcastReceivers` using the `Context.sendBroadcast()` methods. Many of the standard system events are defined as action strings and can be found in the API documentation for the `Intent` class. For instance, if your application needs to be notified whenever the user connects or disconnects the charger to the smartphone, two broadcast actions defined in the `Intent` class do that: `ACTION_POWER_DISCONNECTED` and `ACTION_POWER_CONNECTED`.

The following code shows a simple `BroadcastReceiver` that receives an `Intent` object whenever the user connects or disconnects the power. In this method, the only thing you do is call `Context.startService()` to delegate the event to a service that performs the actual work.

```java
public class ChargerConnectedListener extends BroadcastReceiver {
    public void onReceive(Context context, Intent intent) {
        String action = intent.getAction();

        if (Intent.ACTION_POWER_CONNECTED.equals(action)) {
            context.startService(
                    new Intent(MyService.ACTION_POWER_CONNECTED));
        } else if (Intent.ACTION_POWER_DISCONNECTED.equals(action)) {
            context.startService(
                    new Intent(MyService.ACTION_POWER_DISCONNECTED));
        }
    }
}
```

The default method for implementing `BroadcastReceivers` is to declare them in the manifest. Consequently, it's possible for the `BroadcastReceiver` to notify your service even though the user hasn't started your application. This factor is especially useful for applications that should start on certain system events without user interaction. You could use the following approach to be notified whenever connectivity to Wi-Fi changes. For example, when the user comes home and connects her device to the home Wi-Fi, you could design your application so that it starts to sync data with other devices she has connected to the same network, without her having to manually trigger this action.

```xml
<receiver android:name=".ChargerConnectedListener">
    <intent-filter>
        <action
            android:name="android.intent.action.ACTION_POWER_CONNECTED" />
        <action
            android:name="android.intent.action.ACTION_POWER_DISCONNECTED" />
    </intent-filter>
</receiver>
```

BroadcastReceivers can also be registered programmatically within Activities and Services. Some broadcast Intents can only be registered programmatically, and some only work if you declare them in your manifest. Check the official Android API documentation for details on each action.

When you register a BroadcastReceiver programmatically, as shown in the following example, you must also unregister it in the matching callback. In the this example, the receiver is registered for the two actions in onResume() therefore, you unregister it in onPause().

```java
public class MyActivity extends Activity {
    private ChargerConnectedListener mPowerConnectionReceiver;

    @Override
    protected void onResume() {
        super.onResume();
        IntentFilter intentFilter = new IntentFilter();
        intentFilter.addAction(Intent.ACTION_POWER_CONNECTED);
        intentFilter.addAction(Intent.ACTION_POWER_DISCONNECTED);
        mPowerConnectionReceiver = new ChargerConnecedListener();
        registerReceiver(mPowerConnectionReceiver, intentFilter);
    }

    @Override
    protected void onPause() {
        super.onPause();
        unregisterReceiver(mPowerConnectionReceiver);
    }
}
```

You'll usually want to programmatically register BroadcastReceivers when you're only interested in the events while your application is running and active. This way, your application will consume fewer resources than if you declare them in your manifest and they start every time the event occurs. When your application needs to receive system events, always consider the difference between a BroadcastReceiver registered in the manifest or through Context.registerReceiver() so that you avoid using any more resources than necessary.

Local BroadcastReceivers

If you want to send and receive broadcast only within your own application's process, consider using the LocalBroadcastManager instead of the more generic Context.sendBroadcast() method. This approach is more efficient because no cross-process management is included and you don't have to consider the security issues normally involved with broadcasts. This class is not part of the standard APIs but is contained in the support APIs. The following code exemplifies how to send a local broadcast using the LocalBroadcastManager.

```java
public void sendLocalBroadcast(Intent broadcastIntent) {
    LocalBroadcastManager localBroadcastManager =
            LocalBroadcastManager.getInstance(this);
    localBroadcastManager.sendBroadcast(broadcastIntent);
}
```

To receive a local broadcast, you use the `LocalBroadcastManager` shown in the preceding code. The following example shows a simple `Activity` where you register and unregister for local broadcasts for a certain action.

```
public class LocalBroadcastDemo extends Activity {
    public static final String LOCAL_BRODCAST_ACTION = "localBroadcast";
    private BroadcastReceiver mLocalReceiver;

    @Override
    protected void onResume() {
        super.onResume();
        LocalBroadcastManager localBroadcastManager =
                LocalBroadcastManager.getInstance(this);
        IntentFilter intentFilter = new IntentFilter(LOCAL_BRODCAST_
ACTION);
        mLocalReceiver = new BroadcastReceiver() {
            @Override
            public void onReceive(Context context, Intent intent) {
                // TODO Handle local broadcast...
            }
        };
        localBroadcastManager.registerReceiver(mLocalReceiver,
                                                intentFilter);
    }

    @Override
    protected void onPause() {
        super.onPause();
        LocalBroadcastManager localBroadcastManager =
                LocalBroadcastManager.getInstance(this);
        localBroadcastManager.unregisterReceiver(mLocalReceiver);
    }
}
```

Local broadcast is a convenient way of broadcasting messages and states within your application. Local broadcast is more efficient than standard global broadcasts and is more secure because you can be certain that no data sent this way will leak outside your application. Remember to always unregister these local receivers in the same way you do normal receivers, or you may leak memory.

Normal and Ordered Broadcasts

Broadcasts are divided into two categories, normal and ordered. The normal broadcasts are sent to all receivers asynchronously and are received in an unspecified order, as shown in Figure 8-1. This method is more efficient but lacks some of the advanced features found for ordered broadcasts. No feedback can be sent to the broadcaster with normal broadcasts.

An ordered broadcast is delivered to the registered receivers one at a time in a specified order (see Figure 8-2). You can control the order in which the broadcasts are received by setting the `android:priority` attribute for the relevant `intent-filter` tag in the manifest. Another feature of ordered broadcasts is that by using `abortBroadcast()`, `setResultCode()` and `setResultData()`, a receiver can set a result that is delivered back to the broadcaster or abort the broadcast so that the `Intent` won't be propagated to the next receiver in the queue.

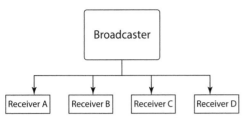

Figure 8-1 Diagram illustrating the asynchronous normal broadcasts to multiple receivers

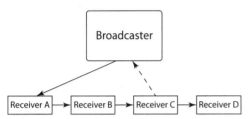

Figure 8-2 Diagram illustrating the sequential propagation of ordered broadcasts

The following code shows the implementation of a receiver that expects an ordered broadcast. You start by checking that the broadcast is in fact ordered and then assign the result code, result data and any extras you want to deliver to the broadcaster. After the onReceive() method returns, the response will be sent back to the broadcaster automatically.

```
public class OrderedReceiver extends BroadcastReceiver {
    public void onReceive(Context context, Intent intent) {
        if(isOrderedBroadcast() {
            setResultCode(Activity.RESULT_OK);
            setResultData("simple response string");
            // Get current response extras, or create new if null.
            Bundle resultExtras = getResultExtras(true);
            // Set our component name for the extras response...
            resultExtras.putParcelable("componentName",
                    new ComponentName(context,getClass()));
        }
    }
}
```

In the following code, you see how to send an ordered broadcast and how responses are handled. You can register for responses by passing a BroadcastReceiver object to the method Context.sendBroadcast(). This receiver will then get a call to onReceive() for every receiver of the original ordered broadcast.

```
public void sendOrderedBroadcastAndGetResponse() {
    Intent intent = new Intent(ACTION_ORDERED_MESSAGE);
    // The broadcast receiver that will handle responses
    BroadcastReceiver responseReceiver = new BroadcastReceiver() {
```

```
        @Override
        public void onReceive(Context context, Intent intent) {
            String resultData = getResultData();
            Bundle resultExtras = getResultExtras(false);
            if (resultExtras != null) {
                ComponentName registeredComponent = resultExtras.
                        getParcelable("componentName");
            }
            // TODO Handle response
        }
    };

    sendOrderedBroadcast(intent, responseReceiver, null,
                    RESULT_OK,null,null);
}
```

You rarely need to send an ordered broadcast in your own applications, but they can be helpful if you'll be communicating with other applications (for instance, plug-ins can have a great use for this). In the Android system, the most common example of ordered broadcasts is when an application listens for incoming SMS messages, which is part of the hidden APIs. I describe this in further detail in Chapter 15.

Sticky Broadcasts

A variation of the normal broadcast is a *sticky* broadcast, which works a little bit differently. The difference is that the `Intent` sent with `Context.sendStickyBroadcast()` will "stay around" after the broadcast is complete, allowing future registrations for the matching `Intent` to receive the same broadcast as well.

One example of such a broadcast is `Intent.ACTION_BATTERY_CHANGED`, which is used to indicate changes in the battery level for the device. Another example is `Intent.ACTION_DOCK_EVENT`, which indicates whether a device is placed in a dock. Check the Android API documentation for other examples of sticky broadcasts. The following code shows an example of a receiver that listens for battery changes. It will also notice whether the sticky broadcast is new or not.

```
public class BatteryChangeListener extends BroadcastReceiver {
    public void onReceive(Context context, Intent intent) {
        String action = intent.getAction();
        if(Intent.ACTION_BATTERY_CHANGED.equals(action)) {
            if(isInitialStickyBroadcast()) {
                // This is an old event from the "sticky" cache
            } else {
                // This is a new event that just occurred...
            }
        }
    }
}
```

This method is especially useful for signaling system-wide states (such as battery status). In order for an application to send this type of broadcast, it must hold the permission `android.permission.BROADCAST_STICKY` and send sticky broadcasts using `Context.sendStickyBroadcast()`.

Use sticky broadcasts with care from your own application, because it will put an additional load on the available system resources.

Directed Broadcasts

Another variation of the normal broadcasts is *directed* broadcasts. These broadcasts use a feature of the `intent-filter` with which you can explicitly specify the receiver by setting the `ComponentName` in the broadcasted `Intent`. This is the combination of the class- and package-name of the registered `BroadcastReceiver`, as shown in the following code :

```
public void sendDirectedBroadcast(String packageName, String className,
                                  String action) {
    Intent intent = new Intent(action);
    intent.setComponent(new ComponentName(packageName, className));
    sendBroadcast(directedBroadcastIntent);
}
```

The result of the previous code is that you send a normal broadcast that will be received only by the specified receiver, even if other receivers are registered for the same `Intent` action. *Note:* You must know both the package-name and the class-name of the receiver for this to work.

The directed broadcast approach can be very useful for applications that provide plug-in functionality. When a plug-in is registered (installed), it can signal to the main application the relevant information for a directed broadcast.

Enabling and Disabling Receivers

When the broadcast you want to listen for is available only for receivers declared in the manifest, you can reduce the impact on the system's load another way. With the `PackageManager`, you can enable and disable components in your application, which is helpful if you have a receiver that you want to be inactive unless the user performs a specific action (for instance, changes a setting).

The two methods that follow illustrate how you can programmatically enable and disable a specific component based on its `ComponentName`. You just set `android:enabled="false"` in the manifest as the default value for that component and later use the following code to change the value to `true`.

```
public void enableBroadcastReceiver() {
    PackageManager packageManager = getPackageManager();
    packageManager.setComponentEnabledSetting(
            new ComponentName(this, ChargerConnecedListener.class),
```

```
                        PackageManager.COMPONENT_ENABLED_STATE_ENABLED,
                        PackageManager.DONT_KILL_APP);
    }

    public void disableBroadcastReceiver() {
        PackageManager packageManager = getPackageManager();
        packageManager.setComponentEnabledSetting(
                new ComponentName(this, ChargerConnecedListener.class),
                        PackageManager.COMPONENT_ENABLED_STATE_DISABLED,
                        PackageManager.DONT_KILL_APP);
    }
```

Notice the use of `PackageManager.DONT_KILL_APP` as the last parameter to `setComponentEnabledSetting()`. This will prevent the platform from killing the application, which is otherwise the default behavior when changing this property.

You can use this method for enabling and disabling components for `Activities` as well (and also `Services` and `ContentProviders`). It's an efficient way to toggle the visibility of your application's icons in the launcher (also called, *home-screen application tray*). You could, for instance, show only the icon for the setup `Activity` after installation and later hide it using this method after the setup is complete. You can also use this method to show the icon for an `Activity` that shouldn't be visible until the user completes the setup.

System Broadcast Intents

The Android API defines many different broadcast actions that relate to different system events. In earlier code examples in this chapter, I've shown a few of these, like changes in battery level or when the power to the devices was connect and disconnected. Because these events are spread out in different places relating to their respective function, finding a broadcast for a specific event can be difficult, even with the Android developer site's search function. Maybe you don't even know that a certain event exists, or perhaps you get too many irrelevant matches. Also, some very useful broadcast `Intent` actions aren't publically specified in the API, and finding them requires some understanding of the hidden Android APIs. (I go into the details of the hidden Android APIs in Chapter 15.)

In this section, you will find some of the most commonly used system events, along with some examples of when to use them. Several others are available, and the only way to find them is to know what you're looking for and search the official Android APIs. A good place to start when looking for their definitions is in the `Intent` class.

Auto-Starting Your Application

One of the frequent questions Android application developers ask me is how they can make their applications start automatically. The short answer is that you can't, not directly. However, you can register for certain events that eventually will be triggered and which you can use to start your application. There is also an event that is sent to an application after it's upgraded from an earlier version (usually after an update is downloaded and installed from Google Play).

The following code shows the declaration of a receiver in the manifest that listens to the `Intent.ACTION_BOOT_COMPLETED` and `Intent.ACTION_MY_PACKAGE_REPLACED` broadcasts. *Note:* The receiver is disabled by default. This is a good practice, especially when listening for `Intent.ACTION_BOOT_COMPLETED`; otherwise your application will start every time the device is booting up, possibly waste your system's resources.

```
<receiver android:name=".StartupListener" android:enabled="false">
    <intent-filter>
        <action android:name="android.intent.action.BOOT_COMPLETED" />
        <action android:name="android.intent.action.MY_PACKAGE_REPLACED"
/>
    </intent-filter>
</receiver>
```

> Enable receivers for these broadcasts only when doing so is necessary, such as after the user changes a setting in your application or enables certain features—for example, an alarm clock application in which the receiver is left disabled until the user schedules an alarm. Use the code from the earlier example for enabling (and disabling) this receiver as needed.

User Presence and Screen State

When a user locks a device (that is, presses the power button to turn off the device), the current `Activity` receives a call to `onPause()`, signifying that it has lost focus. Similarly, the `Activity` receives a call to `onResume()` when it regains focus after the lock screen is disabled. Normally, applications don't need additional information, but what if you have a `Service` that needs to be notified every time the user unlocks the device or when the screen goes on or off? Luckily, there are broadcasts for these events as well, as shown in the following code block.

```
<receiver android:name=".UserPresentListener">
    <intent-filter>
        <action android:name="android.intent.action.SCREEN_OFF" />
        <action android:name="android.intent.action.SCREEN_ON" />
        <action android:name="android.intent.action.USER_PRESENT" />
    </intent-filter>
</receiver>
```

`Intent.ACTION_SCREEN_ON` and `Intent.ACTION_SCREEN_OFF` are sent as the device screen goes on and off, respectively. `Intent.ACTION_USER_PRESENT` is sent when the user deactivates the lock screen. A simple diagram showing how these actions are broadcast is shown in Figure 8-3.

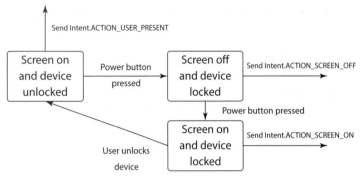

Figure 8-3 A simple diagram illustrating when broadcasts are sent for the events when the screen goes on and off and when the user disables the lock screen

Network and Connectivity Changes

For many Android applications, one of the most important things to keep track of is the state of the network and what kind of connectivity the device currently has. It's good practice to limit your application's use of the network according to the available bandwidth.

Most Android devices have two types of networks, cellular and Wi-Fi. If your application operates heavily on a network, you may want to defer transfers until the device is connected to a Wi-Fi; otherwise, you may incur considerable cost if you transfer data for users of mobile networks such as 3G or LTE. These events can also be useful for detecting when a user connects to a well-known Wi-Fi, like a corporate intranet, where it's safe to transfer sensitive data.

Connectivity and network broadcast actions are handled by different parts of the Android API. The action `ConnectivityManager.CONNECTIVITY_ACTION` is broadcast whenever a general change in network connectivity occurs, such as switching from Wi-Fi to mobile data. When this is received, the `ConnectivityManager` service can be retrieved using `Context.getService()` which lets you gain more detailed information about the current network.

However, to get more fine-grained information about the current network, you also need to listen for broadcast actions from `TelephonyManager` (for cellular mobile data network events) and `WifiManager` (for Wi-Fi–related events). `TelephonyManager` lets you query the type of mobile data connection, and `WifiManager` gives you access to retrieval of the state of the Wi-Fi connection and the different IDs related to a Wi-Fi (SSID and BSSID).

The following code is a simplified example of how to detect when a device enters a preconfigured "home" Wi-Fi, which is effective for applications configured to talk to servers or for media centers that are available only on a specific Wi-Fi.

```
public class CheckForHomeWifi extends BroadcastReceiver {
    public static final String PREFS_HOME_WIFI_SSID = "homeSSID";

    public void onReceive(Context context, Intent intent) {
        SharedPreferences preferences =
```

```
                PreferenceManager.getDefaultSharedPreferences(context);
        String homeWifi = preferences.getString(PREFS_HOME_WIFI_SSID, null);

        if(homeWifi != null) { // Only check if home WiFi is set
            NetworkInfo networkInfo =
                    intent.getParcelableExtra(WifiManager.EXTRA_NETWORK_INFO);

            if(networkInfo != null &&
                networkInfo.getState().equals(NetworkInfo.State.CONNECTED))
{
                WifiInfo wifiInfo =
                    intent.getParcelableExtra(WifiManager.EXTRA_WIFI_INFO);

                if(wifiInfo != null
                    && homeWifi.equals(wifiInfo.getSSID())) {
                    // Success - We're on out home WiFi!
                } else {
                    // Fail - We're on some other WiFi!
                }
            }

        }
    }
}
```

In this following example, you listen for changes from the ConnectivityManager and determine whether you're on a mobile data network. If you receive mobile data, you make an additional check using the TelephonyManager to see if you're on a 3G or LTE network.

```
public class WhenOn3GorLTE extends BroadcastReceiver {
    public void onReceive(Context context, Intent intent) {
        String action = intent.getAction();

        if (ConnectivityManager.CONNECTIVITY_ACTION) {
            boolean noConnectivity = intent.
                    getBooleanExtra(ConnectivityManager.
                            EXTRA_NO_CONNECTIVITY, false);

            if(noConnectivity) {
                // No network at all.. :(
            } else {
                int networkType = intent.
                        getIntExtra(ConnectivityManager.
                                EXTRA_NETWORK_TYPE,
                                ConnectivityManager.TYPE_DUMMY);

                if(networkType == ConnectivityManager.TYPE_MOBILE) {
                    checkfor3GorLte(context);
                }
            }
        }
    }
```

```
private void checkfor3GorLte(Context context) {
    TelephonyManager telephonyManager = (TelephonyManager) context.
        getSystemService(Context.TELEPHONY_SERVICE);

    switch (telephonyManager.getNetworkType()) {
        case TelephonyManager.NETWORK_TYPE_HSDPA:
        case TelephonyManager.NETWORK_TYPE_HSPA:
        case TelephonyManager.NETWORK_TYPE_HSPAP:
        case TelephonyManager.NETWORK_TYPE_HSUPA:
        case TelephonyManager.NETWORK_TYPE_LTE:
            // Yay - we got fast enough mobile data! :)
            break;
        default:
            // Slow mobile network - notify user...
            break;
    }
}
}
```

Device Configuration Changes

Whenever you turn an Android device from portrait to landscape orientation, an event is triggered by the system causing a *configuration change*. Several related triggers all cause this event, such as changing the UI mode on the device or when keyboard visibility changes.

Configuration changes are a little tricky to manage on Android. For an `Activity`, the default behavior is to restart, which means that `onPause()`, `onStop()`, and `onDestroy()` are called and your `Activity` instance is lost, including all its data. To avoid having the `Activity` restart when a certain configuration change occurs, you can declare these events in the `android:configChanges` attribute of the `Activity` tag. As a result, the method `Activity.onConfigurationChanged()` is called with the new `Configuration` object, instead of your `Activity` restarting. Use this method only as a last resort—for instance, if you have a full-screen game or application with custom handling of changes in the device's orientation.

The standard way of handling configuration changes for an `Activity` is through the default behavior: Let the system restart it. This works well for most situations, but in some cases, you may want to avoid restarting your `Activity` because restarting it could have a negative impact on performance and user experience.

For the `Service`, `ContentProvider`, and `Application` components, you can also use the `onConfigurationChanged()` method. The difference is the `Activity` class is called for all configuration changes without you having to add attributes in the manifest. Also, for these components, configuration changes will not force them to restart (which is good because otherwise `Services` would restart when you rotate your device). This allows your `Service`, or some other background component, to detect when the user rotates the device or when another application changes the UI mode.

Summary

In this chapter, I introduced advanced concepts of the `BroadcastReceivers` that Android developers might not be familiar with. These receivers are powerful tools when it comes to reacting to system-wide events and also for communicating within your application, using the `LocalBroadcastManager`, or between multiple applications.

I explained the difference between normal, ordered, sticky, and directed broadcasts and when and how to apply them. Next, I showed how to enable and disable receivers, and other components, in your code to ensure that they're activated only when necessary. This powerful feature in Android should be used more often in applications to reduce their load on the overall system.

Many different broadcast `Intent` actions are defined by the Android platform. I discussed a few of the most useful broadcasts and gave a few examples of when and how to use them. Most of them are documented in the official Android APIs, but some are part of the hidden APIs that I cover in more detail in Chapter 15.

Finally, I covered how to detect configuration changes of the device, including screen orientation, keyboard state, and UI mode. By default, your `Activity` is restarted when a configuration change occurs, but you can override this using the `android:configChanges` attribute in the manifest. You can also listen for these changes by overriding the method `onConfigurationChanged()` in your `Service` components, which can help with receiving notifications about state changes in devices that lack a system broadcast.

`BroadcastReceivers` and configuration changes are often overlooked in Android applications, but as a skilled developer, you can use them to create a smooth user experience and to react to changes that could otherwise cause unexpected behavior in an application.

Further Resources

Documentation

For handling runtime configuration changes, go to `http://developer.android.com/guide/topics/resources/runtime-changes.html`

Chapter 9
Data Storage and Serialization Techniques

This chapter is all about storing and representing data on a local device. Storing data is an important aspect of all software applications. Developers usually use the term *persistence* when talking about storing data, and *serialization* to describe how data is represented in its stored state. Without persistence, data would be able to keep its state only in RAM and would be lost after the relevant process finishes. Achieving persistence often involves compromises among performance, latency, size, and complexity. For instance, if data must be read fast, you'll usually go with a slower than usual write operation. Serialization is all about how the data is structured, both in its persisted state as well as in-memory.

In this chapter, I cover the two most common techniques used in Android applications for persistence and serialization,—namely, SQLite and `SharedPreferences`—as well as two alternative methods that also allow you to transport data over a network or between two devices.

> Storing data on a cloud-storage service such as Google Drive or Dropbox is beyond the scope of this chapter, but you can learn more about storing data on Google Drive in Chapter 19.

Persistence Options for Android

When you store persistent data on an Android device, the standard APIs provide two readymade methods for storing structured data, *preference files* and *SQLite databases*. Preference files are stored in an XML format and managed by the `SharedPreferences` class. SQLite databases have a more complex API and are usually wrapped in a `ContentProvider` component.

The names of these methods indicate what they should be used for. You use `SharedPreferences` for settings, options, user preferences, and other simple values. In preference files, you don't store arrays and tables of values or any binary data. Instead, data represented in Java as lists or arrays is more likely to go into an SQLite database through a `ContentProvider`. There are, of course, exceptions to these rules, so always consider the best choice for your application.

Binary data, which is usually media such as image, video, or audio files, should not be stored directly in an SQLite database or a preference file. It's usually better to store binary data as regular files, either in an app's internal storage or on external public storage. However, in many cases, it may be a good idea to use a `ContentProvider` to handle the persistence of binary files as well; doing so provides convenient ways to deal with files and keep them in sync with the records in your database.

Storing Data in Preference Files

The files backing your `SharedPreferences` objects are regular XML files stored in the app's data directory. The structure is quite simple because it allows only key/value pairs to be stored, but the Android APIs also provide a very convenient abstraction that allows you to read and write data in a type-safe way.

The easiest way to create a `SharedPreferences` object is to use the `PreferenceManager.getDefaultSharedPreferences()` method, which gives you the default preference object for your application. Using this approach as your main storage for preferences is convenient because the framework manages the name of the file. However, if you have multiple preference files in your application, you're better off using the `Context.getSharedPreference()` method, which allows you to freely name the file. If you want to create a preference file that is relevant to only one activity, you can use the `Activity.getPreference()` method, which gets its name from the `Activity` calling the method.

The name for preference files created by `PreferenceManager.getDefaultSharedPreferences()` **is formed by the package name with the suffix _ preferences—for instance,** `com.aapt1.code_preferences`. **Although you rarely need this name, it becomes important when you want to implement a backup agent for this file, as I describe in the section "Application Data Backup" near the end of this chapter.**

The types of values you can store in a preference file using the `SharedPreferences` class are `int`, `float`, `long`, `boolean`, `String`, and a `Set` of `String` objects (string arrays). The name of the key must always be a valid `String`, and the common practice is to use a dot notation for the keys in order to structure multiple keys into groups.

For instance, if your preference file contains values that will be used to configure networking as well as user-interface settings, you can group these values by prefixing each key with the term `network` or `ui`. In this way, you can easily manage and avoid conflicting names. In the following example, you see how to structure preferences this way by using a prefix and defining the keys in a separate Java interface:

```java
public interface Constants {
    public static final String NETWORK_PREFIX = "network.";
    public static final String UI_PREFIX = "ui.";

    public static final String NETWORK_RETRY_COUNT
            = NETWORK_PREFIX + "retryCount";
    public static final String NETWORK_CONNECTION_TIMEOUT
            = NETWORK_PREFIX + "connectionTimeout";
    public static final String NETWORK_WIFI_ONLY
            = NETWORK_PREFIX + "wifiOnly";

    public static final String UI_BACKGROUND_COLOR
            = UI_PREFIX + "backgroundColor";
    public static final String UI_FOREGROUND_COLOR
            = UI_PREFIX + "foregroundColor";
    public static final String UI_SORT_ORDER
            = UI_PREFIX + "sortOrder";
```

```
        public static final int SORT_ORDER_NAME = 10;
        public static final int SORT_ORDER_AGE = 20;
        public static final int SORT_ORDER_CITY = 30;
    }
```

The preceding method is the preferred way for accessing the preference values instead of hardcoding the key names for each access. Doing so removes the chance of misspelling the names of the keys, a common source of bugs.

The following code is an example of using preferences together with a `Constants` class:

```
public class MainActivity extends Activity {
    private void readUiPreferences() {
        SharedPreferences preferences
                = PreferenceManager.getDefaultSharedPreferences(this);
        int defaultBackgroundColor = getResources().
                getColor(R.color.default_background);
        int backgroundColor = preferences.getInt(
                Constants.UI_BACKGROUND_COLOR,
                defaultBackgroundColor);
        View view = findViewById(R.id.background_view);
        view.setBackgroundColor(backgroundColor);
    }
}
```

To change the values in a preference, you first retrieve an `Editor` instance, which provides the appropriate PUT method as well as methods for committing your changes. Prior to Android version 2.3 (API level 9), you committed changes using the `commit()` method, which did the writing to disk synchronously. However, in version 2.3, the `Editor` class provides an `apply()` method that performs the actual disk write operation asynchronously. Because you always want to avoid blocking operations in your main thread as much as possible, the `apply()` method is preferable to the old `commit()` method. This makes it safe to update `SharedPreference` on the main thread directly from a UI operation (for instance, in an `onClick()` method, as shown in the following example).

```
public class MainActivity extends Activity {
    public void doToggleWifiOnlyPreference(View view) {
        SharedPreferences preferences = PreferenceManager.
                getDefaultSharedPreferences(this);
        boolean currentValue = preferences.
                getBoolean(Constants.NETWORK_WIFI_ONLY, false);
        preferences.edit()
                .putBoolean(Constants.NETWORK_WIFI_ONLY, !currentValue)
                .apply();
    }
}
```

The preceding code shows where you use a click listener to toggle the preference value stored in `Constants.NETWORK_WIFI_ONLY`. If you were to use the old `commit()` method, the main thread could have been blocked, causing a degraded user experience. With `apply()`, you no longer have to worry about that issue.

Every preference file has a single instance within the same process. So even though you retrieve a `SharedPreference` object from two different components (but in the same application) with the two objects having the same name, they share the same backing instance, so every change will immediately be reflected in both objects.

In order to get a notification when a value is updated, you can register a callback listener that is triggered whenever `apply()` or `commit()` is called. The most common use for this is when you change a value in a preference from an `Activity` that should affect the behavior of a background service, as shown in this example:

```java
public class NetworkService extends IntentService
        implements SharedPreferences.OnSharedPreferenceChangeListener {
    public static final String TAG = "NetworkService";
    private boolean mWifiOnly;

    @Override
    public void onCreate() {
        super.onCreate();
        SharedPreferences preferences = PreferenceManager
                .getDefaultSharedPreferences(this);
        preferences.registerOnSharedPreferenceChangeListener(this);
        mWifiOnly = preferences.getBoolean(Constants.NETWORK_WIFI_ONLY,
                                            false);
    }

    @Override
    public void onDestroy() {
        super.onDestroy();
        SharedPreferences preferences = PreferenceManager
                .getDefaultSharedPreferences(this);
        preferences.unregisterOnSharedPreferenceChangeListener(this);
    }

    @Override
    public void onSharedPreferenceChanged(SharedPreferences preferences,
                                            String key) {
        if (Constants.NETWORK_WIFI_ONLY.equals(key)) {
            mWifiOnly = preferences
                    .getBoolean(Constants.NETWORK_WIFI_ONLY, false);
            if(mWifiOnly) cancelNetworkOperationIfNecessary();
        }
    }

    @Override
    protected void onHandleIntent(Intent intent) {
        ConnectivityManager connectivityManager
                = (ConnectivityManager)
                getSystemService(CONNECTIVITY_SERVICE);
        NetworkInfo networkInfo
                = connectivityManager.getActiveNetworkInfo();
```

```
        int type = networkInfo.getType();
        if (mWifiOnly && type != ConnectivityManager.TYPE_WIFI) {
            Log.d(TAG, "We should only perform network I/O over WiFi.");
            return;
        }

        performNetworkOperation(intent);
    }
}
```

User Options and Settings UI

In many applications, it's common to provide a separate UI that allows users to change the options and settings of the application. Android provides a set of readymade `Activity` and `Fragment` classes that make creating such a UI easy—`PreferenceActivity` and `PreferenceFragment`.

Start by creating an XML file, placed in the XML resources directory, which follows the `PreferenceScreen` syntax. This is a simple XML structure that specifies all the preferences you'll allow users to change and also how they interact with the preferences. You can provide simple text fields for entering text strings, check boxes, and lists of choices. For each option, you can specify a title and description, and you can group a number of preferences together in different categories. You don't need to deal with saving changed values because that's managed by the `PreferenceFragment`. The instance of the `SharedPreferences` that a `PreferenceFragment` is working against is the same as you get from `PreferenceManaget.getDefaultSharedPreferences()`.

The following code shows a `PreferenceScreen` XML for two user-configurable options relating to the previous examples.

```xml
<?xml version="1.0" encoding="utf-8"?>
<PreferenceScreen xmlns:android="http://schemas.android.com/apk/res/
android">
 <PreferenceCategory android:title="@string/network_preferences_title">
  <CheckBoxPreference
     android:title="@string/network_wifi_only_title"
     android:summaryOn="@string/network_wifi_only_summary_on"
     android:summaryOff="@string/network_wifi_only_summary_off"
     android:key="network.wifiOnly"
     android:defaultValue="false"/>
  <ListPreference
     android:title="@string/network_retry_count_title"
     android:summary="@string/network_retry_count_summary"
     android:key="network.retryCount"
     android:defaultValue="3"
     android:entryValues="@array/network_retry_count_option_values"
     android:entries="@array/network_retry_count_options" />
 </PreferenceCategory>
</PreferenceScreen>
```

Next, you implement a `PreferenceActivity`, add a `PreferenceFragment` as its UI, and then call `PreferenceFragment.addPreferencesFromResource()` to specify the XML used for displaying the settings UI. The Android framework will generate a UI that follows the style and theme of your application (see Figure 9-1).

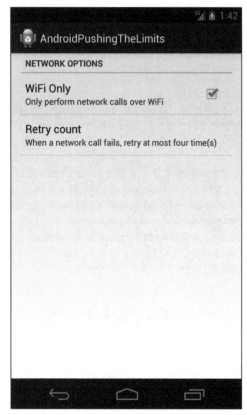

Figure 9-1 The result of a simple `PreferenceScreen`

In the following code, you specify which XML file to use from the resources. You also call `PreferenceManager.setDefaultValues()` so that the preference file is populated with the default values specified in the XML file.

```java
public class SettingsFragment extends PreferenceFragment {
    @Override
    public void onCreate(Bundle savedInstanceState) {
        super.onCreate(savedInstanceState);
        PreferenceManager.setDefaultValues(getActivity(),
                R.xml.preferences, false);
        addPreferencesFromResource(R.xml.preferences);
    }
}
```

The most common way to start this `Activity` is through an `Intent` where you specify the `ComponentName`, instead of using an action string. Also make sure that you set the `android:exported` flag to `false` in the manifest so that it can be started only within your application.

High-Performance ContentProviders

When you choose to store data in an SQLite database, I always recommend that you create a `ContentProvider`, even if you store data only for internal use. My reason is that Android provides several utility and UI-related classes that work on top of `ContentProviders` and make things much easier. Also, these classes provide an easy mechanism for notifying clients whenever an update occurs to the data, which makes it easier for developers to keep the list in the UI in sync with the actual content.

When you create the tables for your database, be sure to consider its main purpose. Will the database mostly be read and displayed in a UI (for instance, a `ListView`), or are you designing a database that will have more write than read operations and that will happen in the background (for instance, an activity logger or a sports application tracking the user's position during training)? Depending on the use, read performance may be more important than fast write operations, or vice versa.

Android Database Design

Design of a relational database is usually done through a process called *database normalization*. This process tries to minimize dependency and redundancy in a database using a number rule called *normal form*. There are a number of normal forms, but in most situations, only the first three are relevant. When a database design fulfills the first three normal forms, it's considered *normalized*.

In many cases, you may want to disregard the traditional database design and normalization rules. Unless you'll be storing hundreds of thousands of records in your database, each containing a huge amount of text and maybe even binary data, you can generally use a much simpler database design. Consider an application that keeps track of tasks. Each task has a name, a date when it was created, a priority, a status, and an owner. If you were to make an optimal database design, it probably would look something like the one shown in Figure 9-2.

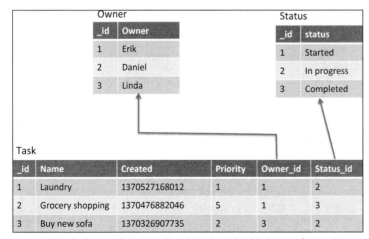

Figure 9-2 A database with three tables where the task table has two foreign keys

This design requires two foreign keys in the task table, which is perfectly okay, but it will make your application code more complex. The choice of statuses isn't likely to change for this application, so the better option would be to remove the extra table and just interpret the column as a reference to a set of constants. The Owner field is at this moment a more complex matter. It may be okay just to store the name—in fact, doing so is okay for most occasions. If you need additional data for each person, you can rely on the ContactsProvider and store a reference to a contact in your table instead. The result is a much simpler table, as illustrated in Figure 9-3.

Task					
_id	Name	Created	Priority	Owner	Status
1	Laundry	1370527168012	1	Erik	1
2	Grocery shopping	1370476882046	5	Erik	3
3	Buy new sofa	1370326907735	2	Linda	2

Figure 9-3 A simplified version of the database for storing tasks

Creating and Upgrading Databases

I recommend that you always wrap your SQLite databases in Android using the ContentProvider component. In this way, you can manage all calls to the database from one place and also use several readymade utilities for working with databases.

In this section, I give an example of a provider that stores tasks that can be given different priorities, status, and owners. I'll start with the basics of creating the actual database.

The following code shows the provider without the query methods (query(), insert(), update(), and delete()). I show some of these in the section "Database Transactions," later in this chapter. The important thing here is the class MyDatabaseHelper that extends SQLiteOpenHelper. This class helps in opening SQLiteDatabase objects and in managing database upgrades. The onCreate() method for this class is called once when the application starts and the provider is accessed the first time—more specifically, the first time getReadableDatabase() or getWritableDatabase() is called.

```
public class TaskProvider extends ContentProvider {
    public static final String AUTHORITY = "com.aptl.code.provider";
    public static final int ALL_TASKS = 10;
    public static final int SINGLE_TASK = 20;
    public static final String TASK_TABLE = "task";
    public static final String[] ALL_COLUMNS =
            new String[]{TaskColumns._ID, TaskColumns.NAME,
                    TaskColumns.CREATED, TaskColumns.PRIORITY,
                    TaskColumns.STATUS, TaskColumns.OWNER};
    public static final String DATABASE_NAME = "TaskProvider";
    public static final int DATABASE_VERSION = 2;
    public static final String TAG = "TaskProvider";
    public static final String CREATE_SQL = "CREATE TABLE "
            + TASK_TABLE + " ("
            + TaskColumns._ID + " INTEGER PRIMARY KEY AUTOINCREMENT, "
            + TaskColumns.NAME + " TEXT NOT NULL, "
```

```
                + TaskColumns.CREATED + " INTEGER DEFAULT NOW, "
                + TaskColumns.PRIORITY + " INTEGER DEFAULT 0, "
                + TaskColumns.STATUS + " INTEGER DEFAULT 0, "
                + TaskColumns.OWNER + " TEXT);";
public static final String CREATED_INDEX_SQL = "CREATE INDEX "
        + TaskColumns.CREATED + "_idx ON " + TASK_TABLE + " ("
        + TaskColumns.CREATED + " ASC);";
public static final String OWNER_INDEX_SQL = "CREATE INDEX "
        + TaskColumns.OWNER + "_idx ON " + TASK_TABLE + " ("
        + TaskColumns.CREATED + " ASC);";
public static UriMatcher mUriMatcher
        = new UriMatcher(UriMatcher.NO_MATCH);
public MyDatabaseHelper mOpenHelper;

static {
    mUriMatcher.addURI(AUTHORITY, "task", ALL_TASKS);
    mUriMatcher.addURI(AUTHORITY, "task/#", SINGLE_TASK);
}

@Override
public boolean onCreate() {
    mOpenHelper = new MyDatabaseHelper(getContext());
    return true;
}

 // Query methods omitted for brevity...

public interface TaskColumns extends BaseColumns {
    public static final String NAME = "name";
    public static final String CREATED = "created";
    public static final String PRIORITY = "priority";
    public static final String STATUS = "status";
    public static final String OWNER = "owner";
}

private class MyDatabaseHelper extends SQLiteOpenHelper {

    public MyDatabaseHelper(Context context) {
        super(context, DATABASE_NAME, null, DATABASE_VERSION);
    }

    @Override
    public void onCreate(SQLiteDatabase database) {
        Log.d(TAG, "Create SQL : " + CREATE_SQL);
        database.execSQL(CREATE_SQL);
        database.execSQL(CREATED_INDEX_SQL);
    }

    @Override
    public void onUpgrade(SQLiteDatabase db,
                          int oldVersion, int newVersion) {
```

```
            if (oldVersion < 2) {
                db.execSQL("ALTER TABLE " + TASK_TABLE
                        + " ADD COLUMN " + TaskColumns.OWNER + " TEXT");
                db.execSQL(OWNER_INDEX_SQL);
            }
        }
    }
}
```

Every time the `MyDatabaseHelper` class is created, it compares the internal version number that the SQLite database currently has (stored in the internal table called `android_metadata`) with the one provided to the constructor of `SQLiteOpenHelper`. Thus you can perform database upgrades and add new columns to existing tables or perform any other SQL commands. This capability is efficient because it doesn't require you to drop all tables and their content when you need to change the database.

In the preceding example, the `Owner` column is part of the `CREATE_SQL` as well as the `ALTER TABLE` statement called in `onUpgrade()`. This is because there are two possible scenarios. In the first scenario, a new installation of the application will first call `onCreate()`, followed by `onUpgrade()`. Because the `if` statement in `onUpgrade()` is false, the `ALTER TABLE` statement won't be called. However, for an upgrade of the application from an older version, `onCreate()` won't be called, and the `if` statement in `onUpgrade()` is `true`, the new column will be created. By incrementally increasing the version number for your database and adding a new `if` statement for each alteration to the database, you have a simple yet powerful method for upgrading the database.

In the code examples in this chapter I use `String` **constants for declaring the SQL statements to make the examples more clear. A better alternative is to store them in text files in the** `raw` **application resources. This makes them easier to work with as well as simplifies testing.**

Implementing Query Methods

When your database is queried (generally using `ContentResolver.query()`), the method `ContentProvider.query()` is called. Your implementation must take care of interpreting the incoming `Uri` to decide which query should be executed and check that all incoming parameters are safe.

The following code shows the implementation of the `query()` method as well as two utility methods used for modifying the `selection` and `selectionArgs` parameters. Also, here you make a simple check to see if the incoming `projection` parameter is `null`, and if so you set it to the default value. The same check is made on the `sortOrder` parameter where you use the column named `priority` as the default for sorting.

```
public static String[] fixSelectionArgs(String[] selectionArgs,
                                        String taskId) {
    if (selectionArgs == null) {
        selectionArgs = new String[]{taskId};
    } else {
        String[] newSelectionArg =
                new String[selectionArgs.length + 1];
```

```
                newSelectionArg[0] = taskId;
                System.arraycopy(selectionArgs, 0,
                        newSelectionArg, 1, selectionArgs.length);
        }
        return selectionArgs;
    }

    public static String fixSelectionString(String selection) {
        selection = selection == null ? TaskColumns._ID + " = ?" :
                TaskColumns._ID + " = ? AND (" + selection + ")";
        return selection;
    }

    @Override
    public Cursor query(Uri uri, String[] projection,
                        String selection, String[] selectionArgs,
                        String sortOrder) {
        projection = projection == null ? ALL_COLUMNS : projection;
        sortOrder = sortOrder == null ? TaskColumns.PRIORITY : sortOrder;
        SQLiteDatabase database = mOpenHelper.getReadableDatabase();

        switch (mUriMatcher.match(uri)) {
            case ALL_TASKS:
                return database.query(TASK_TABLE, projection,
                        selection, selectionArgs,
                        null, null, sortOrder);
            case SINGLE_TASK:
                String taskId = uri.getLastPathSegment();
                selection = fixSelectionString(selection);
                selectionArgs = fixSelectionArgs(selectionArgs, taskId);
                return database.query(TASK_TABLE, projection,
                        selection, selectionArgs,
                        null, null, sortOrder);
            default:
                throw new IllegalArgumentException("Invalid Uri: " + uri);
        }
    }
}
```

The two utility methods for modifying the `selection` and `selectionArgs` parameters are used only when addressing a specific record in the database using an `Uri`. *Note:* You prepend (in the `fixSelectionString()` and `fixSelectionArgs()` methods) the ID column to the existing selection. This makes the query faster because comparison on the primary key column is always very fast and thus speeds up the entire query.

When writing database queries, keep the simplest comparisons in the `WHERE` clause before the more complex ones. Doing so makes the query execute faster because it can determine much earlier whether the record should be included.

Database Transactions

When you execute a piece of SQL on an SQLite database, you always perform a transaction. Unless you specifically manage the transaction yourself, as I show next, it will be created for you automatically for that statement. Because most calls to a ContentProvider result in only one SQL statement, there's little need for handling transactions manually in these cases. However, if your application will execute multiple SQL statements, such as inserting many new records in one batch, always manage your own transactions.

The ContentProvider class provides two methods for transaction management, ContentProvider. bulkInsert() and ContentProvider.applyBatch(). In the following code, you see how to implement the bulkInsert() methods, which will insert multiple records in one single transaction. This approach is significantly faster than calling ContentProvider.insert() for every new piece of data you want to store.

```java
private Uri doInsert(Uri uri, ContentValues values, SQLiteDatabase
database) {
    Uri result = null;
    switch (mUriMatcher.match(uri)) {
        case ALL_TASKS:
            long id = database.insert(TASK_TABLE, "", values);
            if (id == -1) throw new SQLException("Error inserting data!");
            result = Uri.withAppendedPath(uri, String.valueOf(id));
    }
    return result;
}

@Override
public Uri insert(Uri uri, ContentValues values) {
    SQLiteDatabase database = mOpenHelper.getWritableDatabase();
    Uri result = doInsert(uri, values, database);
    return result;
}

@Override
public int bulkInsert(Uri uri, ContentValues[] contentValueses) {
    SQLiteDatabase database = mOpenHelper.getWritableDatabase();
    int count = 0;
    try {
        database.beginTransaction();
        for (ContentValues values : contentValueses) {
            Uri resultUri = doInsert(uri, values, database);
            if (resultUri != null) {
                count++;
            } else {
                count = 0;
                throw new SQLException("Error in bulk insert");
            }
        }
        database.setTransactionSuccessful();
    } finally {
        database.endTransaction();
    }
    return count;
}
```

The semantics for transactions are simple. You begin a new transaction by calling SQLiteDatabase. beginTransaction(). After you insert all the records successfully, you call SQLiteDatabase. setTransactionSuccessful() and then end the transaction with SQLiteException. endTransaction(). If something goes wrong in one of the insertions, you throw a SQLException, and all the previous insertions will be rolled back because the call to SQLiteDatabase. setTransactionSuccessful() was never called.

I highly recommend that you implement this method for your own providers because it will increase the performance on insertions significantly. However, because this method works only for insert operations, you may need to implement another method for handling more complex operations.

If you need to perform multiple update() or delete() statements within a single transaction, you must implement your own version of ContentProvider.applyBatch().

```
@Override
public ContentProviderResult[] applyBatch(ArrayList<ContentProviderOperat
ion>
  operations)
        throws OperationApplicationException {
    SQLiteDatabase database = mOpenHelper.getWritableDatabase();
    ContentProviderResult[] result
                = new ContentProviderResult[operations.size()];
    try {
        database.beginTransaction();
        for (int i = 0; i < operations.size(); i++) {
            ContentProviderOperation operation = operations.get(i);
            result[i] = operation.apply(this, result, i);
        }
        database.setTransactionSuccessful();
    } finally {
        database.endTransaction();
    }
    return result;
}
```

As with the buildInsert() method shown earlier, you begin a transaction, apply the operations, set the transaction successfully, and finally end the transaction. This API is designed for complex providers like the ContactsProvider, where there are many connected tables, each with its own Uri. Also, if you need to perform batch inserts to multiple tables, this API can still be useful in your own application.

Storing Binary Data in ContentProvider

Binary data includes anything that cannot be represented using the simple data types in Java, usually an image or some other media file, though it can be any type of file of a proprietary format. Working with such content can be tricky, but luckily the ContentProvider class provides a number of methods for dealing with this issue. Say that you want to store a JPG photo with each task in your database. First, you need to add another column to your task table with the name _data and the type TEXT, as shown here:

```
db.execSQL("ALTER TABLE " + TASK_TABLE + " ADD COLUMN _data TEXT");
```

The `ContentProvider.openFileHelper()` method uses this internally. You just store the path to the future file belonging to each record at each insertion. To do so, you modify the `doInsert()` method shown earlier.

```
private Uri doInsert(Uri uri, ContentValues values,
                     SQLiteDatabase database) {
    Uri result = null;
    switch (sUriMatcher.match(uri)) {
        case ALL_TASKS:
            long id = database.insert(TASK_TABLE, "", values);
            if (id == -1) throw new SQLException("Error inserting data: "
                                          + values.toString());
            result = Uri.withAppendedPath(uri, String.valueOf(id));

            // Update row with _data field pointing at a file...
            File dataFile = Environment.getExternalStoragePublicDirectory(
                                          Environment.DIRECTORY_
PICTURES);
            dataFile = new File(dataFile, FILE_PREFIX + id + FILE_SUFFIX);
            ContentValues valueForFile = new ContentValues();
            valueForFile.put("_data", dataFile.getAbsolutePath());
            update(result, values, null, null);
    }
    return result;
}
```

In this case, you write the JPG to the `PICTURES` directory on the external storage. Next, you override the method `ContentProvider.openFile()`, which will return a `ParcelFileDescriptor` to the client. You can then use that object for reading and writing directly to the file.

```
@Override
public ParcelFileDescriptor openFile(Uri uri, String mode) throws
    FileNotFoundException {
    if(sUriMatcher.match(uri) == SINGLE_TASK)
        return openFileHelper(uri, mode);
    else
        return super.openFile(uri, mode);
}
```

Using `openFileHelper()` handles the actual opening of the file and passes it to the calling client. When you want to read a `Bitmap` for a certain record in your `ContentProvider`, you can simply use the same `Uri` as for the record, and the framework takes care of the rest, as shown here:

```
public Bitmap readBitmapFromProvider(int taskId, ContentResolver
resolver)
        throws FileNotFoundException {
    Uri uri = Uri.parse("content://" + TaskProvider.AUTHORITY
            + "/" + TaskProvider.TASK_TABLE + "/" + taskId);
    return BitmapFactory.decodeStream(resolver.openInputStream(uri));
}
```

Storing a file works similarly with `ContentResolver.openOutputStream()` with the correct `Uri`. This is especially useful when you want to display data from your `ContentProvider` in a `ListView` that contains both text and images, such as in the preceding example.

Serializing Data for Persistence

Using the `ContentValues` and `Cursor` classes when handling persistent data in your application is fine when working with your `ContentProvider`, but if you ever need to send the data over the Internet or share it with another device, you have a completely different challenge. To resolve this challenge, you need to transform your data to a format that the receiving end can work with and that is suitable for sending over the network. This technique is called *serialization*.

Serialization is the concept of taking an object in memory and writing it to a file (or other output) such that the exact same memory representation can later be read (called *deserialization*). Android provides its internal serialization API with the `Parcelable` interface, but it isn't designed or well-suited for persistent storage on files or for transferring over a network.

In this section, I discuss two suitable formats for persisting complex data, JSON and Google Protocol Buffers. Both are well-supported by Android and have open-source implementations for most platforms, meaning that they're' well-suited for transporting over networks.

JavaScript Object Notation

JSON is an abbreviation for JavaScript Object Notation, and it's a subset of the JavaScript standard. The official Android API has built-in support for reading and writing JSON data. This format is excellent for representing complex objects that don't contain binary values. It has also become somewhat of a de-facto standard for sharing data with web services online.

The following example shows a simple JSON array with three objects containing the same information that was stored in the `TaskProvider` in an earlier example. This format is excellent for sending tasks with an online web service or for sharing directly with a friend.

```
[
    {
        "name": "Laundry",
        "created": 1370527168012,
        "priority": 5,
        "owner": "Erik",
        "status": 1
    },
    {
        "name": "Groceries",
        "created": 1370476882046,
        "priority": 3,
        "owner": "Linda",
        "status": 2
    },
```

```
    {
        "name": "Buy new sofa",
        "created": 1370326907735,
        "priority": 2,
        "owner": "Linda",
        "status": 1
    }
]
```

Reading JSON data from an `InputStream` is best done using the `JsonReader` API, as shown following:

```java
public JSONArray readTasksFromInputStream(InputStream stream) {
    InputStreamReader reader = new InputStreamReader(stream);
    JsonReader jsonReader = new JsonReader(reader);
    JSONArray jsonArray = new JSONArray();
    try {
        jsonReader.beginArray();
        while (jsonReader.hasNext()) {
            JSONObject jsonObject
                    = readSingleTask(jsonReader);
            jsonArray.put(jsonObject);
        }
        jsonReader.endArray();
    } catch (IOException e) {
        // Ignore for brevity
    } catch (JSONException e) {
        // Ignore for brevity
    }

    return jsonArray;
}

private JSONObject readSingleTask(JsonReader jsonReader)
        throws IOException, JSONException {
    JSONObject jsonObject = new JSONObject();
    jsonReader.beginObject();
    JsonToken token;
    do {
        String name = jsonReader.nextName();
        if ("name".equals(name)) {
            jsonObject.put("name", jsonReader.nextString());
        } else if ("created".equals(name)) {
            jsonObject.put("created", jsonReader.nextLong());
        } else if ("owner".equals(name)) {
            jsonObject.put("owner", jsonReader.nextString());
        } else if ("priority".equals(name)) {
            jsonObject.put("priority", jsonReader.nextInt());
        } else if ("status".equals(name)) {
            jsonObject.put("status", jsonReader.nextInt());
        }
```

```
        token = jsonReader.peek();
    } while (token != null && !token.equals(JsonToken.END_OBJECT));
    jsonReader.endObject();
    return jsonObject;
}
```

Although it's also possible to read the entire contents of the `InputStream` to a `String` and then pass that to the constructor of `JSONArray`, the preceding method consumes less memory and will most likely be faster. Likewise, the `JsonWriter` class allows you to efficiently write JSON data to an `OutputStream`, as shown here:

```
public void writeJsonToStream(JSONArray array, OutputStream stream) throws
JSONException {
    OutputStreamWriter writer = new OutputStreamWriter(stream);
    JsonWriter jsonWriter = new JsonWriter(writer);

    int arrayLength = array.length();
    jsonWriter.beginArray();
    for(int i = 0; i < arrayLength; i++) {
        JSONObject object = array.getJSONObject(i);
        jsonWriter.beginObject();
        jsonWriter.name("name").
                value(object.getString("name"));
        jsonWriter.name("created").
                value(object.getLong("created"));
        jsonWriter.name("priority").
                value(object.getInt("priority"));
        jsonWriter.name("status").f
                value(object.getInt("status"));
        jsonWriter.name("owner").
                value(object.getString("owner"));
        jsonWriter.endObject();
    }
    jsonWriter.endArray();
    jsonWriter.close();
}
```

Advanced JSON Handling with Gson

The `JSONObject` and `JSONArray` classes are convenient to work with as value objects in your code, but they have some limitations and usually consume more memory than necessary. Likewise, `JsonReader` and `JsonWriter` result in quite a lot of code if you have several different types of value objects. If you need more advanced serialization and deserialization of JSON data, you can find an excellent open-source library called Gson.

You can find the documentation for Gson at `https://code.google.com/p/google-gson`. To include Gson in your Gradle configuration, add the following to the dependencies: `compile 'com.google.code.gson:gson:2.2.4'`.

This library allows you to convert a Plain Old Java Objects (POJOs) into JSON and back. All you need to do is to define your data as regular Java objects with getters and setters and include the Gson library in your project.

The following class shows a simple Java object that represents a task:

```java
public class Task {
    private String mName;
    private String mOwner;
    private Status mStatus;
    private int mPriority;
    private Date mCreated;

    public Task() {
    }

    public Task(String name, String owner,
                Status status, int priority, Date created) {
        mName = name;
        mOwner = owner;
        mStatus = status;
        mPriority = priority;
        mCreated = created;
    }

    // Getters and setter omitted for brevity...

    @Override
    public boolean equals(Object o) {
        if (this == o) return true;
        if (o == null || getClass() != o.getClass()) return false;
        Task task = (Task) o;
        return mCreated.equals(task.mCreated) && mName.equals(task.mName);
    }

    @Override
    public int hashCode() {
        int result = mName.hashCode();
        result = 31 * result + mCreated.hashCode();
        return result;
    }

    public enum Status {
        CREATED, ASSIGNED, ONGOING, CANCELLED, COMPLETED
    }
}
```

Notice the use of Java enum for the status of the task. This object is much easier to work with in your application than the raw JSONObject.

The following code shows how to read and write a Collection of Task objects. The serialized form is always valid JSON data, so this choice becomes very convenient when working toward web services that publish data in JSON format. When you're also in control of the server-side code and it happens to be written in Java, you can easily share the same set of Java code between your server and Android application.

```java
public Collection<Task> readTasksFromStream(InputStream stream) {
    InputStreamReader reader = new InputStreamReader(stream);
    JsonReader jsonReader = new JsonReader(reader);
    Gson gson =  new Gson();
    Type type = new TypeToken<Collection<Task>>(){}.getType();
    return gson.fromJson(jsonReader, type);
}

public void writeTasksToStream(Collection<Task> tasks, OutputStream
  outputStream) {
    OutputStreamWriter writer = new OutputStreamWriter(outputStream);
    JsonWriter jsonWriter = new JsonWriter(writer);
    Gson gson = new Gson();
    Type type = new TypeToken<Collection<Task>>(){}.getType();
    gson.toJson(tasks, type, jsonWriter);
}
```

To make it simpler to use your POJOs toward a ContentProvider, you can implement two methods that convert your objects to and from ContentValues and Cursor objects, as shown here:

```java
public ContentValues toContentValues() {
    ContentValues values = new ContentValues();
    values.put(TaskProvider.TaskColumns.NAME, mName);
    values.put(TaskProvider.TaskColumns.OWNER, mOwner);
    values.put(TaskProvider.TaskColumns.STATUS, mStatus.ordinal());
    values.put(TaskProvider.TaskColumns.PRIORITY, mPriority);
    values.put(TaskProvider.TaskColumns.CREATED, mCreated.getTime());
    return values;
}

public static Task fromCursor(Cursor cursor) {
    Task task = new Task();
    int nameColumnIdx
            = cursor.getColumnIndex(TaskProvider.TaskColumns.NAME);
    task.setName(cursor.getString(nameColumnIdx));
    int ownerColumnIdx
            = cursor.getColumnIndex(TaskProvider.TaskColumns.OWNER);
    task.setOwner(cursor.getString(ownerColumnIdx));
    int statusColumnIdx
            = cursor.getColumnIndex(TaskProvider.TaskColumns.STATUS);
    int statusValue = cursor.getInt(statusColumnIdx);
    for (Status status : Status.values()) {
        if(status.ordinal() == statusValue) {
            task.setStatus(status);
        }
    }
    int priorityColumnIdx
            = cursor.getColumnIndex(TaskProvider.TaskColumns.PRIORITY);
    task.setPriority(cursor.getInt(priorityColumnIdx));
    int createdColumnIdx
            = cursor.getColumnIndex(TaskProvider.TaskColumns.CREATED);
    task.setCreated(new Date(cursor.getLong(createdColumnIdx)));
    return task;
}
```

If your application will have many different POJOs and tables, it may be easier to integrate an ORM (Object-Relational-Mapping) library to handle the serialization and deserialization between your SQLite database and Java objects. Two ORM libraries present a good option for Android today, **greenDAO** (`http://greendao-orm.com`) **and OrmLight** (`http://ormlite.com`).

Google Protocol Buffers

Google Protocol Buffer, or *protobuf*, is a way of encoding structured data in an efficient and extensible format. It differs from JSON in that it supports binary data mixed with simple data types and also has an advanced and extensible schema support. Protobuf has implementations for most software platforms, including a *lite* Java variant suitable for Android.

You can find documentation, download links, and installation instructions for Google Protocol Buffers at `https://developers.google.com/protocol-buffers`. **Remember that for Android you have to build the *lite* version of the tool, so you cannot use the one found in the central Maven repository. Executing** "`mvn package -P lite`" **in the Java source directory does this**. **Check the installation instructions for further details.**

Although JSON lets you read and write arbitrary data to a `JSONObject`, protobuf requires the use of a schema that defines the data you want to store. The schema defines a number of *messages,* where each message has a number of name-value pair fields. Each field can be either one of the supported built-in primitive data types, an *enum,* or another message. You can also specify whether a field is required or optional as well as some other parameters. Once your protobuf schema is complete, you use the protobuf tools to generate the Java code for your data. The generated Java classes can now be used for reading and writing protobuf data in a convenient way.

The following code is a sample of a simple protobuf schema that defines the information similar to the `TaskProvider` shown earlier:

```
package com.apt1.code.task;

option optimize_for = LITE_RUNTIME;
option java_package = "com.apt1.code.task";
option java_outer_classname = "TaskProtos";

message Task {
    enum Status {
        CREATED = 0;
        ONGOING = 1;
        CANCELLED = 2;
        COMPLETED = 3;
    }
```

```
message Owner {
    required string name = 1;
    optional string email = 2;
    optional string phone = 3;
}

message Comment {
    required string author = 1;
    required uint32 timestamp = 2;
    required string content = 3;
}

required string name = 1;
required uint64 created = 2;
required int32 priority = 3;
required Status status = 4;
optional Owner owner = 5;
repeated Comment comments = 6;
}
```

Note: Declarations in the beginning tell the protobuf tool what Java package and class name to use when generating the code. There is also an instruction to generate a *lite* version that is supported by Android.

Deserializing a `protobuf` object from an `InputStream` is easy, as shown in the following example. The generated Java code gives you a number of functions for merging the content from byte arrays, `ByteBuffer`, and `InputStream` objects.

```
public TaskProtos.Task readBrotoBufFromStream(InputStream inputStream)
        throws IOException {
    TaskProtos.Task task = TaskProtos.Task.newBuilder()
            .mergeFrom(inputStream).build();
    Log.d("ProtobufDemo", "Read Task from stream: "
            + task.getName() + ", "
            + new Date(task.getCreated()) + ", "
            + (task.hasOwner() ?
                task.getOwner().getName() : "no owner") + ", "
            + task.getStatus().name() + ", "
            + task.getPriority()
            + task.getCommentsCount() + " comments.");
    return task;
}
```

In this example, you see how to retrieve the values in a `protobuf` object. *Note:* `Protobuf` objects are immutable. The only way to make a modification is to create a new builder from an existing object, set the new value, and generate a `Task` object that will replace the old one. This makes protobuf a bit harder to work with but forces you to use a better design when working with persistence of complex objects.

The following method shows how to construct a new `protobuf` object for a task. You start by creating a new `Builder` for the specific object you want to construct and then you set the desired values and call `Builder.build()` to create your immutable `protobuf` object.

```
public TaskProtos.Task buildTask(String name, Date created,
                                 String ownerName, String ownerEmail,
                                 String ownerPhone,
                                 TaskProtos.Task.Status status,
                                 int priority,
                                 List<TaskProtos.Task.Comment> comments) {
    TaskProtos.Task.Builder builder = TaskProtos.Task.newBuilder();
    builder.setName(name);
    builder.setCreated(created.getTime());
    builder.setPriority(priority);
    builder.setStatus(status);
    if(ownerName != null) {
        TaskProtos.Task.Owner.Builder ownerBuilder
                = TaskProtos.Task.Owner.newBuilder();
        ownerBuilder.setName(ownerName);
        if(ownerEmail != null) {
            ownerBuilder.setEmail(ownerEmail);
        }
        if(ownerPhone != null) {
            ownerBuilder.setPhone(ownerPhone);
        }
        builder.setOwner(ownerBuilder);
    }

    if (comments != null) {
        builder.addAllComments(comments);
    }

    return builder.build();
}
```

When you need to write a `protobuf` object to a file or to a network stream, the API provides a set of methods for that. In the following code, you see an example where you can serialize (that is, write) a `Task` object to an `OutputStream`.

```
public void writeTaskToStream(TaskProtos.Task task,
                              OutputStream outputStream)
        throws IOException {
    task.writeTo(outputStream);
}
```

The main advantage of protobuf is that it consumes much less memory and is faster to read and write than JSON. `Protobuf` objects are also immutable, which is useful when you want to ensure that the values of the object remain the same during its lifetime.

Application Data Backup

After you resolve all your persistence needs for your application, consider whether your application will benefit from using the backup service for Android provided by Google. This service lets you back up your application's persistence data and restore it if the user performs a factory reset or upgrades to a new Android device.

Android provides a convenient API for managing backups, and it's a feature that will be greatly appreciated by users if they lose their device. The backup is securely stored on a cloud and will be restored only to a device with the same Google ID.

The following XML snippet is a piece from a typical `AndroidManifest.xml` file:

```xml
<application
        android:allowBackup="true"
        android:backupAgent="MyBackupAgent"
        android:icon="@drawable/ic_launcher"
        android:label="@string/app_name"
        android:theme="@style/AppTheme">
    <meta-data android:name="com.google.android.backup.api_key"
        android:value="backup-key-string"/>

...
</application>
```

To enable backup of your application's data, you only need to specify the class name of your backup agent in the `android:backupAgent` attribute. This class deals with the backup and restoration of application data that you choose to back up for the user. The `meta-data` attribute in the preceding example specifies the API key that you get once you register your application on the Google backup service. You can find the site for registering your applications at `https://developer.android.com/google/backup/signup.html`.

When you register and receive your API key, paste it into the `android:value` attribute, as just shown. Although the key is bound to your application's package and cannot be used for other applications (that is, one key per application), you should take care not to share it publicly in any code you publish.

The following class shows a simple backup agent used to back up and restore your default preferences file. *Note:* The filename for the preference file you get from `PreferenceManager.getDefaultPreferences()` is named `<package-name>_preferences`. This is an undocumented detail that makes a big difference when it comes to backing up your preference files.

```java
public class MyBackupAgent extends BackupAgentHelper {
    public static final String PREFS_BACKUP_KEY = "prefsBackup";

    @Override
    public void onCreate() {
        super.onCreate();
```

```
                SharedPreferencesBackupHelper sharedPreferencesBackupHelper
                    = new SharedPreferencesBackupHelper(this,
                    getPackageName() + "_preferences");
                addHelper(PREFS_BACKUP_KEY, sharedPreferencesBackupHelper);
            }
        }
```

The `BackupAgentHelper` class automatically handles both backup and restoration of the preference files you choose to add to this helper. You can also add backup for other, regular files using the class `FileBackupHelper`.

The backup agent provided for Android applications by Google is appropriate for small amounts of data. Although it would be technically possible to back up a SQLite database, you would probably be better off to first dump the contents of the database to a serialized format, compress the file, and perform your backup on that dump.

In the Android SDK, you can find the command-line tool `bmgr` that allows you to force backup and restoration operations on your application. This is useful when you're developing your applications because you can check that everything is working correctly.

Summary

Persisting data is central to most software development. The most common solution for Android applications is either through the `SharedPreference` class or by using a `ContentProvider` with an SQLite database. The `SharedPreferences` and `ContentProvider` API are both powerful and easy to use. Being able to get the most out of these APIs can make a huge difference in the overall user experience.

However, when you need to transport data over the network, a number of options are available that aren't part of the Android APIs. Serializing data with JSON, and more specifically using the Gson library, is a powerful technique that you should master. For the even more advanced situations where performance and size are crucial, using Google Protocol Buffers can help you solve your problems.

Finally, consider the use of a backup agent in your application in order to provide users with a smooth experience when they switch to a new Android device. Use the backup agent to store user preferences and options that let them keep the same configuration between multiple devices.

Further Resources

Documentation

Guide to Settings: `http://developer.android.com/guide/topics/ui/settings.html`

Guide to Content Providers: `http://developer.android.com/guide/topics/providers/content_providers.html`

Websites

Full documentation and information about SQLite: `www.sqlite.org`

Google Gson: `https://code.google.com/p/google-gson`

Google Protocol Buffers—Tutorial for Java: `https://developers.google.com/protocol-buffers/docs/javatutorial`. Also see `https://developers.google.com/protocol-buffers` for additional information

Two ORM frameworks suitable for Android are greeDAO (`http://greendao-orm.com`) and OrmLight (`http://ormlite.com`)

Documentation for the Backup Agent: `https://developer.android.com/google/backup/signup.html`

Chapter 10
Writing Automated Tests

If I had to pick one thing that developers of mobile apps often miss, it would be testing, despite the fact that high-quality software is the result of thorough testing. Consequently, this may be the most important chapter in this book.

The traditional way of developing software has been to design the software architecture, implement the code, and finally test the code, maybe by using automated tests to some degree. However, when testing is the last thing done in the development cycle, often too little testing is done or the wrong things are tested.

Test Driven Development (TDD) takes a different approach to software development, and its principles lead to high-quality software. With TDD, you start by defining your tests based on how your application will be used. Then you start implementing code that fulfills these tests, continuing until all the tests are satisfied. At this point, you can refactor your application code to optimize it for performance and to improve the overall design.

Using TDD involves a number of tools and techniques. First, you need a unit-testing framework for writing the automated tests. This framework, which is included in the Android APIs, is the main focus of this chapter. Second, you need a continuous integration and build server. This server automatically builds your application and performs all the automated tests for every change in the code. Finally, you need a code-coverage tool that tells you how much of the application's code is really being tested.

Android Testing Principles

On Android, you can divide tests into two categories: unit and instrumentation tests. Although within the field of TDD, there are other types of tests (for example, integration, functional, system, and component tests) in the context of Android, I'm focusing on unit and instrumentation tests.

Unit testing works on a very fine-grained level, usually on individual methods and classes with all external dependencies removed. On the other hand, instrumentation tests focus on verifying the behavior of a component (`Activity`, `Service`, `BroadcastReceiver` or `ContentProvider`) in the overall system.

The goal with unit testing is to verify that your methods behave as expected and that they can handle erroneous input without crashing. A framework called JUnit was developed for the Java programming language. JUnit is also part of the official Android APIs in the `junit` package along with the Android-specific testing framework under `android.test`. To do unit testing, you call a method in your application code and test its result for the expected output. This is called, *asserting the result,* and there is a ready-made utility class named `Assert` for this purpose. Each test you write should perform an assertion on the value, which in turn tells the testing framework whether the test passed.

Each test is called a *test case,* and a set of test cases is called a *test suite.* Each test case starts with a setup where all dependencies are created and initialized. When the test case is complete, a teardown is performed to release the resources that were created during setup.

Because the methods in your application code often have dependencies to the system or other components, you need a way to isolate a method when running a test. To do so, you use *mock* objects that simulate the behavior of the dependent objects. The Android API provides a set of mock classes that you can use in your tests. Mock objects are usually created in the setup of each test case and released during teardown.

When using the new Android build system based on Gradle (which I describe in Chapter 1), the default place for all your test code is under `<project root>/src/instrumentTest`. The name of the default package for tests is the same as your application package name with `.test` appended. All of this is configurable in `gradle.build`.

What to Test

When you write your automated tests, test only *your* code. There's no point in writing automated tests that verify system functions and services. For instance, you don't need to write a unit test that verifies a button is pressed. Instead, write a test that verifies the button has an `onClick` listener and that the listener behaves as expected.

Tests for user interfaces are some of the more complex tests you'll write. However, again, keep in mind that you should test your own code, not the functionality of Android's UI classes. For instance, you don't need to write a test that verifies scrolling works in a `ListView`. Instead, focus on writing tests that verify the content of the `ListView` and that a click on a specific element performs the expected action.

Because it's hard to test large and complex methods, keep your tests as limited and focused as possible. Also, make sure you test only one thing at a time, which makes it easier to detect where a bug occurred and to do refactoring. It's better to have many small test cases than a single large, complex test case for your `Activity`. This approach also affects how you write your code because writing small test cases in advance will result in better overall design in your code.

Refactoring your code to extract smaller methods from a single large method is good practice. Use code coverage to detect which methods are covered by your tests and where you need to add additional test cases. Make sure you run all your test cases for every code commit. This is where a continuous integration server comes in handy. Be sure to configure your development environment so that it will trigger a new job on the build server for every commit.

Basic Unit Testing

When you test classes that don't depend on a component lifecycle, do the simplest form of unit testing using the `AndroidTestCase` class. Doing so is useful when you can construct an object independently from any component or other part of the Android framework.

```
public class Util {
    public static int byteArrayToInt(byte[] bytes) {
        return bytes[3] & 0xFF |
                (bytes[2] & 0xFF) << 8 |
                (bytes[1] & 0xFF) << 16 |
                (bytes[0] & 0xFF) << 24;
    }
}
```

Consider the preceding utility class with a method for converting four bytes to an integer. You don't need to perform special setup or teardown for this test because the method takes simple inputs and is static. Only one testing method is needed for the method in the Util class. Running the test on a device generates a pass, and everything looks good.

```
public class UtilTest extends AndroidTestCase {
    public void testBytesToIntConversion() {
        int result = Util.byteArrayToInt(new byte[] {(byte) 127,
                (byte) -1, (byte) -1, (byte) -1});
        assertEquals(Integer.MAX_VALUE, result);
        result = Util.byteArrayToInt(new byte[] {(byte) 0,
                (byte) 0, (byte) 0, (byte) 0});
        assertEquals(0, result);
        result = Util.byteArrayToInt(new byte[] {(byte) -128,
                (byte) 0, (byte) 0, (byte) 0});
        assertEquals(Integer.MIN_VALUE, result);
    }
}
```

The preceding code verifies that the method gives the correct answer given a valid input, but it doesn't test what happens when you give the method an invalid input. To do so, you add three test methods for the possible invalid input: for a null array, for an array that is too short, and for when an array is too long. Here is the code for the three test methods:

```
public void testBytesToIntWithNull() {
    try {
        int result = Util.byteArrayToInt(null);
    } catch (IllegalArgumentException e) {
        return;
    }
    fail();
}

public void testBytesToIntWithTooShortInput() {
    try {
        int result = Util.byteArrayToInt(new byte[] {1,2,3});
    } catch (IllegalArgumentException e) {
        return;
    }
    fail();
}
```

```
public void testBytesToIntWithTooLongInput() {
    try {
        int result = Util.byteArrayToInt(new byte[] {1,2,3,4,5,6,7,8,9});
    } catch (IllegalArgumentException e) {
        return;
    }
    fail();
}
```

You should expect to get an `IllegalArgumentException` when you have invalid input, or the test will fail. If you run the tests now, all three new test methods will fail, indicating that you need to fix your utility method.

In the following code example I've modified the utility method to handle incorrect input. If you run the previous tests again, they should all pass. This is an example of TDD, although very simplified.

```
public class Util {
    public static int byteArrayToInt(byte[] bytes)
            throws IllegalArgumentException {
        if(bytes == null || bytes.length != 4) {
            throw new IllegalArgumentException();
        }
        return bytes[3] & 0xFF |
                (bytes[2] & 0xFF) << 8 |
                (bytes[1] & 0xFF) << 16 |
                (bytes[0] & 0xFF) << 24;
    }
}
```

It's a good practice to write the tests for your classes *before* you implement them completely so that you can verify that they work as expected. As shown here, you should not only check for correct behavior in normal cases but also test what happens when they receive a bad or unexpected input. Using this approach, you'll greatly improve the quality of your code.

Testing Activities

Testing your user interfaces means testing all your `Activity` classes. You'll generally use either `ActivityUnitTestCase` or `ActivityInstrumentationTestCase2` when writing tests for your `Activities`. The first class provides a more isolated testing where you have only a minimal connection to the system infrastructure. This approach is helpful when you test methods in your `Activity` that in turn call methods that interact with the system (such as `Context.startService()`) and you want to limit the scope of your test.

The following code shows a simple `Activity` that sets up a `View` to be displayed, along with the method `startBackgroundJob()` that will be used as a click listener in your view:

```
public class MainActivity extends Activity {
    public static final String ACTION_START_BACKGROUND_JOB
                                = "startBackgroundJob";
```

```
        @Override
        protected void onCreate(Bundle savedInstanceState) {
            super.onCreate(savedInstanceState);
            setContentView(R.layout.activity_main);
        }

        public void startBackgroundJob(View view) {
            Intent backgroundJob = new Intent(ACTION_START_BACKGROUND_JOB);
            startService(backgroundJob);
        }
    }
```

In the XML layout, you assign the click listener using the attribute `android:onClick`:

```xml
<RelativeLayout xmlns:android="http://schemas.android.com/apk/res/android"
    xmlns:tools="http://schemas.android.com/tools"
    android:layout_width="match_parent"
    android:layout_height="match_parent"
    tools:context=".MainActivity">

    <Button android:id="@+id/background_job_btn"
            android:layout_width="wrap_content"
            android:layout_height="wrap_content"
            android:layout_centerInParent="true"
            android:gravity="center"
            android:text="@string/start_background_job_label"
            android:onClick="startBackgroundJob" />
</RelativeLayout>
```

You now have two things to test for in your `Activity`: the existence of a click listener for the `Button` and that the click listener calls `Context.startService()` with the correct `Intent`.

In the following example, you have two test methods, `testIfButtonHasClickListener()` and `testIfClickListenerStartsServiceCorrectly()`.

```java
public class MainActivityTest extends ActivityUnitTestCase<MainActivity> {
    private Intent mServiceIntent;

    public MainActivityTest() {
        super(MainActivity.class);
    }

    public void testIfButtonHasClickListener() {
        startActivity(new Intent(Intent.ACTION_MAIN), null, null);
        View testButton = getActivity().
                          findViewById(R.id.background_job_btn);
        assertTrue("Button is missing onClick listener!",
                testButton.hasOnClickListeners());
    }
```

```
    public void testIfClickListenerStartsServiceCorrectly() {
        setActivityContext(new MyMockContext(getInstrumentation().
            getTargetContext()));
        startActivity(new Intent(Intent.ACTION_MAIN), null, null);
        View testButton = getActivity().
                            findViewById(R.id.background_job_btn);
        TouchUtils.clickView(this, testButton);
        assertEquals("Wrong Intent action for starting service!",
            "startBackgroundJob", mServiceIntent.getAction());
    }

    public class MyMockContext extends ContextWrapper {
        public MyMockContext(Context base) {
            super(base);
        }

        @Override
        public ComponentName startService(Intent serviceIntent) {
            mServiceIntent = serviceIntent;
            return new ComponentName("com.apt1.code", "NetworkService");
        }
    }
}
```

The first test retrieves the `Button` in the current UI layout and verifies that it has a click listener. This is a useful test for `Button` and similar views where you have assigned the click listener using the XML attribute `android:onClick`.

The second test is a bit more complicated. Before the `Activity` in this test is started, you create a mocked `Context` with your own implementation of `Context.startService()` and assign it as the `Activity` context for the test. When the method `Context.startService()` is called in the click listener, your own implementation is the one called. Here you store the incoming `Intent` so you can use it to verify the test. If the `Intent` action string is what you're expecting, then the test passes.

Testing Services

The Android testing APIs provide a class named `ServiceTestCase` that helps with setting up tests for a service. In the following example you can see a very simple `Service` that I've created a test case for. This code implements a simple `Service` according to the local binder pattern explained in Chapter 6:

```
public class MyService extends Service {
    private LocalBinder mLocalBinder = new LocalBinder();

    public IBinder onBind(Intent intent) {
        return mLocalBinder;
    }
```

```
      public class LocalBinder extends Binder {
          public MyService getService() {
              return MyService.this;
          }
      }
  }
}
```

The next code example is a simple `ServiceTestCase` to verify the implementation:

```
public class MyServiceTest extends ServiceTestCase<MyService> {
    public MyServiceTest() {
        super(MyService.class);
    }

    @Override
    public void setUp() throws Exception {
        super.setUp();
        setupService();
    }

    public void testBinder() throws Exception {
        Intent serviceIntent = new Intent(getContext(), MyService.class);
        IBinder binder = bindService(serviceIntent);
        assertTrue(binder instanceof MyService.LocalBinder);
        MyService myService = ((MyService.LocalBinder) binder).
getService();
        assertSame(myService, getService());
    }

    @Override
    public void tearDown() throws Exception {
        shutdownService();
        super.tearDown();
    }
}
```

In this code you call `setupService()` to create all the necessary dependencies for the `Service` being tested. In the `testBinder()` method you call the test-specific `bindService()` method, which returns the `IBinder` instance that should be returned by `onBind()` in `MyService`. After you verify the correct class for the `IBinder` instance, you call `getService()` and verify that the object returned is the same instance as the `Service` already started by the test case.

While this example is very simple, it demonstrates how to use the `ServiceTestCase` for writing tests for `Service` components. You should use this as much as possible for testing the `Services` in your own applications.

Testing ContentProviders

Testing your `ContentProvider` is straightforward when you use the `ProviderTestCase2` class. The goal of testing your provider is to verify its public *contract*, which is to say that you test that a client receives the data it requests.

The `ProviderTestCase2` allows you to do tests on your `ContentProvider` against a `Context` (and database) that is isolated from the default environment of your application. The following example shows a number of tests for the `TaskProvider` that I cover in Chapter 9.

```
public class TaskProviderTest extends ProviderTestCase2<TaskProvider> {
    private Uri ALL_TASKS_URI
                    = Uri.parse("content://com.apt1.code.provider/task");
    private MockContentResolver mResolver;

    public TaskProviderTest() {
        super(TaskProvider.class, TaskProvider.AUTHORITY);
    }

    @Override
    protected void setUp() throws Exception {
        super.setUp();
        mResolver = getMockContentResolver();
    }

    public void testDatabaseCreated() {
        Cursor cursor = null;
        try {
            cursor = mResolver.
                    query(ALL_TASKS_URI, null, null, null, null);
            // Database should be empty
            assertNotNull(cursor);
            assertFalse(cursor.moveToNext());

            // Verify that we got all the columns
            String[] allColumnsSorted
                    = new String[TaskProvider.ALL_COLUMNS.length];
            System.arraycopy(TaskProvider.ALL_COLUMNS, 0,
                    allColumnsSorted, 0, allColumnsSorted.length);
            Arrays.sort(allColumnsSorted);
            String[] columnNames = cursor.getColumnNames();
            Arrays.sort(columnNames);
            assertTrue(Arrays.equals(allColumnsSorted, columnNames));
        } finally {
            if (cursor != null) {
                cursor.close();
            }
        }
    }

    public void testCreateTaskWithDefaults() {
        ContentValues values = new ContentValues();
        values.put(TaskProvider.TaskColumns.NAME, "Do laundry");
```

```
        values.put(TaskProvider.TaskColumns.OWNER, "Erik");
        Uri insertedUri = mResolver.insert(ALL_TASKS_URI, values);
        assertNotNull(insertedUri);

        Cursor cursor = mResolver.query(insertedUri,
                                        null, null, null, null);
        assertNotNull(cursor);
        assertTrue(cursor.moveToNext());

        int nameColumnIdx
            = cursor.getColumnIndex(TaskProvider.TaskColumns.NAME);
        assertEquals(cursor.getString(nameColumnIdx), "Do laundry");

        int ownerColumnIdx
            = cursor.getColumnIndex(TaskProvider.TaskColumns.OWNER);
        assertEquals(cursor.getString(ownerColumnIdx), "Erik");

        int statusColumnIdx
           = cursor.getColumnIndex(TaskProvider.TaskColumns.STATUS);
        assertEquals(cursor.getInt(statusColumnIdx), 0);

        int priorityColumnIdx
         = cursor.getColumnIndex(TaskProvider.TaskColumns.PRIORITY);
        assertEquals(cursor.getInt(priorityColumnIdx), 0);

        int createdColumnIdx
          = cursor.getColumnIndex(TaskProvider.TaskColumns.CREATED);
        SystemClock.sleep(500);
        assertTrue(cursor.getLong(createdColumnIdx)
                    < System.currentTimeMillis());
    }

    public void testInsertUpdateDelete() {
        ContentValues values = new ContentValues();
        values.put(TaskProvider.TaskColumns.NAME, "Do laundry");
        values.put(TaskProvider.TaskColumns.OWNER, "Erik");
        Uri insertedUri = mResolver.insert(ALL_TASKS_URI, values);
        assertNotNull(insertedUri);

        values.put(TaskProvider.TaskColumns.PRIORITY, 5);
        values.put(TaskProvider.TaskColumns.STATUS, 1);
        int updated = mResolver.update(insertedUri, values, null, null);
        assertEquals(updated, 1);

        Cursor cursor = null;
        try {
            cursor = mResolver.query(insertedUri, null, null, null, null);
            assertNotNull(cursor);
            assertTrue(cursor.moveToNext());
            int statusColumnIdx
                = cursor.getColumnIndex(TaskProvider.TaskColumns.STATUS);
            assertEquals(cursor.getInt(statusColumnIdx), 1);
            int priorityColumnIdx
                = cursor.getColumnIndex(TaskProvider.TaskColumns.PRIORITY);
```

```
            assertEquals(cursor.getInt(priorityColumnIdx), 5);
        } finally {
            if (cursor != null) {
                cursor.close();
            }
        }

        try {
            int deleted = mResolver.delete(insertedUri, null, null);
            assertEquals(deleted, 1);

            cursor = mResolver.query(insertedUri, null, null, null, null);
            assertNotNull(cursor);
            assertFalse(cursor.moveToNext());
        } finally {
            if (cursor != null) {
                cursor.close();
            }
        }
    }

    public void testInsertInvalidColumn() {
        try {
            ContentValues values = new ContentValues();
            values.put(TaskProvider.TaskColumns.NAME, "Do laundry");
            values.put(TaskProvider.TaskColumns.OWNER, "Erik");
            values.put("nonExistingColumn", "someData");
            Uri uri = mResolver.insert(ALL_TASKS_URI, values);
            fail("Should throw SQLException on wrong column name.");
        } catch (Exception e) {
            assertTrue(e instanceof SQLException);
        }
    }

    public void testInvalidUri() {
        try {
            Cursor cursor = mResolver.
                    query(Uri.parse("content://"
                            + TaskProvider.AUTHORITY + "/wrongPath"),
                            null, null, null, null);
            fail("Expected IllegalArgumentException!");
        } catch (Exception e) {
            assertTrue(e instanceof IllegalArgumentException);
        }
    }
}
```

These tests verify that the database is created with the expected table and columns. Next, they verify that the default values are created correctly when those columns are excluded in an insert-call. One test verifies that inserts, updates, and deletes work as expected. Finally, you see a test verifying that you cannot insert records using an invalid column name and a test for handling an invalid Uri.

In a real-life application, you would add additional tests that cover many more cases to ensure that everything is handled correctly. Let this serve as a guideline for how to write tests for your own ContentProviders.

Running Tests

To run your test, you can either use the built-in feature of Android Studio or execute Gradle from the command line with the task connectedInstrumentTest. During a normal development cycle, using the built-in runner from Android Studio is recommended because it gives you full integration between the test results and your code. Figure 10-1 shows an example of how to configure a test-runner from within Android Studio.

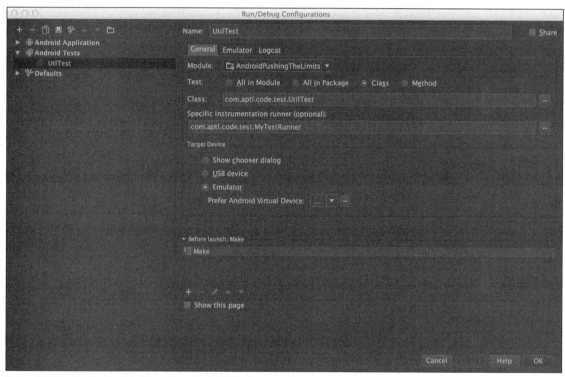

Figure 10-1 Custom test run configuration in Android Studio

When developing a new feature, the temptation to run all your test cases every time you want to verify your code can be impractical because of the time involved in your development cycle. To manage this issue, you can define custom test suites and test runners that execute only a partial set of your tests cases.

The following example shows how to create a test runner that executes only the tests from MainActivityTest shown earlier. This approach is useful when you're focusing on developing a new UI feature and want to perform only the tests that relate to that feature.

```java
public class MyTestRunner extends InstrumentationTestRunner {
    @Override
    public TestSuite getAllTests() {
```

```
          return new TestSuite(MainActivityTest.class);
     }
}
```

You can construct your test runners and test suites multiple ways. Use the classes from `android.unit.suitebuilder` to construct your custom set of tests for your needs.

Continuous Integration

When you have a team of developers working on the same project, it's good practice to use a continuous integration (CI) system for automatically running the tests whenever there is a change committed to your main branch. Several CI servers are available. A free and open-source alternative is Jenkins CI, which you can find at `http://jenkins-ci.org`. It has plug-in support for both the Gradle build system and Android, which makes it a convenient choice.

To configure Jenkins CI to run your project, all you need to do is to setup a free-f-form project in Jenkins CI, add a build step for invoking a Gradle script, and point out the root directory and Gradle build file for your project, as shown in Figure 10-2.

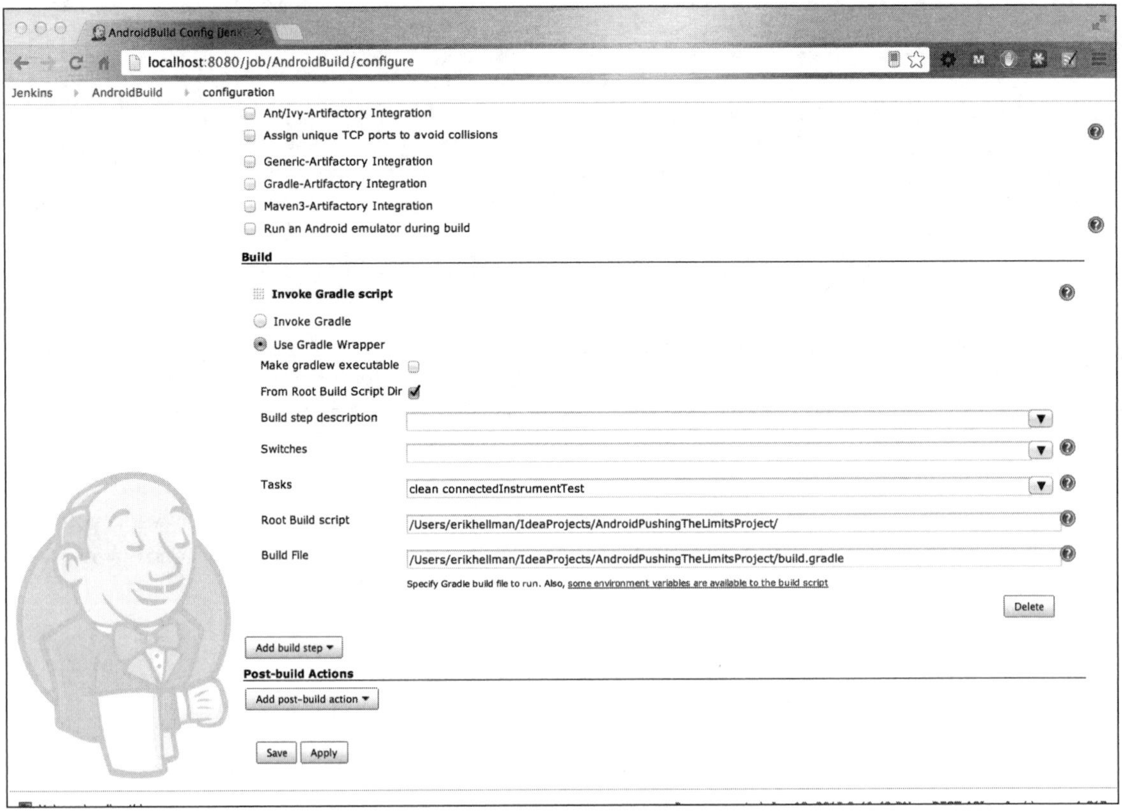

Figure 10-2 Setting up Jenkins CI for executing the Gradle script for an Android project

Summary

In this chapter, I covered how to write automated unit and instrumentation tests for your Android applications. Writing instrumentation tests is the best way to find and eliminate bugs in your code. It is also the only way to verify use-cases that can be very difficult to replicate in real life.

If you're new at testing, below I recommend that you read the "Android Testing Guidelines," as well as find out more about TDD in general.

Further Resources

Android Testing Guidelines

Extensive guidelines for writing tests for Android: `http://developer.android.com/tools/testing/index.html`

Books

Beck, Kent. *Test Driven Development: By Example*. Addison-Wesley, 2002.

Websites

More information about Jenkins CI: `http://jenkins-ci.org`

Part III

Pushing the Limits

Chapter 11

Advanced Audio, Video, and Camera Applications

Although basic APIs are sufficient for working with audio, video, and camera, more advanced applications often require more functionality. Ordinary recording and playback is possible with the Java APIs in Android; however, the latency involved with higher-level APIs may sometimes be too much for them. And working with camera applications such as augmented reality and other real-time scenarios can be difficult.

In this chapter, you find out how to get the most out of different media features in Android. Android allows you to use both high-performance and low-level APIs, such as OpenGL ES for graphics and OpenSL ES for audio. I show you how to use these APIs together and present some cases for using advanced audio, video, and camera features.

Some of the examples in this chapter include native C code, specifically the example related to OpenSL ES. If you are not familiar with using the Android NDK for building applications with native C code, you may want to read Chapter 14 before proceeding with this chapter.

Advanced Audio Applications

Music players were the first audio-centric applications for Android. Some could play music from an online streaming server and some played music from locally stored files. As the Android platform evolved, more advanced audio APIs were needed, and Google added APIs to allow low-latency audio streaming and recording.

The audio APIs in Android today provide some advanced features that you can integrate into your applications. It's now much easier to implement VoIP (*Voice over Internet Protocol*) applications, build custom-streaming music clients, and implement low-latency sound effects for your games. Also available are APIs to provide text-to-speech and speech recognition features, allowing users to interact with applications using audio rather than visual UI or touch technologies.

In this section, I explain how to use these features and provide example code that can help you get started.

Low-Latency Audio

Android has four APIs for doing audio playback (five, if you count MIDI) and three APIs for audio recording. The following sections provide you with a brief overview of these APIs, along with code exemplifying the more advanced ones.

Audio Playback APIs

The default class for audio playback is the MediaPlayer class. This class provides basic audio playback suitable for music players (or video) and a convenient API for playing audio from both streaming sources (such as an online Internet radio) and local files. An advanced state machine is associated with a MediaPlayer class that your application needs to track. You can use this API to embed music or video playback within your application without extra processing or latency requirements.

The second option for audio playback is the SoundPool class, which provides a low-latency support useful for sound effects and other short audio samples. You use this API to play samples of sound in a game. However, it doesn't support audio streaming, so you can't use it for real-time audio streaming applications like VoIP.

The third option for audio playback is the AudioTrack class, which allows you to push a single audio stream as raw PCM buffers to the audio hardware, allowing low-latency playback even for streaming scenarios. AudioTrack usually provides latency low enough to be used in VoIP and similar applications.

The following code shows how to set up an AudioTrack instance for a typical VoIP scenario:

```
public class AudioTrackDemo {

    private final AudioTrack mAudioTrack;
    private final int mMinBufferSize;

    public AudioTrackDemo() {
        mMinBufferSize = AudioTrack.getMinBufferSize(16000,
                AudioFormat.CHANNEL_OUT_MONO,
                AudioFormat.ENCODING_PCM_16BIT);
        mAudioTrack = new AudioTrack(AudioManager.STREAM_VOICE_CALL,
                16000,
                AudioFormat.CHANNEL_OUT_MONO,
                AudioFormat.ENCODING_PCM_16BIT,
                mMinBufferSize * 2,
                AudioTrack.MODE_STREAM);
    }

    public void playPcmPacket(byte[] pcmData) {
        if(mAudioTrack != null
                && mAudioTrack.getState() == AudioTrack.STATE_INITIALIZED)
        {
            if(mAudioTrack.getPlaybackRate()
                    != AudioTrack.PLAYSTATE_PLAYING) {
                mAudioTrack.play();
            }
            mAudioTrack.write(pcmData, 0, pcmData.length);
        }
    }

    public void stopPlayback() {
        if(mAudioTrack != null) {
            mAudioTrack.stop();
            mAudioTrack.release();
        }
    }
}
```

First, you determine the minimum buffer size for the audio stream. To do so, you need to know the sample rate, whether the data is mono or stereo, and whether you will use 8-bit or 16-bit PCM encoding. The sample rate and sample size are the parameters to `AudioTrack.getMinBufferSize()`, which returns the minimum buffer size in bytes for this `AudioTrack` instance.

You create the `AudioTrack` instance with the correct parameters according to your needs. You adapt the first parameter to the type of audio you'll be working with. For a VoIP application, use `STREAM_VOICE_CALL`, and for a streaming music application, use `STREAM_MUSIC`.

The second, third, and fourth parameters for the `AudioTrack` differ according to the situation. These are the sample rate, stereo or mono, and sample size. A VoIP application would use 16 kHz in 16-bit mono while regular music CDs use 44.1 kHz in 16-bit stereo. A high sample rate in 16-bit stereo requires a larger buffer and also more data transfer, but will give you better quality playback. All Android devices support PCM playback in 8, 16, and 44.1 kHz sample rates in either 8- or 16-bit stereo.

The buffer size parameter for the `AudioTrack` should be a multiple of the minimum buffer size. Deciding the size of this buffer depends on your needs and may even vary because of network latency and other factors.

Always avoid having an empty buffer because that will cause glitches in the audio playback.

The final parameter to the constructor determines whether you'll send audio data only once (`MODE_STATIC`) or as a continuous stream of data (`MODE_STREAM`). In the first case, you need to send the entire audio clip at once. When streaming, you can send arbitrary sized pieces of PCM data, which is probably what you want to do when handling streaming music or a VoIP call.

Audio Recording APIs

The first API for recording audio (and also video) is the `MediaRecorder` API. This API is similar to the `MediaPlayer` in that it maintains an internal state that you need to track in your code. With the `MediaRecorder`, it's only possible to capture recording to a file, so this API is not suitable for streaming solutions.

If you need to stream the audio you're recording, you can use the `AudioRecord` API, which is very similar to the `AudioTrack` described in the previous section.

The following example shows how to set up an `AudioRecord` instance for recording 16-bit mono in 16 kHz samples:

```
public class AudioRecordDemo {

    private final AudioRecord mAudioRecord;
    private final int mMinBufferSize;
    private boolean mDoRecord = false;
```

```
public AudioRecordDemo() {
    mMinBufferSize = AudioTrack.getMinBufferSize(16000,
            AudioFormat.CHANNEL_OUT_MONO,
            AudioFormat.ENCODING_PCM_16BIT);
    mAudioRecord = new AudioRecord(
            MediaRecorder.AudioSource.VOICE_COMMUNICATION,
            16000,
            AudioFormat.CHANNEL_IN_MONO,
            AudioFormat.ENCODING_PCM_16BIT,
            mMinBufferSize * 2);
}

public void writeAudioToStream(OutputStream stream) {
    mDoRecord = true;
    mAudioRecord.startRecording();
    byte[] buffer = new byte[mMinBufferSize * 2];
    while(mDoRecord) {
        int bytesWritten = mAudioRecord.read(buffer, 0, buffer.
length);
        try {
            stream.write(buffer, 0, bytesWritten);
        } catch (IOException e) {
            // Ignore for brevity...
            mDoRecord = false;
        }
    }
    mAudioRecord.stop();
    mAudioRecord.release();
}

public void stopRecording() {
    mDoRecord = false;
}
}
```

Because this is very similar to what you do for setting up an `AudioTrack`, this setup makes it useful to combine these two classes when using VoIP and similar applications.

OpenSL ES for Android

Earlier in this chapter, I said there are four APIs for audio playback and three for audio recording. So far, I've covered three for playback and two for recording. In this section, you find out about the final API, OpenSL ES, which supports both playback and recording. This API is a standard from the Khronos Group (the same group responsible for the OpenGL APIs).

This API provides low-level audio hardware access and low-latency features for dealing with audio playback and recording. Whereas the other audio APIs in Android have a convenient Java API, OpenSL ES is currently accessible only in native C using the Android NDK. In this section, I describe only the native part of the OpenSL ES API. You can turn to Chapter 14 to find out how you can use the Android NDK and write JNI code to bridge between Java and native C.

For this section, I assume that you have some knowledge of the C programming language.

The first part of this OpenSL ES example includes the declarations of the required include files and the global objects that will be used in the code, as shown here:

```
#include <pthread.h>

// for native OpenSL ES audio
#include <SLES/OpenSLES.h>
#include <SLES/OpenSLES_Android.h>

static pthread_cond_t s_cond;
static pthread_mutex_t s_mutex;

static SLObjectItf engineObject = NULL;
static SLEngineItf engineEngine;
static SLObjectItf outputMixObject = NULL;
static SLObjectItf bqPlayerObject = NULL;
static SLPlayItf bqPlayerPlay;
static SLAndroidSimpleBufferQueueItf bqPlayerBufferQueue;
```

The following code contains the callback function `bqPlayerCallback()` that's called by the OpenSL ES framework when a sample plays:

```
static void waitForPlayerCallback()
{
    pthread_mutex_lock(&s_mutex);
    pthread_cond_wait(&s_cond, &s_mutex);
    pthread_mutex_unlock(&s_mutex);
}

SLresult enqueueNextSample(short* sample, int size, short waitForCallback)
{
    if(waitForCallback)
    {
        waitForPlayerCallback();
    }
    return (*bqPlayerBufferQueue)->Enqueue(bqPlayerBufferQueue,
                                           nextBuffer,
                                           nextSize);
}

void bqPlayerCallback(SLAndroidSimpleBufferQueueItf bq, void *context)
{
    pthread_cond_signal(&s_cond);
}
```

In this case, you're feeding the output buffer from a different thread through the `enqueueNextSample()` function. In order to synchronize the thread where the callback occurs with the thread calling the `enqueue` function, you use a `pthread_mutex`. A call to `waitForPlayerCallback()` will block the thread until `pthread_cond_signal()` is called in the callback (similar to how `Object.wait()` blocks in Java).

The initialization of the OpenSL ES engine is shown in the following code:

```
SLresult initOpenSLES()
{
    // Use this to check the result of each operation..
    SLresult result;

    int speakers;
    int channels = 2;

    // We first create the mutex needed for our playback later
    pthread_cond_init(&s_cond, NULL);
    pthread_mutex_init(&s_mutex, NULL);

    // Create and realize the engine
    result = slCreateEngine(&engineObject, 0, NULL, 0, NULL, NULL);
    if(result != SL_RESULT_SUCCESS) return result;
    result = (*engineObject)->Realize(engineObject,
                                      SL_BOOLEAN_FALSE);
    if(result != SL_RESULT_SUCCESS) return result;
    result = (*engineObject)->GetInterface(engineObject,
                                           SL_IID_ENGINE,
                                           &engineEngine);
    if(result != SL_RESULT_SUCCESS) return result;

    // Create and realise the output mixer
    const SLInterfaceID outputIds[1] = {SL_IID_VOLUME};
    const SLboolean outputReq[1] = {SL_BOOLEAN_FALSE};
    result = (*engineEngine)->CreateOutputMix(engineEngine,
                                              &outputMixObject,
                                              1,
                                              outputIds,
                                              outputReq);
    if(result != SL_RESULT_SUCCESS) return result;
    result = (*outputMixObject)->Realize(outputMixObject,
                                         SL_BOOLEAN_FALSE);
    if(result != SL_RESULT_SUCCESS) return result;

    // Setup the output buffer and sink
    SLDataLocator_AndroidSimpleBufferQueue bufferQueue =
                    {SL_DATALOCATOR_ANDROIDSIMPLEBUFFERQUEUE, 2};
    speakers = SL_SPEAKER_FRONT_LEFT | SL_SPEAKER_FRONT_RIGHT;
    SLDataFormat_PCM formatPcm = {SL_DATAFORMAT_PCM,
                                  channels,
                                  SL_SAMPLINGRATE_44_1,
                                  SL_PCMSAMPLEFORMAT_FIXED_16,
                                  SL_PCMSAMPLEFORMAT_FIXED_16,
                speakers, SL_BYTEORDER_LITTLEENDIAN};
```

```
    SLDataSource audioSource = {&bufferQueue, &formatPcm};
    SLDataLocator_OutputMix dataLocOutputMix =
                                        {SL_DATALOCATOR_OUTPUTMIX,
                                        outputMixObject};
    SLDataSink audioSink = {&dataLocOutputMix, NULL};

    // Create a realize the player object
    const SLInterfaceID playerIds[] =
                        {SL_IID_ANDROIDSIMPLEBUFFERQUEUE};
    const SLboolean playerReq[] = {SL_BOOLEAN_TRUE};
    result = (*engineEngine)->CreateAudioPlayer(engineEngine,
                                        &bqPlayerObject,
                                        &audioSource,
                                        &audioSink,
                                        1,
                                        playerIds,
                                        playerReq);
    if(result != SL_RESULT_SUCCESS) return result;
    result = (*bqPlayerObject)->Realize(bqPlayerObject,
                                SL_BOOLEAN_FALSE);
    if(result != SL_RESULT_SUCCESS) return result;
    result = (*bqPlayerObject)->GetInterface(bqPlayerObject,
                                        SL_IID_PLAY,
                                        &bqPlayerPlay);
    if(result != SL_RESULT_SUCCESS) return result;

    // Get the player buffer queue object
    result = (*bqPlayerObject)->GetInterface(bqPlayerObject,
            SL_IID_ANDROIDSIMPLEBUFFERQUEUE, &bqPlayerBufferQueue);
    if(result != SL_RESULT_SUCCESS) return result;

    // Register the callback function
    result = (*bqPlayerBufferQueue)->RegisterCallback(bqPlayerBufferQueue,
                                        bqPlayerCallback,
                                        NULL);
    if(result != SL_RESULT_SUCCESS) return result;

    return SL_RESULT_SUCCESS;
}
```

The basic concept for all initialization here is that you first *create* an object (for instance, the engine) and then *realize* it. Next, you retrieve the *interface* to control the object.

In this example, you start by creating the engine, followed by the player object. You also create an output buffer object where you write the audio samples to be played. The player is configured to play 16-bit stereo (2 channels) in 44.1 kHz. Finally, you set the callback for the player buffer. The callback function will be called after the buffer is ready to receive a new sample for playback.

Also notice that in the beginning of this function, you create the objects related to the mutex used in the callback and the function for adding new samples.

The final part of this example gives two functions for controlling the state of the player object (play and pause) and the shutdown function that does the entire cleanup.

The following example shows how to use OpenSL ES for low-latency audio playback. This API is very useful for the extreme low-latency scenarios or when most of your code is already in native C. For recording, you use this API in much the same way as when doing playback but with different interfaces.

```
SLresult pausePlayback()
{
    return (*bqPlayerPlay)->SetPlayState(bqPlayerPlay,
                                          SL_PLAYSTATE_PAUSED);
}

SLresult startPlayback()
{
    return (*bqPlayerPlay)->SetPlayState(bqPlayerPlay,
                                          SL_PLAYSTATE_PLAYING);
}

void shutdownOpenSLES()
{
    if (bqPlayerObject != NULL) {
        (*bqPlayerObject)->Destroy(bqPlayerObject);
        bqPlayerObject = NULL;
        bqPlayerPlay = NULL;
        bqPlayerBufferQueue = NULL;
    }

    if (outputMixObject != NULL) {
        (*outputMixObject)->Destroy(outputMixObject);
        outputMixObject = NULL;
    }

    if (engineObject != NULL) {
        (*engineObject)->Destroy(engineObject);
        engineObject = NULL;
        engineEngine = NULL;
    }

    pthread_cond_destroy(&s_cond);
    pthread_mutex_destroy(&s_mutex);
}
```

Text-to-Speech (TTS)

Although visual feedback is usually the fastest way to provide information to the user, doing so also requires the user's full attention to the device. When the user is not able to look at the device, you need some other means of communicating. Android comes with a powerful API to do text-to-speech (TTS), which enables you to add voice notifications and other spoken feedback in your application that don't require users to look at the screen.

The following code shows how to use the TTS API:

```java
public class TextToSpeechDemo implements TextToSpeech.OnInitListener {
    private final TextToSpeech mTextToSpeech;
    // Used to queue up messages before the TTS engine is initialized...
    private final ConcurrentLinkedQueue<String> mBufferedMessages;
    private Context mContext;
    private boolean mIsReady;

    public TextToSpeechDemo(Context context) {
        mContext = context;
        mBufferedMessages = new ConcurrentLinkedQueue<String>();
        mTextToSpeech = new TextToSpeech(mContext, this);
    }

    @Override
    public void onInit(int status) {
        if (status == TextToSpeech.SUCCESS) {
            mTextToSpeech.setLanguage(Locale.ENGLISH);
            synchronized (this) {
                mIsReady = true;
                for (String bufferedMessage : mBufferedMessages) {
                    speakText(bufferedMessage);
                }
                mBufferedMessages.clear();
            }
        }
    }

    public void release() {
        synchronized (this) {
            mTextToSpeech.shutdown();
            mIsReady = false;
        }
    }

    public void notifyNewMessages(int messageCount) {
        String message = mContext.getResources().
                getQuantityString(R.plurals.msg_count,
                                    messageCount, messageCount);
        synchronized (this) {
            if (mIsReady) {
                speakText(message);
            } else {
                mBufferedMessages.add(message);
            }
        }
    }
}
```

```
        private void speakText(String message) {
            HashMap<String, String> params = new HashMap<String, String>();
            params.put(TextToSpeech.Engine.KEY_PARAM_STREAM,
                    "STREAM_NOTIFICATION");
            mTextToSpeech.speak(message, TextToSpeech.QUEUE_ADD, params);
            mTextToSpeech.playSilence(100, TextToSpeech.QUEUE_ADD, params);
        }
    }
```

Because the initialization of the TTS engine happens asynchronously, you may need to queue up messages before you can perform the actual text-to-speech operation.

You can send several parameters to the TTS engine. In the preceding, you see how to decide which audio stream to use for the spoken message. In this case, you use the same audio stream as the notification sounds.

Finally, if you are going to "speak" multiple messages, it's a good practice to add a brief silence at the end of each message. Doing so makes it clearer to the user when one message ends and another one starts.

Speech Recognition

Besides text-to-speech synthesis, Android can perform speech recognition. This feature is a bit more complicated and doesn't support as many languages as the text-to-speech API. However, it's still a powerful feature for providing an alternative input from the user when touch interaction is limited.

Note: You need to declare the user of the permission `android.permission.RECORD_AUDIO` before you can use the speech recognition feature.

In the following code, you start by creating the `SpeechRecognizer` object and set the listener for the callback. When the click listener `doSpeechRecognition()` is called, the speech recognition is initialized with a language parameter and a flag indicating that you want partial results delivered during the processing.

```
    public class SpeechRecognitionDemo extends Activity {

        private SpeechRecognizer mSpeechRecognizer;

        @Override
        protected void onCreate(Bundle savedInstanceState) {
            super.onCreate(savedInstanceState);
            setContentView(R.layout.speech_recognition_demo);
            mSpeechRecognizer = SpeechRecognizer.createSpeechRecognizer(this);
            mSpeechRecognizer.
                        setRecognitionListener(new MyRecognitionListener());
        }

        @Override
        protected void onDestroy() {
            super.onDestroy();
            mSpeechRecognizer.destroy();
        }

        public void doSpeechRecognition(View view) {
            view.setEnabled(false);
```

```java
        Intent recognitionIntent =
                    new Intent(RecognizerIntent.ACTION_RECOGNIZE_SPEECH);
        recognitionIntent.putExtra(RecognizerIntent.EXTRA_PARTIAL_RESULTS,
                            true);
        recognitionIntent.putExtra(RecognizerIntent.EXTRA_LANGUAGE,
                            "en-US");

        mSpeechRecognizer.startListening(recognitionIntent);
    }

    private class MyRecognitionListener implements RecognitionListener {
        @Override
        public void onReadyForSpeech(Bundle bundle) {
        }

        @Override
        public void onBeginningOfSpeech() {
            ((TextView) findViewById(R.id.speech_result)).setText("");
        }

        @Override
        public void onRmsChanged(float rmsdB) {
            // Not used
        }

        @Override
        public void onBufferReceived(byte[] bytes) {

        }

        @Override
        public void onEndOfSpeech() {
            findViewById(R.id.do_speech_recognition_btn).setEnabled(true);
        }

        @Override
        public void onError(int i) {
            // Something went wrong...
            findViewById(R.id.do_speech_recognition_btn).setEnabled(true);
        }

        @Override
        public void onResults(Bundle bundle) {
            ArrayList<String> partialResults =
          bundle.getStringArrayList(SpeechRecognizer.RESULTS_RECOGNITION);
            if (partialResults != null && partialResults.size() > 0) {
                String bestResult = partialResults.get(0);
                ((TextView) findViewById(R.id.speech_result)).
                                            setText(bestResult + ".");
            }
        }
    }
```

```
        @Override
        public void onPartialResults(Bundle bundle) {
            ArrayList<String> partialResults =
        bundle.getStringArrayList(SpeechRecognizer.RESULTS_RECOGNITION);
            if (partialResults != null && partialResults.size() > 0) {
                String bestResult = partialResults.get(0);
                ((TextView) findViewById(R.id.speech_result)).
                                                setText(bestResult);
            }
        }

        @Override
        public void onEvent(int i, Bundle bundle) {
            // Not used...
        }
    }
}
```

The listener now receives a call to each method in turn. In this example, you display the partially recognized result (best match) in `onPartialResult()` and keep doing so until you get the final result on `onResult()`.

A more advanced application could also interpret the words and listen for certain commands. This way, your application can keep performing speech recognition until the user explicitly tells it to stop—for example, a dictation application that allows the user to add periods between sentences with the single word "stop" followed by a brief silence.

Video Processing with OpenGL ES 2.0

Android supports hardware-accelerated graphics through the OpenGL ES 2.0 and 3.0 APIs. While OpenGL is already used for the standard UI rendering and composition in Android, it is more commonly known as the API used for building graphics-engines for 2D and 3D games. However, as OpenGL ES 2.0 and later require a dedicated GPU for processing, it can also be used for real-time processing of input from a video or a camera feed. In this section I show how to use OpenGL ES 2.0 on Android for adding real-time effects, starting with the video example.

In this section, I assume that the reader has some basic understanding of OpenGL ES 2.0.

In later versions of Android (starting from API level 11), you can use an extension called *streaming texture* to continuously feed streams of images, like a video, to the OpenGL ES 2.0 context as a texture. Although it may be interesting to show a video playing on a rotating cube, a more practical use is to add visual effects to a video. In the following two examples I include only the relevant parts for using the streaming texture feature. For full OpenGL ES 2.0 examples, see the "Further Resources" section as well as the OpenGL ES examples in the Android SDK samples.

In the following code snippet you can see the beginning of a `Renderer` implementation that will be used by a `GLSurfaceView`:public class MyVideoRenderer implements:

```
        GLSurfaceView.Renderer, SurfaceTexture.OnFrameAvailableListener {
    private static int GL_TEXTURE_EXTERNAL_OES = 0x8D65;
    private MediaPlayer mMediaPlayer;
    private float[] mSTMatrix = new float[16];
    private int muSTMatrixHandle;
```

The GL extension used for supporting this feature is called `GL_TEXTURE_EXTERNAL_OES` and is not defined in the Android SDK. However, it's just a constant that you can define yourself in your code as just shown. The renderer also has a reference to the `MediaPlayer` that will be used to playback the video. Finally, a transformation matrix and corresponding shader handle are defined. This matrix is later used when mapping the texture coordinates from the video or camera feed in the fragment shader.

In the `onSurfaceCreated()` method shown in the following example, I show how to set up the texture that will be used as an input.

```
public void onSurfaceCreated(GL10 glUnused, EGLConfig config) {
    ... omitted for brevity ...

    muSTMatrixHandle = GLES20.glGetUniformLocation(mProgram, "uSTMatrix");
    checkGlError("glGetUniformLocation uSTMatrix");
    if (muSTMatrixHandle == -1) {
        throw new RuntimeException("Unable to retrieve uSTMatrix");
    }

    // Setup the texture
    int[] textures = new int[1];
    GLES20.glGenTextures(1, textures, 0);
    mTextureID = textures[0];
    GLES20.glBindTexture(GL_TEXTURE_EXTERNAL_OES, mTextureID);
    GLES20.glTexParameterf(GL_TEXTURE_EXTERNAL_OES,
                           GLES20.GL_TEXTURE_MIN_FILTER,
                           GLES20.GL_NEAREST);
    GLES20.glTexParameterf(GL_TEXTURE_EXTERNAL_OES,
                           GLES20.GL_TEXTURE_MAG_FILTER,
                           GLES20.GL_LINEAR);

    // Define the SurfaceTexture and assign it to our MediaPlayer
    mSurface = new SurfaceTexture(mTextureID);
    mSurface.setOnFrameAvailableListener(this);
    Surface surface = new Surface(mSurface);
    mMediaPlayer.setSurface(surface);
    surface.release();

    synchronized (this) {
        updateSurface = false;
    }

    mMediaPlayer.start();
}
```

Instead of GLES20.GL_TEXTURE2D, you use the constant defined earlier referring to the extension. Next, you create a SurfaceTexture and add it to a Surface object, which in turn is used as the rendering surface for the MediaPlayer. Doing so causes each video frame to be rendered into a streaming texture instead of to the screen. A callback is also added that will update the variable updateSurface as soon as a new frame is available. Finally, you start the playback of the video on the MediaPlayer.

In the onDrawFrame() method shown in the following code, you start by checking whether a new frame is available. If so, the SurfaceTexture is updated and the transformation matrix relevant for this frame is stored in mSTMatrix. This will be used to transform the texture coordinates to the proper sampling location in the frame. Also, note that the binding of the texture is also changed to use the extension constant GL_TEXTURE_EXTERNAL_OES.

```
public void onDrawFrame(GL10 glUnused) {
    synchronized (this) {
        if (updateSurface) {
            mSurface.updateTexImage();
            mSurface.getTransformMatrix(mSTMatrix);
            updateSurface = false;
        }
    }

    ... omitted for brevity ...

    GLES20.glActiveTexture(GLES20.GL_TEXTURE0);
    GLES20.glBindTexture(GL_TEXTURE_EXTERNAL_OES, mTextureID);

    GLES20.glUniformMatrix4fv(muMVPMatrixHandle, 1, false, mMVPMatrix, 0);
    GLES20.glUniformMatrix4fv(muSTMatrixHandle, 1, false, mSTMatrix, 0);

    GLES20.glDrawArrays(GLES20.GL_TRIANGLE_STRIP, 0, 4);
    checkGlError("glDrawArrays");
    GLES20.glFinish();
}
```

In the following code you can see the vertex shader used in this example. Here, the uSTMatrix uniform is used together with the regular transformation matrix and vertex position to calculate the final vTextureCoord.

```
uniform mat4 uMVPMatrix;
uniform mat4 uSTMatrix;
attribute vec4 aPosition;
attribute vec4 aTextureCoord;
varying vec2 vTextureCoord;
void main() {
    gl_Position = uMVPMatrix * aPosition;
    vTextureCoord = (uSTMatrix * aTextureCoord).xy;
}
```

The fragment shader starts by specifying that the GL_OES_EGL_image_external extension is used and is required for this shader to work, as shown in the following code. Next, the sTexture changes its type to samplerExternalOES.

```
#extension GL_OES_EGL_image_external : require
precision mediump float;
varying vec2 vTextureCoord;
uniform samplerExternalOES sTexture;

void main() {
    gl_FragColor = texture2D(sTexture, vTextureCoord);
}
```

This simply renders the video as-is without changes to the screen, as shown in Figure 11-1.

Figure 11-1 Rendering a video using OpenGL ES 2.0 and `SurfaceTexture`

By changing only the fragment shader, you can now achieve some cool effects on the video.

The following code applies a *negative* effect to the video in runtime (see Figure 11-2):

```
#extension GL_OES_EGL_image_external : require
precision mediump float;
varying vec2 vTextureCoord;
uniform samplerExternalOES sTexture;
uniform float uResS;
uniform float uResT;

void main() {
    vec2 onePixel = vec2(1.0 / uResS, 1.0 / uResT);
    float T = 1.0;
    vec2 st = vTextureCoord.st;
    vec3 irgb = texture2D(sTexture, st).rgb;
    vec3 neg = vec3(1., 1., 1.)-irgb;
    gl_FragColor = vec4(mix(irgb, neg, T), 1.);
}
```

This shader takes two extra parameters telling how large the texture is. These two parameters are useful in other types of filter effects as well. Refer to the OpenGL ES 2.0 resource listed in the "Further Resources" section at the end of this chapter for more information.

Figure 11-2 Rendering a video with OpenGL ES 2.0 and using a filter for negative effect

Camera Processing with OpenGL ES 2.0

Using OpenGL ES 2.0, you can follow the same process with the camera as you did with video in the previous section. You can connect the stream of preview frames to the same type of streaming texture and perform real-time processing of these frames. In this way, you can create powerful augmented reality (AR) applications, showing image filters in real time or run some powerful computations on the image that would take much more time if done on the CPU.

```
mSurface = new SurfaceTexture(mTextureID);
mSurface.setOnFrameAvailableListener(this);

try {
    mCamera.setPreviewTexture(mSurface);
    mCamera.startPreview();
} catch (IOException e) {
    e.printStackTrace();
}
```

The only difference from the previous example is in the `onDrawFrame()` method, where instead of working with a `MediaPlayer`, you give the `SurfaceTexture` directly to the `Camera` as a preview texture.

The fragment shader used in this example will perform edge detection on the preview frames. The result of this can be seen in Figure 11-3.

Figure 11-3 The edge detection effect on the camera preview frames running on a Nexus 4

The following code shows the code for this shader:

```
#extension GL_OES_EGL_image_external : require
precision mediump float;
varying vec2 vTextureCoord;
uniform samplerExternalOES sTexture;
uniform float uResS;
uniform float uResT;

void main() {
    vec3 irgb = texture2D(sTexture, vTextureCoord).rgb;
    float ResS = uResS;
    float ResT = uResT;
    vec2 stp0 = vec2(1./ResS, 0.);
    vec2 st0p = vec2(0., 1./ResT);
    vec2 stpp = vec2(1./ResS, 1./ResT);
    vec2 stpm = vec2(1./ResS, -1./ResT);
    const vec3 W = vec3(0.2125, 0.7154, 0.0721);
    float i00 = dot(texture2D(sTexture, vTextureCoord).rgb, W);
    float im1m1 = dot(texture2D(sTexture, vTextureCoord-stpp).rgb, W);
    float ip1p1 = dot(texture2D(sTexture, vTextureCoord+stpp).rgb, W);
    float im1p1 = dot(texture2D(sTexture, vTextureCoord-stpm).rgb, W);
    float ip1m1 = dot(texture2D(sTexture, vTextureCoord+stpm).rgb, W);
    float im10 = dot(texture2D(sTexture, vTextureCoord-stp0).rgb, W);
    float ip10 = dot(texture2D(sTexture, vTextureCoord+stp0).rgb, W);
    float i0m1 = dot(texture2D(sTexture, vTextureCoord-st0p).rgb, W);
    float i0p1 = dot(texture2D(sTexture, vTextureCoord+st0p).rgb, W);
    float h = -1.*im1p1 - 2.*i0p1 - 1.*ip1p1 + 1.*im1m1 + 2.*i0m1 + 1.*ip1m1;
    float v = -1.*im1m1 - 2.*im10 - 1.*im1p1 + 1.*ip1m1 + 2.*ip10 + 1.*ip1p1;
    float mag = length(vec2(h, v));
    vec3 target = vec3(mag, mag, mag);
    gl_FragColor = vec4(mix(irgb, target, 1.0),1.);
}
```

Encoding Media

Android 4.3, more specifically API level 18, includes a number of improvements to the media APIs in Android. The two significant classes in this API are `MediaCodec` and `MediaMuxer`. The `MediaCodec` class, introduced earlier in a more limited version in Android 4.2 (with API level 16), provides application developers access to low-level media codec functionality. With API level 18, the `MediaCodec` class also supports encoding from a `Surface`, which means it is possible to record OpenGL ES 2.0 scenes into a video stream.

The `MediaMuxer` class allows developers to mux raw media streams into a media file for playback. By using both of these classes, you can add the functionality of recording a game session. You can also use these classes with the previous examples of processing a video or camera feed to store the result as a new MP4 file.

Recording an OpenGL Scene

The following example shows the basics of using the `MediaCodec` and `MediaMuxer` for recording the result of an OpenGL ES 2.0 scene to an MP4 file. This method should work with any OpenGL ES 2.0 content. With this code, you create the encoder and the muxer, and use the `MediaFormat` to specify the parameters for the encoder:

```
private void prepareEncoder() {
    mBufferInfo = new MediaCodec.BufferInfo();
    MediaFormat format = MediaFormat.createVideoFormat("video/avc",
            VIDEO_WIDTH, VIDEO_HEIGHT);
    format.setInteger(MediaFormat.KEY_COLOR_FORMAT,
            MediaCodecInfo.CodecCapabilities.COLOR_FormatSurface);
    format.setInteger(MediaFormat.KEY_BIT_RATE, 6000000); // 6 Mbps
    format.setInteger(MediaFormat.KEY_FRAME_RATE, 30);
    format.setInteger(MediaFormat.KEY_I_FRAME_INTERVAL, 10);

    // Create a MediaCodec encoder, and configure it with our format.
    mEncoder = MediaCodec.createEncoderByType(MIME_TYPE);
    mEncoder.configure(format, null, null,
                    MediaCodec.CONFIGURE_FLAG_ENCODE);

    mMuxer = new MediaMuxer(mOutputFile.getAbsolutePath(),
                        MediaMuxer.OutputFormat.MUXER_OUTPUT_MPEG_4);
    mSurface = mEncoder.createInputSurface();
}
```

This example uses H.264 as the output format, with a bitrate of 6 Mbps and 30 frames per second with 10 frames between each I-frame. You also create the `Surface` that will be used as the input for the encoder.

After the encoder and muxer are created, you next set up the EGL context that will be used for recording, as shown in the following code:

```
private static final int EGL_RECORDABLE_ANDROID = 0x3142;

private void recorderEglSetup() {
    mEGLDisplay = EGL14.eglGetDisplay(EGL14.EGL_DEFAULT_DISPLAY);
    if (mEGLDisplay == EGL14.EGL_NO_DISPLAY) {
        throw new RuntimeException("EGL Get Display failed!");
    }
```

```java
    int[] version = new int[2];
    if (!EGL14.eglInitialize(mEGLDisplay, version, 0, version, 1)) {
        mEGLDisplay = null;
        throw new RuntimeException("EGL init error!");
    }

    int[] attribList = {
            EGL14.EGL_RED_SIZE, 8,
            EGL14.EGL_GREEN_SIZE, 8,
            EGL14.EGL_BLUE_SIZE, 8,
            EGL14.EGL_RENDERABLE_TYPE, EGL14.EGL_OPENGL_ES2_BIT,
            EGL_RECORDABLE_ANDROID, 1,
            EGL14.EGL_NONE
    };
    EGLConfig[] configs = new EGLConfig[1];
    int[] numConfigs = new int[1];
    if (!EGL14.eglChooseConfig(mEGLDisplay, attribList,
                               0, configs, 0, configs.length,
                               numConfigs, 0)) {
        throw new RuntimeException("EGL Config error!");
    }

    int[] glAttribs = {
            EGL14.EGL_CONTEXT_CLIENT_VERSION, 2,
            EGL14.EGL_NONE
    };
    mEGLContext = EGL14.eglCreateContext(mEGLDisplay, configs[0],
                                         EGL14.eglGetCurrentContext(),
                                         glAttribs, 0);

    int[] surfaceAttribs = {
            EGL14.EGL_NONE
    };
    mEGLSurface = EGL14.eglCreateWindowSurface(mEGLDisplay, configs[0],
                                        mSurface, surfaceAttribs,
0);
}

public void releaseRecorder() {
    mEncoder.stop();
    mEncoder.release();
    mEncoder = null;

    mMuxer.stop();
    mMuxer.release();
    mMuxer = null;

    EGL14.eglDestroySurface(mEGLDisplay, mEGLSurface);
    EGL14.eglDestroyContext(mEGLDisplay, mEGLContext);
    EGL14.eglReleaseThread();
    EGL14.eglTerminate(mEGLDisplay);
```

```
        mSurface.release();
        mSurface = null;

        mEGLDisplay = null;
        mEGLContext = null;
        mEGLSurface = null;
    }
```

The two most important parts are marked in bold. The constant defined before the method is used when setting up EGL to tell Android that this is a recordable context. The mSurface variable is the same as the one created in the prepareEncoder() method.

The release() method must be called after recording is completed in order to clean up all the resources held by your application. Note that releasing this EGL context doesn't release the same context used for rendering to the display.

Because recording a scene requires two rendering passes, once to the physical display and once to the Surface used for encoding, you need two methods for saving and restoring the rendering state of OpenGL. The following code shows these two methods.

```
    private void storeRenderState() {
        System.arraycopy(mProjMatrix,
                        0, mSavedProjMatrix,
                        0, mProjMatrix.length);
        mSavedEglDisplay = EGL14.eglGetCurrentDisplay();
        mSavedEglDrawSurface = EGL14.eglGetCurrentSurface(EGL14.EGL_DRAW);
        mSavedEglReadSurface = EGL14.eglGetCurrentSurface(EGL14.EGL_READ);
        mSavedEglContext = EGL14.eglGetCurrentContext();
    }

    private void restoreRenderState() {
        if (!EGL14.eglMakeCurrent(mSavedEglDisplay,
                mSavedEglDrawSurface,
                mSavedEglReadSurface,
                mSavedEglContext)) {
            throw new RuntimeException("eglMakeCurrent failed!");
        }
        System.arraycopy(mSavedProjMatrix,
                        0, mProjMatrix, 0, mProjMatrix.length);
    }
```

Next, you need a method for transferring the encoded video stream to the muxer used for writing to the MP4 file:

```
    private void drainEncoder(boolean endOfStream) {
        if (endOfStream) {
            mEncoder.signalEndOfInputStream();
        }

        ByteBuffer[] encoderOutputBuffers = mEncoder.getOutputBuffers();
```

```java
    while (true) {
        int encoderStatus = mEncoder.dequeueOutputBuffer(mBufferInfo, 0);
        if (encoderStatus == MediaCodec.INFO_TRY_AGAIN_LATER) {
            break;
        } else if (encoderStatus ==
                                MediaCodec.INFO_OUTPUT_BUFFERS_CHANGED) {
            encoderOutputBuffers = mEncoder.getOutputBuffers();
        } else if (encoderStatus ==
                                MediaCodec.INFO_OUTPUT_FORMAT_CHANGED) {
            MediaFormat newFormat = mEncoder.getOutputFormat();
            mTrackIndex = mMuxer.addTrack(newFormat);
            mMuxer.start();
            mMuxerStarted = true;
        } else {
            ByteBuffer encodedData = encoderOutputBuffers[encoderStatus];

            if ((mBufferInfo.flags &
                            MediaCodec.BUFFER_FLAG_CODEC_CONFIG) != 0) {
                mBufferInfo.size = 0;
            }

            if (mBufferInfo.size != 0) {
                encodedData.position(mBufferInfo.offset);
                encodedData.limit(mBufferInfo.offset + mBufferInfo.size);

                mMuxer.writeSampleData(mTrackIndex, encodedData,
                                    mBufferInfo);
            }

            mEncoder.releaseOutputBuffer(encoderStatus, false);
            if ((mBufferInfo.flags
                & MediaCodec.BUFFER_FLAG_END_OF_STREAM) != 0) {
                break;
            }
        }
    }
}
```

The while loop in this example will continue until it has exhausted any remaining data from the encoder output.

In the following code you can see a typical onSurfaceChanged() method used for OpenGL ES scenes in Android, with the addition of setting up the encoder and EGL context for recording the scene:

```java
public void onSurfaceChanged(GL10 gl10, int width, int height) {
    GLES20.glViewport(0, 0, width, height);
    float ratio = (float) width / height;
    Matrix.frustumM(mProjMatrix, 0, -ratio, ratio, -1, 1, 3, 7);

    prepareEncoder(mContext);
    if (mEncoder != null) {
```

```
        storeRenderState();
        recorderEglSetup();
        mEncoder.start();
        if (!EGL14.eglMakeCurrent(mEGLDisplay, mEGLSurface,
                                  mEGLSurface, mEGLContext)) {
            throw new RuntimeException("eglMakeCurrent failed");
        }
        restoreRenderState();

        mFrameCount = 0;
    }
}
```

The `onDrawFrame()` method in the following code first draws the scene to the main display, followed by a check to determine if the encoder is valid. The remaining code changes the EGL context, configures the viewport for the second rendering, and draws the scene to the new viewport.

```
public void onDrawFrame(GL10 gl10) {
    drawFrame();

    if(mEncoder != null) {
        storeRenderState();
        if (!EGL14.eglMakeCurrent(mEGLDisplay, mEGLSurface,
                                  mEGLSurface, mEGLContext)) {
            throw new RuntimeException("eglMakeCurrent failed");
        }
        Matrix.orthoM(mProjMatrix, 0,  0, mWidth,
                        0, mHeight,  -1, 1);
        GLES20.glViewport(mViewportXoff, mViewportYoff,
                        mViewportWidth, mViewportHeight);
        drawFrame();
        drainEncoder(false);
        long when = System.nanoTime();
        EGLExt.eglPresentationTimeANDROID(mEGLDisplay, mEGLSurface, when);
        EGL14.eglSwapBuffers(mEGLDisplay, mEGLSurface);
        restoreRenderState();
    }
}
```

After the second drawing is complete the encoder is drained of any data.

The method in the following code shows how to signal to stop the encoder and release all its related resources:

```
public void stopRecording() {
    drainEncoder(true);
    releaseRecorder();
}
```

This method should be called either when the user leaves the application or when recording should be stopped.

Summary

With the later versions of Android, the possibilities for doing advanced media operations in applications have become much better. The examples in this chapter serve to demonstrate some of the more advanced APIs. You can build a complete application from a single example, or combine them into a more complex experience.

While the examples in this chapter are not complete implementations of an application, they should be enough for experienced developers to get started.

Further Resources

Documentation

From the Khronos Group on the OpenSL ES API: `www.khronos.org/opensles`

Specification for the OpenGL extension GL_OES_EGL_image_external: `www.khronos.org/registry/gles/extensions/OES/OES_EGL_image_external.txt`

LittleCheeseCake by Yu Lu using OpenGL ES 2.0 shaders on Android: `http://littlecheesecake.me/blog/13804700/opengles-shader`

Using the `MediaCodec` and `MediaMuxer` in Android: `http://bigflake.com/mediacodec/`

Chapter 12

Secure Android Applications

Security is such a complex topic that it deserves its own chapter in this book. Although security is composed of many aspects, in this chapter I focus on how you as an application developer can manage the security around your application and its data. Because of Andoid's current, excellent API, I also include a section on device administration.

Android Security Concepts

Android has an advanced security model for protecting application data and services from other applications. Every application runs with its own unique user ID that provides basic protection. Each application is signed with its unique key, which works as a foundation around the security model in the Android framework. Moreover, Android's permission system lets a given application share access to its component only to other applications that explicitly declare the right permission in their manifest. Apps can also define permissions such that only apps signed with the same key can use them. Finally, the Android APIs provide methods for verifying signatures, for verifying the user ID of calling processes, and for using strong encryption schemes.

Signatures and Keys

All applications running in Android are signed with a key, including the Android system itself. During normal development, you will use the auto-generated debug key for signing your application (which is done automatically by the Gradle build system or the IDE). When you publish your application on the Google Play Store, be sure to use a unique key that you generate manually using the `keytool` application.

You can use the same key for all the applications you publish, but I recommend that you create a unique key for each application. The only reasons for using the same key for multiple applications is when the applications need to access each other's data directly, or you have defined permissions with the protection level `signature`.

The following command shows how to generate a new, unique key for your application. A good practice is to give the alias the same name as the package name for your application. Also, if you're maintaining application keys for multiple organizations, I suggest you use a separate keystore for each organization.

```
$ keytool -genkey -v -keystore <keystore filename> \
    -alias <alias for key> -keyalg RSA -keysize 2048 -validity 10000
```

When you generate a new key, the `keytool` asks you for a password. If you don't provide a password, anyone with access to the keystore file can create a properly signed application. Thus it's highly recommended that you use a unique password for each keystore file.

Always back up your keystore files online—using, for example, Google Drive or Dropbox. Otherwise, if you lose your keystore file or forget the password, you'll no longer be able to sign new versions of your application and that effectively makes it impossible to provide upgrades for your users.

Android Permissions

Using a feature in Android that requires a special permission is only a matter of adding a `uses-permission` tag in the `AndroidManifest.xml` file. This tells the system that your application requires that particular permission, and notifies the user about this requirement before installation.

Android defines five protection levels: `normal`, `dangerous`, `signature`, `signatureOrSystem`, and `system`. The default level, unless otherwise specified, is `normal`, which is generally used to signal the system that an application requires the functions for this permission. The user is notified before installation (usually in the Google Play Store application) only when the permission is defined as `dangerous`.

A `signature` protection level requires that the application be signed with the same certificate as the application that defined the permission, which can be useful for device vendors because they can define permissions that only applications signed with the same certificate as the system can use. In this way, it's possible for device vendors to release new applications for their devices that use protected system services.

The `signatureOrSystem` and `system` protection levels tell the Android system that applications must reside on the system partition of the device in order to be able to use the permission. The most common examples of this feature are the Google applications (Gmail, Google Play Services, YouTube, and so on) that come pre-installed on the system partition. These applications can use many of the permissions that normal applications cannot reach, even though Google, and not the device manufacturer, signed them. The `signatureOrSystem` is basically a combination of the two protection levels.

Declaring Custom Permissions

In most cases, your application will be self-contained, so there will be little need to declare any new permissions. However, if you will provide an API for other applications to use, for instance a plug-in feature, I recommend defining your own permissions.

The following example shows the relevant parts for defining a read and write permission on a `ContentProvider`.

```xml
<?xml version="1.0" encoding="utf-8"?>
<manifest xmlns:android="http://schemas.android.com/apk/res/android"
    package="com.aaptl.security"
    android:versionCode="1"
    android:versionName="1.0" >
```

```
<permission android:name="com.aapt1.security.READ_DATA"
            android:description="@string/read_perm_desc"
            android:label="@string/read_perm_label"
            android:protectionLevel="dangerous" />

<permission android:name="com.apt1.security.WRITE_DATA"
            android:descriptiona="@string/write_perm_desc"
            android:label="@string/write_perm_label"
            android:protectionLevel="signature" />
...

    <provider
            android:name=".TaskProvider"
            android:authorities="com.aapt1.security.provider"
            android:readPermission="com.aapt1.security.READ_DATA"
            android:writePermission="com.aapt1.security.WRITE_DATA"
            android:exported="true"/>

...
</manifest>
```

The read permission's protection level is set to `dangerous`, which will show up when the user wants to install an application that uses this permission. The write permission, on the other hand, has its protection level set to `signature`, which limits the user of this permission to applications signed with the same certificate.

You can also add the attribute `android:permissionFlags="costsMoney"`, **which signals the user that an application using this permission will generate a cost. Common examples are applications that want to send SMS. Whenever your application provides an API that could result in a monetary cost for users, protect the API with a permission that has this flag set.**

Protecting User Data

If your application creates content that shouldn't be accessible to other applications, store it in the default data directory for the application. Storing data on external storage is never safe, unless you encrypt the content (see the section "Client-Side Data Encryption," later in this chapter). Files stored in an application's data directory can be accessed only by that application or an application with the same user ID (which requires the applications to be signed by the same certificate).

When you create databases using the `SQLiteOpenHelper`, as shown in Chapter 9, they end up in the application's data directory by default, so these SQLite databases are always protected from other applications. To create ordinary files, however, you use the method `Context.openFileOutput()`, which creates a new file (or opens an existing file for appending data) in the application's data directory.

The following method is an example of how to append data to a private file.

```
public static void appendStringToPrivateFile(Context context,
                                        String data, String filename)
{
    FileOutputStream outputStream
            = context.openFileOutput(filename,
                              Context.MODE_APPEND|Context.MODE_PRIVATE);
    outputStream.write(data.getBytes("UTF-8"));
    outputStream.close();
}
```

You open files for reading using `Context.openFileInput()`. Notice the use of both `Context.MODE_APPEND` and `Context.MODE_PRIVATE` as flags to `openFileOutput()`. These flags will make the file always append data to the end when writing and accessible only to your application, respectively. To protect your data, always use `MODE_PRIVATE` (which is also the default flag). To provide a file that other applications can read, you should instead use a `ContentProvider` and define the appropriate permissions.

The two flags `Context.MODE_WORLD_READABLE` and `Context.MODE_WORLD_WRITABLE` make files in the application's data directory world readable and writable. However, these flags are now deprecated, and you're strongly encouraged not to use them.

Because the `MODE_PRIVATE` flag sets the correct Linux file permissions, they protect files from being accessed by other applications. However, simply using the method described in the preceding example should not be considered a secure solution. If you're storing very sensitive information on a device, I strongly advise applying some encryption to the files.

Verifying Calling Applications

Although permissions provide a way of ensuring that the user accepts that an application can access your services or providers, at times it's necessary to identify the application of an incoming call. Consider a `ContentProvider` that provides a way for third-party applications to add (insert) data. However, you want applications to be capable of accessing only the records they've created, so you need some way of securely identifying the remote process in each call to `query()`, `insert()`, `update()`, and `delete()`.

The following method shows how to use the `Binder` to retrieve the UID (User ID) for the calling applications. From there, you can retrieve the package names (that is, applications) that have this UID.

```
private String getPackageNameForCaller(Context context) {
    int callingUid = Binder.getCallingUid();
    PackageManager packageManager = context.getPackageManager();
    String[] packages = packageManager.getPackagesForUid(callingUid);
    if(packages != null && packages.length > 0) {
        return packages[0]; // Return the first matching package...
    }
    return null;
}
```

Because you can have the same UID for multiple applications, signed with the same key, by using the `android:sharedUserId` attribute in the manifest, you may receive multiple package names in this lookup. So, in the public documentation of your provider, you need to state that applications using your API can't share the UID with another application.

After you get the package name for the application, you can use it when querying the database. For each insert, make sure that you populate a column with the value of the calling application's package name. In the query, update and delete, you modify the selection and selection argument so that the package name is prepended, as shown here:

```
private String prependSelection(String selection) {
    return Columns.PACKAGE_NAME + " = ? AND (" + selection + ")";
}

private String[] prependSelectionArgs(String[] selectionArgs) {
    String[] newSelArgs = new String[selectionArgs.length + 1];
    System.arraycopy(selectionArgs, 0, newSelArgs, 1, selectionArgs.
length);
    newSelArgs[0] = getPackageNameForCaller(getContext());
    return newSelArgs;
}
```

In this way, you can provide a single `ContentProvider` that other applications can work with while simultaneously providing protection so that data cannot leak. This approach is suitable for applications that aggregate data from different sources and in which you enable the use of plug-ins from third-party developers.

Client-Side Data Encryption

Imagine an app that syncs user-generated data to a cloud service. However, in this case, the data stored on the cloud service must be encrypted so that no one but the user can decrypt the data. This scenario means that the encryption and decryption must happen on the client-side. A couple of examples today are LastPass, which manages all your passwords, and Wuala, a cloud-storage service where all data is encrypted on the client-side, which effectively protects the user's data even if the cloud service is compromised.

The challenge with such an application is that you wouldn't want to store anything on the device that isn't encrypted. For instance, if you have a notebook application for storing secure notes, you can't store decrypted notes in the application's data directory, because if the user were to lose the device, it wouldn't take much effort for a hacker to gain access to the file system and read the unencrypted files. To solve this problem, only keep unencrypted data in memory. Although it's still possible to read the state of a memory, doing so is significantly harder than reading the file system.

In this section, I explain how to encrypt and decrypt data using a password and how to create a memory-based database that you can use in your application like any other `ContentProvider`.

Android Crypto API

The API for encrypting and decrypting data in Android is based on the API found in the `javax.crypto` package in Java SE. The actual implementation is based on the open-source Bouncy Castle Crypto APIs, a clean room implementation of the JCE 1.2.1 specification. As a result, you can use most Java libraries that use the `javax.crypto` APIs from Java SE when writing Android applications.

Generating a Key

When using encryption and decryption functions, you need to generate a key that is secure, unique, and capable of being re-created based on the user's input (that is, a password or other secure method).

The following code shows how to generate a `SecretKey` for the AES algorithm, which is secure enough for most situations. The `salt` is the input to the generation of the key that you need to keep track of. In cryptography, a *salt* is a random piece of data used as input for the one-way function in the encryption algorithms.

```
public static SecretKey generateKey(char[] password, byte[] salt)
        throws Exception {
    int iterations = 1000;
    int outputKeyLength = 256;
    SecretKeyFactory secretKeyFactory
                    = SecretKeyFactory.getInstance("PBKDF2WithHmacS
HA1");
    KeySpec keySpec = new PBEKeySpec(password, salt,
                                    iterations, outputKeyLength);
    byte[] keyBytes = secretKeyFactory.generateSecret(keySpec).
getEncoded();
    return new SecretKeySpec(keyBytes, "AES");
}
```

Encrypting Data

To encrypt data, you must generate the salt and an initialization vector as an input to the `Cipher` used for encrypting.

The following method generates a salt of 8 bytes using the `SecureRandom` class. *Note:* You never manually seed the `SecureRandom` class because the system takes care of that for you. You create an initialization vector, initiate the `Cipher`, and encrypt your plain text to a byte array. When you have your cipher data, you generate a normal `String` from those bytes by using the `Base64` utility class. You append the initialization vector and salt in the same way, separated by a non-base64 character.

```
public static String encryptClearText(char[] password, String plainText)
        throws Exception {
    SecureRandom secureRandom = new SecureRandom();
    int saltLength = 8;
    byte[] salt = new byte[saltLength];
    secureRandom.nextBytes(salt);
    SecretKey secretKey = generateKey(password, salt);
```

```
Cipher cipher = Cipher.getInstance("AES/CBC/PKCS5Padding");
byte[] initVector = new byte[cipher.getBlockSize()];
secureRandom.nextBytes(initVector);
IvParameterSpec ivParameterSpec = new IvParameterSpec(initVector);
cipher.init(Cipher.ENCRYPT_MODE, secretKey, ivParameterSpec);
byte[] cipherData = cipher.doFinal(plainText.getBytes("UTF-8"));
return Base64.encodeToString(cipherData,
                            Base64.NO_WRAP | Base64.NO_PADDING)
        + "]" + Base64.encodeToString(initVector,
                            Base64.NO_WRAP | Base64.NO_PADDING)
        + "]" + Base64.encodeToString(salt,
                            Base64.NO_WRAP | Base64.NO_PADDING);
}
```

The returned String can be securely sent over the network or stored on the external storage. An application using this approach for securing data should require the user to input a password that is secure enough. How to choose such a password is beyond the scope of this book, but I recommend using a regular expression for checking the complexity of a password. A good source for various regular expressions that you can use is available at http://regexlib.com/.

Decrypting Data

Decrypting data works very much like encryption. You take the String generated by a previous call to encryptClearText() and split it on the separator that you choose.

In the following method, you see how the Cipher, the initialization vector, and the SecretKey are re-created from the input string. As long as the passwords match, you'll be able to decode the encoded data.

```
public static String decryptData(char[] password, String encodedData)
        throws Exception {
    String[] parts = encodedData.split("]");
    byte[] cipherData = Base64.decode(parts[0], Base64.DEFAULT);
    byte[] initVector = Base64.decode(parts[1], Base64.DEFAULT);
    byte[] salt = Base64.decode(parts[2], Base64.DEFAULT);

    Cipher cipher = Cipher.getInstance("AES/CBC/PKCS5Padding");
    IvParameterSpec ivParams = new IvParameterSpec(initVector);
    SecretKey secretKey = generateKey(password, salt);
    cipher.init(Cipher.DECRYPT_MODE, secretKey, ivParams);
    return new String(cipher.doFinal(cipherData), "UTF-8");
}
```

This method is useful for fairly small sets of data. If you need to encrypt and decrypt larger files, check the CipherInputStream and CipherOutputStream as they support streaming data that is too large to fit in memory all at once.

Working with Encrypted Data

After you encode the data, you can safely write it to a file or send it over the network without the risk of leaking the user's private information. The only one who can decrypt the data is the person who knows the password, which means that you could basically store the encrypted data on a public server without anyone, including yourself, being able to read its content. This is a great way to gain your users' trust—as long as you can explain it in terms that nontechnical people can grasp. A couple of services already use this capability as their main selling point.

Considering the example of a secure notebook application, you could use the approach just described for encrypting and decrypting the notes. When the user makes an update to his notes, you can upload the file to his Google Drive or similar service, and the notes will then be accessible from his other devices. (See Chapter 19 for an example of storing data in Google Drive.)

Consider the following Java object for representing notes in a notebook application:

```java
public class NoteData {
    private UUID mID;
    private String mTitle;
    private String mContent;
    private String mCategory;
    private Date mLastChange;

    public NoteData() {
        mID = UUID.randomUUID();
    }

    // Getters and setters omitted for brevity...
}
```

You can use Google Gson, as shown in Chapter 9, to serialize and deserialize objects of this class to the JSON format. The JSON data can be represented as a normal `String` object, which you then can use for encrypting your notes. Decrypting and deserializing works the same way.

The following example shows a simplified method for use in a notebook application that securely encrypts and decrypts the users' notes based on their passwords. The encrypted data can then be transferred online, which I cover in more detail in Chapter 17.

```java
public String encryptNoteDataCollection(Collection<NoteData> notes,
                                         char[] password) {
    StringWriter writer = new StringWriter();
    JsonWriter jsonWriter = new JsonWriter(writer);
    Gson gson = new Gson();
    Type type = new TypeToken<Collection<NoteData>>(){}.getType();
    gson.toJson(notes, type, jsonWriter);
    String clearText = writer.toString();
    try {
        return encryptClearText(password, clearText);
    } catch (Exception e) {
        // Ignore for brevity
        return null;
    }
}
```

```
public static Collection<NoteData> decryptAndDecode(char[] password,
                                                    String encryptedData)
{
    try {
        String jsonData = decryptData(password, encryptedData);
        Gson gson =  new Gson();
        Type type = new TypeToken<Collection<NoteData>>(){}.getType();
        JsonReader jsonReader = new JsonReader(new
StringReader(jsonData));
        return gson.fromJson(jsonReader, type);
    } catch (Exception e) {
        // Ignore for brevity...
        return null;
    }
}
```

If you prefer to work toward a `ContentProvider`, you can create an SQLite database in memory using the following code:

```
mDatabase = SQLiteDatabase.create(null);
```

This database instance will be destroyed as soon as the database object is closed. This means that your application should store the encrypted content to a local file for every change (insert, update or delete) to the database and must repopulate the database content each time it is opened.

Android Key Chain Management

A feature that was long missing from Android was central secure credential storage and a way to control the system's trusted Certificate Authorities, which are crucial in order to build secure applications for enterprise and other sensitive services.

In this section I'm assuming that you're familiar with the basics of certificates, CA and PKI. If not, refer to the "Further Resources" section at the end of this chapter. Although permissions can protect the data from other applications and encryption can prevent access of the data even when the file is copied from the device, your application still needs a secure method for verifying that the remote host it communicates with is indeed the one it claims to be. Because you cannot assume that the user will always be on a safe, well-known, and secure network, you need to verify any host that you communicate with using its certificates.

Explaining the details of certificate authority, key chains, and how they make the Internet secure is beyond the scope of this book. However, I do show how you can use the key chain API that was made available in Android 4.0/ICS to store a new key pair, as well as how to verify the source of the data and sign it so that a recipient can verify its authenticity.

First, you need to generate a new certificate that you can use for testing your application, which you do using the same `keytool` shown earlier in this chapter for creating the signature for your application.

The following example shows how to generate a simple certificate using the `keytool` command. The result is written to a file named `MyKeyStore.pfx`. In a real-world situation, the IT department of a company usually generates these certificates for each user and distributes them securely. Next, the enterprise application imports this certificate and stores it in the central credential storage.

```
$ keytool -genkeypair -alias MyCertificate -keystore MyKeyStore.pfx
  -storepass thepassword -validity 10000 -keyalg RSA -keysize 2048
  -storetype pkcs12
What is your first and last name?
  [Unknown]:  Erik Hellman
What is the name of your organizational unit?
  [Unknown]:  Development
What is the name of your organization?
  [Unknown]:  Hellsoft
What is the name of your City or Locality?
  [Unknown]:  Malmoe
What is the name of your State or Province?
  [Unknown]:  Skaane
What is the two-letter country code for this unit?
  [Unknown]:  SE
Is CN=Erik Hellman, OU=Development, O=Hellsoft, L=Malmoe, ST=Skaane,
  C=SE correct?
  [no]:  yes
```

In the following code, you see how to install a certificate from a file (represented as a byte array).

```java
public class SigningActivity extends Activity {
    private static final int INSTALL_CERT_CODE = 1001;
    private static final String CERT_FILENAME = "MyKeyStore.pfx";
    private static final String CERTIFICATE_NAME = "MyCertificate";

    @Override
    protected void onActivityResult(int requestCode, int resultCode,
                                    Intent data) {
        if(requestCode == INSTALL_CERT_CODE) {
            if(resultCode == RESULT_OK) {
                // Certificate successfully installed
            } else {
                // User cancelled certificate installation
            }
        }
    }

    // click-listener for installing certificate
    public void doInstallCertificate(View view) {
        byte[] certData = readFile(CERT_FILENAME);
        Intent installCert = KeyChain.createInstallIntent();
        installCert.putExtra(KeyChain.EXTRA_NAME, CERTIFICATE_NAME)
        installCert.putExtra(KeyChain.EXTRA_PKCS12, certificateData);
        startActivityForResult(installCert, INSTALL_CERT_CODE);
    }

    ...
}
```

The code will activate a dialog box where a user can enter the password for the chosen keystore. Next, another dialog box, as shown in Figure 12-1, is activated in which the user can choose the alias for the certificate.

Figure 12-1 Dialog box asking for the name of the certificate that is being installed by the application

When your application wants to use a certificate, it must first ask users which one they want to use, which is done by calling `KeyChain.choosePrivateKeyAlias()`, as shown in the following code.

```
public void doSignNoteData(View view) {
    KeyChain.choosePrivateKeyAlias(this, new KeyChainAliasCallback() {
        @Override
        public void alias(String alias) {
            EditText editText = (EditText) findViewById(R.id.input_text);
            String textToSign = editText.getText().toString();
            new MySigningTask().execute(textToSign, alias);
        }
    }, null, null, null, -1, null);
}
```

This activates a system dialog box, as shown in Figure 12-2.

Figure 12-2 System dialog box that allows the user to
pick a certificate from the trusted storage

The preceding callback will receive the alias for the chosen certificate, and you can now continue with retrieving the certificate and the signing process. *Note:* The callback is executed on a `Binder` thread and not on the main thread. Because the signing process could potentially block the thread it's running on, you use an `AsyncTask` for the actual signing.

The following method shows how to retrieve the private key of the certificate pair and use it to create a signature of the `String` you want to sign. You use the same approach as in the earlier encryption example to build two `Base64` encoded `Strings` with a separator.

```
public String createSignedNote(String textToSign, String alias) {
    try {
        byte[] textData = textToSign.getBytes("UTF-8");
        PrivateKey privateKey
                = KeyChain.getPrivateKey(getApplicationContext(), alias);
        Signature signature
                = Signature.getInstance("SHA1withRSA");
        signature.initSign(privateKey);
        signature.update(textData);
        byte[] signed = signature.sign();
        return Base64.encodeToString(textData,
                Base64.NO_WRAP | Base64.NO_PADDING)
                + "]" + Base64.encodeToString(signed,
                Base64.NO_WRAP | Base64.NO_PADDING);
    } catch (Exception e) {
        Log.e(TAG, "Error signing data.", e);
    }
    return null;
}
```

To verify the signature of signed data, your application must first retrieve the `PublicKey` from the certificate. In the following code, it's assumed that the chain contains only one entry, but in real-life situations, you will probably have at least two entries (one for the organization and one for the user).

```
private boolean verifySignature(String dataAndSignature, String alias) {
    try {
        String[] parts = dataAndSignature.split("]");
        byte[] decodedText = Base64.decode(parts[0], Base64.DEFAULT);
        byte[] signed = Base64.decode(parts[1], Base64.DEFAULT);
        X509Certificate[] chain = KeyChain.getCertificateChain(this,
alias);
        PublicKey publicKey = chain[0].getPublicKey();
        Signature signature = Signature.getInstance("SHA1withRSA");
        signature.initVerify(publicKey);
        signature.update(decodedText);
        return signature.verify(signed);
    } catch (Exception e) {
        Log.e(TAG, "Error verifying signature.", e);
    }
    return false;
}
```

You can also use the public and private keys to encrypt data. If two parties (for instance, the company server and an application on an employee's smartphone) need to communicate securely, you use the receiving party's public key to encrypt data, which then can be decrypted only by using the private key.

Most webservers today support the secure HTTP protocol called HTTPS. This protocol has built-in support to set up the connection between the client and the server using this approach, so all you do is provide the client-side certificate. Refer to the documentation for the `HttpsURLConnection` for more information on this topic.

Device Management API

Although encrypting and verifying data are important parts of security, they're often not enough for most organizations. Within the domain of enterprise applications is a need to set certain restrictions on a device before allowing it to communicate with a company's intranet. This situation is resolved via a Device Management API available in Android that provides a number of functions to handle enterprise requirements. This API provides a number of policies that an application can apply to a device to ensure that it is secure. There are policies for limiting and resetting the password, for locking and wiping a device, and for encrypting the storage. Check the documentation for the Device Administration API (see `http://developer.android. com/guide/topics/admin/device-admin.html`) for a full list of policies.

The first thing you need to enable this in your application is an XML file in the resources that defines which device policies your application needs to apply.

The following example shows a simple device policy XML that you store in the XML resources. It enables your application to register when a user logs in (unlocks the device), to limit and reset the password, to force the device to lock down, and to encrypt the storage when required.

```xml
<?xml version="1.0" encoding="utf-8"?>
<device-admin xmlns:android="http://schemas.android.com/apk/res/android">
    <uses-policies>
        <watch-login/>
        <force-lock/>
        <limit-password/>
        <encrypted-storage/>
        <reset-password/>
    </uses-policies>
</device-admin>
```

Next, you need to define a `BroadcastReceiver` that will be called when the device administration is enabled for your application.

```xml
<receiver
        android:name=".MyDeviceAdminReceiver"
        android:label="@string/device_admin_label"
        android:description="@string/device_admin_description"
        android:permission="android.permission.BIND_DEVICE_ADMIN">
```

```
<meta-data
        android:name="android.app.device_admin"
        android:resource="@xml/device_admin"/>
<intent-filter>
    <action android:name="android.app.action.DEVICE_ADMIN_ENABLED"/>
</intent-filter>
</receiver>
```

Now you need to implement a custom `BroadcastReceiver` (extending `DeviceAdminReceiver`) where you configure the manifest entry, as in the preceding example. First, you specify that the permission for the receiver and add a meta-data tag that specifies the XML also shown in the preceding example.

```
public class MyDeviceAdminReceiver extends DeviceAdminReceiver {
    @Override
    public void onEnabled(Context context, Intent intent) {
        super.onEnabled(context, intent);
        PackageManager packageManager = context.getPackageManager();
        ComponentName deviceAdminService
                = new ComponentName(context, MyDeviceAdminService.class);
        packageManager.setComponentEnabledSetting(deviceAdminService,
                PackageManager.COMPONENT_ENABLED_STATE_ENABLED, 0);
        context.startService(new Intent(context,
                                        MyDeviceAdminService.class));
    }

    @Override
    public void onDisabled(Context context, Intent intent) {
        super.onDisabled(context, intent);
        context.stopService(new Intent(context,
                                        MyDeviceAdminService.class));
        PackageManager packageManager = context.getPackageManager();
        ComponentName deviceAdminService
                = new ComponentName(context, MyDeviceAdminService.class);
        packageManager.setComponentEnabledSetting(deviceAdminService,
                PackageManager.COMPONENT_ENABLED_STATE_DISABLED, 0);
    }
}
```

The receiver is notified when device administration for your application is enabled or disabled. There are also callbacks for certain device policy events, such as password expiration. In the preceding example, you see how to enable and disable a service in your application, depending on the state of device administration for this application.

To enable device administration for your application, you need to start a system `Activity` that asks for the user's permission (see Figure 12-3).

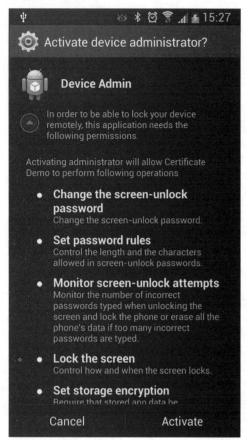

Figure 12-3 The system `Activity` that asks for permission
to enable device administration rights for an application.
The first paragraph under the title is the same as the text in
the `EXTRA_ADD_EXPLANATION` parameter.

The following example shows how to request the user to enable device administration for your application.
Note: You send the `ComponentName` for the receiver and you can add an extra explanation that is displayed
to the user. This is recommended for applications using the Device Administration API; otherwise, what the
prompted dialog box means may be confusing.

```
public static void enableDeviceAdmin(Context context) {
    Intent enableDeviceAdmin
            = new Intent(DevicePolicyManager.ACTION_ADD_DEVICE_ADMIN);
    ComponentName deviceAdminReceiver
            = new ComponentName(context, MyDeviceAdminReceiver.class);
    enableDeviceAdmin.putExtra(DevicePolicyManager.EXTRA_DEVICE_ADMIN,
            deviceAdminReceiver);
    enableDeviceAdmin.putExtra(DevicePolicyManager.EXTRA_ADD_EXPLANATION,
            context.getString(R.string.device_admin_explanation));
    context.startActivity(enableDeviceAdmin);
}
```

After the user accepts the device administration request, your application can start applying its policies and control the device to a certain degree.

The following method is a simple example in which you reset the password and lock the device immediately.

```
private void changePasswordAndLockDevice(String password) {
    mDevicePolicyManager = (DevicePolicyManager)
            getSystemService(DEVICE_POLICY_SERVICE);
    if(mDevicePolicyManager.resetPassword(password, 0)) {
        mDevicePolicyManager.lockNow();
    }
}
```

Doing so can be useful for a remote security feature. By sending a verified message (as shown earlier in this chapter) to the device, the user or someone with the right authorization can lock the device if it's stolen or lost. The message could come from an SMS, which I describe in Chapter 15, or from a Google Cloud Messaging (GCM) service, which I cover in Chapter 19.

Summary

In this chapter, I described how you can use the Android permissions to restrict what and how other applications can access your application. I also showed how to identify the calling application in order to isolate data you receive from multiple applications. This feature is especially powerful when your application is working with aggregated data from several sources.

I then demonstrated how to encrypt and decrypt data using the crypto APIs in Android, which can often provide enough security when the user's data for your application is stored externally or on a remote server.

If your application will involve external parties, such as a remote server, simply performing encryption of the data may not be enough. You also need to be able to verify that data your application receives is coming from a verified source. The new Key Chain API in Android 4.0 and later provides secure and trusted storage for application-specific certificates.

Finally, I showed how to use the Device Administration API in order to programmatically control the security features. As a result, you can write applications that can lock a device or reset the password. The Device Administration API combined with the other security features described in this chapter give you a set of powerful tools for creating applications that fulfill the security requirements of most enterprises.

Further Resources

Books

Adams, Carlisle, and Steve Lloyd. *Understanding PKI: Concepts, Standards, and Deployment Considerations,* 2nd edition. Addison-Wesley, 2002.

Documentation

Documentation on the Device Administration APIs: `http://developer.android.com/guide/topics/admin/device-admin.html`

Websites

Android Developers Blog. "Using Cryptography to Store Credentials Safely": `http://android-developers.blogspot.se/2013/02/using-cryptography-to-store-credentials.html`

Android Developers Blog. "Unifying Key Store Access in ICS": `http://android-developers.blogspot.se/2012/03/unifying-key-store-access-in-ics.html`

Android Explorations. "Using the ICS KeyChain API": `http://nelenkov.blogspot.se/2011/11/using-ics-keychain-api.html`

"Sample CodeC for Using the ICS KeyChain API and Related Articles": `https://github.com/nelenkov/keystore-test#readme`

Chapter 13

Maps, Location, and Activity APIs

In May 2013, at the annual Google IO conference, Google presented something slightly different for Android developers. Google used to focus on new platform features and Android versions at this event, but at this conference, they presented a new service API for location-based apps that works on older Android versions as well. This new API allows developers to use the new and advanced Location and Activity API for Android, which is part of the Google Play Services, on most Android devices deployed into the market today.

In this chapter, I cover the features of the new Location API and how you can integrate it into your applications.

Fused Location Manager

Google managed to provide a new unified Location API that works for older Android versions by *fusing* input from all the sensors and other inputs into one library. Figures 13-1 and 13-2 show the differences between the use of the old location-based APIs and the new fused Location Manager. The new library checks for the existence of all the possible inputs and sensors and manages all the specifics for each Android version.

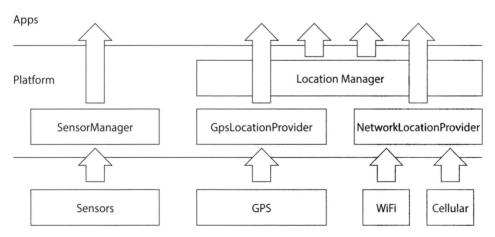

Figure 13-1 The old location-based APIs in the Android platform. Using these APIs requires a great deal of effort from developers who also have to consider the different Android platforms.

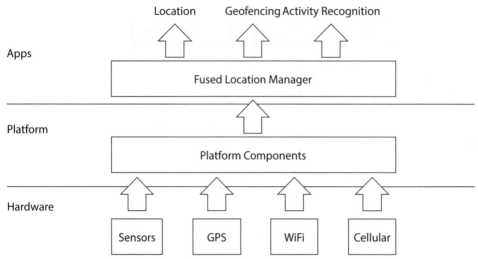

Figure 13-2 The fused Location Manager combines sensors, GPS, Wi-Fi, and cellular into a single API for location-based applications.

There are several advantages to using the new approach, but the most obvious one is that Google can provide updates and fixes for bugs that otherwise would have to be rolled out by each handset manufacturer. Also, it allows you to build advanced maps and location-enabled applications on older devices, as long as they have Google Play Services installed. For details on how to verify that Google Play Services is installed and working correctly, refer to Chapter 19.

Google Maps v2 Integration

To integrate the Google Maps API on Android, you need to create a new project in the Google API Console at `https://code.google.com/apis/console`. You should create a new project here for each Android application that will use the Google Play Services APIs (see Figure 13-3). (I go into more detail about how to work with the API console and Google Play Services in Chapter 19.) The first thing you need to do after you create the project is to enable the Google Maps Android API v2 under Services and create a new Android key under API Access.

You generate the key by entering the `SHA1` value for the key used for signing your APK, as shown in Figure 13-4. Usually you will have two keys. One is used during development (debug key) that is usually shared among multiple applications and considered insecure (usually found under `$HOME/.android/debug.keystore`). The second one is your release key, which you should always keep secure. I recommend that you create two API keys for each application, one for the development version and one for the release version.

You get the `SHA1` by using the `keytool` in the terminal, as shown here with the relevant text shown in bold:

```
$ keytool -list -v -keystore ~/.android/debug.keystore -alias
androiddebugkey
  -storepass android -keypass android
```

```
Alias name: androiddebugkey
Creation date: May 15, 2013
Entry type: PrivateKeyEntry
Certificate chain length: 1
Certificate[1]:
Owner: CN=Android Debug, O=Android, C=US
Issuer: CN=Android Debug, O=Android, C=US
Serial number: 5193e7a1
Valid from: Wed May 15 21:53:05 CEST 2013 until: Fri May 08 21:53:05 CEST
   2043
Certificate fingerprints:
   MD5:  09:AF:DA:16:0B:94:71:67:61:5B:C3:7D:9E:12:53:A0
   SHA1: A0:D6:9F:F7:6E:F0:AD:B3:70:0B:74:91:13:E8:57:C3:C9:80:6D:EA
   Signature algorithm name: SHA1withRSA
   Version: 3
```

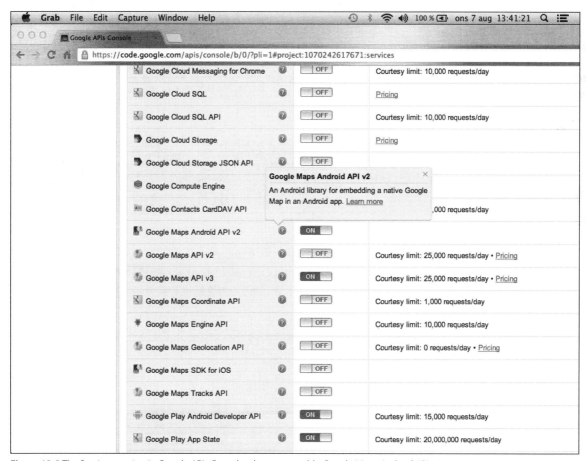

Figure 13-3 The Services section in Google APIs Console where you enable Google Maps Android API v2

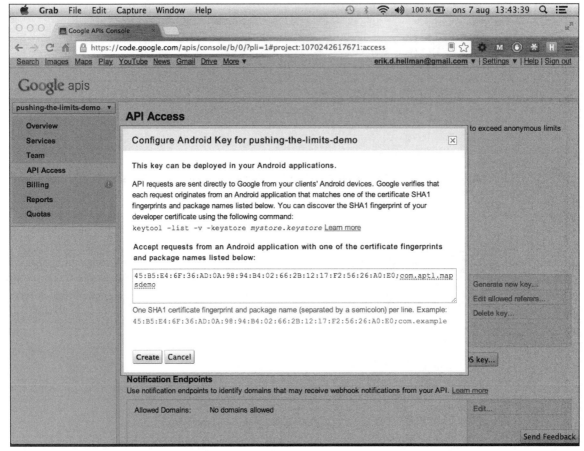

Figure 13-4 Creating a new Android key for the Google Maps API access

Copy the text and paste it into the dialog for configuring a new Android key on the API Console (as shown in Figure 13-4). After the SHA1 value, you append a semicolon followed by the package name for your application. When you click Create, the key will be generated and you can copy it into your manifest. This process is covered in more detail in Chapter 19.

You need to add the API key as a metadata element in the manifest, as shown in the following example, with the API key shown in bold.

```
<application
    android:allowBackup="true"
    android:icon="@drawable/ic_launcher"
    android:label="@string/app_name"
    android:theme="@style/AppTheme" >
    ...
    <meta-data
            android:name="com.google.android.maps.v2.API_KEY"
            android:value="AIzaSyCXNWDY7nx-_0vnwMW-6mXryYD5BTblyVM"/>
</application>
```

Working with Google Maps

Working with the new (version 2) Google Maps API is simple and straightforward. In the following example, you see how Java code adds Google Maps to your application:

```
protected void onCreate(Bundle savedInstanceState) {
    super.onCreate(savedInstanceState);
    setContentView(R.layout.activity_main);
    mMapFragment = (MapFragment) getFragmentManager().
                                findFragmentById(R.id.map);
    GoogleMap map = mMapFragment.getMap();
    map.setTrafficEnabled(true);
    CameraPosition cameraPosition = new CameraPosition.Builder().
                                                target(MY_HOME).
                                                zoom(17).
                                                bearing(90).
                                                tilt(30).build();
    map.animateCamera(CameraUpdateFactory.
        newCameraPosition(cameraPosition));
    map.setMapType(GoogleMap.MAP_TYPE_NORMAL);
    map.setMyLocationEnabled(true);
    map.setIndoorEnabled(true);
}
```

The `GoogleMap` object is the central piece when working with the maps. In this example, you also move the camera for the map to `MY_HOME` (a predefined `LatLng` constant) and tell the `GoogleMap` object to enable "My location" on the map as well as indoor positioning and maps.

The following XML layout is an example of how you can define the initial map in an XML layout:

```
<fragment xmlns:android="http://schemas.android.com/apk/res/android"
          xmlns:map="http://schemas.android.com/apk/res-auto"
          android:id="@+id/map"
          android:layout_width="match_parent"
          android:layout_height="match_parent"
          android:name="com.google.android.gms.maps.MapFragment"
          map:cameraBearing="112.5"
          map:cameraTargetLat="55.59612590"
          map:cameraTargetLng="12.98140870"
          map:cameraTilt="30"
          map:cameraZoom="13"
          map:mapType="normal"
          map:uiCompass="true"
          map:uiRotateGestures="true"
          map:uiScrollGestures="true"
          map:uiTiltGestures="true"
          map:uiZoomControls="true"
          map:uiZoomGestures="true"/>
```

You'll find this using the XML layout useful if your application needs to display a default location on the maps because the values here can be localized as any other resource can.

To interact with a `GoogleMap` object, you can register a number of listeners for certain events.

Markers on Maps

A `Marker` is the simplest thing you can add to a `GoogleMap` object (see Figure 13-5). You simply need a `LatLng` object with the coordinates of its position.

The following code shows how to add a new `Marker` to a `GoogleMap` object.

```
mMap.addMarker(new MarkerOptions().
        position(latLng).
        title(mMarkerTitle).
        snippet(mMarkerSnippet).
        icon(mMarkerDrawable));
```

The only required attribute for a marker is the position. It is also possible to define a draggable `Marker` that the user can move around. You do so by calling `draggable(true)` on the `MarkerOptions` object and ensuring that you've set the `Marker` drag listener on the map with `GoogleMap.setOnMarkerClickListener()`.

Figure 13-5 Placing markers on a map. Note the marker with the custom icon.

Drawing Circles

Drawing circles on a `GoogleMap` is done in the same way as placing `Markers`.

Following is an example of how to use the `onMapClick()` callback on a `GoogleMap` to place a red circle with the radius of 40 meters on the map where the user taps (see the result in Figure 13-6).

```
public void onMapClick(LatLng latLng) {
    mMap.addCircle(new CircleOptions().
                radius(40).
                center(latLng).
                fillColor(Color.RED).
                strokeColor(Color.BLACK).
                strokeWidth(6));
}
```

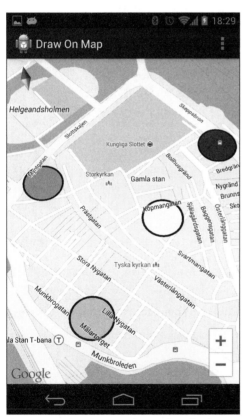

Figure 13-6 A Google map with a number of circles

Drawing Polygons

Polygons are complex geometrical objects formed by a number of points. You can use polygons to cover an area of a map (as shown in Figure 13-7).

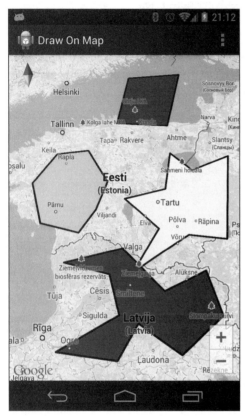

Figure 13-7 A Google map with a number of different polygons drawn on top

The following is a simple example where a quick tap on the maps adds a new point for the polygon and where a long tap completes the polygon:

```
@Override
public void onMapClick(LatLng latLng) {
    if (mNewPolygon == null) {
        mNewPolygon = new PolygonOptions().add(latLng);
    } else {
        mNewPolygon.add(latLng);
    }
}
```

```
@Override
public void onMapLongClick(LatLng latLng) {
    Log.d(TAG, "Closing polygon at " + latLng.toString());
    mNewPolygon.add(latLng).
            fillColor(getColor()).
            strokeColor(Color.BLACK).
            strokeWidth(6);
    mMap.addPolygon(mNewPolygon);
    mNewPolygon = null;
    mDrawState = null;
}
```

Useful Location API Utilities

A common operation in location-based applications is to find out whether a certain location (latitude and longitude) is close to another location.

The following method takes two LatLng parameters and returns the approximate distance between them in meters.

```
public float distanceBetween(LatLng latLng1, LatLng latLng2) {
    float[] results = new float[3];
    Location.distanceBetween(latLng1.latitude,
            latLng1.longitude,
            latLng2.latitude,
            latLng2.longitude,
            results);
    return results[0];
}
```

Another operation common for location-based applications is to determine if you are inside a certain area or not. The most common case is to define an area as a rectangle formed by two coordinates. However, sometimes you have a number of coordinates around which you first want to form the smallest bounding rectangle.

```
public LatLngBounds getBoundsForPoints(List<LatLng> coordinates) {
    LatLngBounds.Builder builder = LatLngBounds.builder();
    for (LatLng coordinate : coordinates) {
        builder.include(coordinate);
    }
    return builder.build();
}

public boolean isWithinBound(LatLng latLng, LatLngBounds bounds) {
    return bounds.contains(latLng);
}
```

The two preceding methods demonstrate how you can use the class LatLngBounds to create a rectangle around a number of points. You can then use the LatLngBounds.contains() method to determine whether another LatLng object is contained within that rectangle.

Geocoding

At this point you should be familiar with the `GoogleMaps` class and how to work with locations in Android using the new Location API. However, locations are defined as latitude and longitude, which is rarely useful for users of your application. Most users are more familiar with streets, city names, and names of places. To find a useful name for a certain latitude and longitude, Android provides the `Geocoder` class:

```
public static Address getAddressForLocation(Context context, Location
    location) {
    try {
        Geocoder geocoder = new Geocoder(context);
        List<Address> addresses = geocoder.
            getFromLocation(location.getLatitude(),
                    location.getLongitude(),
                    1);
        if(addresses != null && addresses.size() > 0) {
            return addresses.get(0);
        } else {
            return null;
        }
    } catch (IOException e) {
        return null;
    }
}

public String getStreetNameForAddress(Address address) {
    String streetName = address.getAddressLine(0);
    if(streetName == null) {
        streetName = address.getThoroughfare();
    }
    return streetName;
}
```

The first method shows how to retrieve the first matching `Address` for a certain `Location`. There can be multiple matches, so one alternative could be to provide the user with a list from which they can select the address that matches.

The `Address` object is a bit vague on what the different fields represent because they can vary depending on your country and location.

The second method usually gives you the current street name. However, always assume that the fields returned from an `Address` object can be null.

Using the LocationClient

The new fused Location Manager is accessed through the `LocationClient` class. This class is used to listen for location updates and to perform geofencing operations. I recommend that you create this instance in `onCreate()` and release the API in `onDestroy()`.

Initialize the Location API as shown in the following code:

```
@Override
protected void onCreate() {
    super.onCreate();
    setContentView(R.layout.activity_main);
    MapFragment mapFragment = (MapFragment) getFragmentManager().
                                                findFragmentById(R.id.map);
    mMap = mapFragment.getMap();
    mLocationCallbacks = new MyLocationCallbacks();
    mLocationClient = new LocationClient(this,
            mLocationCallbacks, mLocationCallbacks);
    mLocationClient.connect();
}

@Override
protected void onDestroy() {
    super.onDestroy();
    if (mLocationClient != null && mLocationClient.isConnected()) {
        mLocationClient.disconnect();
        mLocationClient = null;
    }
}
```

This is an asynchronous API, so you need to register the relevant callbacks as well. Remember to disconnect the LocationClient in the correct callback as well:

```
private class MyLocationCallbacks
        implements GooglePlayServicesClient.ConnectionCallbacks,
        GooglePlayServicesClient.OnConnectionFailedListener,
        LocationListener {


    @Override
    public void onConnected(Bundle bundle) {
        LocationRequest locationRequest = new LocationRequest();
        locationRequest.setSmallestDisplacement(TWENTYFIVE_METERS);
        locationRequest.setExpirationDuration(FIVE_MIUTES);
        mLocationClient.requestLocationUpdates(locationRequest, this);
    }

    @Override
    public void onDisconnected() {

    }

    @Override
    public void onConnectionFailed(ConnectionResult connectionResult) {
        // TODO Error handling...
    }
```

```
    @Override
    public void onLocationChanged(Location location) {
        LatLng latLng = new LatLng(location.getLatitude(),
                location.getLongitude());
        CameraPosition cameraPosition = new CameraPosition.Builder()
                .target(latLng)
                .zoom(17)
                .bearing(90)
                .tilt(30)
                .build();
        mMap.animateCamera(CameraUpdateFactory.
                              newCameraPosition(cameraPosition));
    }
}
```

The callback just shown requests location updates every 25 meters for the next 5 minutes. After you receive the call to `onConnected()`, you cannot perform any operations on the `LocationClient`. Also, it's good practice to set the expiration duration for your `LocationRequest` to a low number and renew the request if needed. Doing so reduces the risk of unnecessary battery consumption.

When a callback to `onLocationChanged()` is triggered, you update the camera position for the `GoogleMap` object. In this example, you perform an animation of the camera movement to the new location, which is an efficient way of displaying the map as soon as possible and moving the camera as soon as the asynchronous location request is complete.

Geofencing

One of the best features of the new Location API for Android is geofencing. Basically, geofencing allows you to define a circle that represents a virtual fence around a specific location (longitude and latitude). Whenever the device comes within the area of that circle, it will notify your application. A `Geofence` is defined by the latitude, longitude, and a radius in meters, which is then registered using the new Location API with expiration time, transition type ("enter" or "exit") and an ID.

The following is the callback method you can set for long taps on a `GoogleMap` object:

```
public void onMapLongClick(LatLng latLng) {
    Geofence.Builder builder = new Geofence.Builder();
    builder.setCircularRegion(latLng.latitude,
                              latLng.longitude,
                              TWENTYFIVE_METERS);
    builder.setExpirationDuration(ONE_WEEK);
    // For now, use the lat/long as ID.
    String geofenceRequestId = latLng.latitude + ","
                             + latLng.longitude;
    builder.setRequestId(geofenceRequestId);
    // Only interested in entering the geofence for now...
    builder.setTransitionTypes(Geofence.GEOFENCE_TRANSITION_ENTER);
    List<Geofence> geofences = new ArrayList<Geofence>();
```

```
                    geofences.add(builder.build());
                    Intent intent = new Intent(MyIntentService.
                                                  ACTION_NOTIFY_ENTERED_GEOFENCE);
                    PendingIntent pendingIntent = PendingIntent.getService(this,
                                                                     1001,
                                                                     intent,
                                                                     0);
             mLocationClient.addGeofences(geofences, pendingIntent,
                        new LocationClient.OnAddGeofencesResultListener() {
                            @Override
                            public void onAddGeofencesResult(int status,
                                                        String[] strings) {
                                if (status == LocationStatusCodes.SUCCESS) {
                                    double latitude = Double.parseDouble(strings[0])
                                    double longitude = Double.parseDouble(strings[0])
                                    LatLng latLng = new LatLng(latitude, longitude);
                                    Circle circle = mMap.addCircle(new
             CircleOptions().
                                            fillColor(Color.GREEN).
                                            strokeWidth(5).
                                            strokeColor(Color.BLACK).
                                            center(latLng).
                                            visible(true).
                                            radius(TWENTYFIVE_METERS));
                                    mGeoReminders.add(circle);
                                } else {
                                    // TODO: Error handling...
                                }
                            }
                    });
             }
```

Here, you add a new `Geofence` at the position where the user performs a long tap. As with the other operations on the `LocationClient`, this is an asynchronous call. After the callback is triggered, you check the result and if the addition of the new `Geofence` was a success, you create a circle on the `GoogleMap` object indicating where the `Geofence` is registered.

This example shows how to combine drawing objects on top of a `GoogleMap` with the `Geofence` API. The `PendingIntent` in the preceding example contains information about the `Geofences` that was triggered.

The following `IntentService` will, in this case, show a notification to the user that a `Geofence` has been triggered:

```
public class MyIntentService extends IntentService {
    public static final String TAG = "MyIntentService";
    public static final String ACTION_NOTIFY_ENTERED_GEOFENCE =
                        "com.aptl.locationandmapsdemo.NOTIFY_ENTER_
GEOFENCE";
    private int mNextNotificationId = 1;
```

```
    public MyIntentService() {
        super(TAG);
    }

    @Override
    protected void onHandleIntent(Intent intent) {
        String action = intent.getAction();

        if (LocationClient.hasError(intent)) {
            // TODO: Error handling...
        } else {
            List<Geofence> geofences =
                             LocationClient.
getTriggeringGeofences(intent);
            for (Geofence geofence : geofences) {
                showNotification(geofence);
            }
        }
    }

    private void showNotificat(Geofence geofence) {
        // TODO: Show notification to user
    }
}
```

Activity Recognition

The final part of the new Location API is Activity Recognition. This feature is controlled by the class `ActivityRecognitionClient` that works much as the `LocationClient` does.

In the following example, you can see a simple `Activity` that initiates and connects to the `ActivityRecognitionClient`:

```
public class ActivityRecognition extends Activity implements
        GooglePlayServicesClient.ConnectionCallbacks,
        GooglePlayServicesClient.OnConnectionFailedListener {
    private static final long THIRTY_SECONDS = 1000 * 30;
    private static final long FIVE_SECONDS = 1000 * 5;
    private boolean mActivityRecognitionReady = false;
    private ActivityRecognitionClient mActivityRecognitionClient;
    private PendingIntent mPendingIntent;

    @Override
    protected void onCreate(Bundle savedInstanceState) {
        super.onCreate(savedInstanceState);
        mActivityRecognitionReady = false;
        setContentView(R.layout.activity_recognition);
        mActivityRecognitionClient =
                new ActivityRecognitionClient(this, this, this);
        mActivityRecognitionClient.connect();
    }
```

```
    @Override
    protected void onDestroy() {
        super.onDestroy();
        if (mActivityRecognitionClient != null
                && mActivityRecognitionClient.isConnected()) {
            mActivityRecognitionClient.disconnect();
            mActivityRecognitionClient = null;
        }
    }

    public void doStartActivityRecognition(View view) {
        if (mActivityRecognitionReady) {
            Intent intent = new Intent(MyIntentService.
                    ACTION_NOTIFY_ACTIVITY_DETECTED);
            mPendingIntent =
                    PendingIntent.getService(this, 2001, intent, 0);
            mActivityRecognitionClient.
                    requestActivityUpdates(FIVE_SECONDS,
                            mPendingIntent);
        }
    }

    @Override
    public void onConnected(Bundle bundle) {
        mActivityRecognitionReady = true;
        findViewById(R.id.start_activity_recognition_btn).
setEnabled(false);
    }

    @Override
    public void onDisconnected() {
        mActivityRecognitionReady = false;
        findViewById(R.id.start_activity_recognition_btn).
setEnabled(true);
    }

    @Override
    public void onConnectionFailed(ConnectionResult connectionResult) {
        mActivityRecognitionReady = false;
        findViewById(R.id.start_activity_recognition_btn).
setEnabled(true);
        // Error handling...
    }
}
```

The click listener (doStartActivityRecognition()) starts the request for activity (not to be confused with the Activity component) changes and provides a PendingIntent that will be sent to the same IntentService as shown earlier, but with modifications for handling activity changes as well. When requesting activity changes, a frequency of 5 seconds is selected. You adapt this frequency depending on the needs of your application. The higher the frequency, the more battery your application will consume.

```java
protected void onHandleIntent(Intent intent) {
    String action = intent.getAction();

    if (ACTION_NOTIFY_ACTIVITY_DETECTED.equals(action)){
        if (ActivityRecognitionResult.hasResult(intent)) {
            ActivityRecognitionResult result = ActivityRecognitionResult.
                    extractResult(intent);
            DetectedActivity detectedActivity =
                                        result.getMostProbableActivity();
            Log.d(TAG, "Detected activity: " + detectedActivity);
            if(detectedActivity.getType() != mLastDetectedActivity) {
                mLastDetectedActivity = detectedActivity.getType();
                showNotification(detectedActivity);
            }
        }
    } else if (ACTION_NOTIFY_ENTERED_GEOFENCE.equals(action)) {
        ... Geofencing detection showed in previous section...
    }
}

private void showNotification(DetectedActivity detectedActivity) {
    Notification.Builder builder = new Notification.Builder(this);
    builder.setContentTitle("Activity change!");
    builder.setContentText("Activity changed to: "
            + getActivityName(detectedActivity.getType()));
    builder.setSmallIcon(R.drawable.ic_launcher);
    NotificationManager manager =
            (NotificationManager) getSystemService(NOTIFICATION_SERVICE);
    manager.notify(2001, builder.build());
}

private String getActivityName(int type) {
    switch (type) {
        case DetectedActivity.IN_VEHICLE:
            return "In vehicle";
        case DetectedActivity.ON_BICYCLE:
            return "On bicycle";
        case DetectedActivity.ON_FOOT:
            return "On foot";
        case DetectedActivity.STILL:
            return "Still";
    }
    return "Unknown";
}
```

The three preceding methods show how the `IntentService` listens to both geofencing and activity changes. When an activity change occurs, the result is retrieved through `ActivityRecognitionResult.extractResult()`. From that point, you can inspect the type and the confidence of the detection result.

This API can provide you with very accurate information about the users' behavior and the context they are in at the moment. If a user is on a bicycle or in a vehicle, you could adapt the interface of the application and rely more on speech recognition and text-to-speech. If the device reports that it is still for a while, you can make further assumptions and adapt the behavior of your application accordingly.

Summary

The new Location API provided by Google doesn't enable anything that Android developers didn't have access to before. There has always been a Location API in the Android platform, and there have been third-party libraries that estimate the users' activity by reading the sensors. However, with the new API, you have an easy-to-use solution that works across all Android devices and is guaranteed to work as long as the device has Google Play Services installed. The new API is very easy to use and can easily be integrated into any existing application with little effort.

By combining the new Maps and Location API with Geofencing and Activity Recognition, you have a set of really powerful tools for building context- and location-aware applications that otherwise could take months to develop. You can now build new types of location-based social games much easier than ever possible before.

When your application is aware of the current context for the users, you can create a much richer user experience and provide a user interface that varies depending on the situation.

However, beware of overusing these APIs because they do have an impact on battery consumption. Requesting too frequent updates will consume a lot of power. Experiment and see what rate suits your application best.

Further Resources

Documentation

Google Maps Android API v2: `https://developers.google.com/maps/documentation/android`

Websites

The Google APIs Console for setting up API access and new keys for your project: `https://code.google.com/apis/console`

Developer guidelines for location-aware applications: `http://developer.android.com/training/location/index.html`

Chapter 14

Native Code and JNI

Although the Java-based APIs available for Android are usually sufficient for most applications, a time will come when you need to go native. You'll find several reasons for having to use native code in your application. Perhaps you have an existing proprietary native library that you need to integrate with an application on Android and re-implementing it in Java would take too much time. Another common reason is performance. Most performance-critical code in Android is already running in native, not within the Dalvik VM. When you need to use a performance-critical library, it's often better to use the native version than trying to find, or port, a Java version.

I begin this chapter by explaining how to write pure native applications for Android. Because games are the most common reason for writing pure native applications, I also show how to use OpenGL ES 2.0 for Android in C. Next, I show how you can mix Java and native code to get the best from both worlds. Then I introduce the basics of the Java Native Interface (JNI) and how you can use it in your code. Finally, I take you through an example of how to integrate an existing native C library in your Java application using the stand-alone toolchain.

For this chapter, I assume that you have at least a basic knowledge of the C programming language. However, even if you don't, this chapter can help you understand how to work with native code for your Android application.

A Note on CPU Architecture

When you build a piece of native code with the Android NDK, it will match a specific application binary interface (ABI). These ABIs represent the different types of CPU architectures that Android supports. At the time of this writing, the vast majority of Android devices run on ARM CPUs, or more specifically, ARMv7a. This is an extension of the standard ARM architecture, but it supports a number of more advanced features such as hardware floating-point computation. The ABIs supported by the Android NDK are *armeabi* (basic 32-bit ARM support), *armeabi-v7a* (ARMv7), *x86* (32-bit Intel x86 or IA-32), and *mips* (MIPS32 revision 1).

When you're building your native code, consider which CPU architecture (ABI) your application needs to support. If you compile your code only for ARMv7, your application won't be visible on the Google Play Store for devices with the other CPU architectures. In this way you can use native libraries as a sort of filter for the Google Play Store as well.

You're now probably asking why you shouldn't build your native code for every possible platform because you just need to specify which ABIs you target in the build script (see "Android NDK Build Scripts," later in this chapter). The reason for not choosing to support all ABIs is that the native code you're compiling may not support some platforms. For instance, if your native code uses a specific CPU feature, porting your code to other architectures may require a bit of extra work.

Writing Android Applications in C

The C programming language is one of the oldest programming languages still in use. Dennis Ritchie originally developed it between 1969 and 1973 at AT&T Bell Labs. The language was standardized as ANSI C or C89 in 1989 and has since received several updates, named according to the year of release—for example, C90, C99, and C11. The latest version, C11, was approved in December 2011.

In this chapter, I've intentionally focused on writing native code in C and excluded instructions and examples for C++. Although a lot of the code here will work for C++, in some situations, C++ requires different handling, and mixing the instructions for both of these languages can be confusing. Refer to the official Android NDK documentation on how to use C++ to write native code for your applications.

Android has support for writing all or parts of your application in native C. To get started, you first need to download the Android Native Development Kit (NDK) from the Android Developers site, which comes as a ZIP file that you extract in your home directory.

You can find the full instructions on downloading and installing the Android NDK at http://developer.android.com/tools/sdk/ndk.

Android NDK Build Scripts

After you download and extract the Android NDK, you can start developing native-only applications. However, you still need the standard Android SDK to package your code into a working APK. You need to place all the native code that your application will run in the `jni` directory of the main sources in your project.

In order for Android to understand how to compile your native code, you need to provide the NDK with the proper build scripts. These files use the same syntax as the normal GNU makefiles, but their names differ from what you find in source code you compile for Linux desktops or similar UNIX-based operating systems.

The only file required is `Android.mk`. Here is a simple example of such a file:

```
LOCAL_PATH := $(call my-dir)

include $(CLEAR_VARS)

LOCAL_MODULE    := native-activity
LOCAL_SRC_FILES := main.c
LOCAL_LDLIBS    := -llog -landroid -lEGL -lGLESv1_CM
LOCAL_STATIC_LIBRARIES := android_native_app_glue

include $(BUILD_SHARED_LIBRARY)

$(call import-module,android/native_app_glue)
```

This example is taken from the native-activity sample application found in the Android NDK (<ndk root>/ samples/native-activity/). I'm using this sample code as a foundation for explaining how a native-only Android application works. Notice the line starting with LOCAL_STATIC_LIBRARIES that tells the build system to include a local static library when building this code, a detail I get back to in the section "Porting a Native Library to Android."

The second file is Application.mk, which describes which native modules are needed by your application. Here you also can define additional build parameters, as shown in this example:

```
APP_ABI := all
APP_PLATFORM := android-10
```

Note in the preceding example that the contents of Application.mk. APP_ABI are used to tell which ABIs this application supports—in this case, all the ABIs supported by the current NDK. APP_PLATFORM is similar to the uses-sdk element in the manifest and specifies which Android API level is supported.

Native Activities

After you define the build files, you can move on to the code for your application. The example in this section is still based on the native-activity sample found in the Android NDK.

```
<activity
        android:name="android.app.NativeActivity"
        android:label="@string/app_name"
        android:configChanges="orientation|keyboardHidden">
    <meta-data
            android:name="android.app.lib_name"
            android:value="native-activity"/>
    <intent-filter>
        <action android:name="android.intent.action.MAIN"/>
        <category android:name="android.intent.category.LAUNCHER"/>
    </intent-filter>
</activity>
```

Note: How you define the main Activity in your manifest differs from Java-based applications. A native Activity will always use the name android.app.NativeActivity.

Next, you specify which native library should be loaded through the meta-data element with the name android.app.func_name. This library must be the same as what you specified for LOCAL_MODULE in the Android.mk file.

When writing a native-only application using the NativeActivity, you have a number of choices. The native-activity sample found in the Android NDK shows the method that most developers are likely to be interested in. It uses the API provided by android_native_app_glue.h, which makes it easier to handle the threading and also shows how to set up sensor and event input.

```
#include <jni.h>
#include <errno.h>
```

```
#include <EGL/egl.h>
#include <GLES/gl.h>

#include <android/sensor.h>
#include <android/log.h>
#include <android_native_app_glue.h>
```

In the preceding code, notice the included headers from the file `main.c` in the native-activity sample. By including `android_native_app_glue.h` in your native code and also including the local static library `android_native_app_glue` in `Android.mk`, you get a lot of boilerplate code for free. As a result, you can focus on the actual work of your application, instead of having to set up everything yourself and manage all the threading.

The following function is the entry point for your native `Activity` when using the `android_native_app_glue` library. Because of the amount of code involved, I didn't include the actual code from the native-activity sample, but you can refer to the sample in the Android NDK for the specific details.

```
void android_main(struct android_app* state) {
    // Application initialization and setup goes here...

    state->onInputEvent = engine_handle_input;

    while(1) {
        // Application thread loops here...
    }
}
```

The parameter state has the type of an `android_app` pointer, which points to a `struct` where you can access application data and set callback functions. In the preceding code, you see how to give a pointer to a previously declared function that implements the input event handling. Here is an example of how such a function is declared:

```
static int32_t engine_handle_input(struct android_app* app, AInputEvent*
event) {
    // Handle input events here...
}
```

The examples in this section provide a brief introduction for implementing your native-only Android application. Refer to the native-activity sample in the Android NDK for further details and additional examples of how to use OpenGL ES on the native side for your application.

Working with JNI

When writing an application with both native C and managed Java code, you need to use the Java Native Interface (JNI) for bridging. This is a software layer and API that allows native code to call methods on Java objects and Java methods to call native functions.

On the Java side, you only need to declare the methods that connect to a native function with the prefix `native`. Doing so causes the VM to look up a native function, as I show in the next section. In order for native code to invoke a method on a Java object, more work is involved, which I show in the section "Calling a Java Method from Native," later in this chapter.

Calling Native Functions from Java

To call a native function from a Java method, you need to declare a special method in your class with the keyword `native` that will work as a bridge to the native side. This declaration causes the JVM to look up a native function with the name formed by the package, class, and method name whenever that native method is invoked.

```
public class NativeSorting {

    static {
        System.loadLibrary("sorting_jni");
    }

    public NativeSorting() {

    }

    public void sortIntegers(int[] ints) {
        nativeSort(ints);
    }

    private native void nativeSort(int[] ints);
}
```

The preceding is a simplified example of a class that provides a method for sorting an array of `int`. There are two methods, besides the constructor, in this class. The first, `sortIntegers()`, is the one that you call from your other Java classes, and it's a regular Java method. The second, `nativeSort()`, is the method that points to a function in your native code. Although you can have native methods declared as public, it's good practice to keep them private and wrap their call in a Java method that can manage error handling.

Although you can write the native code from scratch, a tool called `javah` found in the Java SDK (not the Android SDK) can help you with this. This command-line tool generates a C header file with the function declaration that your native methods map to. Run the following command in the `src/main` directory of your project. Make sure you compile the Java code for your application first.

```
$ $ javah -classpath ../../build/classes/release/ -d jni/ com.aptl.
jnidemo.NativeSorting
```

The following command shows how to generate a header file for the `NativeSorting` class shown in the previous code example. The `-classpath` points to the compiled class files (usually under the `<project path>/build` directory), not the DEX file, and the `-d` parameter points to the output directory for the generated headers (usually your `jni` directory in your project). This command generates a file named `com_aptl_jnidemo_NativeSorting.h` in the `jni` directory that contains the declaration of the native function.

```
/* DO NOT EDIT THIS FILE - it is machine generated */
#include <jni.h>
/* Header for class com_apt1_jnidemo_NativeSorting */

#ifndef _Included_com_apt1_jnidemo_NativeSorting
#define _Included_com_apt1_jnidemo_NativeSorting
#ifdef __cplusplus
extern "C" {
#endif
/*
 * Class:      com_apt1_jnidemo_NativeSorting
 * Method:     nativeSort
 * Signature: ([F)V
 */
JNIEXPORT void JNICALL Java_com_apt1_jnidemo_NativeSorting_nativeSort
  (JNIEnv *, jobject, jintArray);

#ifdef __cplusplus
}
#endif
#endif
```

This code shows the generated files. As the comment on the first line says, you shouldn't edit this file. You only copy the method declaration to the .c files that implement the function.

The following code shows the implementation of the JNI function declared in the header file com_apt1_jnidemo_NativeSorting.h. This example doesn't do much in the JNI_OnLoad function, other than return a constant indicating that this code follows JNI version 1.6, which is the one supported by the Dalvik VM.

```
#include <jni.h>
#include <android/log.h>
#include "com_apt1_jnidemo_NativeSorting.h"

void quicksort(int *arr, int start, int end);

JNIEXPORT jint JNI_OnLoad(JavaVM *vm, void *reserved) {
    return JNI_VERSION_1_6;
}

JNIEXPORT void JNICALL Java_com_apt1_jnidemo_NativeSorting_nativeSort
  (JNIEnv *env, jobject obj, jintArray data) {
    jint* array = (*env)->GetIntArrayElements(env, data, 0);
    jint length = (*env)->GetArrayLength(env, data);
    quicksort(array, 0, length);
    (*env)->ReleaseIntArrayElements(env, data, array, 0);
}

void quicksort(int *arr, int start, int end)
{
    // Left out as an exercise for your upcoming interview at Google...
}
```

In this example, the calls to `GetIntArrayElements`, `GetArrayLength`, and `ReleaseIntArray Elements` are the JNI-specific code. The first function call retrieves a pointer to the internal data of the array that can be passed to regular C function. The second one gives you the size of the array. Finally, the third one tells the JVM that the native side is done with the array and that it can copy back its content. These function calls are needed because the complex data types (arrays and objects) that are passed from Java to native through JNI must be accessed through the `JNIEnv` object.

Note: The call to `GetIntArrayElements` returns a `jint` pointer, which points to the data within the `jintArray` received in the function, and you can treat the `jint` pointer as a normal `int` pointer.

The preceding JNI example is for demonstration purposes only; you should always perform sorting of this kind using `Arrays.sort()` or `Collections.sort()`. **Normally, you won't need to perform sorting on the native side because the Java implementation is fast enough.**

Calling a Java Method from Native

Calling a Java method from the native side is a bit more complicated than calling a native function from Java. Because Java is object-oriented, every method call must be made toward a Java object (or toward a Java class for static methods). Thus you need to get a reference not only to the method but also to the object you want to call the method on. This is where the `JNIenv`, `JavaVM`, and `jobject` parameters shown in the earlier examples become important.

Consider the example of native sorting in the previous section. Everything in that example is happening on the same thread, and the native function call will block until the sorting is completed. You can modify this so that the sorting will happen asynchronously. A callback object is passed to the native method, which will then be called by the native code using JNI functions, as shown here:

```
public void sortIntegersWithCallback(int[] ints, Callback callback) {
    nativeSortWithCallback(ints, callback);
}

private native void nativeSortWithCallback(int[] ints, Callback callback);

public interface Callback {
    void onSorted(int[]sorted);
}
```

The preceding methods show the Java side of the modified native sorting. With the following, you generate the header file as before using the `javah` tool.

```
/* DO NOT EDIT THIS FILE - it is machine generated */
#include <jni.h>
/* Header for class com_aptl_jnidemo_NativeSorting */

#ifndef _Included_com_aptl_jnidemo_NativeSorting
#define _Included_com_aptl_jnidemo_NativeSorting
#ifdef __cplusplus
```

```
extern "C" {
#endif
/*
 * Class:     com_apt1_jnidemo_NativeSorting
 * Method:    nativeSortWithCallback
 * Signature: ([ILcom/apt1/jnidemo/NativeSorting/Callback;)V
 */
JNIEXPORT void JNICALL Java_com_apt1_jnidemo_NativeSorting_
nativeSortWithCallback
  (JNIEnv *, jobject, jintArray, jobject);

#ifdef __cplusplus
}
#endif
#endif
```

Note: The function declaration contains a `jobject` parameter. This is a JNI reference to the callback object you'll use for returning the result.

The following is the new implementation of the native code for your sorting, divided into multiple parts to make things clearer. The changes from the previous example are shown in bold:

```
#include <jni.h>
#include <android/log.h>
#include <pthread.h>
#include "com_apt1_jnidemo_NativeSorting.h"

JavaVM *g_vm;

struct thread_args {
    int* data;
    int data_size;
    jobject callback;
};

void quicksort(int *arr, int start, int end);
void background_sorting(void* args);

JNIEXPORT jint JNI_OnLoad(JavaVM *vm, void *reserved) {
    g_vm = vm;
    return JNI_VERSION_1_6;
}
```

As you can see, first you include the pthread library that provides the native API for threading. Next, you declare two global variables, a reference to the `JavaVM` and a `struct` that will be used to pass arguments to the new thread. The `JavaVM` variable is assigned in the `JNI_OnLoad` function. Also note the declaration of the function `background_sorting`. This function is passed to the new thread.

```
JNIEXPORT void JNICALL
  Java_com_apt1_jnidemo_NativeSorting_nativeSortWithCallback
  (JNIEnv *env, jobject obj, jintArray data, jobject callback) {
    jint* array;
```

```
    jint length;
    jmethodID callbackMethodId;
    jclass callbackClass;
    pthread_t thread;
    struct thread_args* myThreadData = malloc(sizeof(struct thread_args));

    array = (*env)->GetIntArrayElements(env, data, 0);
    length = (*env)->GetArrayLength(env, data);
    myThreadData->data = array;
    myThreadData->data_size = length;
    myThreadData->callback = (*env)->NewGlobalRef(env, callback);

    (*env)->ReleaseIntArrayElements(env, data, array, JNI_COMMIT);

    pthread_create(&thread, NULL, (void*)background_sorting,
                    (void*) myThreadData);
}
```

In the preceding example the new JNI function mapping to your native method first allocates a new `struct thread_args` that will contain the parameters for the new thread. Next, you create a global reference to the callback object through the call to `NewGlobalRef()`, which you must do because all references in a JNI function are valid only on the current thread. This is followed by a call to `ReleaseIntArrayElements`, which notifies the VM that you're done with the `jintArray`. However, the difference between this example and the one shown in "Calling Native Functions from Java" is that you pass `JNI_COMMIT` as the last parameter—to prevent the VM from freeing the array variable that contains the data. Finally, you call `pthread_create()` to start the new thread. The third argument to `pthread_create()` is a pointer to the function that will run on the new thread, and the fourth argument is the argument passed to that function.

The following code shows the function that will execute on the background native thread:

```
void background_sorting(void* arg) {
    struct thread_args *data = (struct thread_args *) arg;
    JNIEnv* env = NULL;
    jclass callbackClass;
    jmethodID callbackMethodId;
    jintArray result;

    quicksort(data->data, 0, data->data_size);

    (*g_vm)->AttachCurrentThread(g_vm, &env, NULL);

    result = (*env)->NewIntArray(env, data->data_size);
    (*env)->SetIntArrayRegion(env, result, 0, data->data_size, data->data);

    callbackClass = (*env)->GetObjectClass(env, data->callback);
    callbackMethodId = (*env)->GetMethodID(env, callbackClass,
                                        "onSorted", "([I)V");
    (*env)->CallVoidMethod(env, data->callback, callbackMethodId, result);

    free(data->data);
    free(data);
```

```
        (*env)->DeleteGlobalRef(env, data->callback);
        (*g_vm)->DetachCurrentThread(g_vm);
}
```

First, you cast the argument back to a pointer of the expected type. You can now call `quicksort()` using these arguments to sort the array. Next, you need to connect to the Java VM, create a Java array for the result, find the callback method and invoke it, and finally free all the resources.

The call to `AttachCurrentThread()` tells the Java VM that the current thread should be connected and the `JNIEnv` argument will be assigned to a valid instance. Now you can make calls on the `JNIEnv` object and create a new Java `int` array. To find the callback method, you need to look up the class by a call to `GetObjectClass()` with the global `jobject` reference as an argument. Next, you retrieve a `jmethodID` by calling `GetMethodID()` with the `jclass`, the name of the method, and its native signature as arguments. With a `jmethodID` and a `jobject`, you can call `CallVoidMethod()` to invoke the Java method.

> The signature of a Java method is a string that identifies the arguments and the return value. You can read more about type signatures at `http://docs.oracle.com/javase/6/docs/technotes/guides/jni/spec/types.html#wp16432`.

Lastly, you free the data allocated in the `struct`, delete the global reference to the callback object, and detach the VM from this thread.

The example in this section doesn't include error handling and is used only to illustrate how to pass Java objects between two threads and how to invoke methods from a native `pthread`. The important thing to remember is to free all resources properly to avoid the most common cause of errors when using JNI.

Android Native APIs

Whether you're writing an application entirely in native C or by combining native code with Java using JNI, you will most likely need to use some of the native APIs for Android. In this section, I cover some of these APIs and how you can include them in your code.

Using a native API requires you to do two things: Add a reference in the `Android.mk` file so that your shared library will link to it and include the correct header file in your C code.

To see the full documentation for the supported native APIs, refer to the NDK documentation (`<ndk root>/documentation.html`).

The C Library

The C programming language has a standard library named C library, or *libc*. The Android implementation of this library is called Bionic and is slightly different from the standard libc implementation found on regular Linux distributions.

The Android NDK build system always links to the C library, so all you need to do when using this library is include the correct header file (`stdio.h`, `stdlib.h`, and so on). Also, the `pthread` and math libraries are automatically linked in the same way.

Native Android Logging

The logging functionality used in Android through the Java class `Log` is also available in native C through the log library. To include support for this in your native code, add the following to your `Android.mk` file:

```
LOCAL_LDLIBS := -llog
```

In your C code, you need to include the header file as follows:

```
#include <android/log.h>
```

To simplify your code, wrap the functions declared in the Android log library in a macro. Use the following code in your C code to define log macros to be used throughout your native code:

```
#define TAG "native-log-tag"
#define LOGI(...) ((void)__android_log_print(ANDROID_LOG_INFO, TAG,
    __VA_ARGS__))
#define LOGW(...) ((void)__android_log_print(ANDROID_LOG_WARN, TAG,
    __VA_ARGS__))
#define LOGE(...) ((void)__android_log_print(ANDROID_LOG_ERROR, TAG,
    __VA_ARGS__))
#define LOGD(...) ((void)__android_log_print(ANDROID_LOG_DEBUG, TAG,
    __VA_ARGS__))
```

Native OpenGL ES 2.0

If you'll be writing a pure native application, you will most likely implement the user interface for your `Activity` using OpenGL ES 2.0, as shown in an earlier example in the section "Native Activities." To use this API in your native code, add `-lGLESv2` to `LOCAL_LDLIBS` in your `Android.mk` file and include the headers `GLES2/gl2.h` and `GLES2/gl2ext.h` in your C code.

It's also a good idea to include the EGL library in order to set up a GL context. Use `-lEGL` in the `Android.mk` file and include `EGL/egl.h` and `EGL/eglext.h` in your code.

Native Audio with OpenSL ES

The native audio API in Android is based on the OpenSL ES 1.0.1 from Khronos Group. This API provides a way to perform native audio operations that is generally faster than the Java alternatives. If your application requires very low-latency audio, use this API. To include the API, use the following flag in your `Android.mk` file:

```
LOCAL_LDLIBS += -lOpenSLES
```

Use the following `include` statements in your code to utilize both the standard OpenSL ES API and the Android-specific extensions:

```
#include <SLES/OpenSLES.h>
#include <SLES/OpenSLES_Platform.h>
#include <SLES/OpenSLES_Android.h>
#include <SLES/OpenSLES_AndroidConfiguration.h>
```

Porting a Native Library to Android

Often you will have the source code for an existing, usually open-source, library that you want to integrate into your application. However, doing so can be difficult because these libraries are often built around the traditional build system (usually a GNU makefile generated by the tools Autoconf and Automake) for Linux or other UNIX operating systems. You could copy all the required source files and write a new `Android.mk` file from scratch that configures the build and includes the right headers. However, this approach can prove very time-consuming and error-prone, but luckily there's a way around this issue.

The Android NDK provides the capability to generate a stand-alone toolchain that works in the same way as the standard toolchain on your computer. By referring to this toolchain when building the library, you can use the build system the source code is configured for and build a binary library that you can include in your application. This process makes it easy to port an existing native library written in C/C++ and reduces the complexity of your builds as well.

To build the stand-alone toolchain, run the following command:

```
$NDK/build/tools/make-standalone-toolchain.sh --platform=android-5
--install-dir=<install path>
```

This command creates a new stand-alone toolchain for the ARM ABI and Android API level 5. If you don't provide the `install-dir` parameter, a compressed archive with the toolchain is placed in your system's `temp` directory.

Building a Native Library

The library for the example in this section is the audio codec library called *Opus*. This is a free, open-source audio codec that provides an excellent result for interactive speech as well as streaming music over the Internet. This library uses technology from both the SILK codec from Skype and the CELT codec from Xiph.org. I don't go into the details of how Opus works; instead, I focus on the fact that you can encode and decode between a large audio frame recorded in PCM format and a much smaller Opus packet.

You can download the source code and read more about the Opus codec at http://opus-codec.org.

Even though this example uses the Opus audio codec, the same method applies to most other native libraries that support Linux. Simply download your library and perform the same operations shown in this section.

After you download and extract the library, you need to configure your environment before building.

```
$ export PATH=$TOOLCHAINS/arm-linux-androideabi-4.6/bin/:${PATH}
$ export CC=arm-linux-androideabi-gcc
$ export CXX=arm-linux-androideabi-g++
```

These commands prefix your path so that the binaries in your toolchain have precedence over the default ones for your operating system. It will also set two environment variables used by the build systems to determine which compiler architecture to use.

Install all your stand-alone toolchains in a common directory and assign an environment variable. This way, you can easily refer to a specific toolchain.

This command generates the file `Makefile` used for compiling and installing the library at the specified position (note that `<project path>` requires an absolute path).

```
opus-1.0.2 $ ./configure --prefix=<project path>/jni/libopus --host=
arm-eabi
```

The preceding command needs to be executed in the directory where you extracted the Opus source code and in the same terminal where you configured your environment. It sets up the build parameters for your sources. The host parameter tells the configure script which CPU is to be targeted. The prefix parameter decides where the compiled binaries and header files are installed. Use the directory of your Android application as a prefix if that is where you wish the compiled library to be placed. Note that if the `jni` and `libopus` directories are missing, they will be created.

Before you can continue and build the library, you probably need to manually edit the generated makefile. In a normal UNIX environment, you can have several versions of the same library installed, which are identified by an internal version number as well as their filename (for instance, `libXYZ.1.2.3.so`). The Android NDK doesn't support this version information, so before you build the library, you need to tell the build system to avoid applying any version information. You do so by editing the file `Makefile` that was generated by the configure script. Open the file in a text editor and find the line that appears as follows:

```
libopus_la_LDFLAGS = -no-undefined -version-info 3:0:3
```

Now remove the `-version-info` argument and replace it with the argument `-avoid-version`, which tells the build system not to add this information in the compiled result. The result will appear as follows:

```
libopus_la_LDFLAGS = -no-undefined -avoid-version
```

Now you're ready to compile and install your library in your project's `jni` directory:

```
opus-1.0.2 $ make ; make install
```

The preceding line is actually two commands, make and make install. The first command compiles the code according to the configuration set up by the configure script. make install copies all the resulting binaries and other files to the installation directory. You have now successfully installed the compiled Opus as an ARM binary in the jni directory of your project. You're ready to configure the NDK makefiles and implement the JNI bridge to call the library.

Static Library Module

The library you just built consists of the actual library binary named libopus.so as well as a number of C header files. The header files are required in order to call the functions inside the library itself. When building your native code with the NDK, be sure to define a separate module for the native library. This is why the output path was <project path>jni/libopus and not simply <project path>/jni. The Android.mk file you place in the libopus directory looks like this:

```
LOCAL_PATH := $(call my-dir)
include $(CLEAR_VARS)
LOCAL_MODULE := libopus
LOCAL_SRC_FILES := libopus.so
LOCAL_EXPORT_C_INCLUDES := $(LOCAL_PATH)/include
include $(PREBUILT_SHARED_LIBRARY)
```

The makefile configuration described in the preceding examples defines the module as a shared library and exports the include files found in the include directory. Because no sources need to be compiled for this module (you already did that in the previous section), you specify only the libopus.so file as the source files to be included.

JNI Module for Native Library

It's time to create a new directory named opus_jni next to the libopus directory. This is where your JNI wrapper module for the native library is implemented. Start with the Android.mk file that will import your module.

```
LOCAL_PATH := $(call my-dir)
include $(CLEAR_VARS)
LOCAL_MODULE     := opus_jni
LOCAL_SRC_FILES := opus_jni.c
LOCAL_LDLIBS := -llog
LOCAL_SHARED_LIBRARIES := libopus
include $(BUILD_SHARED_LIBRARY)
$(call import-module,libopus)
```

This Android.mk file tells the NDK to include the static local library libopus in your build, just as was done in the native-activity sample shown in "Android NDK Build Scripts," earlier in this chapter. The next step is to define the Java class that will provide the native methods.

The following class loads the library named opus_jni, and for each new instance, a new encoder and a new decoder are initialized. You then have two public methods, encodePcm() and decodeOpus(), that do the actual codec work. Finally, there is a destroy() method that frees up the memory used by the codec. You now use the javah tool, as shown earlier, to generate the header file for these functions. After you have the header file, you can start implementing the JNI code.

```java
public class OpusCodec {

    {
        System.loadLibrary("opus_jni");
    }

    public OpusCodec(int sampleRate, int channels) {
        initOpusEncoder(sampleRate, channels);
        initOpusDecoder(sampleRate, channels);
    }

    private native void initOpusDecoder(int sampleRate, int channels);
    public native int decodeOpus(byte[] encodedData,
                                 int encodedLength,
                                 short[] pcmOutput,
                                 int pcmLength);
    private native void initOpusEncoder(int sampleRate, int channels);
    public native int encodePcm(short[] pcmData,
                                int pcmLength,
                                byte[] encodedData,
                                int encodedLength);

    public native void destroy();
}
```

Here is the entire JNI code, piece by piece, starting with the header files and definitions:

```c
#include <opus/opus.h>
#include <opus/opus_defines.h>
#include <opus/opus_types.h>
#include <opus/opus_multistream.h>
#include <android/log.h>
#include <string.h>
#include <stdlib.h>
#include <time.h>
#include "com_apt1_opus_OpusCodecTest_OpusCodec.h"

#define LOG_TAG "OpusTest"
#define LOGD(LOG_TAG, ...) __android_log_print(ANDROID_LOG_DEBUG, LOG_TAG,
    __VA_ARGS__)
#define LOGV(LOG_TAG, ...) __android_log_print(ANDROID_LOG_VERBOSE, LOG_
TAG,
    __VA_ARGS__)
#define LOGE(LOG_TAG, ...) __android_log_print(ANDROID_LOG_ERROR, LOG_TAG,
    __VA_ARGS__)

OpusDecoder* gOpusDecoder;
OpusEncoder* gOpusEncoder;

JNIEXPORT jint JNI_OnLoad(JavaVM *vm, void *reserved) {
    return JNI_VERSION_1_6;
}
```

As shown here, the locally generated header files for the JNI functions and the headers for the Opus codec that are located in the `libopus` module are included. The two global variables, `OpusDecoder` and `OpusEncoder`, are the references to the decoder and encoder objects in the Opus library.

You also define the shorter log functions as well as the default `JNI_OnLoad` function to tell the system that it supports the correct JNI version.

```
/*
 * Class:     com_aptl_opus_OpusCodecTest_OpusCodec
 * Method:    initOpusDecoder
 * Signature: (II)I
 */
JNIEXPORT void JNICALL Java_com_aptl_opus_OpusCodecTest_OpusCodec_
initOpusDecoder
  (JNIEnv *env, jobject obj, jint sampleRate, jint channels) {
    int error;
    gOpusDecoder = opus_decoder_create(sampleRate, channels, &error);
    LOGD(LOG_TAG, "Decoder initialized: %d", error);
}

/*
 * Class:     com_aptl_opus_OpusCodecTest_OpusCodec
 * Method:    initOpusEncoder
 * Signature: (II)I
 */
JNIEXPORT void JNICALL Java_com_aptl_opus_OpusCodecTest_OpusCodec_
initOpusEncoder
  (JNIEnv *env, jobject obj, jint sampleRate, jint channels) {
      int error;
      gOpusEncoder = opus_encoder_create(sampleRate, channels,
                                OPUS_APPLICATION_VOIP, &error);
}
```

The two `init` functions call the respective `create` function from the Opus library. In this example, you provide the encoder with a parameter telling it to optimize its processing for VoIP applications.

```
/*
 * Class:     com_aptl_opus_OpusCodecTest_OpusCodec
 * Method:    decodeOpus
 * Signature: ([BI[BIZ)I
 */
JNIEXPORT jint JNICALL Java_com_aptl_opus_OpusCodecTest_OpusCodec_
decodeOpus
  (JNIEnv *env, jobject obj, jbyteArray in, jint inLength, jshortArray
out,
  jint outLength) {
    opus_int32 encodedBytes;
    jbyte* jniIn;
    jshort* jniOut;

    if(in != NULL) {
```

```
            jniIn = (*env)->GetByteArrayElements(env, in, NULL);
            jniOut = (*env)->GetShortArrayElements(env, out, NULL);

            encodedBytes = opus_decode(gOpusDecoder,
                                       jniIn,
                                       inLength,
                                       jniOut,
                                       outLength, 0);

            (*env)->ReleaseByteArrayElements(env, in, jniIn, JNI_ABORT);
            (*env)->ReleaseShortArrayElements(env, out, jniOut, 0);
        } else {
            jniOut = (*env)->GetShortArrayElements(env, out, NULL);

            encodedBytes = opus_decode(gOpusDecoder,
                                       NULL,
                                       0,
                                       jniOut,
                                       (*env)->GetArrayLength(env, out), 1);

        }

    return encodedBytes;
}
```

The decode function allows the input to the opus_decode function to be null, which handles situations where you're missing an incoming packet of Opus data because of network latency and want the decoder to handle the situation. The Opus library is designed to handle such cases and will generate a PCM package to fill out missing audio.

```
/*
 * Class:     com_apt1_opus_OpusCodecTest_OpusCodec
 * Method:    encodePcm
 * Signature: ([BI[BI)I
 */
JNIEXPORT jint JNICALL Java_com_apt1_opus_OpusCodecTest_OpusCodec_
encodePcm
  (JNIEnv *env, jobject obj, jshortArray in, jint inLength, jbyteArray
out,
   jint outLength) {
    opus_int32 encodedBytes;
    jshort* jniIn;
    jbyte* jniOut;

    jniIn = (*env)->GetShortArrayElements(env, in, NULL);
    jniOut = (*env)->GetByteArrayElements(env, out, NULL);

    encodedBytes = opus_encode(gOpusEncoder,
                               jniIn,
                               inLength,
                               jniOut,
                               outLength);
```

```
        if(encodedBytes == OPUS_BAD_ARG) {
            LOGE(LOG_TAG, "OPUS_BAD_ARG");
        } else if(encodedBytes == OPUS_BUFFER_TOO_SMALL) {
            LOGE(LOG_TAG, "OPUS_BUFFER_TOO_SMALL");
        } else if(encodedBytes == OPUS_INTERNAL_ERROR) {
            LOGE(LOG_TAG, "OPUS_INTERNAL_ERROR");
        } else if(encodedBytes == OPUS_INVALID_PACKET) {
            LOGE(LOG_TAG, "OPUS_INVALID_PACKET");
        } else if(encodedBytes == OPUS_UNIMPLEMENTED) {
            LOGE(LOG_TAG, "OPUS_UNIMPLEMENTED");
        } else if(encodedBytes == OPUS_INVALID_STATE) {
            LOGE(LOG_TAG, "OPUS_INVALID_STATE");
        } else if(encodedBytes == OPUS_ALLOC_FAIL) {
            LOGE(LOG_TAG, "OPUS_ALLOC_FAIL");
        }

        (*env)->ReleaseShortArrayElements(env, in, jniIn, JNI_ABORT);
        (*env)->ReleaseByteArrayElements(env, out, jniOut, 0);

        return encodedBytes;
    }
```

The `encode` function takes PCM data represented as an array of short and encodes. The result ends up in the byte array that the Java side can work with.

The `destroy` function is the last part in this file. It's important to call this native method from your Java code as follows once you're done with the `OpusCodec` instance; otherwise, you'll leak memory.

```
/*
 * Class:     com_apt1_opus_OpusCodecTest_OpusCodec
 * Method:    destroy
 * Signature: ()V
 */
JNIEXPORT void JNICALL Java_com_apt1_opus_OpusCodecTest_OpusCodec_destroy
    (JNIEnv *env, jobject obj) {
        opus_decoder_destroy(gOpusDecoder);
        opus_encoder_destroy(gOpusEncoder);
}
```

You now have a fully functioning JNI wrapper for the Opus codec optimized for VoIP applications. With just some small modifications, you can craft this implementation to your own needs and build your own VoIP application or adapt it for streaming music.

Summary

In this chapter, I introduced you to the Android NDK and how you can use it to write and build native code for your Android applications. You can choose to write your entire application in native, which is many times the case when it comes to 3D games where there's an existing 3D engine available, or you can combine it with Java code and write native C code where further optimization is needed. Also, thousands of open-source libraries are on the Internet that you may find useful, and with the techniques shown in this chapter, you can easily port them to Android and create a simple JNI wrapper to access them from Java.

This chapter certainly isn't a comprehensive discussion of all things regarding the NDK and JNI. However, for further details, please refer to the official documentation in the Android NDK as well as the JNI specifications from Oracle, and check out "Further Resources," below.

Further Resources

Android Developers Site

"JNI Tips" specific to Android development: `http://developer.android.com/training/articles/perf-jni.html`

Oracle Websites

Oracle. "Java SE Documentation." Here you can find information on JNI Documentation: `http://docs.oracle.com/javase/7/docs/technotes/guides/jni/index.html`

Oracle. "Java Native Interface Documentation." Here you can find specification for JNI: `http://docs.oracle.com/javase/7/docs/technotes/guides/jni/spec/jniTOC.html`

Chapter 15

The Hidden Android APIs

Android developers know that tons of features in the platform aren't accessible through the official and public APIs. For instance, although Android has classes for sending SMS (`SmsManager` and `SmsMessage`), there is no official API for receiving them. Nevertheless, you can find several applications on the Google Play Store site that provide full-featured SMS clients, and many apps are built around incoming SMS. Although a simple Google search will give the necessary information for how to receive SMS in an Android application, you'll come upon many other cases where the hidden platform APIs in Android could be useful in applications.

In this chapter, I explain how and where to find hidden APIs. I also describe different methods for accessing them and how to do so in a safe and secure way.

Most of the hidden Android APIs are also protected by permissions that have a `protectionLevel` of `signature` or `system` (refer to Chapter 12). Although you can't use these APIs in regular applications you publish on the Google Play Store, you can still use them in applications you write for a custom firmware. Doing so allows you to access these APIs without changing the Android platform. (See Chapter 16 for more on how to build a custom firmware.)

Official and Hidden APIs

The official APIs are all the classes, interfaces, methods, and constants found in the SDK documentation. Although these APIs are usually enough for most applications, at times you'll want to access something more, but don't know how to find them in the official APIs.

When Google publishes the Android SDK, it contains a JAR file (`android.jar`) that you use as a reference when compiling your code. You can find this file via `<sdk root>/platforms/android-<API level>/`. The file contains only *empty* classes, meaning that it includes only the public and protected declarations and all code within the methods has been scrubbed away. This JAR file is generated as part of the SDK when you build the platform.

The scrubbed `android.jar` file is generated when the SDK is built by inspecting each source file and excluding every field (such as constants), method, and class with the JavaDoc annotation `@hide` (see Figure 15-1). This means that these symbols are still accessible to the implementation running on the device but they aren't visible at compile time.

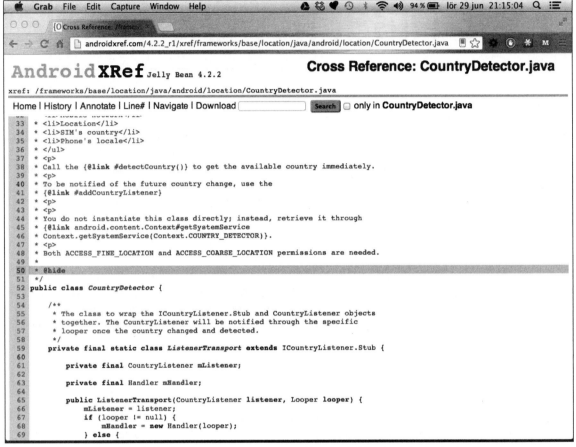

Figure 15-1 The source code for the hidden class `CountryDetector`. Note the `@hide` annotation for the JavaDoc.

Some APIs in Android are hidden automatically, without the `@hide` annotation. You can usually find these APIs in the package `com.android.internal`, which is never part of the `android.jar` but does contain lots of code for internal use in Android. You can find some of the other hidden APIs in the system applications. These APIs usually have `ContentProvider` information for the system providers that isn't included in the official SDK.

Discovering Hidden APIs

The easiest way to find the hidden APIs is to search for them in the Android source code. The source code for the Android platform is vast, but fortunately several online sites have indexed the code and made it searchable. One such site is AndroidXRef (`http://androidxref.com`), which allows you to search all the open source code for all officially released Android versions (see Figure 15-2).

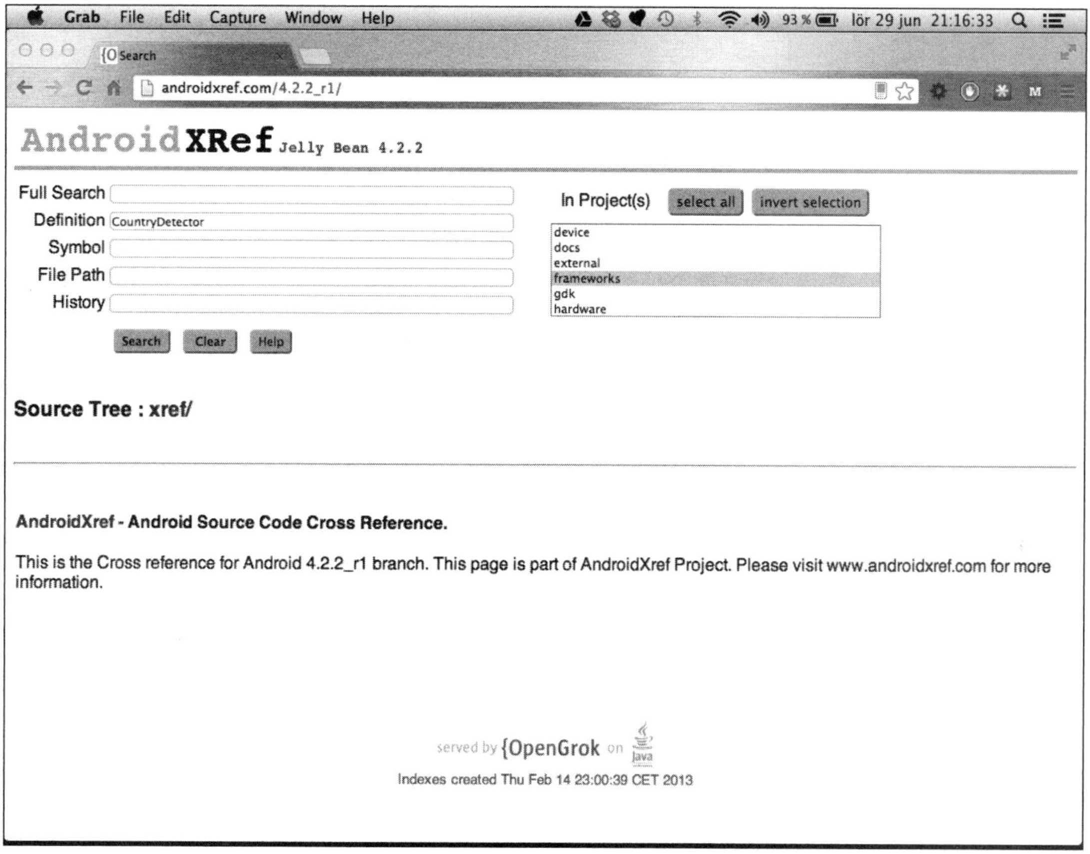

Figure 15-2 The Search dialog box at AndroidXRef

Another way to look for hidden APIs is through the View Source link on the Android API reference site (see Figure 15-3). This site doesn't provide a search method like AndroidXRef does, but it's easier to access directly from the official API documentation.

Although searching is good if you know where and what to look for, finding the code that does what you need can be difficult. You can find most of the hidden APIs in the *frameworks* project. All of the APIs in the `android` package can be found here as well as most of the APIs in `com.android.internal`.

Often the hidden API you're looking for is part of a class that is public. For instance, the `WifiManager` has several public, unhidden, methods but also a number of useful hidden methods and fields. In other cases, the class is hidden from the public API, such as the `CountryDetector` class shown earlier in Figure 15-1.

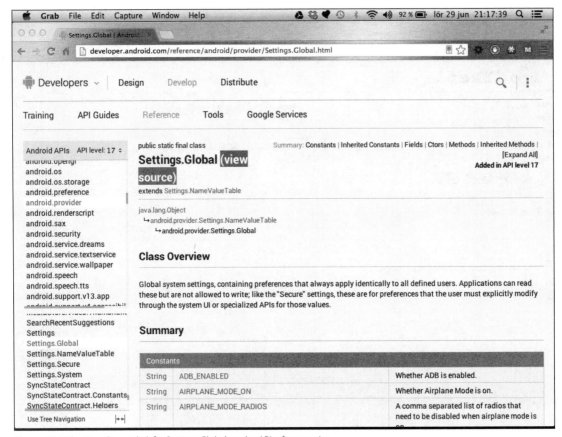

Figure 15-3 The View Source link for Settings.Global on the API reference site

Safely Calling Hidden APIs

Constant fields, such as broadcast actions or provider `Uri`, are major parts of the useful hidden APIs. You can copy these fields into your own code and use them just as they are. The easiest way to do so is to copy the entire class (for instance, directly from AndroidXRef) and place it in your project. If these hidden APIs have been changed in the different Android API levels, you can keep a copy of each version in its own package. This way, you can use a hidden API and still target multiple Android versions.

For most situations in which you need to use a hidden API that consists of constants (such as broadcast actions), I recommend copying the hidden constants from the Android source code.

For APIs that require compile-time linking—that is, interfaces, classes, and methods—you have two choices. You can compile your application with a modified SDK that contains a JAR file with all the classes and interfaces you need. The other solution is to use the Reflection API in Java to dynamically look up the classes and methods you want to call. Each method has its pros and cons, and your choice will depend on the situation.

Modifying the SDK will effectively bind your code to the device you use when generating the modified `android.jar` (see the section "Extracting Hidden APIs from Device") and could result in your code crashing on other devices if you're not careful. However, there's no performance penalty with this solution. Using the Reflections API allows you to target multiple Android versions but can penalize performance because it requires a runtime lookup of classes and methods. I discuss both these approaches in the following sections.

Extracting Hidden APIs from a Device

To do compile-time linking to the hidden APIs, you first need to extract and process the libraries from a device. You can extract these libraries either from an emulator instance or from a device because they'll be used only for compiling your code. Because this work requires a number of files from a device, I recommend that you create an empty working directory. Since you may want to perform this task for multiple API versions, you can create one working directory per API level.

```
$ adb pull /system/framework .
pull: building file list...
pull: <files pulled from device>
63 files pulled. 0 files skipped.
4084 KB/s (35028810 bytes in 8.374s)
```

Run the preceding command from your working directory, and you'll see that it pulls all the files from the directory `/system/framework` on the device. Once the extraction is completed, you can list the files, and the output should look somewhat like the following (it may vary depending on the device's manufacturer and the version of Android you're using):

```
$ ls
am.jar                                    ext.jar
am.odex                                   ext.odex
android.policy.jar                        framework-res.apk
android.policy.odex                       framework.jar
android.test.runner.jar                   framework.odex
android.test.runner.odex                  ime.jar
apache-xml.jar                            ime.odex
apache-xml.odex                           input.jar
bmgr.jar                                  input.odex
bmgr.odex                                 javax.obex.jar
bouncycastle.jar                          javax.obex.odex
bouncycastle.odex                         mms-common.jar
bu.jar                                    mms-common.odex
bu.odex                                   monkey.jar
com.android.future.usb.accessory.jar      monkey.odex
com.android.future.usb.accessory.odex     pm.jar
com.android.location.provider.jar         pm.odex
com.android.location.provider.odex        requestsync.jar
com.android.nfc_extras.jar                requestsync.odex
com.android.nfc_extras.odex               send_bug.jar
com.google.android.maps.jar               send_bug.odex
com.google.android.maps.odex              services.jar
com.google.android.media.effects.jar      services.odex
com.google.android.media.effects.odex     settings.jar
com.google.widevine.software.drm.jar      settings.odex
```

```
com.google.widevine.software.drm.odex        svc.jar
content.jar                                  svc.odex
content.odex                                 telephony-common.jar
core-junit.jar                               telephony-common.odex
core-junit.odex                              uiautomator.jar
core.jar                                     uiautomator.odex
core.odex
```

These files are all the Java-based system libraries on your Android device. They are the optimized DEX files that are loaded by the Dalvik VM. The next step is to decide which file contains the hidden APIs you want to convert back to Java class files that you can use when compiling your application. Most of the hidden APIs are placed in `framework.odex`, whereas the crypto-libraries are in the `bouncycastle.odex` file.

Starting with Android 4.2, several hidden APIs that used to be in `framework.odex` are now placed in other files. For instance, the hidden `Telephony` class is now optional (because not all Android devices have telephony support) and can now be found in `telephony-common.odex`.

Once you know which file you need to convert, you download a tool named Smali that can convert the optimized DEX files (`.odex`) to an intermediate format (`.smali`). You can then convert this intermediate format back to Java class files using another tool named dex2Jar. You can download Smali at `https://code.google.com/p/smali`, and you can find dex2Jar at `https://code.google.com/p/dex2jar`. Download both and extract them to an appropriate location (for instance, next to your working directory). Start by converting the ODEX file to the intermediate format as shown here:

```
$ mkdir android-apis-17
$ java -jar ~/Downloads/baksmali-2.0b5.jar -a 17 -x framework.odex -d . -o
android-apis-17
```

When you run this command from the same directory where you pulled the files from the device, the file `framework.odex` is converted to a number of SMALI files placed in the correct package structure in the directory `android-apis-17`. Next, you need to convert these files into a single DEX file.

```
$ java -jar ~/Downloads/smali-2.0b5.jar -a 17 -o android-apis-17.dex
android-apis-17
```

You can repeat the two preceding steps for each file you need to convert. For instance, on Android 4.2, the hidden `Telephony` class is placed in `telephony-common.odex`. This way, you can create a single JAR file in the end with all the hidden classes you need, even if they're contained in different ODEX files from the start.

Finally, you need to use the dex2Jar tool to convert the DEX file into a JAR file containing all the Java class files.

```
$ ~/Downloads/dex2jar-0.0.9.15/d2j-dex2jar.sh android-apis-17.dex
dex2jar android-apis-17.dex -> android-apis-17-dex2jar.jar
```

The resulting JAR file contains all the classes, both hidden and public, from the original ODEX file (or files). To use this file instead of the default `android.jar` in your SDK, simply rename it to `android.jar` and replace it with the one in your SDK (for instance, `<sdk root>/platforms/android-17/android.jar`). Remember to back up the original file in case you want to revert to the original SDK without the hidden APIs.

> This approach provides you with a set of platform APIs that are guaranteed to work only on the device you extracted the files from. Because this is the baseline for all other Android devices, I recommend doing this only from a Nexus device with an official factory image. Perform this only on a non-Nexus device if you need to use the hidden, proprietary APIs implemented by the device's manufacturer (for instance, a hidden camera extension API or something similar).

Error Handling for Modified SDK

When utilizing the approach for using the hidden APIs described previously, it's difficult to know whether the method signatures from your extracted classes match the ones that users have on their devices. Although modifying the SDK may work on the device you use for development, a user who installs your application may have a device where the hidden APIs are modified by the vendor. When that happens, your application will throw a `NoSuchMethodException` or `ClassNotFoundException`.

You can deal with this situation a couple of ways. You can combine this approach with the use of reflections (described in the next section) to detect the presence of your hidden APIs. In this way, you have the benefit of both solutions, which I recommend. Another way is to simply catch the exception so that you can perform some graceful degradation of the functionality.

Whatever you do, be sure to perform some error handling when calling hidden APIs. At the very least, you can limit the availability of your application to the devices you've tested on. You always want to avoid having your application crashing on a user's device.

Calling Hidden APIs Using Reflections

The Reflections API in Java (found in the `java.lang.reflect` package) gives you a safer approach than modifying the SDK does because you can use it to detect the presence of an API (or lack thereof) before calling it. However, because all binding and invocation of hidden APIs occur in runtime, this method is also slower than the alternative method described in the previous section.

Calling a hidden API using Reflections is a two-step process. First, you need to look up the class and methods you want to call and store a reference to the `Method` object. After you have this reference, you can invoke the method on an object. The two steps are shown in the following code, where you look up the method for checking the state of Wi-Fi tethering:

```
public Method getWifiAPMethod(WifiManager wifiManager) {
    try {
        Class clazz = wifiManager.getClass();
        return clazz.getMethod("isWifiApEnabled");
    } catch (NoSuchMethodException e) {
        throw new RuntimeException(e);
    }
```

```
    }

    public boolean invokeIsWifiAPEnabled(WifiManager wifiManager,
                            Method isWifiApEnabledMethod) {
        try {
            return (Boolean) isWifiApEnabledMethod.invoke(wifiManager);
        } catch (IllegalAccessException e) {
            throw new RuntimeException(e);
        } catch (InvocationTargetException e) {
            throw new RuntimeException(e);
        }
    }
}
```

The preceding example shows a fairly simple invocation using the Reflections API. If the hidden method takes parameters, you need to provide the classes for those in the call to `Class.getMethod()`. Also, in this example, the only error handling is to throw a `RuntimeException`. In your own application, you should handle errors properly and do a graceful degradation of your application's feature set.

Never assume that methods you retrieve using Reflections are available on all devices. If they're hidden, the manufacturer may have modified them and changed their signature (number of parameters, for instance). In the early days of Android, this situation was quite common because many features were missing in the platforms added by manufacturers. However, now you can usually expect the API to be there, just take care to do proper error handing and feature fallback when using the hidden APIs.

Examples of Hidden APIs

In this section, I show a few examples of how hidden APIs are used. These are some of the typical scenarios I've discovered that developers are asking for.

Receiving and Reading SMS

The most commonly requested hidden API in Android is related to receiving and reading SMS. Although the public API contains two permissions, RECEIVE_SMS and READ_SMS, the actual API for performing these actions is hidden.

An application that must be able to receive an SMS must declare the use of the RECEIVE_SMS permission and implement a `BroadcastReceiver` that is triggered for incoming SMS.

```
public class MySmsReceiver extends BroadcastReceiver {
    // Hidden constant from Telephony.java
    public static final String SMS_RECEIVED_ACTION
            = "android.provider.Telephony.SMS_RECEIVED";

    public static final String MESSAGE_SERVICE_NUMBER = "+461234567890";
    private static final String MESSAGE_SERVICE_PREFIX = "MYSERVICE";

    public void onReceive(Context context, Intent intent) {
        String action = intent.getAction();
        if (SMS_RECEIVED_ACTION.equals(action)) {
```

```
                // "pdus" is the hidden key for the SMS data
                Object[] messages =
                        (Object[]) intent.getSerializableExtra("pdus");
                for (Object message : messages) {
                    byte[] messageData = (byte[]) message;
                    SmsMessage smsMessage =
                            SmsMessage.createFromPdu(messageData);
                    processSms(smsMessage);
                }
            }
        }

        private void processSms(SmsMessage smsMessage) {
            String from = smsMessage.getOriginatingAddress();
            if (MESSAGE_SERVICE_NUMBER.equals(from)) {
                String messageBody = smsMessage.getMessageBody();
                if (messageBody.startsWith(MESSAGE_SERVICE_PREFIX)) {
                    // TODO: Message verified - start processing...
                }
            }
        }
    }
```

The preceding code shows a `BroadcastReceiver` that listens for the `Intent` action `android.provider.Telephony.SMS_RECEIVED` (remember to add this to the `intent-filter` in the manifest as well). The only "hidden" parts in this example are this `Intent` action and the `String` to retrieve SMS data from the `Intent` ("pdus").

For reading already received SMS, you need to query a hidden `ContentProvider` and declare the use of the permission `READ_SMS`. The hidden class `Telephony`, found in the `android.provider` package, provides all of the information needed. The best way to use this class is to simply copy it to your own projects and refactor it to suit your package structure. Because it also contains calls to other hidden classes and methods, you must either remove or refactor these calls to make your code compile. Depending on how much of this hidden API you'll need to use, sometimes it's enough to simply copy a number of constant declarations instead of the entire class.

```
    @Override
    public void onActivityCreated(Bundle savedInstanceState) {
        super.onActivityCreated(savedInstanceState);

        mAdapter = new SimpleCursorAdapter(this,
                R.layout.sms_list_item, null,
                new String[] {Telephony.Sms.ADDRESS, Telephony.Sms.BODY,
Telephony.Sms.DATE},
                new int[] {R.id.sms_from, R.id.sms_body, R.id.sms_received},
                CursorAdapter.FLAG_REGISTER_CONTENT_OBSERVER);
        setListAdapter(mAdapter);
        getLoaderManager().initLoader(0, null, this);
    }

    public Loader<Cursor> onCreateLoader(int id, Bundle args) {
        Uri smsUri = Telephony.Sms.CONTENT_URI;
```

```
    return new CursorLoader(getActivity(), smsUri, new String[] {
            Telephony.Sms._ID,
            Telephony.Sms.ADDRESS,
            Telephony.Sms.BODY,
            Telephony.Sms.DATE},
            null, null, Telephony.Sms.DEFAULT_SORT_ORDER);
}
```

Here are two methods shown from a custom `ListFragment`, which loads a `Cursor` from the `Content Provider` for SMS and loads that into a `SimpleCursorAdapter`. The `Uri` for the provider and the name of the columns are all the content used from the `Telephony` class.

Wi-Fi Tethering

Android smartphones can enable Wi-Fi tethering, which makes it possible to create a mobile Wi-Fi hotspot that allows other devices (usually your laptop) to connect to the Internet when you're traveling. This feature is a very popular one on Android, but it has caused some problems for application developers.

When the user enables Wi-Fi tethering, the state of the Wi-Fi is neither on nor off, but "unknown" if you query it through the public API. In a previous example (see the "Calling Hidden APIs Using Reflections" section), I showed how to detect whether Wi-Fi tethering is enabled using hidden method `isWifiApEnabled()`. A number of other hidden methods in the `WifiManager` class provide you with more information about Wi-Fi tethering.

```
private WifiConfiguration getWifiApConfig() {
    WifiConfiguration wifiConfiguration = null;
    try {
        WifiManager wifiManager =
                (WifiManager) getSystemService(WIFI_SERVICE);
        Class clazz = WifiManager.class;
        Method getWifiApConfigurationMethod =
                clazz.getMethod("getWifiApConfiguration");
        return (WifiConfiguration)
                getWifiApConfigurationMethod.invoke(wifiManager);
    } catch (NoSuchMethodException e) {
        Log.e(TAG, "Cannot find method", e);
    } catch (IllegalAccessException e) {
        Log.e(TAG, "Cannot call method", e);
    } catch (InvocationTargetException e) {
        Log.e(TAG, "Cannot call method", e);
    }
    return wifiConfiguration;
}
```

The preceding code shows how you can retrieve the `WifiConfiguration` for the Wi-Fi tethering settings on a device. Note that calling these methods requires that your application have the permission `android. permission.ACCESS_WIFI_STATE`. All Wi-Fi networks that an Android device has configured (that is, connected to) can be enumerated as a list of `WifiConfiguration` objects through the `WifiManager. getConfiguredNetworks()`. In each of the `WifiConfiguration` objects retrieved through this method, the `preSharedKey` is set to `null` for obvious security reasons. However, when retrieving the `WifiConfiguration` object for the Wi-Fi tethering settings as shown in the preceding code, you'll find the clear-text password present in the `preSharedKey` variable. In this way, your application can retrieve both the name for the access point that is created when you activate Wi-Fi tethering and the password.

Although this feature can be considered a security flaw, it's good to know that the permission needed to activate Wi-Fi tethering requires your application to be signed with the system certificate. Thus, even if an application can read the password, there's no way for it to activate Wi-Fi tethering without the user's consent.

Hidden Settings

An Android device has hundreds of different settings that are available through the class `Settings`. Besides providing access to the value for each setting, it publishes a number of `Intent` actions that you can use to launch a specific part of the settings UI. For instance, to launch the settings for airplane mode, you use `Settings.ACTION_AIRPLANE_MODE_SETTINGS` when creating the `Intent`. Figure 15-4 shows how the file `Settings.java` looks like when viewed through AndroidXRef.

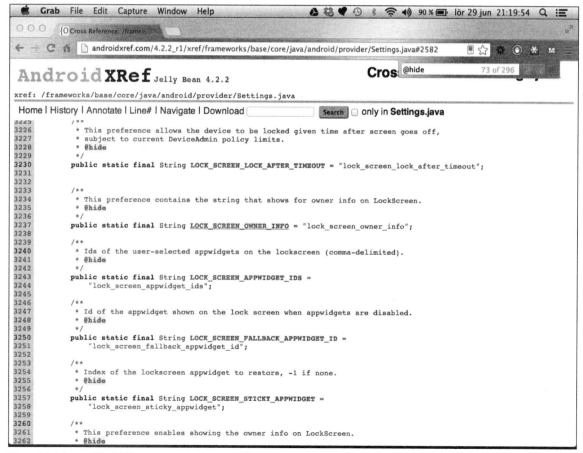

Figure 15-4 Some of the hidden constants in the source file `Settings.java`

A number of hidden setting keys and `Intent` actions are in the `Settings` class, some of which can be very useful when your application needs to figure out details about the device or when you want to present a shortcut within your application to a certain system setting.

Summary

This chapter introduced how you can discover and use the hidden APIs in the Android platform. Although only a few examples are shown, the number of available hidden APIs is quite large. Most of these APIs are not only hidden but also protected with permissions with the `signature` or `system` protection level, which makes them unusable for most Android developers. However, as you will see in the next chapter, they can be an efficient method for building advanced applications with access to system APIs if you build them for a device with a custom firmware.

Some of the APIs are simple constants used to access `ContentProviders`, `Intent` actions for launching `Activities` or settings keys for reading hidden system settings, whereas others are methods that you need to invoke.

Although most applications will never require these APIs, in some situations, you'll benefit by using an API that is officially unavailable. Using the hidden APIs in a smart way will allow you to further enhance your apps.

Further Resources

Websites

An index of all the Android source code sorted according to specific versions: `http://android xref.com`

The Java tutorials on the Reflection API: `http://docs.oracle.com/javase/tutorial/reflect`

The utility for converting ODEX files to DEX format: `https://code.google.com/p/smali`

The utility for converting DEX files to JAR files with Java classes: `https://code.google.com/p/dex2jar`

Chapter 16

Hacking the Android Platform

Although I expect most of you will be developing Android applications, sometimes using the NDK (refer to Chapter 14) and sometimes using hidden APIs (refer to Chapter 15), some of you may have specific reasons to modify the Android platform. Google provides the source code for the Android platform as an open-source project called (you guessed it) Android Open Source Project (AOSP) just so third-party developers can experiment and modify Android to suit their needs.

You can download all the code and compile it, but you also need a supported device if you want to test your modifications on real hardware. Fortunately, all the devices announced under the Google Nexus brand allow you to do so, and many manufacturers, such as Sony Mobile and HTC, allow you to unlock their devices and flash them with a custom firmware as well. A company working on a low-level software feature that it intends to license to handset manufacturers can use this approach to demonstrate its products on real devices, for example.

Until Google released Android as an open-source project and provided open devices, this approach required expensive development platforms from chipset vendors like Qualcomm and Texas Instruments. Today, hundreds of independent developers spend a significant amount of time hacking on their own version of the Android platform. Some of these developers have organized themselves into community groups focusing on building custom firmware for Android devices that users can download and install.

In this chapter, I describe how you can build your own firmware or a custom ROM for an Android device, including how to access and download the AOSP source code, set up the build environment, compile the code, and flash the firmware to a device. In this chapter, I'm using the Galaxy Nexus, but you can use any of the Google Nexus-branded devices with the same instructions. I also provide some general directions on how to proceed with building custom firmware for other manufacturers' devices.

In addition, I describe how to modify and extend the Android platform. Because the Android source code is very large, I selected a few simple examples that will introduce you to the platform's design. If your company is developing custom solutions for the Android platform, you should find this information valuable.

I end this chapter talking about how you can contribute your changes to the Android platform to the AOSP. If you think a feature is missing and not prioritized by Google, you can use this approach to make it happen. (*Note:* This isn't a guarantee Google will accept your patch, but you'll never know unless you try.)

A word of caution: **The things described in this chapter can, if you're not careful, break your device. If you need to do this, use a device that is not your primary phone and know that your actions could render the device unusable or break the warranty. When you flash your device, all its content will be deleted, so be sure to back up content you want to save.**

Several of the major Android device manufacturers allow you to flash a custom firmware on their devices, which you do by unlocking the bootloader so that the device will accept firmware images with signatures other than the device's manufacturer. Doing so usually affects the warranty of the device, but if your goal is to demonstrate a new low-level feature to that manufacturer, it might be worth doing. I briefly cover some of the major manufacturers approach to unlocking the bootloader later in this chapter.

Unlocking Your Device

All Android devices come with a locked bootloader that you need to unlock before you can flash them with new firmware (this also applies to flashing the factory firmwares from the link in the section "Flashing Factory Images"). You can unlock all Google Nexus devices with a simple command. The following instructions apply to Google Nexus devices.

Start by connecting your device to your computer and ensure that USB Debugging is enabled (see Chapter 1). Next, reboot the device to the bootloader using `adb` as shown here:

```
$ adb reboot-bootloader
```

Your device will reboot into the bootloader, as shown in Figure 16-1, where you can issue `fastboot` commands, which are used to unlock the device and flash new firmware images.

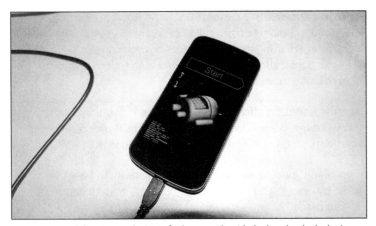

Figure 16-1 A Galaxy Nexus device in fastboot mode with the bootloader locked

Next, perform the following command, which unlocks the bootloader so you can flash your custom firmware images:

```
$ fastboot oem unlock
```

It's also possible to lock the bootloader again by issuing the command `fastboot oem lock`.

The screen of the device changes (see Figure 16-2) and shows information about the effects of unlocking the bootloader. Press Volume Up/Down to select your choice and press the Power button to confirm. When unlocked, the device returns to the fastboot mode and allows you to flash a new firmware image.

Figure 16-2 The warning box presented when you try to unlock the bootloader on a Galaxy Nexus device

Flashing Factory Images

When you build your custom firmware and test your new features, the device is likely to crash. Although generally you can return to fastboot mode and flash a new firmware image, sometimes it may be useful to flash the factory image to the device. You may also want to do so when testing an older version of Android. Download the factory image for your device from `https://developers.google.com/android/nexus/images` and extract the archive into an empty directory.

In the directory, you'll find a shell script named `flash-all.sh`, which will flash the entire factory firmware to the device and restore it to its original state. After the process is complete (it could take a few minutes, depending on the device and your computer), the device reboots into the freshly installed Android image.

Unlocking Non-Google Nexus Devices

Most Android devices on the market aren't Google Nexus brands, and not all of these device's manufacturers allow you to unlock the bootloader and flash a custom firmware. However, more and more manufacturers are realizing the positive benefits of allowing advanced users and third-party companies to unlock and flash their devices with custom firmware, so the list of officially unlockable devices is growing all the time.

Sony Mobile was the first manufacturer to announce that its devices could be unlocked, beginning with its 2011 device. Not every device after 2011 from Sony Mobile can be unlocked, and sometimes the devices sold through operators can't be unlocked. You can find more information about unlocking the Sony Mobile Android devices at `http://unlockbootloader.sonymobile.com`.

HTC also provides an official method for unlocking its devices. Some devices require a firmware update before they can be unlocked. More information is available at `http://www.htcdev.com/bootloader`.

Motorola has an official bootloader unlock program covering some of its devices. To find out if this program covers your device, visit `https://motorola-global-portal.custhelp.com/app/standalone/bootloader/unlock-your-device-a`.

Other manufacturers may also allow you to unlock your device. Visit their support sites for more information. Also, even if there is no official way of unlocking your device, there may be an unofficial workaround. A good place to start is on the XDA Developers forum (`http://www.xda-developers.com`). Remember that unlocking your device this way will usually void the warranty. Also, even if you manage to unlock the device, most manufacturers don't provide a full set of hardware drivers necessary to build a working custom firmware. Refer to the each manufacturer's information on the details.

Community-Supported Firmwares

Ever since the first Android devices were released, a stable and growing community of developers has worked on releasing custom firmware that users can download and flash onto their own devices. The most well-known group is CyanogenMod, and it has custom firmware for a wide selection of devices. You can find more information about its work at `http://www.cyanogenmod.org`.

Other groups have focused on devices from specific vendors. For instance, a group called the FreeXperia Project is building high-quality community firmware for the Sony Mobile Xperia devices. Visit its site at `http://freexperiaproject.com` for more information.

You can usually find the best source for community-developed custom firmware at the XDA Developer forums (see `http://forum.xda-developers.com`). At this site, you can find information about most devices that have been released.

The Android Source Code

The Android Open Source Project is the publically available source code for the Android platform, and Google provides it at `http://source.android.com`. This site includes not only the source code for the Android platform, but also for the SDK and other development tools. The project is structured around a number of Git modules. Each module is part of the overall system, such as the Linux kernel, native libraries, the Dalvik VM, or a system application.

Setting Up the Build Environment

You can work with the Android Open Source Project on Linux and Mac OS X. The build instructions tend to be updated on a regular basis, with support for new versions of the host operating systems and updated development tools, so I'm not covering the instructions on how to set up the environment on your system. You can find the latest instructions for setting up the build environment for AOSP at `http://source.android.com/source/initializing.html`.

Because the default partition on OS X is case-insensitive, for Mac OS X, you need to create a new case-sensitive disk image. Also, downloading the source code (using `repo sync`) the first time will take quite a while—a lot of code must be downloaded.

Nexus Binaries

Although the Android platform is open-source, all the hardware drivers for the Nexus devices are not. For instance, the graphics driver for Galaxy Nexus is a proprietary library from Imagination Technologies, and the source code for this hasn't been released yet. Therefore, you will also need to download all the binary drivers for your Nexus device before you proceed with building a custom firmware. You can find the available binaries at `https://developers.google.com/android/nexus/drivers`.

You download all the binary drivers available for your device to the root of the Android platform projects you've just downloaded. Run the following command to extract the archive, and you'll be prompted with a license agreement:

```
$ tar xzvf imgtec-maguro-jdq39-bb3c4e4e.tgz
x extract-imgtec-maguro.sh
$ sh ./extract-imgtec-maguro.sh

The license for this software will now be displayed.
You must agree to this license before using this software.

-n Press Enter to view the license
```

After you agree to the terms of the license, you have new projects under the `vendor` directory. These are usually only headers, makefiles, and binary `.so` files that will be installed on the custom firmware when you finish building.

It's important to include all the binary drivers available, or the custom firmware you've built probably won't boot correctly.

Building and Flashing

After all the source code is downloaded and the development environment is set up, you can start building the custom firmware. Make sure `ccache` is installed and configured (see `http://source.android.com/source/initializing.html#setting-up-ccache`) because it will speed up subsequent builds.

Building the platform the first time will take a bit of time (about 1½ hours on my MacBook Pro with 16GB RAM).

First, you need to load the build environment into your current shell and tell the build system which device and configuration you want to build.

```
$ source build/envsetup.sh
$ lunch full_maguro-userdebug
```

The first command loads the build system and sets all the right environment variables. The `lunch` command lets you select the build target (when it's called without arguments, you can manually select the target). In this case, you want to build the `userdebug` configuration for the Galaxy Nexus ("maguro"). The `userdebug` configuration allows you to access `adb` with root access and provides more privileges that enable you to debug the device and write to the system partition, which is useful if you want to install a new system application later on.

Because building can take a significant amount of time, I suggest building on a high-end computer with a fast disk (preferably a SSD)—although it's possible to compile the platform on a low-end computer. To speed things up, instruct the build system to use additional threads while building by giving the argument $-jN$ to the `make` command, where N is twice the number of hardware threads your computer supports. Generally, computers can support two hardware threads per CPU core (using hyper-threading), so a computer with one CPU with four cores will support eight threads.

```
$ make -j8
```

This is a good time to go and make some more coffee.

When the build is complete and, hopefully, successful, you can reboot your connected device in fastboot mode and flash the firmware.

```
$ adb reboot-bootloader
$ fastboot flashall -w
```

When the process is complete, your device should boot up with your new custom firmware. Try running the following commands from a terminal to confirm that you have root access:

```
$ adb root
restarting adbd as root
$ adb remount
remount succeeded
$ adb shell
root@android:/ #
```

The first command restarts the `adb` daemon on the device to run as root, giving it additional privileges. The second command remounts the system partition on the device in read/write mode, allowing you to install new system applications under `/system/app`. The final command simply confirms that you have root access by opening a shell on the device. If the command line starts with `root@android`, you know that you have root access.

Congratulations, you now have your very own custom firmware on which you have full root control and the possibility to install new system and platform-signed applications.

Writing System Applications

As I describe in Chapter 3 and 12, Android's permission system has various `protectionLevels` that describe who can use a specific permission. If the permission has its `protectionLevel` set to system, the application that uses this permission must initially be installed on the system partition (`/system/app`, to be specific). In this way, third-party developers can build applications that the manufacturer installs on the system partition and which then have access to system-level permissions. Note that updates to this application will retain the same permissions, even though the updates are placed on the data partition. This is how Google's Android applications (such as Gmail, Google+, and Google Map) can gain additional permissions even though the device manufacturer doesn't sign them.

As a third-party developer, as long as you can get your application in the system partition for a device, you can provide upgrades to users through the Google Play Store.

> **Along with the challenge of getting your system application on a manufacturer's device, you should also define a new system permission that the manufacturer then adds to the system permissions. By using this permission in your system application, you can effectively filter the application on Google Play to make it invisible to users who don't have these modifications.**

To install an APK as a system application, you need to have write access to the system partition (see the end of the "Building and Flashing" section). Then you can push the new APK to the system application folder as shown here:

```
$ adb push <apk file> /system/app
```

After the application is placed on the system partition, the package manager sets it up properly. Your application can now use permissions requiring `protectionLevel system`, even though it isn't signed with the manufacturer's platform certificate.

The `signature permissionLevel` is usually set for even more-sensitive permissions. For instance, the permission `android.permission.FORCE_STOP_PACKAGES` has its `protectionLevel` set to `signature`, meaning that only applications signed with the vendor platform certificate can use APIs that require this. Third-party developers who want to sell their solution to a manufacturer, which requires `signature` permissions can do so by providing a project for the platform build with an unsigned APK, similar to how hardware drivers are distributed for the Nexus devices.

Platform Certificates

You can find the default test keys used to sign your custom firmware under `<aosp root>/build/target/product/security`. Because these keys are available publically, never consider them safe. Refer to the `README` file in this directory for additional information and instructions on how to generate your own platform keys. However, you can use them for developmental purposes when you want to test new system applications. The format of these keys is different from the one used to sign Android applications using the Android SDK or Android Studio, so before you can use them in your development environment, you need to convert them.

```
$ openssl pkcs8 -inform DER -nocrypt -in platform.pk8 -out platform.pem
$ openssl pkcs12 -export -in platform.x509.pem -inkey platform.pem -out
  platform.p12 -name android-platform -password pass:<password>
$ keytool -importkeystore -destkeystore platform.keystore -srckeystore
  platform.p12 -srcstoretype PKCS12
```

You now have a keystore with the format recognized by the Android development tools. Simply use this keystore when you want to sign your application with the platform certificate. Doing so allows your application to use all permissions requiring signature `permissionLevel`. Also, you can now set the `sharedUserId` attribute in the manifest to `android.uid.system`, which gives the application the same user ID as the system server and grants access to additional system-level APIs.

To use this certificate in your application, copy the keystore to your application and add the following to your Gradle build:

```
android {
    signingConfigs {
        debug {
            storeFile file("platform.keystore")
            storePassword "password"
            keyAlias "android-platform"
            keyPassword "password"
        }
    }

    // ... omitted for brevity ..
}
```

Now subsequent debug builds from Android Studio must use the extracted platform key when signing your application.

Remember: **Never use this certificate for applications published on the Google Play Store. Only use it for testing and demonstration.**

Writing Signature-Signed Applications

In Chapter 15, I discuss how to use the hidden platform APIs in the `WifiManager` to detect whether tethering is enabled. Using some of the additional hidden APIs together with the platform key, you can build your own application for controlling Wi-Fi tethering, as shown in the following example:

```
<?xml version="1.0" encoding="utf-8"?>
<manifest xmlns:android="http://schemas.android.com/apk/res/android"
    package="com.aptl.systemlevelapps"
    android:sharedUserId="android.uid.system"
    android:versionCode="1"
    android:versionName="1.0" >
```

```xml
    <uses-permission android:name="android.permission.CHANGE_WIFI_STATE"
/>
    <uses-sdk
        android:minSdkVersion="17"
        android:targetSdkVersion="17" />

    <application
        android:allowBackup="true"
        android:icon="@drawable/ic_launcher"
        android:label="@string/app_name"
        android:theme="@style/AppTheme" >
        <activity
            android:name=".EnableTetheringActivity"
            android:label="@string/app_name" >
            <intent-filter>
                <action android:name="android.intent.action.MAIN" />
                <category android:name="android.intent.category.LAUNCHER" />
            </intent-filter>
        </activity>
    </application>
</manifest>
```

First, you add `sharedUserId` with the value `android.uid.system` to the manifest element to give your application the correct user ID for controlling the Wi-Fi. Even though your application is now signed with the platform certificate, you still need to declare the permissions your application requires, which is why you need to add the permission `CHANGE_WIFI_STATE` to the manifest.

```java
    public class EnableTetheringActivity extends Activity {
        private static final String TAG = "EnableTetheringActivity";
        private WifiManager mWifiManager;
        private Method mSetWifiApEnabledMethod;

        @Override
        protected void onCreate(Bundle savedInstanceState) {
            super.onCreate(savedInstanceState);
            mWifiManager = (WifiManager) getSystemService(WIFI_SERVICE);
            try {
                Class clazz = WifiManager.class;
                mSetWifiApEnabledMethod = clazz.getMethod("setWifiApEnabled",
                                    WifiConfiguration.class, boolean.class);
            } catch (NoSuchMethodException e) {
                Log.e(TAG, "Error retrieving method setWifiApEnabled()", e);
            }
            setContentView(R.layout.activity_main);
        }

        public void doEnableWifiTethering(View view) {
            try {
                if(mWifiManager.isWifiEnabled()) {
                    mWifiManager.setWifiEnabled(false);
                }
```

```
        EditText ssidNameView = (EditText) findViewById(R.id.ssid_name);
        String ssidName = ssidNameView.getText().toString();
        EditText wifiPasswordView =
                        (EditText) findViewById(R.id.wifi_password);
        String wifiPassword = wifiPasswordView.getText().toString();
        WifiConfiguration wifiConfiguration = new WifiConfiguration();
        wifiConfiguration.SSID = ssidName;
        wifiConfiguration.preSharedKey = wifiPassword;
        mSetWifiApEnabledMethod.invoke(mWifiManager,
                                wifiConfiguration, true);
    } catch (IllegalAccessException e) {
        Log.e(TAG, "Illegal access.", e);
    } catch (InvocationTargetException e) {
        Log.e(TAG, "Invocation error.", e);
    }
  }
}
```

The `Activity` shown here retrieves the hidden method `setWifiApEnabled()` from the `WifiManager` class. When the click-callback `doEnableWifiTethering()` is called, the SSID and password are retrieved and used to construct a default `WifiConfiguration`, which is then used as a parameter when invoking the `Method` object.

You now have a way of controlling the state of Wi-Fi tethering through a standard Android application, which just happens to be signed with the platform certificate.

Hacking the Android Platform

In this section, I describe how to work with the AOSP source code. The code examples are in Java, but the same approach applies to native development as well.

Setting Up Your IDE

Although Android Studio works fine for developing regular Android applications, I recommend using IntelliJ IDEA CE (Community Edition) for working with the AOSP source code. You can find this IDE at `www. jetbrains.com/idea`. It's also possible to work with AOSP in Eclipse, but I recommend IntelliJ IDEA CE because of its superior performance and code navigation support.

Before opening the IDE and importing the source code, make a complete build as described in the section "Building and Flashing" earlier in this chapter. Doing so generates the Java source files for platform resources, which makes it easier to work with from the IDE.

After you have a complete build, you can generate the IntelliJ project files (and Eclipse `.classpath` file) by executing the following command in the project root directory:

```
$ development/tools/idegen/idegen.sh
Read excludes: 3ms
Traversed tree: 50027ms
```

Now, you have two IntelliJ IDEA files in the root named `android.ipr` and `android.iml`.

Start IntelliJ IDEA CE and open the project file (`android.ipr`)—the first time you do this, IntelliJ will build an index of all the source code, so it will take some time.

You can now start hacking the AOSP source code.

Android Projects

The Android platform consists of a number of projects, each in its own Git repository. Because there are more than 300 of them, there's not enough room in this book to cover and explain every project in the AOSP source code. Instead, I'll describe some of the more important ones, based on their path in the file system. Some consist of several Git repositories (for instance, the `packages` project).

You can find a complete list of the projects in the file `<aosp root>/.repo/project.list`.

Frameworks/base

The central (and according to some, most important) project in the Android platform is `frameworks/base`. This project contains most of the sources for the system server as well as many other components running on an Android device. Here, you'll also find the implementation of most of the Android APIs (except those belonging to the `java` and `javax` packages). If you want to add a new system service or modify the Android APIs, you make your changes here.

Packages

You'll find all of the standard system applications in the `packages` project, divided into `apps`, `inputmethods`, `providers`, `screensavers`, and `wallpapers` folders. The `apps` folder contains the applications the user can see in the launcher, such as Email, Phone, and Calculator. The `Providers` folder contains the system `ContentProviders`, such as the media or contacts provider. The `Inputmethods` folder contains the default soft keyboards found in Android.

If you want to modify one of the existing system applications, this is where you start. Developers often start modifying the default launcher application in the AOSP sources. You can find this app under `packages/apps/Launcher2`.

Vendor

The `vendor` directory is not a single project but the place where vendor-specific platform projects are contained. This is usually where the binary hardware drivers are placed. If you intend to provide a manufacturer with your own project for the Android platform, such as a shared library with some proprietary implementations, place it in this directory as well. Also, it's best to place vendor-specific applications that should be preinstalled in this directory. In fact, most vendor-specific code should end up here; this way, device manufacturers can keep the Android Open Source Project code clean from source code that isn't open-source.

Here is the `Android.mk` for the Wi-Fi and Bluetooth drivers from Broadcom for the Galaxy Nexus:

```
LOCAL_PATH := $(call my-dir)

ifeq ($(TARGET_DEVICE),maguro)

include $(CLEAR_VARS)
LOCAL_MODULE := bcm4330
LOCAL_MODULE_OWNER := broadcom
LOCAL_SRC_FILES := bcm4330.hcd
LOCAL_MODULE_TAGS := optional
LOCAL_MODULE_SUFFIX := .hcd
LOCAL_MODULE_CLASS := ETC
LOCAL_MODULE_PATH := $(TARGET_OUT_VENDOR)/firmware
include $(BUILD_PREBUILT)

endif
```

You can find this makefile in `<aosp root>/vendor/broadcom/maguro/prebuilt`. The content of this file is very similar to what a normal `Android.mk` looks like when you're doing native development using the Android NDK. The source is the binary file `bcm4330.hcd`, and its output is in the `firmware` directory on the device.

When building your own vendor extension, refer to the existing build files for other projects and construct your own. For Android applications (APK) that you want to include in the system partition, refer to the build files found in the `packages` directory for examples of how your `Android.mk` should look.

Android Linux Kernel

When you're building Android for a Nexus device, note that the Linux kernel is usually prebuilt and can be found under `<aosp root>/device` (for instance, `<aosp root>/device/samsung/tuna` for the Galaxy Nexus). If you need to modify the kernel for your device, you must download the Linux source code for that device, modify the build configuration, build the image, and copy it to the right location.

The Linux kernel has a different license (GPLv2) than the Android platform (usually Apache License v2). The interesting thing with the Linux kernel is that this license guarantees that you can get access to the source code for every single Android device. While modifying the Linux kernel for your own custom firmware is beyond the scope of this book, you can refer to the instructions from the chipset vendor for each device to learn more about kernel development on its hardware platform.

Adding a System Service

When modifying the Android platform, a common task is to add a new system service. These are the services that Android developers get when calling `Context.getSystemService()`. In the following code, I show you how to add a new system service by modifying the code in `frameworks/base`. I call this service `HomeDetector`, and its task is to send a broadcast when the device enters the location defined as *home*. This class belongs to the location APIs; thus it is placed in the `android.location` package.

```java
public class HomeDetector {
    private static final String TAG = "HomeDetector";

    /**
     * Sticky broadcast indicating that the device arrives
     * or leave the defined home wifi.
     *
     */
    public static final String ACTION_HOME_LOCATION_CHANGED =
                              "android.location.HOME_LOCATION_CHANGED";
    /**
     * Extra <code>boolean</code> indicating if the device arrived
     * to the home location or not.
     */
    public static final String EXTRA_AT_HOME = "atHome";

    private IHomeDetector mHomeDetectorService;

    public HomeDetector(IHomeDetector homeDetector) {
        mHomeDetectorService = homeDetector;
    }

    /**
     * Set the home wifi.
     *
     * @param homeWifi
     * @hide Should only be available to system applications
     */
    public void setHomeWifi(WifiInfo wifiInfo) {
        try {
            mHomeDetectorService.setHomeWifi(wifiInfo);
        } catch(RemoteException e) {
            Log.e(TAG, "setHomeLocation.", e);
        }
    }
}
```

The class `HomeDetector` will be the class that is returned when an application calls `Context.getSystemService()` with the parameter `Contex.HOME_DETECTOR` (which you also need to add to the `Context` class). This class takes an instance of `HomeDetectorService` as a constructor parameter, which will contain the actual implementation for the service.

When adding a new system service in Android, the standard approach is to define an AIDL file that will be used internally by the system server. You create this AIDL in the same package as the `HomeDetector` class (`android.location`).

```java
package android.location;

import android.location.Location;
```

```
oneway interface IHomeDetector {
    void setHomeWifi(in WifiInfo homeWifi);
}
```

The AIDL is compiled as an ordinary application-specific AIDL and allows you to implement the other parts of your new system service.

The following code goes into `SystemServer.run()` in the package `com.android.server`. This is the central class for all system services.

```
try {
    Slog.i(TAG, "Home Detector");
    homeDetector = new HomeDetectorService(context);
    ServiceManager.addService(Context.HOME_DETECTOR, homeDetector);
} catch (Throwable e) {
    reportWtf("starting Home Detector", e);
}
```

The preceding code simply creates an instance of `HomeDetectorService` and starts the service.

Here is the actual implementation of the new service:

```
public class HomeDetectorService extends IHomeDetector.Stub  {

    private static final String TAG = "HomeDetectorService";
    public static final String HOME_WIFI_SSID = "homeDetector.ssid";
    public static final String HOME_WIFI_BSSID = "homeDetector.bssid";
    public static final String SET_HOME_WIFI_PERMISSION
            = "android.permission.SET_HOME_WIFI";
    private Context mContext;
    private boolean mCurrentState = false;

    public HomeDetectorService(Context context, WifiManager wifiManager) {
        mContext = context;
        WifiInfo wifiInfo = wifiManager.getConnectionInfo();

        if(wifiInfo != null) {
            String ssid = SystemProperties.get(HOME_WIFI_SSID);
            String bssid = SystemProperties.get(HOME_WIFI_BSSID);
            mCurrentState = wifiInfo.getSSID().equals(ssid)
                                    && wifiInfo.getBSSID().
equals(bssid);
        }
        sendHomeDetectionBroadcast(mCurrentState);

        IntentFilter intentFilter =
                new IntentFilter(WifiManager.NETWORK_STATE_CHANGED_
ACTION);
        mContext.registerReceiver(new WifiListener(), intentFilter);
    }
```

```
    public void setHomeWifi(WifiInfo homeWifi) throws RemoteException {
        mContext.enforceCallingPermission(SET_HOME_WIFI_PERMISSION,
                "Missing permission " + SET_HOME_WIFI_PERMISSION);
        SystemProperties.set(HOME_WIFI_SSID, homeWifi.getSSID());
        SystemProperties.set(HOME_WIFI_BSSID, homeWifi.getBSSID());
    }

    public void sendHomeDetectionBroadcast(boolean state) {
        Intent homeDetectorBroadcast =
                    new Intent(HomeDetector.ACTION_HOME_LOCATION_
CHANGED);
        homeDetectorBroadcast.putExtra(HomeDetector.EXTRA_AT_HOME, state);
        mContext.sendStickyBroadcast(homeDetectorBroadcast);
    }

    class WifiListener extends BroadcastReceiver {

        @Override
        public void onReceive(Context context, Intent intent) {
            NetworkInfo networkInfo = intent.
                        getParcelableExtra(WifiManager.EXTRA_NETWORK_
INFO);
            boolean newState = false;
            if(networkInfo.getState().equals(NetworkInfo.State.CONNECTED))
{
                String ssid = SystemProperties.get(HOME_WIFI_SSID);
                String bssid = SystemProperties.get(HOME_WIFI_BSSID);
                WifiInfo  wifiInfo =
                    intent.getParcelableExtra(WifiManager.EXTRA_WIFI_
INFO);
                newState = wifiInfo.getSSID().equals(ssid) &&
                                        wifiInfo.getBSSID().
equals(bssid);
            }

            // Only send new broadcast if changed
            if(newState != mCurrentState) {
                mCurrentState = newState;
                sendHomeDetectionBroadcast(mCurrentState);
            }
        }
    }
}
```

The usual place to put a new system service is under com.android.server.<category>, where <category> is the type of service you created (in this case, location). Note the call to Context. enforceCallingPermission(), which verifies that the calling process has the right to call this method.

In this case, I created a passive service, but if your service needs to run its own thread, you need to implement the Runnable interface and initialize a new Looper in the run() method, as shown here:

```
@Override
public void run() {
    // Set the correct thread priority
    Process.setThreadPriority(Process.THREAD_PRIORITY_BACKGROUND);
    Looper.prepare(); // Prepare the Looper
    // Create a custom Handler for processing
    mServiceHandler = new MySystemServiceHandler();
    init(); // Perform initialization
    Looper.loop(); // Start this thread as a Looper
}
```

With the `run()` method just shown, your background service can post `Messages` to the custom `Handler` that has its own dedicated thread. In this way, you can perform blocking operations in your service that otherwise could block the entire system.

The final step is to declare the new permission required for the `setHomeWifi()` method, which you do by editing the `AndroidManifest.xml` of the system server, located in `<aosp root>/frameworks/base/core/res/`. Locate the permissions belonging to the location group (`android.permission-group.LOCATION`) and add the new permission there.

```
<!-- Allow an application to set the WiFi which should
    be considered "home" -->
<permission android:name="android.permission.SET_HOME_WIFI"
    android:permissionGroup="android.permission-group.LOCATION"
    android:protectionLevel="signature|system"
    android:label="@string/permlab_setHomeWifi"
    android:description="@string/permdesc_setHomeWifi" />
```

In this case, only `system` or `signature` applications are allowed to use this permission. If you want to create a new public API that anyone can access, consider whether the `protectionLevel` should be `normal` or `dangerous`.

Speeding Up the Platform Development Cycle

After you add your new system service, you're ready to build the code and push the changes onto your device. Because building the entire platform from scratch every time would take a significant amount of time, you can use some tricks to reduce the turnaround time for this kind of development.

For example, instead of building the entire platform, build only the project you've changed. In the earlier example in "Adding a System Service," you modified the project `frameworks/base`, so give this project as a parameter to the `make` command so that only that part is rebuilt.

```
$ make -j8 frameworks/base
```

This command compiles the code and builds the binaries for that specific project. Then you can push only the changed binaries onto the Android device with the following commands:

```
$ adb shell stop
$ adb sync
$ adb shell start
```

The first command stops the Android system server, allowing you to safely push the new binaries onto your devices without crashing them. The second command pushes the actual binaries. This command can also take a second parameter stating which directory you want to synchronize. Finally, you call the third command to restart the system server. Your newly modified system server will now start up together with the new service you just added. This procedure lets you iterate through the development cycle quickly and try out small changes to the system service and libraries, without the time-consuming task of having to shut down the phone and flash a new firmware.

The preceding procedure doesn't produce a new firmware image for each build. To do this, you have to perform a new, full build. However, because you (hopefully) have enabled `ccache` **and haven't deleted your build output directory, the second time around shouldn't take too long.**

Contributing to AOSP

Google is doing most of the new development on the Android platform, but a significant amount of code is contributed by other companies and individuals through the Android Open Source Project. Manufacturers of Android devices and chipset vendors are the largest contributors, but smaller companies also fix many bugs and develop small features. Although Google has the final say in what ends up in the Android platform, it is always interested in high-quality features that others are willing to contribute.

The first thing to do is visit the Android contribution discussion forum (`https://groups.google.com/forum/?fromgroups#!forum/android-contrib`) and describe your new proposal there. If you want to fix a bug, visit the issue tracker for the Android platform (`https://code.google.com/p/android/issues/list`) and report it there (don't forget to check if it has already been reported!). When you feel comfortable that your proposed fix is okay, you can start your contribution process.

Contributions to one of the Android projects are described in detail at `http://source.android.com/source/contributing.html`. Remember that your fix needs to maintain high-quality standard and conform to the Android Code Style Guidelines (see `http://source.android.com/source/code-style.html`). Don't expect that your contribution will get accepted right away or that the processing will go fast. Google deals with a huge number of contributions, and most never make it into the platform for various reasons. Be patient and make sure that your code is well-tested and documented.

Figure 16-3 shows the workflow of a patch. As you can see, you must take a number of steps before your contribution is accepted, but these steps help to guarantee that your code and feature is of high quality.

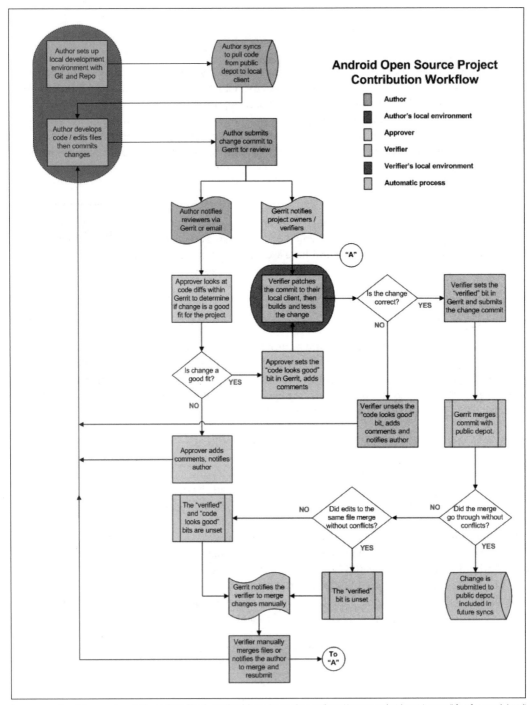

Image reproduced from work created and shared by the Android Open Source Project (http://source.android.com/source/life-of-a-patch.html) and used according to terms described in the Creative Commons 2.5 Attribution License.

Figure 16-3 The Android Open Source Project Contribution Workflow

Summary

In this chapter, I explained the basics of developing the Android platform. I showed how you can unlock your Google Nexus device and flash it with a custom firmware and how you can download the entire Android platform source code and relevant binary drivers to build your own version. I explained some of the reasons for doing so from a business perspective. By working closely with a device manufacturer, your business can get its proprietary third-party solutions that require system-level access onto a device and still be able to upgrade the application through the Google Play Store.

I showed how you can build a system application and push it onto the system partition to test it on your custom firmware. Next, I explained the steps for signing an application with the platform certificate in order to gain access to permissions requiring `signature permissionLevel`.

I completed this chapter with an example for modifying the Android platform by adding a new system service. Although the example is very simple and could just as well be created as a normal application, it demonstrates how and where you should place your new code in the Android platform.

I believe that all Android developers would benefit from a full understanding of how the Android platform is built and works, as well as how the platform certificates protect the sensitive platform APIs.

If you come up with a new feature for the Android platform, consider contributing it back to the Android Open Source Project. There's no guarantee it will be accepted by Google and merged into the Android source code, but it's a good way to practice participating in a large open-source project. Doing so also is great experience in developing high-quality code—because the requirements from Google are very high.

Further Resources

Websites

Developing for the Android Open Source Project: `http://source.android.com`

The Gerrit site for reviewing patches to AOSP: `https://android-review.googlesource.com`

The main discussion group for Android platform and technologies: `https://groups.google.com/forum/?fromgroups#!forum/android-platform`

The main discussion group for help with building the Android source code: `https://groups.google.com/forum/?fromgroups#!forum/android-building`

The discussion group for those who want to port Android to a new device: `https://groups.google.com/forum/?fromgroups#!forum/android-porting`

The main discussion group for those who want to contribute to the Android platform through AOSP: `https://groups.google.com/forum/?fromgroups#!forum/android-contrib`

The public issue tracker for bugs in the Android platform: `https://code.google.com/p/android/issues/list`

XDA Developers forums: `http://forum.xda-developers.com`

Chapter 17

Networking, Web Service, and Remote APIs

A majority of all Android applications perform some kind of network communication over the Internet. Even single-player games today provide social integration with an online web service. So, the data an application generates should be stored online so that users will have access to the same data from other devices.

As a developer of Android applications, you need to consider all aspects of networking. If your application wastes networking resources, it will consume more power and possibly increase the cost to users because of mobile data charges.

In this chapter, I cover how to perform network calls as efficiently as possible. I introduce my favorite APIs for HTTP-based communication. Then I move on to describe three different types of web services and how you can integrate them into your application. If you'll be using a web service in your application, you can likely integrate it by using a technique very similar to one of the three I describe.

I complete this chapter with guidelines for reducing the power your application consumes in regard to network operations. All network calls come with an additional drain on the battery, and you want to reduce this drain as much as possible.

Android Networking

Although Android supports both TCP and UDP communication, most of the network calls for applications are done over HTTP, which is built on top of TCP. In this section, I write mostly about HTTP communication and related topics. I briefly cover connectionless protocols, like mDNS, in Chapter 18.

The first and most important rule to remember when it comes to networking on Android is: *Never perform network calls on the main thread.* Starting with Android version 3.0 (Honeycomb), the main thread is protected by the system, and your application will crash if it tries to do a network call from the main thread.

Second, and almost as important: *Always do networking on Android from a* `Service` *and avoid performing network calls from within an* `Activity`. There are several reasons for doing so, but the most important one is that you need to consider the fast changes in the `Activity` state if you perform network operations there. The user might press Home in the middle of a network call, just to return to your application a second later. By moving all network operations to a `Service`, you can avoid this issue. It also makes for a better overall design because with this approach, you reduce the amount of code in your `Activities`, making it less complicated.

However, in many cases you will be forced to perform network operations directly from an `Activity`, as I show later in this chapter in the section "Foursquare API Using OAuth2" Please consider these cases as exceptions to the rule. As much as possible, try to perform the network calls from a `Service`.

I recommend using either a callback interface or the `LocalBroadcastManager` to communicate network results between the `Activity` and the `Service`. Another way is to store the results from a network call directly into a `ContentProvider` and let the provider notify registered clients about the changes to any data, as shown in Figure 17-1.

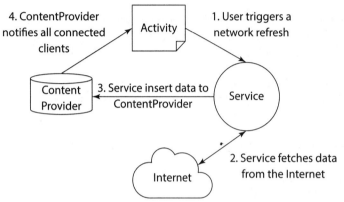

Figure 17-1 Network calls from a `Service` inserting data into a `ContentProvider` that notifies an `Activity`

HttpUrlConnection

The Android API has two APIs for HTTP communication, the Apache `HttpClient` and `HttpUrlConnection`. Both have the same level of support in regard to features, but only `HttpUrlConnection` is recommended because it's the one being actively maintained by Google. Google has also implemented a number of useful features that you otherwise would have to implement yourself, such as transparent response compression and response cache.

```
private void enableHttpResponseCache() {
    try {
        long httpCacheSize = 10 * 1024 * 1024; // 10 MiB
        File httpCacheDir = new File(getCacheDir(), "http");
        Class.forName("android.net.http.HttpResponseCache")
            .getMethod("install", File.class, long.class)
            .invoke(null, httpCacheDir, httpCacheSize);
    } catch (Exception httpResponseCacheNotAvailable) {
    }
}
```

The response cache is available from Android 4.0 (ICS) on, so if your application will also run on an earlier version of Android, use the preceding approach to initiate the cache using Reflections. If your application will target Android 4.0 at the minimum, you can use the following code to install the response cache:

```
try {
    HttpResponseCache httpResponseCache = HttpResponseCache.
            install(new File(getCacheDir(), "http"), CACHE_SIZE);
} catch (IOException e) {
    Log.e(TAG, "Error installing response cache!", e);
}
```

Choose a suitable cache size for your application. If you're retrieving only small amounts of data, pick a cache of only a few megabytes. The cache is application-private, so you don't have to worry about leaking cached responses to other applications on the device.

A Simple HTTP GET

Most network calls from applications will be in the form of simple HTTP GET requests. Here is an example of how to perform such a request:

```
public JSONObject getJsonFromServer(URL url,
                                    long lastModifiedTimestamp) {
    try {
        HttpURLConnection urlConnection = url.openConnection();
        urlConnection.setRequestMethod("GET");
        urlConnection.setInstanceFollowRedirects(true);
        urlConnection.setIfModifiedBecause(lastModifiedTimestamp);
        urlConnection.setUseCaches(true);
        urlConnection.connect();
        if (urlConnection.getResponseCode()
                == HttpURLConnection.HTTP_OK) {
            if (urlConnection.getContentType().
                    contains("application/json")) {
                int length =
                        (HttpURLConnection) urlConnection.
                        getContentLength();
                InputStream inputStream = urlConnection.
                        getInputStream();
                String jsonString = readStreamToString(inputStream, length);
                return new JSONObject(jsonString);
            }
        } else {
            // TODO: Error handling...
        }
    } catch (IOException e) {
        Log.e(TAG, "Error perform HTTP call!", e);
    } catch (JSONException e) {
        Log.e(TAG, "Error parsing JSON!", e);
    }
    return null;
}

private String readStreamToString(InputStream inputStream, int length)
                                                throws IOException {
    try {
        BufferedReader bufferedReader =
```

```
                    new BufferedReader(new InputStreamReader(inputStream));
            StringBuilder stringBuilder = new StringBuilder(length);
            char[] buffer = new char[length];
            int charsRead;
            while ((charsRead = bufferedReader.read(buffer)) != -1) {
                stringBuilder.append(buffer, 0, charsRead);
            }
            return stringBuilder.toString();
        } finally {
            inputStream.close();
        }
    }
}
```

This example is a typical one for using `HttpUrlConnection` to make an HTTP GET and parse the response to a `JSONObject`. The important thing to note here is the `readStreamToString()` method. Although you may find code examples for how to read an `InputStream` to a `String` online, the preceding shows the correct way of reading from a stream. Without any exception, you should always exhaust an `InputStream` when reading. If you don't, you leave data waiting in the lower layers of the platform that could waste resources and keep your device from going to power saver mode, which is one of the most common mistakes when doing network calls, so keep this in mind whenever you're reading from an `InputStream`.

Uploading Files to a Server

Many applications will send data, like images or other files, to an online server. This has turned out to be one of the more complex issues for developers because the standard Java APIs (including Android) doesn't provide an obvious, straightforward method for this issue. Sending data using HTTP involves doing an HTTP POST request with the data in the body. However, the body requires some special formatting, and a number of header fields must be set correctly.

The following example shows the necessary steps for posting a file to a server using HTTP POST.

```
public int postFileToURL(File file, String mimeType, URL url)
                                                throws IOException {
    DataOutputStream requestData = null;
    try {
        long size = file.length();
        String fileName = file.getName();

        // Create a random boundary string
        Random random = new Random();
        byte[] randomBytes = new byte[16];
        random.nextBytes(randomBytes);
        String boundary = Base64.
                encodeToString(randomBytes, Base64.NO_WRAP);

        HttpURLConnection urlConnection
                = (HttpURLConnection) url.openConnection();
        urlConnection.setUseCaches(false);
        urlConnection.setDoOutput(true);
        urlConnection.setRequestMethod("POST");
```

```java
        // Set the HTTP headers
        urlConnection.setRequestProperty("Connection", "Keep-Alive");
        urlConnection.setRequestProperty("Cache-Control", "no-cache");
        urlConnection.setRequestProperty("Content-Type",
                "multipart/form-data;boundary=" + boundary);

        // If larger than MAX_FIXED_SIZE - use chunked streaming
        if (size > MAX_FIXED_SIZE) {
            urlConnection.setChunkedStreamingMode(0);
        } else {
            urlConnection.setFixedLengthStreamingMode((int) size);
        }

        // Open file for reading...
        FileInputStream fileInput = new FileInputStream(file);
        // Open connection to server...
        OutputStream outputStream = urlConnection.getOutputStream();
        requestData = new DataOutputStream(outputStream);

        // Write first boundary for this file
        requestData.writeBytes("--" + boundary + CRLF);
        // Let the server know the filename
        requestData.writeBytes("Content-Disposition: form-data; name=\""
                + fileName + "\";filename=\"" + fileName + CRLF);
        // ...and the MIME type of the file
        requestData.writeBytes("Content-Type: " + mimeType + CRLF);

        // Read the local file and write to the server in one loop
        int bytesRead;
        byte[] buffer = new byte[8192];
        while ((bytesRead = fileInput.read(buffer)) != -1) {
            requestData.write(buffer, 0, bytesRead);
        }

        // Write boundary indicating end of this file
        requestData.writeBytes(CRLF);
        requestData.writeBytes("--" + boundary + "--" + CRLF);
        requestData.flush();

        return urlConnection.getResponseCode();
    } finally {
        if (requestData != null) {
            requestData.close();
        }
    }
}
```

The important part here is to understand the boundary that is used to tell the server where the file data starts and ends in the request body. Also, notice the check on whether the file size is larger than MAX_ FIXED_SIZE (in bytes), where chunked streaming or fixed-length streaming mode is used. For chunked streaming, the parameter 0 means "system default" for the chunk size, which is what most clients should use in this mode. Chunking basically means that the data is sent to the server in parts, with each part prepended with the size. Chunked streaming can be more efficient for memory use and reduces the risk of getting an `OutOfMemoryException`. However, using fixed-length streaming mode is usually faster, although it requires more memory while performing the streaming.

Volley

The standard `HttpUrlConnection` works well for most occasions, but it easily becomes quite complex when you're doing a lot of different HTTP requests. You still need to perform the requests on a background thread and to ensure that everything is closed and shut down properly when your application is done. To make things a bit easier, Google has started working on a new HTTP library that intends to make networking for Android applications easier and faster. You can retrieve the latest version of the Volley library by cloning the Git repository.

```
$ git clone https://android.googlesource.com/platform/frameworks/volley
```

The Volley library is currently under development but is already stable enough for use in applications. It provides a very easy-to-use API for doing the typical network calls, and it handles all background threading and other low-level things for you.

The following example shows how you can use Volley in a `Service` that makes HTTP GET calls and treats the response as JSON data:

```java
public class VolleyExample extends Service {
    private LocalBinder mLocalBinder = new LocalBinder();
    private RequestQueue mResponseQueue;

    @Override
    public void onCreate() {
        super.onCreate();
        mResponseQueue = Volley.newRequestQueue(this);
        mResponseQueue.start();
    }

    @Override
    public void onDestroy() {
        super.onDestroy();
        mResponseQueue.stop();
        mResponseQueue = null;
    }

    public void doJsonRequest(String url,
                              Response.Listener<JSONObject> response,
                              Response.ErrorListener error) {
        JsonObjectRequest jsonObjectRequest
            = new JsonObjectRequest(Request.Method.GET,
                url, null, response, error);
        mResponseQueue.add(jsonObjectRequest);
    }
```

```
    @Override
    public IBinder onBind(Intent intent) {
        return mLocalBinder;
    }

    public class LocalBinder extends Binder {
        public VolleyExample getService() {
            return VolleyExample.this;
        }
    }
}
```

You pass in two callbacks, one for a successful response and one for error. You don't need to worry about starting a new background thread for the network call or initiating the connection yourself; this is all taken care of by the Volley library. All you need to do is add the new request to the `RequestQueue` so that it gets processed.

```
public void doJsonUpdateRequest() {
    Response.Listener<JSONObject> responseListener
            = new Response.Listener<JSONObject>() {
        @Override
        public void onResponse(JSONObject response) {
            handleJsonResponse(response);
        }
    };
    Response.ErrorListener errorListener
            = new Response.ErrorListener() {
        @Override
        public void onErrorResponse(VolleyError error) {
            handleError(error);
        }
    };
    mService.doJsonRequest(API_URL, responseListener, errorListener);
}
```

In the preceding example, you define a callback for a successful response and an error callback. Both of these will run on a thread other than the main thread, so if you intend to modify your UI, be sure to post that update using a `Handler` or an `AsyncTask`.

Currently, the Volley library doesn't support uploading arbitrary binary files. If you need to do uploading, use the method described in the earlier section, "Uploading Files to a Server." However, continue to use Volley for other requests if possible.

If you're doing lots of different HTTP requests, I highly recommend using the Volley library. Because it's also hosted as a part of the Android Open Source Project, it's likely to become a central part of the Android platform in the future.

OkHttp and SPDY

A big problem with HTTP is that it allows only one request and response at a time per connection, which forces browsers and other clients to spawn multiple sockets in order to perform requests in parallel. This issue is less problematic for clients because there will be relatively few connections from one application at any given time; however, it makes a huge difference for servers. In 2009, Google started working on an updated HTTP protocol to address these issues. The result was a new wire protocol named SPDY (pronounced *speedy*) that allows multiple HTTP requests to be multiplexed over a single socket connection. This protocol has become a de facto open standard for the next generation of HTTP. This protocol doesn't replace HTTP; instead, it modifies how requests and responses are sent over the wire. The IETF working group for HTTP has announced that it will start the work on HTTP 2.0 and use the SPDY protocol as a starting point.

If you have full control of both the clients and the server, it may be worth investigating the use of SPDY as an alternative to regular HTTP/1.1—doing so will greatly reduce the network's load and increase the performance. SPDY is already seeing good support in the major web browsers, and there are several implementations for different platforms available, including Android.

If you choose to use SPDY as your communication protocol, I recommend that you choose the third-party library called OkHttp, which is developed by Square, Inc., and available as open source on GitHub (http://square.github.io/okhttp). The library is available as a Maven dependency by including the following line in your Gradle script:

```
compile 'com.squareup.okhttp:okhttp:1.1.1'
```

This library is simply a new and improved HTTP client with support for the SPDY protocol. It uses the `HttpUrlConnection` interface, so switching to this in your existing code should require little work.

The following code shows how you can use the OkHttp library in Android:

```java
public class OkHttpExample {
    private final OkHttpClient mOkHttpClient;

    public OkHttpExample() {
        mOkHttpClient = new OkHttpClient();
    }

    public String okHttpDemo(URL url) throws IOException {
        HttpURLConnection urlConnection = mOkHttpClient.open(url);
        InputStream inputStream = null;
        urlConnection.setRequestMethod("GET");
        urlConnection.connect();
        if (urlConnection.getResponseCode()
                        == HttpURLConnection.HTTP_OK) {
            inputStream = urlConnection.getInputStream();
            return readStreamToString(inputStream,
                            urlConnection.getContentLength());
        }
        return null;
    }
}
```

```java
    private String readStreamToString(InputStream inputStream,
                                      int length)
                                      throws IOException {
        try {
            BufferedReader bufferedReader =
                    new BufferedReader(new InputStreamReader(inputStre
am));
            StringBuilder stringBuilder = new StringBuilder(length);
            char[] buffer = new char[length];
            int charsRead;
            while ((charsRead = bufferedReader.read(buffer)) != -1) {
                stringBuilder.append(buffer, 0, charsRead);
            }
            return stringBuilder.toString();
        } finally {
            inputStream.close();
        }
    }
}
```

When you create a new instance of the `OkHttpClient`, it will set up everything you need, such as connection polling and response cache. This implementation is extremely fast even on regular HTTP requests, so using it may it be a good idea in general. When using OkHttp for SPDY communication, you'll notice a huge improvement in performance for your network calls.

Web Sockets

Web Sockets is the latest darling of the web and is an extension running on top of standard HTTP. It allows for asynchronous message-based communication between a client and a server. It starts with a regular HTTP GET request that contains special HTTP headers indicating that the client wants to upgrade the connection to a Web Socket connection.

Here is an example of the clients GET request for initiating a Web Socket connection:

```
GET /websocket HTTP/1.1
Host: myserver.com
Upgrade: websocket
Connection: Upgrade
Sec-WebSocket-Key: MjExMjM0MTI0MTI0MTI0MTIzCg==
Sec-WebSocket-Protocol: chat
Sec-WebSocket-Version: 13
Origin: http://myserver.com
```

If the client request is accepted, the server responds with the following:

```
HTTP/1.1 101 Switching Protocols
Upgrade: websocket
Connection: Upgrade
Sec-WebSocket-Accept: HSmrc0sMlYUkAGmm5OPpG2HaGWk=
Sec-WebSocket-Protocol: chat
```

> The values in the preceding headers aren't valid for every case but should be calculated according to the Web Socket protocol specification. Normally, you don't need to bother about these details when using a readymade library for Web Socket communication.

When a Web Socket is established, both sides (client and server) can send messages to each other asynchronously. More importantly, you now have a way to quickly notify the client from your server. Messages can be either text or binary and are usually quite small. If you need to transmit a large file between the client and server, stick to standard HTTP instead. Web Sockets is intended for sending notifications with a relatively small payload.

I recommend that you choose a suitable data format when communicating over Web Sockets. In most cases, JSON is sufficient and allows for a simple implementation. JSON messages should be sent as text-messages over Web Sockets. For more advanced scenarios with mixed-type data, I recommend using Google Protocol Buffers, as I describe in Chapter 9.

Although you can implement your own Web Sockets client using the standard `Socket` class in Android, I highly recommend that you use one of the many third-party libraries available. You can choose from several; the one I show here is the one I consider most stable at the moment, the Web Socket implementation for Java by Nathan Rajlich (also known as *TooTallNate*), which you can find at `http://java-websocket.org`. In addition, it contains a server implementation for Web Sockets, which is useful in Chapter 18. To use this library, simply include the following dependency in your Gradle file:

```
compile 'org.java-websocket:Java-WebSocket:1.3.0'
```

When using Web Sockets through this library, you don't use the `HttpUrlConnection`: instead, you create a `WebSocketClient` and connect to a URI.

The following code is a complete example of using this library to connect to a Web Socket online:

```
public class ChatService extends Service {
    private static final String TAG = "ChatService";
    private ChatWebSocketClient mChatWebSocketClient;
    private ChatClient mChatClient;
    private LocalBinder mLocalBinder = new LocalBinder();

    public IBinder onBind(Intent intent) {
        return mLocalBinder;
    }

    public IBinder onBind(Intent intent) {
        return null;
    }

    public void connectToChatServer(URI serverUri) {
        new ChatWebSocketClient(serverUri).connect();
    }
```

```java
    public void disconnect() {
        if (mChatWebSocketClient != null) {
            mChatWebSocketClient.close();
        }
    }

    public void setChatClient(ChatClient chatClient) {
        mChatClient = chatClient;
    }

    public void sendMessage(String message) {
        if(mChatWebSocketClient != null) {
            mChatWebSocketClient.send(message);
        }
    }

    public boolean isConnected() {
        return mChatWebSocketClient != null;

    public interface ChatClient {
        void onConnected();
        void onMessageReceived(String from, String body, Date timestamp);
        void onDisconnected();
    }

    private class ChatWebSocketClient extends WebSocketClient {

        public ChatWebSocketClient(URI serverURI) {
            super(serverURI);
        }

        @Override
        public void onOpen(ServerHandshake serverHandshake) {
            // Called when the Web Socket is connected
            mChatWebSocketClient = this;
            if(mChatClient != null) {
                mChatClient.onConnected();
            }

            Notification notification = buildNotification();
            startForeground(1001, notification);
        }

        @Override
        public void onMessage(String message) {
            // Called when a text message is received
            if(mChatClient != null) {
                try {
                    JSONObject chatMessage = new JSONObject(message);
                    String from = chatMessage.getString("from");
                    String body = chatMessage.getString("body");
```

```
                    Date timestamp =
                            new Date(chatMessage.getLong("timestamp"));
                    mChatClient.onMessageReceived(from, body, timestamp);
                } catch (JSONException e) {
                    Log.e(TAG, "Malformed message!", e);
                }
            }
        }

        @Override
        public void onMessage(ByteBuffer bytes) {
            // Called when a binary message is received
        }

        @Override
        public void onClose(int code, String reason, boolean remote) {
            // Called when the connection is closed
            mChatWebSocketClient = null;
            if(mChatClient != null) {
                mChatClient.onDisconnected();
            }

            stopForeground(true);
        }

        @Override
        public void onError(Exception e) {
            // Called on in case of communication error
        }
    }

    private class LocalBinder extends Binder {
        public ChatService getService() {
            return ChatService.this;
        }
    }
}
```

This is a guide for implementing Web Socket support in your code. In a real-life application, you should add additional security and error checks. The important thing here is that when you call WebSocketClient.connect(), it spawns a new thread on which this Web Socket will live, which means you don't have to do the background thread yourself when using this library.

The ChatClient extends the WebSocketClient class and implements the different event callbacks. All these callbacks occur on the thread that the Web Socket is running on, so never block these calls because doing so will stall any other traffic on the same Web Socket.

It's good practice to use the onOpen() and onClose() callbacks for determining when the you can start communicating over the Web Socket. In the preceding example, the mChatClient member is set and reset (to null) in the respective method, allowing for a simple null check when sending a message.

I return to the topic of Web Sockets in Chapter 18, where I describe how you can communicate directly between two devices.

Integrating Web Services

Most web services that you will use in your Android app usually fit into one of three categories: those that don't require authentication for a user, those that do require authentication for a user but lack a native SDK for Android, and those that require user authentication and provide an SDK for Android. In this section, I provide three examples that illustrate each of these categories.

Google Static Maps v2

In Chapter 13, I cover the use of the new and powerful Location API for Android. Although it's fairly easy to use, it may sometimes be more than you need. If your application needs to show only a static map that the user won't interact with, you can use Google Static Maps v2 API instead, which is a web service from Google that allows you to fetch a piece of Google Maps as a bitmap image (PNG, GIF, or JPEG).

Here is a simple static method for retrieving a static map:

```
public class StaticMapsFetcher {
    public static final String BASE_URL
            = "http://maps.googleapis.com/maps/api/staticmap";
    // TOOD Create this before release!
    public static final String API_KEY = null;
    public static final String UTF8 = "UTF-8";
    private static final String TAG = "StaticMapsFetcher";

    public static Bitmap fetchMapWithMarkers(String address,
                                             int width,
                                             int height,
                                             String maptype,
                                             List<String> markers) {
        HttpURLConnection urlConnection = null;
        try {
            StringBuilder queryString = new StringBuilder("?");

            if (address != null) {
                queryString.append("center=").
                        append(URLEncoder.encode(address, UTF8)).
                        append("&");
            }
            if (width > 0 && height > 0) {
                queryString.append("size=").
                        append(String.format("%dx%d", width, height)).
                        append("&");
            }
            if (maptype != null) {
                queryString.append("maptype=").
                        append(maptype).append("&");
            }
```

```
                if (markers != null) {
                    for (String marker : markers) {
                        queryString.append("markers=").
                                append(URLEncoder.encode(marker, UTF8));
                    }
                }
                if (API_KEY != null) {
                    queryString.append("key=").append(API_KEY).append("&";
                }

                queryString.append("sensor=false");

                URL url = new URL(BASE_URL + queryString.toString());
                urlConnection = url.openConnection();
                urlConnection.connect();
                if (urlConnection.getResponseCode()
                        == HttpURLConnection.HTTP_OK) {
                    BufferedInputStream bufferedInputStream
                            = new BufferedInputStream(urlConnection.
    getInputStream());
                    return BitmapFactory.decodeStream(bufferedInputStream);
                } else {
                    return null;
                }
            } catch (IOException e) {
                Log.e(TAG, "Error fetching map!", e);
            } finally {
                if (urlConnection != null) {
                    urlConnection.disconnect();
                }
            }
        }
    }
```

Note that the API_KEY is left as null; this is allowed, but not recommended, for the Google Static Maps API. Before you release an application that uses this API, you should create a new API key using the Google API Developer Console.

Also note how the use of URLEncoder.encode() for the values of each parameter. This guarantees that whatever the value is, it will be encoded properly in the URL. When a web service is called, an error stating a bad request is common because the server cannot parse the request parameters properly.

This example shows how the simplest web services can be integrated into an Android application. They are one-way, don't require authentication, and have only a few parameters. You can find more information about the parameters for Google Static Maps API API at https://developers.google.com/maps/documentation/staticmaps.

Foursquare API Using OAuth2

When you use a web service that requires a user account, you need to authenticate the user in some way. However, because your application will be a third-party client for this service, you need some way to provide authentication that doesn't compromise the user's credentials, meaning the username and password shouldn't pass through your code. To solve this issue, a standard named OAuth was developed. This standard is now on its second version and is called OAuth2. It was designed so that web applications can allow one website to integrate with a second one on behalf of a user. To use it on Android, you route the authentication through a `WebView` that displays the service authentication web page for the user.

Although it's possible to implement all of the steps for OAuth2 yourself, I recommend using a third-party library that hides away some of the complexity. The one I recommend is called Scribe and can be found at `https://github.com/fernandezpablo85/scribe-java`. Scribe provides a simple wrapper on top of the `HttpUrlConnection` class for OAuth2-enabled services, so it's an excellent use for Android.

In this OAuth2 example, the user's friends are displayed on Foursquare. Although many of the API calls for Foursquare don't require authentication (like searching for venues), getting a list of Foursquare friends will obviously require authentication by the user.

The following code shows an `Activity` that you can use to get authorization for a user's Foursquare account using OAuth2:

```
public class OAuthActivity extends Activity {
    public static final String CLIENT_ID
            = "<Client ID from foursquare.com/developer>";
    public static final String CLIENT_SECRET
            = "<Client SECRET from foursquare.com/developer>";
    public static final Token EMPTY_TOKEN = null;
    public static final String ACCESS_TOKEN = "foursquare.access_token";
    private static final String TAG = "FoursquareOAuth2";
    private OAuthService mOAuthService;

    @Override
    protected void onCreate(Bundle savedInstanceState) {
        super.onCreate(savedInstanceState);
        setContentView(R.layout.activity_main);
    }

    @Override
    protected void onResume() {
        super.onResume();
        mOAuthService = new ServiceBuilder()
                .provider(Foursquare2Api.class)
                .apiKey(CLIENT_ID)
                .apiSecret(CLIENT_SECRET)
                .callback("oauth://foursquare")
                .build();
        String authorizationUrl =
                        mOAuthService.getAuthorizationUrl(EMPTY_TOKEN);
        WebView webView = (WebView) findViewById(R.id.oauth_view);

        WebViewClient webViewClient = new WebViewClient() {
            @Override
            public boolean shouldOverrideUrlLoading(WebView view,
```

```
                                            String url) {
            if (url.startsWith("oauth")) {
                Uri uri = Uri.parse(url);
                String oauthCode = uri.getQueryParameter("code");
                Verifier verifier = new Verifier(oauthCode);
                new GetTokenAccess().execute(verifier);
                return true;
            }
            return super.shouldOverrideUrlLoading(view, url);
        }
    };
    webView.setWebViewClient(webViewClient);
    webView.getSettings().setJavaScriptEnabled(true);
    webView.loadUrl(authorizationUrl);
}

class GetTokenAccess extends AsyncTask<Verifier, Void, Token> {
    @Override
    protected Token doInBackground(Verifier... verifiers) {
        Token accessToken = mOAuthService.
                getAccessToken(EMPTY_TOKEN, verifiers[0]);
        return accessToken;
    }

    @Override
    protected void onPostExecute(Token token) {
        if (token != null) {
            Intent intent = new Intent();
            intent.putExtra(ACCESS_TOKEN, token.getToken());
            setResult(RESULT_OK, intent);
        } else {
            setResult(RESULT_CANCELED);
        }
        finish();
    }
}
}
```

The actual authentication and authorization toward Foursquare goes through a custom `WebViewClient`. The custom `WebViewClient` overrides the method `shouldOverrideUrlLoading()`, which allows you to capture all calls to a URL that this `WebView` will do. In this case, you monitor for all calls that match the callback URL, which will contain the access token needed for signing API requests.

The example needs to use an `AsyncTask` because you cannot do direct network calls on the main thread. `OAuthService.getAccessToken()` will perform a network call to retrieve the access token used for the API calls that require a signed-in user.

The following code uses the `Activity` from the previous example:

```
public class FoursquareActivity extends Activity {
    public static final String TAG = "FoursquareActivity";
```

```java
public static final int OAUTH_REQUEST_CODE = 1001;
public static final String FRIENDS_URI =
                    "https://api.foursquare.com/v2/users/self/friends";
private SharedPreferences mPreferences;

@Override
protected void onCreate(Bundle savedInstanceState) {
    super.onCreate(savedInstanceState);
    setContentView(R.layout.foursquare_main);
    mPreferences = PreferenceManager.
            getDefaultSharedPreferences(this);
}

@Override
protected void onResume() {
    super.onResume();
    if (mPreferences.contains(OAuthActivity.ACCESS_TOKEN)) {
        new GetFoursquareFriends().execute("55.59612590", "12.98140870");
    } else {
        startActivityForResult(new Intent(this, OAuthActivity.class),
                OAUTH_REQUEST_CODE);
    }
}

@Override
protected void onActivityResult(int requestCode,
                                int resultCode,
                                Intent data) {
    if (requestCode == OAUTH_REQUEST_CODE) {
        if (resultCode == RESULT_OK) {
            String accesToken = data.
                    getStringExtra(OAuthActivity.ACCESS_TOKEN);
            mPreferences.edit().
                    putString(OAuthActivity.ACCESS_TOKEN,
                            accesToken).apply();
        } else {
            mPreferences.edit().
                    remove(OAuthActivity.ACCESS_TOKEN).apply();
        }
    }
}

class GetFoursquareFriends extends AsyncTask<String, Void, JSONObject> {

    @Override
    protected JSONObject doInBackground(String... lngLat) {
        OAuthService service = new ServiceBuilder()
                .provider(Foursquare2Api.class)
                .apiKey(OAuthActivity.CLIENT_ID)
                .apiSecret(OAuthActivity.CLIENT_SECRET)
                .callback("oauth://foursquare")
                .build();
```

```
        String accessToken = mPreferences.
                getString(OAuthActivity.ACCESS_TOKEN, null);
        OAuthRequest request = new OAuthRequest(Verb.GET,
                FRIENDS_URI);
        request.addQuerystringParameter("oauth_token",
                accessToken);

        Token token = new Token(accessToken,
                OAuthActivity.CLIENT_SECRET);
        service.signRequest(token, request);
        Response response = request.send();

        if (response.isSuccessful()) {
            try {
                return new JSONObject(response.getBody());
            } catch (JSONException e) {
                Log.e(TAG, "Error building JSONObjet!", e);
            }
        } else {
            Log.d(TAG, "Bad request: "
                    + response.getCode()
                    + " "
                    + response.getMessage());
        }
        return null;
    }


    @Override
    protected void onPostExecute(JSONObject response) {
        if (response != null) {
            try {
                JSONArray friends = response.
                        getJSONObject("response").
                        getJSONObject("friends").
                        getJSONArray("items");
                Log.d(TAG, "Friends: " + friends);
            } catch (JSONException e) {
                Log.e(TAG, "JSON Exception", e);
            }
        }
    }
}
}
```

You start by checking whether an access token is already stored; if not, the OAuth2 `Activity` is started with `Activity.startActivityForResult()`. When the OAuth2 process is completed, successful or not, `onActivityResult()` from the preceding example is called with the results.

Using the `AsyncTask` from the preceding example, you can set up an `OAuthRequest` with the new access token. In this case, an array of all the user's friends on Foursquare is retrieved.

I use the preceding code only to illustrate how to use Scribe and OAuth2 in your application. Because OAuth2 requires user interaction, this is one of the few cases where you must perform network operations from an `Activity`.

You can use the Scribe library for any API that supports OAuth2 for authorization. Check the documentation of the library for officially supported services.

Facebook SDK for Android

Because OAuth2 was designed for the web, it's not a perfect match for a native Android application. Many services have solved this problem in a similar way using a native Android app instead. For instance, Facebook has a great web service that allows you to integrate its Graph API and other Facebook APIs into your Android application. Because users who want to use the Facebook integration in your application most likely will have the Facebook app installed as well, they perform a similar authorization process by using Android `Activities`.

The Facebook SDK for Android (version 3.0 and later) allows you to easily integrate Facebook authorization and authentication for your application using its library project. You can then use this API to simply track users in your application or integrate with Facebook services and send messages and photos. The Facebook SDK for Android is available at `https://developers.facebook.com/android`.

First, you need to register your application on the Facebook Developer site (`https://developers.facebook.com/apps`). Click Create New App and enter the name of your app while leaving the rest of the fields empty or in their default. Next, open the Native Android app section and fill in the details related to your app, as shown in Figure 17-2.

The key hash for your application is generated with the following command in your terminal:

```
$ keytool -exportcert -alias androiddebugkey –keystore  ~/.android/debug.
keystore | openssl sha1 -binary | openssl base64
```

When the online registration is complete, copy the app ID and add it as a String resource in your application's resources. Then you add a `metadata` element that points to this value as well as a reference to the Facebook `LoginActivity`.

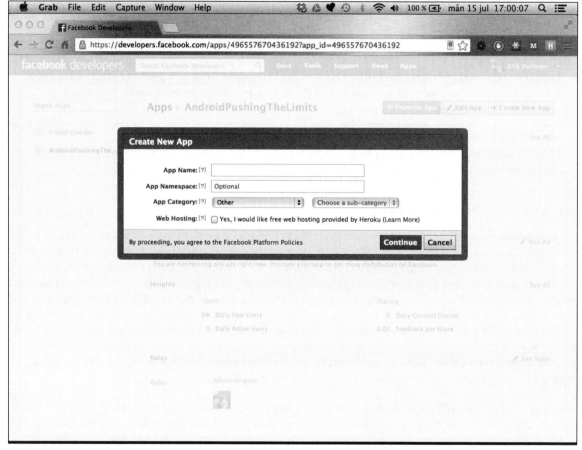

Figure 17-2 Creating a new Facebook app with Android support using the Facebook Developer console

Here is a snippet from the `AndroidManifest.xml` where the necessary components and metadata for Facebook integration (marked in bold) are added:

```
<application
    android:allowBackup="true"
    android:icon="@drawable/ic_launcher"
    android:label="@string/app_name"
    android:theme="@style/AppTheme" >

    <uses-permission android:name="android.permission.INTERNET" />

    <activity
        android:name="com.aptl.myfacebookdemo.MainActivity"
        android:label="@string/app_name" >
        <intent-filter>
            <action android:name="android.intent.action.MAIN" />
            <category android:name="android.intent.category.LAUNCHER" />
        </intent-filter>
    </activity>
```

```
        <activity android:name="com.facebook.LoginActivity"/>
        <meta-data android:name="com.facebook.sdk.ApplicationId"
                    android:value="@string/facebook_app_id" />
</application>
```

Next, you need to implement the Facebook callbacks in `MainActivity`. Also, don't forget to add the `INTERNET` permission as just shown.

The `UiLifecycleHelper` class takes care of all the state changes related to your `Activity` states. All you need to do is override the `onCreate()`, `onResume()`, `onActivityResult()`, `onPause()`, and `onDestroy()` and do the equivalent callback on the helper class, as shown here:

```java
public class MainActivity extends Activity
                            implements Session.StatusCallback {
    private UiLifecycleHelper mUiLifecycleHelper;

    @Override
    protected void onCreate(Bundle savedInstanceState) {
        super.onCreate(savedInstanceState);
        setContentView(R.layout.activity_main);
        LoginButton authButton =
                            (LoginButton) findViewById(R.id.authButton);
        authButton.setReadPermissions(Arrays.asList("user_birthday",
                                            "friends_birthday"));
        mUiLifecycleHelper = new UiLifecycleHelper(this, this);
        mUiLifecycleHelper.onCreate(savedInstanceState);
    }

    @Override
    protected void onResume() {
        super.onResume();
        mUiLifecycleHelper.onResume();
    }

    @Override
    protected void onPause() {
        super.onPause();
        mUiLifecycleHelper.onPause();
    }

    @Override
    protected void onDestroy() {
        super.onDestroy();
        mUiLifecycleHelper.onDestroy();
    }

    @Override
    protected void onSaveInstanceState(Bundle outState) {
        super.onSaveInstanceState(outState);
        mUiLifecycleHelper.onSaveInstanceState(outState);
    }
```

```
    @Override
    protected void onActivityResult(int requestCode, int resultCode,
                                    Intent data) {
        super.onActivityResult(requestCode, resultCode, data);
        mUiLifecycleHelper.onActivityResult(requestCode, resultCode,
data);
    }

    @Override
    public void call(Session session, SessionState state,
                     Exception exception) {
        // Callback for session state changes...
    }
}
```

Note the `LoginButton` that's added to the layout for this `Activity`. You can use it to provide a default Facebook Login button to your application. It's also possible to pass extra parameters, such as necessary permissions and such, which will then be passed on to the authentication process. When the user taps the Login button, a dialog box appears asking the user if she wants to allow your application to get the permissions it has requested, as shown in Figure 17-3.

Figure 17-3 Dialog box asking the user for permissions to access her specific Facebook data

You can add the Facebook Login button in the XML layout for your `Activity` as shown in the following. This way, you can control where the button should appear while at the same time provide a familiar entry point for the user to log in to Facebook.

```
<com.facebook.widget.LoginButton
        android:id="@+id/authButton"
        android:layout_width="wrap_content"
        android:layout_height="wrap_content"
        android:layout_gravity="center_horizontal"
        android:layout_marginTop="5dp" />
```

Once you have a valid authentication toward Facebook, you can use the `Request` class from the Facebook SDK to perform requests. The methods provided by this class come in many different versions, some are asynchronous and perform the network call on a separate background thread, while others are synchronous and allow you to control the background threading yourself. In the following code example you can see a request for the user's friends made using the asynchronous method.

```
public void doLoadFriendList(View view) {
    if(SessionState.OPENED_TOKEN_UPDATED.
            equals(mSessionState)
            || SessionState.OPENED.equals(mSessionState)) {
        Request.executeMyFriendsRequestAsync(mSession,
                new Request.GraphUserListCallback() {
            @Override
            public void onCompleted(List<GraphUser> friends,
                                    Response response) {
                Log.d(TAG, "Friends loaded: " + friends.size());
                mFriendListAdatper.clear();
                mFriendListAdatper.addAll(friends);
                mFriendListAdatper.notifyDataSetChanged();
            }
        });
    }
}
```

Using the Facebook SDK for Android to add Facebook integration to your application is significantly simpler than using the web-based OAuth2 approach shown in the previous section. Facebook SDK for Android allows you to provide a secure method for authorization without having to break the Android UI paradigm.

Finding Online Web Services and APIs

It's impossible to provide a complete list for all the available web services online, mostly because that list changes every day. However, a number of useful resources are online where you can find web services for different things. A good place to start is at www.programmableweb.com, which provides an online directory for many different web services and APIs. Two other very good directory resources for online web services and APIs are www.apis.io and www.mashape.com.

If you need an online service, rest assured that you'll be able to find some exiting web services or online APIs. Although most of these services provide a free tier, several require you either to pay a fee (usually based on usage or a monthly fee) or to contact the provider in order to set up a contract for their use. Often, it may be cheaper to pay for an existing service than try to implement one from scratch, unless that's your core business.

Network and Power Consumption

When it comes to power consumption, the second biggest cause of battery drain is often related to network traffic (the display usually comes first). Users who disable mobile data will see an immediate decrease in battery drain, but will also lose all features requiring online connectivity. Smartphone manufacturers, chipset vendors, and Google have all implemented a number of ways to reduce the amount of network traffic and battery drain in order to increase the battery's life. However, unless application developers follow the guidelines and use the tools at their disposal, these improvements are all in vain.

Because of the openness of the Android platform, a single application can keep the mobile radio in high-drive mode more than needed, thus draining the battery faster. In later versions of Android, users can track the network usage for each application (see Figure 17-4). Although network traffic from your app will not cost you anything, excessive use will cost the user through battery loss and data traffic charges, probably resulting in a very bad review rating. It's in your best interest to make sure you don't use more data than is absolutely necessary.

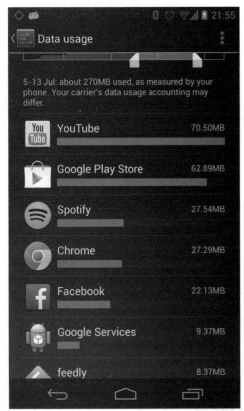

Figure 17-4 Data Usage from the Settings application shows how much data each application used during a certain period

The radio hardware on a smartphone, that is the Wi-Fi and the cellular chip, has built-in power-saving features on the hardware level that automatically kicks in when no network traffic is active (that is, no incoming or outgoing data packages) and reduces the consumption of power to a very low level. When an application wants to send data or when an application is waiting for incoming data and a package is received, the network hardware will disable the power saving in order to be able to send data as fast and efficiently as possible.

If only one application on a device is making network calls, there's no problem with consumption of power. The problem occurs when many applications want to access the network, and they're doing so in random order.

General Guidelines

Before performing a network call, first consider whether the user really needs this data right now. For instance, if the data your application fetches is quite small, it's probably okay to fetch it when the user launches the application instead of continuously updating the data at regular intervals or when your app gets a notification (either through Google Cloud Messaging or some other push notification service). Unnecessary network requests is the most common mistake for applications that fetch data online. In many situations, you can wait until the user explicitly requests the data (for instance, when the application is launched).

Second, consider how much data you need to retrieve. For example, in an e-mail application, it's usually enough to fetch only the ten latest e-mail headers, which could be more difficult to implement, especially on the server-side, but will save data traffic and reduce the time required for the network call to complete. Using different types of caches (like the response cache introduced for `HttpUrlConnection` in Android 4/ICS) and retrieving smaller pages of data from the service will greatly reduce your application's network traffic.

Also, because the `HttpUrlConnection` class now supports transparent compressions, make sure that the data retrieved from the server is gzip-compressed if possible—this compress/decompress feature is enabled by default by most major public web services. Another way to optimize the amount of data is to choose a better data format, which usually involves a balance between size optimization and how dynamic the format is. If you can, choose a format that allows you to extend your data definition without losing backward-compatibility. Although JSON is good enough for most situations, and also allows you to use the same backend for web clients, the best choice in terms of size is probably Google Protocol Buffers.

Finally, my third tip is related to the first one. If you need to notify the user about a new message or some other online information that requires the user's attention, you cannot wait until the user starts the application to perform the network call. In such cases, you have two choices: polling the service at regular intervals or letting the server push the information down to the client.

Power Efficient Network Polling

Network polling has several drawbacks but is sometimes the only viable way for you to check whether there's something new to fetch from an online service. Fortunately, Android provides a convenient API for doing recurring polling through the `AlarmManager` API.

Following is an example of a method for scheduling a recurring polling at 15-minute intervals. Note the use of `ELAPSED_REALTIME` as the type of alarm:

```
public void scheduleNetworkPolling() {
    AlarmManager alarmManager = (AlarmManager)
            getSystemService(ALARM_SERVICE);
    int alarmType = AlarmManager.ELAPSED_REALTIME;
    long interval = AlarmManager.INTERVAL_FIFTEEN_MINUTES;
    long start = System.currentTimeMillis() + interval;

    Intent pollIntent
            = new Intent(MyNetworkService.ACTION_PERFORM_POLL);
    PendingIntent pendingIntent
            = PendingIntent.getService(this, 0, pollIntent, 0);

    alarmManager.setInexactRepeating(alarmType,
            start, interval, pendingIntent);
}
```

If you need to awaken the device from a suspended mode, change `ELAPSED_REALTIME` to `ELAPSED_REALTIME_WAKEUP`. Doing so, however, causes the device to consume more battery because it will go out of suspend mode every 15 minutes.

The way the `setInexactRepeating()` works is that all applications that register for a wakeup using this service with the same interval will be awakened at the same time. Regardless of when an application registered for a 15-minute wakeup interval, it will receive its `PendingIntent` at the same time the other registered applications do.

Although this approach doesn't consume less battery, it will reduce the device's overall consumption of power if all applications that need a recurring polling interval use it. This will then ensure that no network polling happens between the 15-minute intervals.

Server-Side Push

The best solution for reducing the number of network calls is to use a server-side push. This technique allows the server to actively notify a client that there is new data to retrieve. The server-side push notification can come in many forms. It can be an out-of-bounds message that comes through a messaging service not directly connected to the Internet, like SMS, or it can be a regular TCP socket with a long keep-alive.

The most obvious choice for server-side push notifications is Google Cloud Messaging, which I explain in detail in Chapter 19. However, two other solutions are available for server-side push.

SMS Push Notifications

As I explain in Chapter 15, you can register a `BroadcastReceiver` to receive incoming SMS as part of the hidden Android APIs. This solution can work as an out-of-bounds server-side push notification that wakes up the device and notifies it that there is new data to fetch online. Although this solution has a certain monetary cost for the service provider, it can be used for notifications that happen less frequently or when you're able to send SMS for free (for instance, if you're writing an application for a telecom operator).

The following code is a slightly modified version of the example in Chapter 15. In this case, the method `processSms()` will return `true` or `false` depending on whether it's a push notification

SMS you're expecting. If `true`, the network service starts and you call `abortBroadcast()` and `setResultData(null);` to ensure that the SMS is not propagated to the other receivers.

```java
public class MySmsPushNotifier extends BroadcastReceiver {
    // Copied from Telephony.java
    public static final String SMS_RECEIVED_ACTION
            = "android.provider.Telephony.SMS_RECEIVED";
    public static final String MESSAGE_SERVICE_NUMBER = "+461234567890";
    private static final String MESSAGE_SERVICE_PREFIX = "MYSERVICE";

    public void onReceive(Context context, Intent intent) {
        String action = intent.getAction();
        if (SMS_RECEIVED_ACTION.equals(action)) {
            Object[] messages =
                    (Object[]) intent.getSerializableExtra("pdus");
            for (Object message : messages) {
                byte[] messageData = (byte[]) message;
                SmsMessage smsMessage =
                        SmsMessage.createFromPdu(messageData);
                if (processSms(smsMessage)) {
                    Intent networkIntent
                            = new Intent(MyNetworkService.
                            ACTION_PERFORM_NETWORK_CALL);
                    context.startService(networkIntent);
                    abortBroadcast();
                    setResultData(null);
                }
            }
        }
    }

    private boolean processSms(SmsMessage smsMessage) {
        String from = smsMessage.getOriginatingAddress();
        if (MESSAGE_SERVICE_NUMBER.equals(from)) {
            String messageBody = smsMessage.getMessageBody();
            if (messageBody.startsWith(MESSAGE_SERVICE_PREFIX)) {
                return true;
            }
        }
        return false;
    }
}
```

In order for your receiver to take priority over the default SMS receiver, you also need to modify the priority of the `intent-filter` as shown here:

```xml
<receiver android:name=".MySmsPushNotifier">
    <intent-filter android:priority="9999">
        <action android:name="android.provider.Telephony.SMS_RECEIVED" />
    </intent-filter>
</receiver>
```

Web Sockets for Server-Side Push

I describe how to use Web Sockets earlier in this chapter. You can create a light-weight server-side push notification service using Web Sockets. This method is not foolproof, and you need to adjust the timeout on the socket on both the server and the client for this method to be efficient.

In the following example, the callbacks signal which state the push-notification socket is in:

```
class PushNotificationSocket extends WebSocketClient {

    public PushNotificationSocket(URI serverURI) {
        super(serverURI);
    }

    @Override
    public void onOpen(ServerHandshake serverHandshake) {
        // Web Socket opened - now registered for notifications
    }

    @Override
    public void onMessage(String message) {
        try {
            JSONObject jsonObject = new JSONObject(message);
            parseNotification(jsonObject);
        } catch (JSONException e) {
            Log.e(TAG, "Error parsing notification message!", e);
        }
    }

    @Override
    public void onClose(int code, String reason, boolean remote) {
        // Socket closed - reopen if this was unintentional
        // due to a network timeout or similar
    }

    @Override
    public void onError(Exception e) {
        // Error, possibly due to timeout.
        // Reconnect if possible.
    }
}
```

This code is only partially complete but illustrates how Web Sockets can be used for a light-weight server-side push notification. You also need a server that can respond to Web Socket requests. In Chapter 18, I provide an example of such a server using the same Web Socket library used in this chapter. You can also use this library on a server-side Java application.

Summary

In this chapter, I explained the best way to use a number of different APIs and libraries for doing networking communication over HTTP. The standard `HttpUrlConnection` is sufficient for most situations, but if you will do a lot of networking calls, you should take a look at the alternatives covered in this chapter.

I also discussed how to integrate three different types of web services, from the simplest ones that don't require any authentication to the more complicated ones that require OAuth2 or a native Android SDK. Most of the web services you'll encounter can fit into one of these three categories.

In the final part of this chapter, I provided some guidelines on what to consider when it comes to power consumption and network operations. If possible, try to use Google Cloud Messaging from a server to notify your application when new data is available. However, when server-side push is not possible, you should use the periodic scheduling from the `AlarmManager`, which will help applications perform their network polling at the same time, thus keeping the device in a suspended mode longer.

Networking is a complicated topic, and this chapter's space doesn't allow coverage of all options. Before performing network calls, make sure that the network is available and listen for changes in the connectivity using a `BroadcastReceiver`, as I describe in Chapter 8. If your application transmits large amounts of data, like high-resolution photos, consider having an option to disable network communication for your application when on a mobile network and only allow the traffic to occur over Wi-Fi. This is best done through some settings UI, as I describe in Chapter 9. Finally, always assume that any network operation you initiate could fail and produce a faulty or abnormal response. Implementing proper and thorough error-handling in your network calls is very important. I highly recommend that you write automated unit tests, as I describe in Chapter 10, to verify your code as much as possible.

Further Resources

Documentation

> For the HTTP protocol: `http://www.w3.org/Protocols/`

Websites

> SPDY specification and whitepaper: `http://dev.chromium.org/spdy/spdy-whitepaper`

> The latest draft for HTTP/2.0, based on SPDY: `http://http2.github.io/http2-spec`

> The OAuth Bible from Mashape: `https://github.com/Mashape/mashape-oauth/blob/master/FLOWS.md`

> How OAuth2 works by Aaron Parecki: `http://aaronparecki.com/articles/2012/07/29/1/oauth2-simplified`

> How to perform regular updates without draining the battery: `http://developer.android.com/training/efficient-downloads/regular_updates.html`

> How to make more energy and network efficient apps: `http://developer.sonymobile.com/knowledge-base/tutorials/android_tutorial/how-to-develop-energy-and-network-efficient-apps-tutorial`

Chapter 18

Communicating with Remote Devices

The most common use of network communication in Android applications is when calling online web services, which I cover in Chapter 17. However, another area of communication is between your Android device and some other local device. The second device can be another Android smartphone, an activity tracker, a heartbeat monitor, a wireless weather station, or simply a regular laptop. A number of different technologies on Android support communication with these devices. You can use a USB-cable from your Android smartphone to the device, Bluetooth Low Energy for short-range and power-efficient wireless communication, or WiFi Direct for high-speed peer-to-peer networking.

In this chapter, I cover some of the different communication technologies supported by Android (USB, Bluetooth Low Energy, and Wi-Fi). I continue with some more advanced solutions using the WiFi Direct technology supported by Android, which lets you do peer-to-peer connectivity between multiple devices using high-speed Wi-Fi. Next, I show how you can announce and discover services on a Wi-Fi (or WiFi Direct) network using the built-in discovery service in the Android APIs. Finally, I show how you can implement your own web server in an Android application and how to publish an API on top of it, either using RESTful web services or an asynchronous Web Socket server.

Android's Connectivity Technologies

Most Android devices support a number of connectivity technologies. Basically, these are USB, Bluetooth, and Wi-Fi. Furthermore, these technologies can be divided into subcategories. For instance, you can use the APIs in Android to perform raw serial communication over USB, or you can use the Android Open Accessory Protocol defined by Google specifically for hardware accessories targeting Android devices. The Android Open Accessory Protocol is supported through the Accessory Development Kit (ADK).

All Android devices support the Classic Bluetooth profiles, which are suitable for more battery-intensive operations such as audio streaming. With Android 4.3, you now have support for Bluetooth Low Energy devices and the Bluetooth Smart technology, which enables you to write applications that can discover and communicate with devices that support the GATT profile (like heart monitors, step counters, and other low-power accessories).

For the more data-intensive communication scenarios, you can use Wi-Fi. Android has three modes in which its Wi-Fi can operate: infrastructure (standard Wi-Fi connected to an access point), tethering (Android device acting as a Wi-Fi access point to other devices), and WiFi Direct. Infrastructure is what you generally use when your device is connected to a Wi-Fi and you access the Internet. For the purpose of this chapter, just know that this works well when all devices are connected to the same Wi-Fi network, which usually means at home, at work or when using a public Wi-Fi somewhere. Tethering can only be activated by the user through the Network menu in the Settings application (unless you have access to the platform certificate, as I describe in Chapter 16), which means it is of little interest for most developers.

WiFi Direct is one of the most interesting technologies for Android, because on later devices it can be active in parallel with the infrastructure mode (that is, you can use WiFi Direct while connected to your home Wi-Fi). WiFi Direct allows an application to set up a peer-to-peer Wi-Fi network that works without the need for a dedicated access point. This makes WiFi Direct very attractive for network communication between devices in a more ad hoc scenario. It also provides high-speed connectivity that cannot be achieved by routing the communication over a server on the Internet. For instance, if you want to create a multiplayer game that doesn't require Internet connectivity or if you need a fast and secure way of sharing data (like photos) between two friends, WiFi Direct is a very suitable solution.

Android USB

USB on Android is supported through the APIs found in the package `android.hardware.usb`. There is also a library for supporting USB accessories available for devices running Android 2.3.4. In this chapter, I focus on the *host mode* for USB communication. For information about USB accessory mode, see `http://developer.android.com/guide/topics/connectivity/usb/accessory.html`.

USB is designed so that one device acts as a *host* to a number of other devices. Among other things, the host can supply power to the connected devices, which is why you don't need an extra battery for USB mice or why you can charge your Android smartphone using the USB port on your laptop.

An Android device can also act as a USB host, allowing you to power external devices, which means you can connect to things like card readers, finger print scanners, and other USB connected peripherals to your Android devices.

To enable an application to communicate over USB, first you define the `Activity` that starts when you connect your USB device. In the following code, you see an example of how this can look in the manifest. Note the `metadata` element that defines an XML file, which acts as a filter to select which USB devices your application will trigger on.

```
<activity
    android:name=".MyUsbDemo"
    android:label="@string/app_name" >
    <intent-filter>
        <action
            android:name="android.hardware.usb.action.USB_DEVICE_ATTACHED"
/>
    </intent-filter>
    <meta-data
            android:name="android.hardware.usb.action.USB_DEVICE_ATTACHED"
            android:resource="@xml/device_filter" />
</activity>
```

The `device_filter.xml` can look like the following example. In this case, it will filter on an Arduino Uno board and start your `Activity` when you plug in such a device on your Android smartphone.

```
<resources>
    <usb-device vendor-id="9025" product-id="67" />
</resources>
```

The onResume() method shown in the following code example demonstrates how you can get the UsbDevice instance from the Intent that will launch your Activity.

```
protected void onResume() {
    super.onResume();
    Intent intent = getIntent();
    UsbDevice device = (UsbDevice) intent.
            getParcelableExtra(UsbManager.EXTRA_DEVICE);
    Log.d(TAG, "Found USB Device: " + device.toString());
    new Thread(new UsbCommunciation(device)).start();
}
```

After you have the UsbDevice object, you can start communicating with the device by opening a connection, claiming its interface and retrieving the endpoints for reading and writing. In the following example, I continuously write the same message to the device and read a response, using the buildTransfer() method.

```
private class UsbCommunciation implements Runnable {
    private final UsbDevice mDevice;

    UsbCommunciation(UsbDevice dev) {
        mDevice = dev;
    }

    @Override
    public void run() {
        UsbDeviceConnection usbConnection
                        = mUsbManager.openDevice(mDevice);
        if (!usbConnection.claimInterface(mDevice.getInterface(1),
                                    true)) {
            return;
        }
        // Arduino USB serial converter setup
        usbConnection.controlTransfer(0x21, 34, 0, 0, null, 0, 0);
        usbConnection.controlTransfer(0x21, 32, 0, 0,
                                new byte[]{(byte) 0x80, 0x25, 0x00,
                                        0x00, 0x00, 0x00, 0x08},
                                7, 0);

        UsbEndpoint output = null;
        UsbEndpoint input = null;

        UsbInterface usbInterface = mDevice.getInterface(1);
        for (int i = 0; i < usbInterface.getEndpointCount(); i++) {
            if (usbInterface.getEndpoint(i).getType() ==
                UsbConstants.USB_ENDPOINT_XFER_BULK) {
                if (usbInterface.getEndpoint(i).getDirection() ==
                    UsbConstants.USB_DIR_IN) {
                    input = usbInterface.getEndpoint(i);
                }
                if (usbInterface.getEndpoint(i).getDirection() ==
                    UsbConstants.USB_DIR_OUT) {
                    output = usbInterface.getEndpoint(i);
                }
```

```
                }
            }

            byte[] readBuffer = new byte[MAX_MESSAGE_SIZE];
            while (!mStop) {
                usbConnection.bulkTransfer(output, TEST_MESSAGE,
                                            TEST_MESSAGE.length, 0);
                int read = usbConnection.bulkTransfer(input, readBuffer,
                                                    0, readBuffer.length,
                                                    0);

                handleResponse(readBuffer, read);
                SystemClock.sleep(1000);
            }

            usbConnection.close();
            usbConnection.releaseInterface(usbInterface);
        }
    }
```

USB communication in Android can be handy in situations where wireless interfaces aren't sufficient. It can also be a simple solution for when you need to start prototyping on a new accessory where you don't have a working Bluetooth or Wi-Fi stack ready.

Bluetooth Low Energy

With Android 4.3, Google introduced support for Bluetooth Smart, which also includes support for Bluetooth Low Energy (BLE) devices like heart rate monitors and activity trackers. This opens up the possibility for you to build new and exciting features by extending your apps with support from a wide range of devices.

Figure 18-1 illustrates how the BLE services are structured. A device can have a number of services, such as battery, heart rate monitor, and cycling speed. Each service has a number of characteristics, such as the body location of the heart rate monitor or the number of RPMs for your bicycle. Some characteristics, such as current time, support writing from the client (your Android device), whereas others support only reading and/or notifications. Furthermore, each characteristic can have a number of descriptors attached to it. Descriptors work as additional information about the characteristic they're attached to.

To support BLE, you first need to add the BLUETOOTH and BLUETOOTH_ADMIN permissions to your application, as shown next. You should also declare the use of the bluetooth_le feature so that your app is available only to devices that support it.

```
<uses-permission android:name="android.permission.BLUETOOTH"/>
<uses-permission android:name="android.permission.BLUETOOTH_ADMIN"/>

<uses-feature android:name="android.hardware.bluetooth_le"
              android:required="true"/>
```

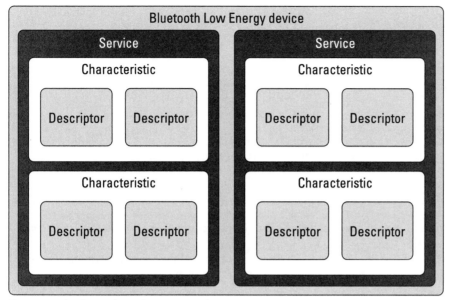

Figure 18-1 The Bluetooth Low Energy system design

Before performing a Bluetooth operation (LE or Classic), you need to verify that it is enabled. The following method checks whether Bluetooth is enabled and, if Bluetooth isn't enabled, displays the system dialog asking the user to activate it.

```
protected void onResume() {
    super.onResume();
    if(!mBluetoothAdapter.isEnabled()) {
        Intent enableIntent  = new Intent(BluetoothAdapter.
                                            ACTION_REQUEST_ENABLE);
        startActivityForResult(enableIntent, ENABLE_REQUEST);
    }
}
```

Next, you can start the scanning of BLE devices, as shown here:

```
public void doStartBtleScan() {
    mLeScanCallback = new MyLeScanCallback();
    BluetoothManager bluetoothManager =
            (BluetoothManager) getSystemService(Context.BLUETOOTH_
SERVICE);
    mBluetoothAdapter = bluetoothManager.getAdapter();
    mBluetoothAdapter.startLeScan(mLeScanCallback);
}
```

After a BLE device is found, you'll receive a callback where you can continue and complete the connection to the device. In the following code, I stop further scanning of devices and initiate a connection.

```
private class MyLeScanCallback implements BluetoothAdapter.LeScanCallback {
    @Override
    public void onLeScan(BluetoothDevice bluetoothDevice,
                         int rssi, byte[] scanRecord) {
        // TODO: Verify that we have the correct device...
        mBluetoothAdapter.stopLeScan(this);
        mMyGattCallback = new MyGattCallback();
        mGatt = bluetoothDevice.connectGatt(BtleDemo.this,
                                            false, mMyGattCallback);
    }
}
```

If your application will connect to a specific type of device, you can inspect the device here before connecting.

The callback method `onConnectionStateChange()` receives a call once the connection is made. At this point, you can discover the services available on the remote device, as shown here:

```
private class MyGattCallback extends BluetoothGattCallback {
    @Override
    public void onConnectionStateChange(BluetoothGatt gatt,
                                        int status, int newState) {
        super.onConnectionStateChange(gatt, status, newState);
        if(newState  == BluetoothGatt.STATE_CONNECTED &&
            status == BluetoothGatt.GATT_SUCCESS) {
          Log.d(TAG, "Connected to " + gatt.getDevice().getName());
          gatt.discoverServices();
        }
    }
}
```

When the BLE service discovery is completed for the device, as shown in the following code example, you can iterate over the services and its characteristics. For each characteristic, you check whether it supports reading and notifications, and if so call the respective method.

```
@Override
public void onServicesDiscovered(BluetoothGatt gatt, int status) {
    super.onServicesDiscovered(gatt, status);
    if(status == BluetoothGatt.GATT_SUCCESS) {
        List<BluetoothGattService> services = gatt.getServices();
        for (BluetoothGattService service : services) {
            Log.d(TAG, "Found service: " + service.getUuid());
            for (BluetoothGattCharacteristic characteristic :
                                        service.getCharacteristics()) {
                Log.d(TAG, "Found characteristic: " +
                        characteristic.getUuid());

                if(hasProperty(characteristic,
                        BluetoothGattCharacteristic.PROPERTY_READ)) {
```

```
                    Log.d(TAG, "Read characteristic: " +
                            characteristic.getUuid());
                    gatt.readCharacteristic(characteristic);
                }

                if(hasProperty(characteristic,
                        BluetoothGattCharacteristic.PROPERTY_NOTIFY)) {
                    Log.d(TAG, "Register notification for characteristic: "
                            + characteristic.getUuid());
                    gatt.setCharacteristicNotification(characteristic,
                                                    true);
                }
            }
        }
    }

    }
}

public static boolean hasProperty(BluetoothGattCharacteristic
    characteristic, int property) {
    int prop = characteristic.getProperties() & property;
    return prop == property;
}
```

The read operation on a characteristic is asynchronous, so you have to read the value in the callback. The registration for notifications will also use a callback from the same interface to notify your application of its updates. The following code shows how you can read the signed 32-bit integer value from this characteristic, both for asynchronous reading and for notifications.

```
@Override
public void onCharacteristicRead(BluetoothGatt gatt,
    BluetoothGattCharacteristic characteristic, int status) {
    super.onCharacteristicRead(gatt, characteristic, status);
    if(status == BluetoothGatt.GATT_SUCCESS) {
        Integer value =
    characteristic.getIntValue(BluetoothGattCharacteristic.FORMAT_SINT32,
                            0);
        // TODO Handle read value...
    }
}

@Override
public void onCharacteristicChanged(BluetoothGatt gatt,
BluetoothGattCharacteristic characteristic) {
    super.onCharacteristicChanged(gatt, characteristic);
    Integer value = characteristic.
                        getIntValue(BluetoothGattCharacteristic.
                        FORMAT_SINT32, 0);
    // TODO Handle value from notification...
}
```

Be sure to refer to the comprehensive Bluetooth specifications, which you can find at the Bluetooth Working Group website at `https://developer.bluetooth.org/gatt/Pages/default.aspx`.

Android Wi-Fi

Wi-Fi is the general name for the collection of technology standards managed by the Wi-Fi Alliance. WiFi Direct is an additional technology that runs on top of the 802.11n standard. It enables devices to communicate without the need for a dedicated access point, which makes it very similar to Bluetooth, except that it uses high-speed Wi-Fi communication.

However, even if you have your devices on the same Wi-Fi, you still need to discover them in order to set up a connection. Discovery means to find the IP address of the device running the service you want to use. Android has built-in support for network discovery on both standard Wi-Fi (infrastructure) and WiFi Direct that lets devices find services that are announced using the DNS-SD protocol.

Network Service Discovery

USB and Bluetooth provide an automatic discovery of the service you're providing, but it's not the same with web services published on a Wi-Fi network. However, there are standard discovery mechanisms supported by Android that allow you to announce your service as well as discover services on a local network. The implementation consists of two standards: mDNS and DNS-SD. The first (mDNS) is a multicast protocol for announcing and discovering hosts using the UDP multicast protocol. DNS-SD is a service discovery protocol for announcing and discovering services running on remote hosts (usually limited to the local network). Both are available in Android through the `android.net.nsd` package and through the `NsdManager` system service.

The following code will declare a service that you have on your device:

```
private void announceService() {
    NsdManager nsdManager = (NsdManager) getSystemService(NSD_SERVICE);
    NsdServiceInfo nsdServiceInfo = new NsdServiceInfo();
    nsdServiceInfo.setPort(8081);
    nsdServiceInfo.setServiceName("MyService");
    nsdServiceInfo.setServiceType("_http._tcp.");
    mRegistrationListener = new MyRegistrationListener();
    nsdManager.registerService(nsdServiceInfo,
            NsdManager.PROTOCOL_DNS_SD,
            mRegistrationListener);
}
```

Note that if you skip setting a host for the `NsdServiceInfo`, the IP of your device on the Wi-Fi will be used. The service type for mDNS must be of a valid type. If the service you're announcing is implemented as a web server (or a Web Socket), you can use the type in the preceding example. For a detailed description of the mDNS protocol and how to construct valid service types, see `http://files.dns-sd.org/draft-cheshire-dnsext-dns-sd.txt`. After you call `NsdManager.registerService()`, the `NsdManager` starts announcing your service on the local Wi-Fi and triggers the callbacks in `mRegistrationListsner` when the state of your registration changes.

When you want to discover a service, you use the same API but call `NsdManager.discoverServices()` instead, as shown here:

```
private void discoverService() {
    mDiscoveryListener = new MyDiscoveryListener();
    NsdManager nsdManager = (NsdManager) getSystemService(NSD_SERVICE);
    nsdManager.discoverServices("_http._tcp.",
            NsdManager.PROTOCOL_DNS_SD,
            mDiscoveryListener);
}
```

Note that you provide the service type as the search query and you'll receive callbacks once something is found, lost, or discovery started and stopped.

After a service is found, you need to resolve it to gain full information about it. To do so, you call `NsdManager.resolveService()`, as shown in the following code.

```
@Override
public void onServiceFound(NsdServiceInfo serviceInfo) {
    NsdManager nsdManager = (NsdManager) getSystemService(NSD_SERVICE);
    nsdManager.resolveService(serviceInfo, mResolveListener);
}
```

When the resolve is finished, you receive a callback, as shown in the following code, where you can extract the host and the port of the remote service that you've discovered.

```
@Override
public void onServiceResolved(NsdServiceInfo serviceInfo) {
    mRemoteHost = serviceInfo.getHost();
    mRemotePort = serviceInfo.getPort();
}
```

Using the network service discovery through the `NsdManager` allows you to communicate with devices on the local Wi-Fi without forcing the user to enter an IP address manually. This can be very useful when you create an application that wants to share data, like a photo album, or when setting up a local multiplayer game between friends.

In the section "On-Device Web Services," I show two examples of how to implement a web service running on the device. By combining on-device web services with the mDNS features shown in this section, you can create powerful services that work across devices with little or no user interaction.

WiFi Direct

WiFi Direct is part of the Wi-Fi Alliance 802.11 standards and allows high-speed Wi-Fi communication between devices without the need for a dedicated access point. It's basically a peer-to-peer protocol using Wi-Fi technology. All Android devices running version 2.3/Gingerbread or later support WiFi Direct, but with Android 4.1 and the introduction of the network service discovery APIs for WiFi Direct, WiFi Direct became *really* interesting for application developers.

On Android devices running version 4 or later, it's usually possible to run WiFi Direct in concurrent mode, meaning that the device can support both WiFi Direct and regular Wi-Fi simultaneously.

First, you register a `BroadcastReceiver` programmatically that will be notified about the connection and peer changes on the WiFi Direct network, as shown in the following code.

```
protected void onCreate(Bundle savedInstanceState) {
    super.onCreate(savedInstanceState);
    setContentView(R.layout.wifi_direct_services);
    IntentFilter intentFilter = new IntentFilter(WifiP2pManager.
                            WIFI_P2P_PEERS_CHANGED_ACTION);
    intentFilter.addAction(WifiP2pManager.
                        WIFI_P2P_CONNECTION_CHANGED_ACTION);
    mReceiver = new MyWifiDirectReceiver();
    registerReceiver(mReceiver, intentFilter);
}
```

Next, on the device that will publish a service you initialize a WiFi Direct channel, create a `WifiP2pServiceInfo` that identifies your service, and add it as a local service. That's all you need to set up WiFi Direct on the server side. In the following code you can see a method that performs these actions.

```
private void announceWiFiDirectService() {
    Log.d(TAG, "Setup service announcement!");
    mWifiP2pManager = (WifiP2pManager) getSystemService(WIFI_P2P_SERVICE);
    HandlerThread handlerThread = new HandlerThread(TAG);
    handlerThread.start();
    mWFDLooper = handlerThread.getLooper();
    mChannel = mWifiP2pManager.initialize(this, mWFDLooper,
            new WifiP2pManager.ChannelListener() {
                @Override
                public void onChannelDisconnected() {
                    Log.d(TAG, "onChannelDisconnected!");
                    mWFDLooper.quit();
                }
            });
    Map<String, String> txtRecords = new HashMap<String, String>();
    mServiceInfo = WifiP2pDnsSdServiceInfo.newInstance(SERVICE_NAME,
            "_http._tcp",
            txtRecords);
    mWifiP2pManager.addLocalService(mChannel, mServiceInfo,
                            new WifiP2pManager.ActionListener() {
        @Override
        public void onSuccess() {
            Log.d(TAG, "Service announcing!");
        }

        @Override
        public void onFailure(int i) {
            Log.d(TAG, "Service announcement failed: " + i);
        }
    });
}
```

On the device that will act as a client, you perform a similar setup, but instead of publishing a service, you tell the `WifiP2pManager` that you want to listen for peer devices and also give it a `WifiP2pServiceRequest` to search for. The following code shows this method.

```
private void discoverWiFiDirectServices() {
    mWifiP2pManager = (WifiP2pManager) getSystemService(WIFI_P2P_SERVICE);
    HandlerThread handlerThread = new HandlerThread(TAG);
    handlerThread.start();
    mWFDLooper = handlerThread.getLooper();
    mChannel = mWifiP2pManager.initialize(this, mWFDLooper,
            new WifiP2pManager.ChannelListener() {
                @Override
                public void onChannelDisconnected() {
                    Log.d(TAG, "onChannelDisconnected!");
                    mWFDLooper.quit();
                }
            });
    mServiceRequest = WifiP2pDnsSdServiceRequest.newInstance("_http._tcp");
    mWifiP2pManager.addServiceRequest(mChannel, mServiceRequest, null);
    mWifiP2pManager.setServiceResponseListener(mChannel, this);
    mWifiP2pManager.setDnsSdResponseListeners(mChannel, this, this);
    mWifiP2pManager.discoverPeers(mChannel,
                                    new WifiP2pManager.ActionListener() {
        @Override
        public void onSuccess() {
            Log.d(TAG, "Peer discovery started!");
        }

        @Override
        public void onFailure(int i) {
            Log.d(TAG, "Peer discovery failed: " + i);
        }
    });
    mWifiP2pManager.discoverServices(mChannel,
                                        new WifiP2pManager.ActionListener() {
        @Override
        public void onSuccess() {
            Log.d(TAG, "Service discovery started!");
        }

        @Override
        public void onFailure(int i) {
            Log.d(TAG, "Service discovery failed: " + i);
        }
    });
}
```

When a service matching your `WifiP2pServiceRequest` is found, the following callback will be invoked:

```
@Override
public void onDnsSdServiceAvailable(String instanceName,
                                    String registrationType,
                                    WifiP2pDevice srcDevice) {
```

```
        Log.d(TAG, "DNS-SD Service available: " + srcDevice);
        mWifiP2pManager.clearServiceRequests(mChannel, null);
        WifiP2pConfig wifiP2pConfig = new WifiP2pConfig();
        wifiP2pConfig.deviceAddress = srcDevice.deviceAddress;
        wifiP2pConfig.groupOwnerIntent = 0;
        mWifiP2pManager.connect(mChannel, wifiP2pConfig, null);
    }
```

In the preceding example, you cancel any further service discovery for WiFi Direct and connect to the device. The configuration used here lets the device know that it has a very low intention to become the group owner. It also contains the network address (specifically, the MAC address, not the IP address) of the remote device. When the connect() method is called, the device on the other end (that is, the server device) displays a dialog asking the user to confirm the connection (see Figure 18-2).

Figure 18-2 The confirmation dialog that appears on the remote device when a client requests a connection

On both devices, once the connection is established, a broadcast will trigger the BroadcastReceiver that was registered earlier. In the following code, I check whether the device is the group owner and if not, get the InetAddress so that a TCP connection can be made to the service on the remote device:

```java
public class MyWifiDirectReceiver extends BroadcastReceiver {
    @Override
    public void onReceive(Context context, Intent intent) {
        String action = intent.getAction();
        if(WifiP2pManager.WIFI_P2P_CONNECTION_CHANGED_ACTION.
equals(action)
            && mWifiP2pManager != null) {
            mWifiP2pManager.requestConnectionInfo(mChannel, this);
        }
    }

    @Override
    public void onConnectionInfoAvailable(WifiP2pInfo wifiP2pInfo) {
        Log.d(TAG, "Group owner address: " + wifiP2pInfo.
groupOwnerAddress);
        Log.d(TAG, "Am I group owner: " + wifiP2pInfo.isGroupOwner);
        if(!wifiP2pInfo.isGroupOwner) {
            connectToServer(wifiP2pInfo.groupOwnerAddress);
        }
    }
}
```

In this procedure, the tricky thing is to understand that you can get only the IP address of the group owner. After a connection is made, you need to verify which device is the owner of the new P2P group and set up the communication with that device. Hopefully the device that hosts the service (HTTP server or similar) will be the group owner, but if that is not the case, you must provide the IP for the service host to the client in some other way.

The main reason for using WiFi Direct is, of course, that you don't need existing Wi-Fi infrastructure. Also, because the setup doesn't require additional PIN codes or passphrases, it's much easier to connect devices this way.

On-Device Web Services

When two remote devices need to communicate, one of them usually has to act as the server. (The exception is when using UDP multicasting or similar techniques; however, because I usually propose building device-to-device communication using an existing and familiar standard like HTTP, I don't include that broader discussion in this chapter.)

Communication can be either synchronous, which we normally associate with standard HTTP requests and responses, or asynchronous, which is when you need something like Web Sockets to solve things.

The actual task for your on-device web service can be anything imaginable. A Wi-Fi–enabled camera could upload photos to a simple RESTful web service that stores new photos in the album of your phone; the web browser on your laptop could connect to your phone and receive notifications of incoming phone calls; and SMS or another Android device could connect to your device in order to set up a simple chat session. Whatever service you choose to provide, most of services can be implemented using the HTTP protocol.

RESTful with Restlet

There are several options for implementing a web server in an Android application. Because the most common use for implementing a web server is to provide a REST-based web service, I advise using a software component that makes these kinds of operations easier. The one I usually choose is Restlet; it's a lightweight Java-based web server with good support for building RESTful web services. You can find more information about Restlet at `http://restlet.org`.

The following is an example of using the Restlet engine for implementing a simple web service in an Android application that will give the current location of the device:

```
public class RestletService extends Service
        implements LocationListener {
    public static final String ACTION_START_SERVER
            = "com.aptl.myrestletdemo.START_SERVER";
    public static final String ACTION_STOP_SERVER
            = "com.aptl.myrestletdemo.STOP_SERVER";
    private static final int SERVER_PORT = 8081;
    public static final long ONE_MINUTE = 1000 * 60;
    public static final float MIN_DISTANCE = 50;
    private static final String TAG = "RestletService";
    private HandlerThread mLocationThread;
    private Location mLocation;
    private Component mServer;

    public IBinder onBind(Intent intent) {
        return null;
    }

    @Override
    public int onStartCommand(Intent intent, int flags, int startId) {
        String action = intent.getAction();

        if(ACTION_START_SERVER.equals(action)) {
            new Thread(new Runnable() {
                @Override
                public void run() {
                    initRestlet();
                }
            }).start();
        } else if(ACTION_STOP_SERVER.equals(action)) {
            if (mServer != null) {
                shutdownRestlet();
            }
        }

        return START_REDELIVER_INTENT;
    }

    private void initRestlet() {
        try {
            mLocationThread = new HandlerThread("LocationUpdates");
            mLocationThread.start();
```

```
            LocationManager locationManager =
                    (LocationManager) getSystemService(LOCATION_SERVICE);
            mLocation = locationManager.
                    getLastKnownLocation(LocationManager.GPS_PROVIDER);
            Criteria criteria = new Criteria();
            criteria.setAccuracy(Criteria.ACCURACY_FINE);
            criteria.setCostAllowed(true);
            criteria.setSpeedRequired(true);
            criteria.setAltitudeRequired(true);
            locationManager.requestLocationUpdates(ONE_MINUTE,
                    MIN_DISTANCE,
                    criteria,
                    this,
                    mLocationThread.getLooper());

            mServer =  new Component();
            mServer.getServers().add(Protocol.HTTP, SERVER_PORT);
            Router router = new Router(mServer.getContext()
                    .createChildContext());
            router.attachDefault(new Restlet() {
                @Override
                public void handle(Request request,
                                    Response response) {
                    response.setStatus(Status.CLIENT_ERROR_FORBIDDEN);
                }
            });
            router.attach("/location", new LocationRestlet());
            mServer.getDefaultHost().attach(router);
            mServer.start();
        } catch (Exception e) {
            Log.e(TAG, "Error starting server.", e);
        }
    }

    private void shutdownRestlet() {
        if (mServer != null) {
            try {
                mServer.stop();
            } catch (Exception e) {
                Log.e(TAG, "Error stopping server.", e);
            }
        }

        LocationManager locationManager =
                (LocationManager) getSystemService(LOCATION_SERVICE);
        locationManager.removeUpdates(this);
        if (mLocationThread != null) {
            mLocationThread.getLooper().quit();
            mLocationThread = null;
        }
    }

    @Override
```

```
    public void onLocationChanged(Location location) {
        mLocation = location;
    }

    @Override
    public void onStatusChanged(String s, int i, Bundle bundle) {

    }

    @Override
    public void onProviderEnabled(String s) {

    }

    @Override
    public void onProviderDisabled(String s) {

    }

    public class LocationRestlet extends Restlet {
        @Override
        public void handle(Request request, Response response) {
            if(Method.GET.equals(request.getMethod())) {
                try {
                    JSONObject jsonObject = new JSONObject();
                    jsonObject.put("latitude", mLocation.getLatitude());
                    jsonObject.put("longitude", mLocation.getLongitude());
                    jsonObject.put("time", mLocation.getTime());
                    jsonObject.put("altitude", mLocation.getAltitude());
                    jsonObject.put("speed", mLocation.getSpeed());
                    response.setStatus(Status.SUCCESS_OK);
                    response.setEntity(jsonObject.toString(),
                            MediaType.APPLICATION_JSON);
                } catch (JSONException e) {
                    response.setStatus(Status.SERVER_ERROR_INTERNAL);
                }
            } else {
                response.setStatus(Status.CLIENT_ERROR_BAD_REQUEST);
            }
        }
    }
}
```

In the preceding code example the server port is hard coded. While this is technically okay, there might be other applications running on the device that open the same port. Therefore, you should have a proper error-handling for the cases where the port might be busy. Use the discovery services described in the "Network Discovery Service" section to announce the port for your web server.

After setting up the server, you only need to provide your custom `Restlet` objects that respond to different paths you register using the `Router` object.

The Restlet API makes it easy to implement these kinds of RESTful web services. You can add variables to the path you register the `Restlet` instance on and then retrieve the variables in the `handle()` method, as shown here (note the variable in bold):

```
router.attach("/contact/{contactId}", new ContactsRestlet());

...

public class ContactsRestlet extends Restlet {
    @Override
    public void handle(Request request, Response response) {
        String contactId = String.valueOf(request.
                getAttributes().get("contactId"));

        JSONObject contact = new JSONObject();
        // TODO: Read contact with contactId from provider...

        response.setEntity(contact.toString(), MediaType.APPLICATION_
JSON);
    }
}
```

Restlet is an excellent software library to use when you need to provide a simple HTTP-based interface to your application running on a device. Combined with the network discovery service from the previous section, you have a powerful method for publishing services on the local Wi-Fi.

Web Socket Server

Although Restlet allows you to implement RESTful services that are always synchronous, you sometimes need a method for supporting asynchronous communication instead. As I show in Chapter 17, Web Sockets provide an easy-to-use method for doing asynchronous communication on top of HTTP. Also, since it is a Web standard, it allows web browsers to interact with this service as well. In this section I show how to use the server-side part of the same Web Sockets library used in Chapter 17 in order to build an asynchronous web service for your application.

The following is a simple implementation for a `Service` that handles a Web Socket server. The callback in `MyWebSocketServer` can be used to register new clients connecting (and removing those that disconnect).

```
public class WebSocketService extends Service {
    private static final String TAG = "WebSocketService";
    private Set<WebSocket> mClients;
    private MessageListener mMessageListener;
    private MyWebSocketServer mServer;
    private LocalBinder mLocalBinder = new LocalBinder();

    public IBinder onBind(Intent intent) {
        return mLocalBinder;
    }
```

```java
@Override
public void onCreate() {
    super.onCreate();
    mClients = Collections.synchronizedSet(new HashSet<WebSocket>());
}

@Override
public void onDestroy() {
    super.onDestroy();
    stopWebSocketServer();
}

public void startWebSocketServer() {
    if (mServer == null) {
        InetSocketAddress serverAddress = new InetSocketAddress(8081);
        mServer = new MyWebSocketServer(serverAddress);
        mServer.start();
    }
}

public void stopWebSocketServer() {
    if (mServer != null) {
        try {
            mServer.stop();
        } catch (IOException e) {
            Log.e(TAG, "Error stopping server.", e);
        } catch (InterruptedException e) {
            Log.e(TAG, "Error stopping server.", e);
        }
    }
}

public void sendBroadcast(String message) {
    for (WebSocket client : mClients) {
        client.send(message);
    }
}

public void setMessageListener(MessageListener messageListener) {
    mMessageListener = messageListener;
}

public interface MessageListener {
    void onMessage(WebSocket client, String message);
}

class MyWebSocketServer extends WebSocketServer {

    public MyWebSocketServer(InetSocketAddress address) {
        super(address);
    }
```

```
        @Override
        public void onOpen(WebSocket webSocket,
                           ClientHandshake clientHandshake) {
            mClients.add(webSocket);
        }

        @Override
        public void onClose(WebSocket webSocket,
                            int code,
                            String reason,
                            boolean remote) {
            mClients.remove(webSocket);
        }

        @Override
        public void onMessage(WebSocket webSocket,
                              String message) {
            if(mMessageListener != null) {
                mMessageListener.onMessage(webSocket, message);
            }
        }

        @Override
        public void onError(WebSocket webSocket,
                            Exception e) {
            webSocket.close();
            mClients.remove(webSocket);
        }
    }

    public class LocalBinder extends Binder {
        public WebSocketService getService() {
            return WebSocketService.this;
        }
    }
}
```

By providing a simple callback interface, you can have an `Activity` register for new incoming messages. This way you can build a simple chat server that works on your local Wi-Fi (or over WiFi Direct).

Summary

In this chapter, I covered the three supported methods for communicating between devices: USB, Bluetooth, and Wi-Fi. Although Bluetooth and Wi-Fi are wireless, USB still has some advantages because it's a secure and more reliable communication. Bluetooth, especially Bluetooth Low Energy, provides a very power-efficient method for exchanging data between devices. The support for BLE is quite new in Android, but I expect it to be fairly widespread in the months to come.

Finally, Wi-Fi provides high-speed communication using the standard TCP or UDP protocols that we're used to on the Internet. Android also provides convenient discovery APIs for both standard Wi-Fi and WiFi Direct.

After you connect the devices on the same Wi-Fi, or in a WiFi Direct group, you can set up a web service or an asynchronous Web Socket server to exchange data between the device running as a server and the one running as a client.

Further Resources

Websites

Android Developer guidelines for USB communication: `http://developer.android.com/guide/topics/connectivity/usb/index.html`

Android Developer guidelines for Bluetooth Low Energy: `http://developer.android.com/guide/topics/connectivity/bluetooth-le.html`

The GATT specifications for Bluetooth Low Energy services: `https://developer.bluetooth.org/gatt/Pages/GATT-Specification-Documents.aspx`

Android Developer guidelines for WiFi Direct: `http://developer.android.com/guide/topics/connectivity/wifip2p.html`

Information about Multicast DNS: `http://www.multicastdns.org`

A list of different service types for DNS-SD: `http://www.dns-sd.org/ServiceTypes.html`

The main site for the Restlet Java Framework: `http://restlet.org`

The main site for the Java-based Web Socket library used in this chapter: `https://github.com/TooTallNate/Java-WebSocket`

Chapter 19
Google Play Services

Google provides a wide range of online services that can be used on websites, desktop applications, or mobile applications like Android. In Chapter 17, I discuss how to integrate online web services with your application, but in those examples, I use third-party services outside the Google ecosystem. In this chapter, I focus on online services managed by Google.

You now have available a set of APIs called Google Play Services that lets you integrate Google APIs with very little effort, and I cover a some of those services in this chapter.

The new Location API covered in Chapter 13 is also part of Google Play Services. However, as the Location API is a bit different from the ones covered here, it deserves its own chapter.

In this chapter, you find out how to get authorization to the online services such as Google Drive, services running on the Google Cloud Platform, and the new Google Play Games APIs. You also discover how to set up push notifications for your application using the Google Cloud Messaging service.

You can include the Google Play Services APIs in your project by adding the following to your Gradle build-file dependencies section:

```
compile 'com.google.android.gms:play-services:3.1.36'
```

Authorization

Before you can start using any of the Google Play Services, or any other Google services, you need to retrieve an authorization token for the Google account of the user. To do so, you first need to fetch the account name for the user.

The easiest way to retrieve the account name for a user is to use the following code:

```
public void doConnectAccounts(MenuItem menuItem) {
    Intent intent = AccountPicker.newChooseAccountIntent(null, null,
            new String[] {"com.google"}, false,
            "Pick one of your Google accounts to connect.",
            null, null, null);
    startActivityForResult(intent, ACCOUNT_REQUEST);
}
```

Calling `AccountPicker.newChooseAccountIntent()` starts an `Activity` that returns the chosen account. By passing `"com.google"` as one of the allowed account types, the picker will filter out all other account types. If multiple accounts are available, the user will see a dialog box where he can select the one he wants to use (see Figure 19-1).

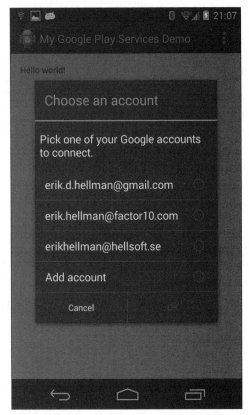

Figure 19-1 The dialog box presented when there are multiple Google accounts available

After the picker `Activity` returns with a result, you check whether the call was successful and retrieve the selected account name, as shown in the following code:

```
protected void onActivityResult(int requestCode, int resultCode,
                                Intent data) {
    super.onActivityResult(requestCode, resultCode, data);
    if(requestCode == ACCOUNT_REQUEST) {
        if(resultCode == RESULT_OK) {
            String accountName
                    = data.getStringExtra(AccountManager.KEY_ACCOUNT_
NAME);
            mPrefs.edit().putBoolean(PREFS_IS_AUTHORIZED, true)
                    .putString(PREFS_SELECTED_ACCOUNT, accountName).apply();
```

```
                Log.d(TAG, "Picked account: " + accountName);
                invalidateOptionsMenu();
                authorizeAccount(accountName);
            } else {
                Log.e(TAG, "No account picked...");
            }
        }
    }
}
```

In this case, you also store the account name in a `SharedPreferences` along with a flag indicating that the user successfully selected an account.

Before you request an auth token, you must decide on the scope of the permissions you need for the services you'll use. These scopes are standard OAuth2 scopes, and you can find them for each Google API in their respective online documentation. In this case, you request access to the user's App Data on Google Drive (see the section "Google Drive Application Data" later in this chapter), the user information (such as full name), and the user's Google+ information. The following code shows how such a `String` should look.

```
public static final String AUTH_SCOPE =
        "oauth2:https://www.googleapis.com/auth/drive.appdata " +
            "https://www.googleapis.com/auth/userinfo.profile " +
            "https://www.googleapis.com/auth/plus.me";
```

After you have the account name, you can fetch an auth token using the class `GoogleAuthUtil`. This operation must run off the main thread because it performs network operations, so as shown in the following code, you wrap it in an `AsyncTask`:

```
class MyAuthTokenTask extends AsyncTask<String,Void,String> {

    @Override
    protected String doInBackground(String... accountName) {
        String authToken = null;
        try {
            authToken = GoogleAuthUtil.getToken(ServicesDemo.this,
                    accountName[0], AUTH_SCOPE);
        } catch (IOException e) {
            Log.e(TAG, "Error getting auth token.", e);
        } catch (UserRecoverableAuthException e) {
            Log.d(TAG, "User recoverable error.");
            cancel(true);
            startActivityForResult(e.getIntent(), TOKEN_REQUEST);
        } catch (GoogleAuthException e) {
            Log.e(TAG, "Error getting auth token.", e);
        }
        return authToken;
    }

    @Override
    protected void onPostExecute(String result) {
        // Auth token acquired - start performing API requests
```

```
            if (result != null) {
                mPrefs.edit().putString(PREFS_AUTH_TOKEN, result).apply();
            }
        }
    }
```

This operation will always fail on the user's first attempt (unless she authorized this application on another device earlier), so you need to catch the `UserRecoverableAuthException` and call `startActivityFor Result()` using the `Intent` contained in the exception. This brings up another dialog where the user is informed about the API permissions your application has requested (not to be confused with standard Android permissions). The following code shows how the `onActivityResult()` callback method looks in this case:

```
protected void onActivityResult(int requestCode, int resultCode, Intent
data) {
    super.onActivityResult(requestCode, resultCode, data);
    if(requestCode == ACCOUNT_REQUEST) { // Account picked
        if(resultCode == RESULT_OK) {
            String accountName
                    = data.getStringExtra(AccountManager.KEY_ACCOUNT_
NAME);
            mPrefs.edit().putBoolean(PREFS_IS_AUTHORIZED, true)
                    .putString(PREFS_SELECTED_ACCOUNT, accountName).
                    apply();
            invalidateOptionsMenu();
            new MyAuthTokenTask().execute(accountName);
        } else {
            Log.e(TAG, "No account picked...");
        }
    } else if(requestCode == TOKEN_REQUEST) { // Token requested
        if(resultCode == RESULT_OK) {
            // Try again...
            new MyAuthTokenTask().
                    execute(mPrefs.getString(PREFS_SELECTED_ACCOUNT,
null));
        }
    }
}
```

Note that you modify the earlier `onActivityResult()` to handle recovery from errors that might occur on the first call to `GoogleAuthUtil.getToken()`. All you do here is retry the execution of `MyAuthTokenTask` because you should now have the right permissions.

Google Drive Application Data

Every Android user who has a Google account also has access to the Google Drive cloud storage service. This service has a number of convenient APIs for reading and writing files and data to the user's Google Drive storage. With this the Google Drive API, you can store data in Google Drive that can be seen or accessed by only one application. If you want your application to provide the capability of syncing its working data online, you'll find that this API is very handy.

This application data feature should not be confused with the backup features built into Android, where the developer cannot control when files are backed up. This is also different from the Game Cloud Save API, which is focused on saving game states across devices. You should use Google Drive and the Application Data features for larger amounts of data that is only valid for your application—for instance, a sketching application that saves files in a proprietary format.

As with the Location API described in Chapter 13, you need to add your application's package name and SHA1 key string in the Google API Console, as shown in Figure 19-2. Create a new Client ID and add the information needed. After this is done, your application (the package name you specified) will be authorized to access Google Drive on behalf of users.

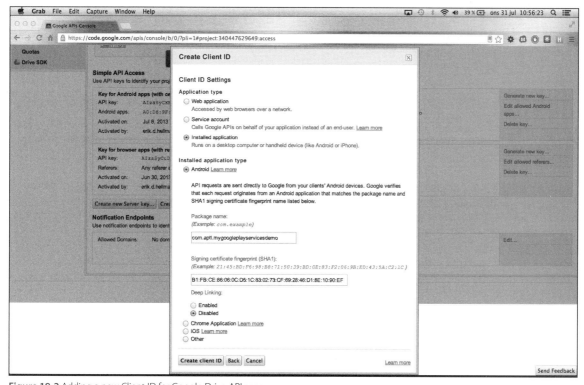

Figure 19-2 Adding a new Client ID for Google Drive API access

Before you get started with the Android code, you need to add the necessary dependencies to your Gradle build file.

```
compile 'com.google.api-client:google-api-client-android:1.16.0-rc'
compile 'com.google.apis:google-api-services-drive:v2-rev89-1.15.0-rc'
```

The first line adds the generic Google Client for Android library. The second line adds the Google Drive–specific library that you will use in this case.

Because your applications have already received an auth token from the authorization step (shown in the previous section), you can now create a `GoogleAccountCredentials` that will be used by the Drive API.

The returned `Drive` instance will be authorized to access the user's private App Data. The following code shows the `createDriveService()` that implements this:

```
public Drive createDriveService(accountName) {
    try {
        GoogleAccountCredential googleAccountCredential =
                GoogleAccountCredential.usingOAuth2(this,
                        Arrays.asList(DriveScopes.DRIVE_APPDATA));
        googleAccountCredential.setSelectedAccountName(accountNAme);
        Drive.Builder builder =
                    new Drive.Builder(AndroidHttp.newCompatibleTransport(),
                                new AndroidJsonFactory(),
                                googleAccountCredential);
        return builder.build();
    } catch (IOException e) {
        Log.e(TAG, "Error", e);
    } catch (GoogleAuthException e) {
        Log.e(TAG, "Error", e);
    }
    return null;
}
```

When you want to store data that is private to your application in the App Data folder in Google Drive, you simply create a `File` object (note that this is not the `java.io.File` class, but one specific for Google Drive API) and populate it with the relevant metadata. You provide it with the content (in this case, a `ByteArrayContent`) and insert the file into Google Drive. The result will be a file that is hidden in the user interface of Google Drive. The following code shows how to add a new file to the App Data "folder" of Google Drive:

```
class MyGoogleDriveAppDataTask extends AsyncTask<JSONObject, Void,
Integer> {

    @Override
    protected Integer doInBackground(JSONObject... jsonObjects) {
        String accountName = mPrefs.getString(PREFS_SELECTED_ACCOUNT,
                                            null);
        Drive drive = createDriveService(accountName);
        int insertedFiles = 0;
        for (JSONObject jsonObject : jsonObjects) {
            String dataString = jsonObject.toString();
            String md5 = getMD5String(dataString.getBytes());
            File file = new File();
            file.setTitle(md5);
            String mimeType = "application/json";
            file.setMimeType(mimeType);
            file.setParents(Arrays.
                    asList(new ParentReference().setId("appdata")));

            ByteArrayContent content
                    = new ByteArrayContent(mimeType,
                                        dataString.getBytes());

            try {
                drive.files().insert(file, content).execute();
```

```
                    insertedFiles++;
            } catch (IOException e) {
                Log.e(TAG, "Failed to insert file with content "
                            + dataString, e);
            }
        }
        return insertedFiles;
    }

    private String getMD5String(byte[] data) {
        MessageDigest mdEnc = null;
        try {
            mdEnc = MessageDigest.getInstance("MD5");
        } catch (NoSuchAlgorithmException e) {
            Log.e(TAG, "Error retrieving MD5 function!", e);
            return null;
        }
        mdEnc.update(data, 0, data.length);
        return new BigInteger(1, mdEnc.digest()).toString(16);
    }

}
```

The user can see the space used by your application, delete its content, and disconnect your app from her Google Drive account through the Manage Apps menu in the Google Drive settings (see Figure 19-3).

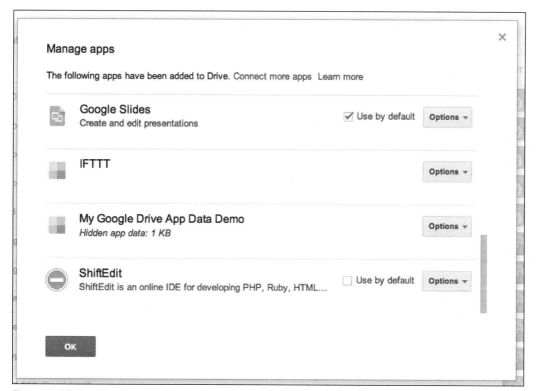

Figure 19-3 The apps connected to the user's Google Drive account

Reading and updating files is done through the same API as just shown. Note that all of the operations require network access, so remember to perform these operations off the main thread.

Google Cloud Endpoints

Google has gathered all its cloud-based developer resources and called it *Google Cloud Platform*. This is basically an improved interface for App Engine, Compute Engine, Cloud Datastore, and all the other online services that Google provides. Most of these services have a free tier, so getting started with building a cloud backend for your mobile application is very easy. To get started, visit `https://cloud.google.com/console` and create a new project.

The easiest way to get started with your own Cloud Platform backend is to generate a basic App Engine backend from Android Studio (see Figure 19-4).

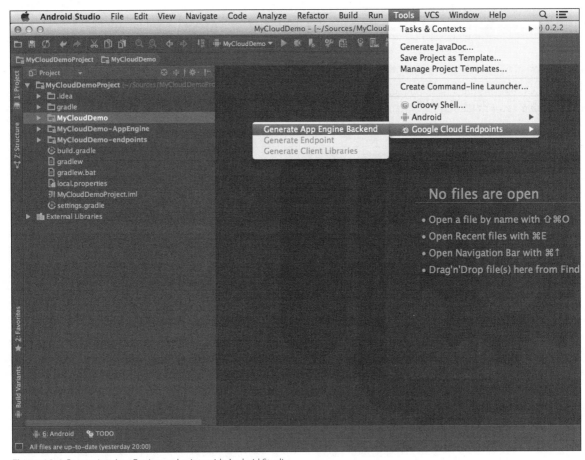

Figure 19-4 Generating App Engine endpoints with Android Studio

After the code generation is complete, you'll have two new modules ending with "endpoint" and "AppEngine." You can now start to add new POJOs (Plain Old Java Objects) with getters and setters that can be queried, inserted, updated, and deleted from your Android application.

The following code is an example of a simple POJO for storing tasks:

```
@Entity
public class TaskInfo {
    @Id
    private String id;
    private String title;
    private String content;


    public TaskInfo() {
    }

    public TaskInfo(String id, String title, String content) {
        this.id = id;
        this.title = title;
        this.content = content;
    }

    public String getId() {
        return id;
    }

    public void setId(String id) {
        this.id = id;
    }

    public String getTitle() {
        return title;
    }

    public void setTitle(String title) {
        this.title = title;
    }

    public String getContent() {
        return content;
    }

    public void setContent(String content) {
        this.content = content;
    }
}
```

Following this example, you add this `TaskInfo` class to the AppEngine module in the project and then run "Generate endpoint" followed by "Generate Client Libraries" from the Tools menu again. This creates the client-side libraries that you can use in your application.

The `AsyncTask` shown next is an example of how to add a new `TaskInfo`:

```
class AddTaskInfo extends AsyncTask<TaskInfo, Void, Void> {
    @Override
    protected Void doInBackground(TaskInfo... taskInfos) {
        mTaskInfoEndpoint = CloudEndpointUtils.
                updateBuilder(new Taskinfoendpoint.Builder(
                        AndroidHttp.newCompatibleTransport(),
                        new JacksonFactory(),
                        new HttpRequestInitializer() {
                            public void initialize(HttpRequest
                                                    httpRequest) {

                            }
                        })
                ).build();
        for (TaskInfo taskInfo : taskInfos) {
            try {
                mTaskInfoEndpoint.insertTaskInfo(taskInfo).execute();;
            } catch (IOException e) {
                Log.e(TAG, "Error inserting task.", e);
            }
        }
        return null;
    }
}
```

Note: Because they will perform network calls that would otherwise block the main thread, all these calls need to happen on a dedicated thread.

The following shows how to use the same endpoint to query for all `TaskInfo` instances stored in your App Engine instance:

```
class GetAllTaskInfo extends AsyncTask<Void, Void, List<TaskInfo>> {

    @Override
    protected List<TaskInfo> doInBackground(Void... voids) {
        try {
            mTaskInfoEndpoint = CloudEndpointUtils.
                    updateBuilder(new Taskinfoendpoint.Builder(
                            AndroidHttp.newCompatibleTransport(),
                            new JacksonFactory(),
                            new HttpRequestInitializer() {
                                public void initialize(HttpRequest
                                                        httpRequest) {
                                }
                            })).build();
            return mTaskInfoEndpoint.listTaskInfo().execute().getItems();
        } catch (IOException e) {
            Log.e(TAG, "Error performing query.", e);
            cancel(true);
        }
        return null;
    }
```

```
    @Override
    protected void onPostExecute(List<TaskInfo> taskInfos) {
        super.onPostExecute(taskInfos);
        mTaskInfoArrayAdapter.clear();
        mTaskInfoArrayAdapter.addAll(taskInfos);
        mTaskInfoArrayAdapter.notifyDataSetChanged();
    }
}
```

The same approach can be used for updating and deleting existing `TaskInfo` objects.

Integrating a simple cloud backend can introduce some great features in your application. When the data your application uses can be shared across all the user's devices, including the user's web browser, you can create very powerful user experiences.

Google Cloud Messaging

When your application communicates with an online backend, such as a service implemented using Google Cloud Endpoints, consider using server-side push notifications to notify the application when new data is available. This reduces the need for devices to send unnecessary polling requests to your service, which drains battery fast and also increases the load on your servers.

Google supports push notifications through the Google Cloud Messaging (GCM) service, which is part of Google Play Services. Implementing GCM in your application allows you to send messages to the devices running your application. The most common use for this is to let Android applications know that there's new data to fetch online; this is called a *tickle* and eliminates the need for doing recurring polling operations from the application. You can also send application data with a payload of up to 4K using GCM.

To integrate GCM in your application, you must enable it in your Google API Console and set up a Server key for your application under API Access. Also make sure that Google Cloud Messaging is enabled for your project.

GCM Client

On the client-side of your GCM integration, which is your Android application, you need to add a number of elements to your manifest.

Here's an example of how the manifest looks for the application with the package name `gom.aptl. myclouddemo`.

```
<?xml version="1.0" encoding="utf-8"?>
<manifest xmlns:android="http://schemas.android.com/apk/res/android"
        package="com.aptl.myclouddemo"
        android:versionCode="1"
        android:versionName="1.0">

    <uses-sdk
            android:minSdkVersion="18"
            android:targetSdkVersion="18"/>
```

```
    <uses-permission
            android:name="com.google.android.c2dm.permission.RECEIVE"/>
    <uses-permission android:name="android.permission.INTERNET"/>
    <uses-permission android:name="android.permission.GET_ACCOUNTS"/>
    <uses-permission android:name="android.permission.WAKE_LOCK"/>

    <permission
            android:name="com.apt1.myclouddemo.permission.C2D_MESSAGE"
            android:protectionLevel="signature"/>
    <uses-permission
            android:name="com.apt1.myclouddemo.permission.C2D_
MESSAGE"/>

    <application
            android:allowBackup="true"
            android:icon="@drawable/ic_launcher"
            android:label="@string/app_name"
            android:theme="@style/AppTheme">
        <activity
                android:name=".CloudPlatformDemo"
                android:label="@string/app_name">
            <intent-filter>
                <action android:name="android.intent.action.MAIN"/>
                <category android:name="android.intent.category.
LAUNCHER"/>
            </intent-filter>
        </activity>
        <receiver
                android:name=".MyGcmReceiver"
                android:permission="com.google.android.c2dm.SEND">
            <intent-filter>
                <action
                    android:name="com.google.android.c2dm.intent.
RECEIVE"/>
                <category android:name="com.apt1.myclouddemo"/>
            </intent-filter>
        </receiver>
        <service android:name=".MyGcmService"/>
    </application>

</manifest>
```

Note that the new permission declared prevents other applications from receiving the same incoming message. Also, the permission on the `receiver` tag ensures that no other application can send a fake message to your application.

The first time your application starts, you need to call `GoogleCloudMessaging.register()` using the sender ID, as shown in the following example:

```
class RegisterGcm extends AsyncTask<Void, Void, Void> {
    @Override
    protected Void doInBackground(Void... voids) {
```

```
        try {
            GoogleCloudMessaging cloudMessaging =
                    GoogleCloudMessaging.getInstance(CloudPlatformDemo.this);
            String registrationID = cloudMessaging.register(SENDER_ID);
            SharedPreferences preferences
                    = PreferenceManager
                    .getDefaultSharedPreferences(CloudPlatformDemo.this);
            preferences.edit().
                    putString(PREFS_GCM_REG_ID, registrationID).
                    apply();
            cloudMessaging.close();
        } catch (IOException e) {
            Log.e(TAG, "GCM Error.", e);
        }
        return null;
    }
}
```

The sender ID is the same as the *project number* that you can find on the Google Cloud Console. You will also need to refresh the registration because it eventually times out. The default timeout for a GCM registration is seven days.

Whenever your server sends a GCM message to your client, it triggers a call to the receiver registered for the GCM messages. Following is a simple example where the message, stored as a `Bundle` in the `Intent`, is passed to an `IntentService` for further processing:

```
public class MyGcmReceiver extends BroadcastReceiver {
    public void onReceive(Context context, Intent intent) {
        GoogleCloudMessaging cloudMessaging =
                GoogleCloudMessaging.getInstance(context);
        String messageType = cloudMessaging.getMessageType(intent);

        if(GoogleCloudMessaging.MESSAGE_TYPE_MESSAGE.equals(messageType))
        {
            // Pass the message to the IntentService for processing...
            Intent serviceIntent = new Intent(context,
                                                MyGcmService.class);
            serviceIntent.putExtras(intent.getExtras());
            context.startService(serviceIntent);
        }

        setResultCode(Activity.RESULT_OK);
    }
}
```

Before your server can send GCM messages to a user's device, the application must provide its registration ID to the server. The easiest way to do so is to use the `DeviceInfoEndpoint` that's generated by the Google Cloud Endpoint features in Android Studio.

The `AsyncTask` shown next illustrates how to use the generated endpoint for delivering the registration ID to the client:

```
class SendRegistrationId extends AsyncTask<Void, Void, Void> {
    @Override
    protected Void doInBackground(Void... voids) {
        try {
            SharedPreferences preferences
                    = PreferenceManager
                    .getDefaultSharedPreferences(CloudPlatformDemo.this);
            String registrationId = preferences.
                                    getString(PREFS_GCM_REG_ID,
                                        null);
            DeviceInfo deviceInfo = new DeviceInfo();
            deviceInfo.setDeviceRegistrationID(registrationId);
            deviceInfo.setTimestamp(System.currentTimeMillis());
            deviceInfo.setDeviceInformation("Device Info...");
            Deviceinfoendpoint deviceinfoendpoint =
                    CloudEndpointUtils.updateBuilder(
                        new Deviceinfoendpoint.Builder(
                            AndroidHttp.newCompatibleTransport(),
                            new JacksonFactory(),
                            new HttpRequestInitializer() {
                                public void initialize(HttpRequest
                                                    httpRequest)
{
                                }
                            })
                    ).build();
            deviceinfoendpoint.insertDeviceInfo(deviceInfo).execute();
        } catch (IOException e) {
            Log.e(TAG, "Error inserting device info.", e);
        }
        return null;
    }
}
```

The final part is sending the GCM message from the server to the clients whenever a new `TaskInfo` has been inserted (see previous section). The easiest way to do so is to modify the method `TaskInfoEndpoint.insertTaskInfo()` in the App Engine module, as shown in the following code. The added code is shown in bold. In this case, a simple tickle message is sent, telling the client that new data is available online.

```
@ApiMethod(name = "insertTaskInfo")
public TaskInfo insertTaskInfo(TaskInfo taskInfo) throws IOException {
    EntityManager mgr = getEntityManager();
    try {
        if (containsTaskInfo(taskInfo)) {
            throw new EntityExistsException("Object already exists");
        }
        mgr.persist(taskInfo);

        Sender sender = new Sender(API_KEY);
        CollectionResponse<DeviceInfo> deviceInfos
                = endpoint.listDeviceInfo(null, 10);
        Message message = new Message.Builder().
                addData("message", "Task Inserted").build();
```

```
        for (DeviceInfo deviceInfo : deviceInfos.getItems()) {
            sender.send(message, deviceInfo.getDeviceRegistrationID(), 5);
        }
    } finally {
        mgr.close();
    }
    return taskInfo;
}
```

Google Play Game Services

At Google IO 2013, developers were introduced to the new online services for games. Google Play Game Services let developers include social elements such as achievements and leaderboards, but also real-time multiplayer support in their games.

In this section, I cover the use of the real-time multiplayer support. This is the most technically advanced feature in this service, and by mastering it, you should have no problem integrating the other features as well.

The core of the real-time multiplayer consists of two basic concepts: a virtual room where the game takes place and a number of participants. Players can be invited to a room or automatically matched (auto-matching of random players). A room is created when the first player wishes to start a new multiplayer session. All players in a multiplayer game are participants in the same room. One player can send invitations to other players from their Google+ circles.

The easiest way to implement the real-time multiplayer service in your game is to add the `BaseGameUtils` library project to your application, which can be found at `https://github.com/playgameservices/android-samples`. Here, you'll find the class `BaseGameActivity`, which you should extend instead of the standard `Activity` class, and the `GameHelper`, which contains a number of useful helper methods.

Next, you need to enable the Google Play Games Services for your game. You can either follow the instructions found at `https://developers.google.com/games/services/console/enabling`, or you can sign in to the Google API Console, enable the necessary services for your project (Google+ API, Google Play Game Services, Google Play Game Management, and Google Play App State), and create a new Client ID for installed applications, as shown in Figure 19-2. Next, take the first part of the Client ID (the numbers, followed by `.apps.googleusercontent.com`) and add that as a string resource value in your application.

Now, you add a new metadata tag inside your applications tag of your manifest, as shown next. This connects the Google Play Games Services to your application.

```
<meta-data android:name="com.google.android.gms.games.APP_ID"
           android:value="@string/app_id" />
```

In the UI shown at startup, you add a button for the user to log in to Google+ with your game. If possible, use the readymade `SignInButton` in your XML layout, as shown here:

```
<com.google.android.gms.common.SignInButton
        android:id="@+id/sign_in_button"
        android:layout_centerHorizontal="true"
```

```
android:layout_width="wrap_content"
android:layout_height="wrap_content"
android:onClick="doSignIn" />
```

In the click-callback shown next, you simply call the method `beginUserInitiatedSignIn()` from the base class `BaseGameActivity`, and the user can sign in:

```
public void doSignIn(View view) {
    beginUserInitiatedSignIn();
}
```

You'll have two callbacks for the sign-in process, `onSignInFailed()` and `onSignInSucceeded()`, which are used to process the result. If sign-in is successful, you can proceed by displaying a UI for inviting players or seeing existing invitations.

In the two click-callbacks shown in the following code, you invite new players or display existing invitations by starting the games client `Activity`:

```
public void doInvitePlayers(View view) {
    Intent intent = getGamesClient().getSelectPlayersIntent(1, 3);
    startActivityForResult(intent, INVITE_PLAYERS_RC, null);
}

public void doSeeInvitations(View view) {
    Intent intent = getGamesClient().getInvitationInboxIntent();
    startActivityForResult(intent, SEE_INVITATIONS_RC, null);
}
```

When inviting players, you must specify the maximum and minimum number of players for a game. These calls open a new `Activity` from the Google Play Game Services framework that lets the user either pick opponents or invite additional players.

Because there are two ways to start a multiplayer game, either through an invitation or by inviting players, you need two different methods for creating the room for this game session. The following code shows how to handle these two cases:

```
private void handlePlayersInvited(Intent intent) {
    ArrayList<String> players = intent.
            getStringArrayListExtra(GamesClient.EXTRA_PLAYERS);

    int minAutoMatchPlayers = intent.
            getIntExtra(GamesClient.EXTRA_MIN_AUTOMATCH_PLAYERS, 0);
    int maxAutoMatchPlayers = intent.
            getIntExtra(GamesClient.EXTRA_MAX_AUTOMATCH_PLAYERS, 0);
    Bundle autoMatchCriteria = null;
    if (minAutoMatchPlayers > 0 || maxAutoMatchPlayers > 0) {
        autoMatchCriteria =
                RoomConfig.createAutoMatchCriteria(minAutoMatchPlayers,
                        maxAutoMatchPlayers, 0);
    }
```

```
        RoomConfig.Builder roomConfigBuilder
                = RoomConfig.builder(this);
        roomConfigBuilder.addPlayersToInvite(players);
        roomConfigBuilder.setMessageReceivedListener(this);
        roomConfigBuilder.setRoomStatusUpdateListener(this);
        if (autoMatchCriteria != null) {
            roomConfigBuilder.setAutoMatchCriteria(autoMatchCriteria);
        }

        getGamesClient().createRoom(roomConfigBuilder.build());
    }

    private void handleInvitationResult(Intent intent) {
        Bundle bundle = intent.getExtras();
        if (bundle != null) {
            Invitation invitation =
                bundle.getParcelable(GamesClient.EXTRA_INVITATION);
            if(invitation != null) {
                RoomConfig.Builder roomConfigBuilder
                = RoomConfig.builder(this);
                roomConfigBuilder
                        .setInvitationIdToAccept(invitation.getInvitationId())
                        .setMessageReceivedListener(this)
                        .setRoomStatusUpdateListener(this);
                getGamesClient().joinRoom(roomConfigBuilder.build());
            }
        }
    }
}
```

The two interfaces `RoomStatusUpdateListener` and `RoomUpdateListener` provide a set of callback methods for the different state changes of your multiplayer session. How you use these callbacks depends completely on your game. The simplest solution is to direct all callbacks to the same handler where you determine the state of the game, as shown in the following code:

```
@Override
public void onPeerJoined(Room room, List<String> arg1) {
    updateRoom(room);
}

public void updateGameState(Room room) {
    mParticipants = room.getParticipants();

    // TODO: Implement change of game state here...
}
```

The first method shown here is one of the callbacks from `RoomStatusUpdateListener`. In this case, you simply call `updateGameState()` with the `Room` as a parameter. In this method, you get the current list of participants and then update the game state accordingly. Remember that a participant can disconnect from an ongoing game at any time, so your code needs to deal with this and act accordingly.

During the game, each player will perform actions that will result in an update being sent to the other players.

The following code shows how to send a real-time message to all participants in a room.

```
public void sendGameUpdate(byte[] data, Room room) {
    getGamesClient().sendUnreliableRealTimeMessageToAll(data,
                                               room.getRoomId());
}
```

Data Messaging

The messaging part of the real-time multiplayer API is very interesting. It allows you to send messages with data between players in a `Room` without any additional servers or other infrastructure needed by you. Three types of communication are supported by this API:

- **Reliable messaging:** Allows you to send a message with a maximum of 1400 bytes with reliable data delivery, integrity, and ordering. This means that all messages will arrive and in the right order. However, because of network latency and such, there can be a significant delay between two messages. This should be used for data that needs to be delivered but where latency is not an issue.

- **Unreliable messaging:** This allows you to send messages with a maximum of 1168 bytes. There is no guarantee of delivery or data arriving in order. Integrity of individual messages is preserved, but you need to implement your game logic so that it doesn't depend on every one of these messages being delivered or if they're delivered in the right order. These messages usually have a much lower latency than the reliable messages and can thus be used for a real-time scenario.

- **Socket-based messaging:** This enables streaming of data between players, instead of delivering distinct messages. The socket-based messaging has the same limits as unreliable messaging, but usually has lower latency than reliable messaging. However, this method of communication is more complex, and you should use unreliable or reliable messaging as much as possible.

All three types of messaging are done through the `GameClient` class. Receiving messages is handled by adding a `RealTimeMessageReceivedListener` to the `Room` before starting a game session.

Messaging Strategy

When using the real-time multiplayer API, your players can connect across networks. Google's infrastructure behind these services allows players to be on completely different networks and still be able to send messages with relatively low latency.

However, you still need a smart strategy for sending messages between participants in a game. Although the name of the service implies real-time aspects, that's not altogether the case. There may be hundreds of milliseconds or even seconds in latency between two players, depending on their respective network configuration.

The goal is to send as few messages as possible and only with data that's absolutely necessary. For instance, in the case of a multiplayer racing game, you need to communicate two things from a participant: current velocity (speed and direction) and current position. Each instance of the game then calculates the position of the local player's cars and updates the view accordingly. The position of the different players won't match exactly between the players, but it will be close enough for the game to feel consistent.

When a player changes the speed or direction of his car, your game will send an update with this information to the other participants. Because this will change frequently, these messages should be sent as *unreliable messages* to reduce latency. When receiving one of these messages, the game will update the speed and direction of the local representation of that participant accordingly. Because the order for these messages isn't guaranteed, they should also contain a sequence number so that your game can discard messages that arrive out of order.

Because unreliable messages might also be lost, you also need to send a few *reliable messages* that can be used as more reliable checkpoints in the game. This way, even if one participant drops a number of messages with speed and direction updates, the other players will eventually receive the correct position for that player.

The following example uses the class `Car` to represent each participant in the racing game:

```
class Car {
    String participantId;
    Point position;
    Point velocity;
}

public static final byte POSITION_DATA = 1;
public static final byte VELOCITY_DATA = 2;
private HashMap<String, Car> mCars = new HashMap<String, Car>();

@Override
public void onRealTimeMessageReceived(RealTimeMessage realTimeMessage) {
    String participantId = realTimeMessage.getSenderParticipantId();
    Car car = mCars.get(participantId);
    byte[] messageData = realTimeMessage.getMessageData();
    switch (messageData[0]) {
        case POSITION_DATA:
            car.position.set(messageData[1], messageData[2]);
            break;
        case VELOCITY_DATA:
            car.velocity.set(messageData[1], messageData[2]);
            break;
    }
}


public void simpleRaceGameLoop() {
    for (Car car : mCars.values()) {
        car.position.offset(car.velocity.x, car.velocity.y);
    }
    SystemClock.sleep(100);
}
```

Whenever a message arrives, you check the first `byte` to see if it's an update to a car's position or its velocity. Here, you update the state of the variable for that `Car`.

Meanwhile, the `simpleRaceGameLoop()` loops continuously during the game and updates the position of each car using the last known velocity. This method is called *dead-reckoning* and is used in many types of multiplayer games.

For a real game, you need to add additional information to these messages and also implement some logic to handle the cases when the player crashes the car. Also, you need to have a separate message to determine who the winner is, and in this case, the easiest way is to let each participant game calculate his finishing time and broadcast it. This way, each participant constructs the final result using the input from the other participants.

The preceding example uses the raw byte array directly for the necessary data, which can work fine if you have only a small variation of your messages and don't send complex data structures. However, as soon as your messages increase in complexity, I highly recommend that you use Google Protocol Buffers. See Chapter 9 for details on how to integrate this into your application.

Implementing real-time multiplayer games is usually very complicated. But with the new Google Play Game Services APIs, implementation has now became much easier. You no longer need to deal with all the difficult aspects of networking and can focus on the actual game content, thus I expect a lot of really innovative multiplayer games to appear.

Summary

By adding a cloud backend to your application, you can greatly enhance the user experience. Many users have more than one device, and by utilizing the online services available for syncing data or interacting with existing Google services, your application can fit more seamlessly into the entire ecosystem.

The Google Play Services APIs for Android provide a set of very powerful APIs for authorization, real-time multiplayer integration, and push notifications using GCM, to name a few. You can select the parts of these services and APIs that are most appropriate for your application.

Because most of these services have a free tier on the Google Cloud Platform, you can start experimenting to get a better understanding of how they work and what they can provide.

Further Resources

Websites

Main site for Google Play Services: `http://developer.android.com/google/index.html`

Main site for Google Cloud Platform: `https://cloud.google.com`

Google Play Game Services samples and helper libraries: `https://github.com/playgameservices/android-samples`

Multiplayer API for Google Play Games Services: `https://developers.google.com/games/services/common/concepts/realtimeMultiplayer`

Synchronized stopwatch demo using Google Cloud Endpoints and Cloud Messaging: `http://bradabrams.com/2013/06/google-io-2013-demo-android-studio-cloud-endpoints-synchronized-stopwatch-demo`

Chapter 20
Distributing Applications on Google Play Store

Publishing Android applications has become very easy thanks to all the improvements made to the Google Play Store. Google provides a number of useful tools, guides, and checklists that will help you in the process of getting your application out to your users. In order to gain access to the Google Play Console, you must first register for a publisher account and set up a Google Wallet Merchant Account if you want to sell apps or support in-app purchases. You do this through the Google Play Developer Console, which you can find at `https://play.google.com/apps/publish` (see Figure 20-1).

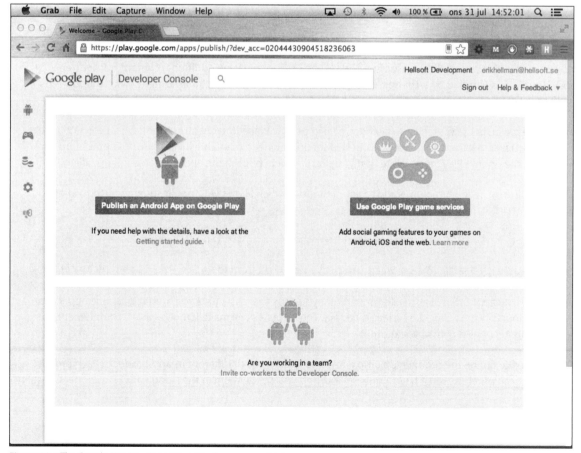

Figure 20-1 The Google Play Developer Console after a successful sign-up

Google Play supports additional features such as an advanced In-app Billing service that lets you sell digital content from within your application and provides the means by which users can sign up for a subscription for a service within your application. Both of these features are managed by the In-app Billing APIs that I cover in this chapter.

If you don't want to charge for your application or for digital in-app content but still want to have some revenue from your application, you can integrate ads. You do so by using the Google AdMob Ads SDK, which lets you place ad banners in your application as standard Android View objects.

In some situations, you may want to verify that your paid application is licensed to run on the most current device. To support this, Google provides the Google Play Licensing Service, which lets you perform automatic verifications on the purchase state of an application. You'll find a guide for integrating this service in this chapter.

Android limits APK files distributed through Google Play to 50MB. Some games and apps require resources that exceed this limit, which is why Google Play supports the use of APK extension files. I provide a guide for using this service in the section, "APK Expansion Files," later in this chapter.

In-app Billing

Although selling your application is the most obvious way of monetizing your application, sometimes it's more efficient to provide your application for free and rely on users purchasing additional content from within your application. This is handled by an In-app Billing service that lets users buy digital content or subscriptions for a specific application.

To get started with in-app purchases, you need a valid Google Wallet Merchant Account, which you find in the Google Play Developer Console. Once you get this set up, you need to enable billing for your application and upload it to the Google Play Store. (Note that you don't need to publish the app to enable in-app billing.)

Start by adding the following permission to your manifest, which allows your application to perform in-app purchases:

```
<uses-permission android:name="com.android.vending.BILLING" />
```

Next, you must copy the file `IInAppBillingService.aidl` from the `play_billing` directory in the Android SDK extras and place it in the package `com.android.vending.billing` under the `aidl` sources directory of your application. I also recommend that you copy the `util` package from the sample application TrivialDrive found in the `play_billing` directory. These classes will make it much easier to implement the In-app Billing API in your own application.

You also need to define the product IDs (also known as SKUs) for your different in-app products. Each product that the user can purchase must have a unique SKU, and you define them in the Google Play Developer Console as follows:

```
public static final String APPLE_SKU = "apple";
public static final String BANANA_SKU = "banana";
public static final String ORANGE_SKU = "orange";
public static final String AVOCADO_SKU = "avocado";
public static final String LIME_SKU = "lime";
public static final String[] FRUIT_SKUS = new String[] {APPLE_SKU,
                                                        BANANA_SKU,
                                                        ORANGE_SKU,
                                                        AVOCADO_SKU,
                                                        LIME_SKU};
private Inventory mInventory;
private Set<String> mOwnedFruits = new HashSet<String>();
```

When your application starts, you create the `IabHelper` class that you copied from the TrivialDrive samples application, as shown in the following code:

```
@Override
protected void onCreate(Bundle savedInstanceState) {
    super.onCreate(savedInstanceState);
    setContentView(R.layout.activity_main);
    mHelper = new IabHelper(this, BASE_64_PUBLIC_KEY);
    mHelper.startSetup(new IabHelper.OnIabSetupFinishedListener() {
        @Override
        public void onIabSetupFinished(IabResult result) {
            if(!result.isSuccess()) {
                // TODO Error handling of In-App Billing integration!
            }
        }
    });
}
```

Load the current `Inventory` for all the products, as shown next. This class is also part of the `utility` package that you copied from the samples. This query also allows you to check whether the current user has purchased a specific SKU.

```
private void loadFruitInventory() {
    mHelper.queryInventoryAsync(true,
            new IabHelper.QueryInventoryFinishedListener() {
        @Override
        public void onQueryInventoryFinished(IabResult result,
                                             Inventory inventory) {
            if(result.isSuccess()) {
                mInventory = inventory;
                mOwnedFruits.clear();
                for (String fruitSku : FRUIT_SKUS) {
                    if(inventory.hasPurchase(fruitSku)) {
                        mOwnedFruits.add(fruitSku);
                    }
                }
            }
        }
    });
}
```

In-app purchases are asynchronous because they will start an `Activity` in the Google Play Store application. The following is the code for launching the purchase flow for buying a fruit. Note that you also have to implement `onActivityResult()` and call `handleActivityResult()` on the helper class.

```
@Override
protected void onActivityResult(int requestCode, int resultCode, Intent
data) {
    if(!mHelper.handleActivityResult(PURCHASE_FRUIT, resultCode, data)) {
        super.onActivityResult(requestCode, resultCode, data);
    }
}

private void purchaseFruit(String sku) {
    // User doesn't own this fruit yet
    if (!mOwnedFruits.contains(sku)) {
        mHelper.launchPurchaseFlow(this, sku, PURCHASE_FRUIT,
                new IabHelper.OnIabPurchaseFinishedListener() {
                @Override
                public void onIabPurchaseFinished(IabResult result,
                                                    Purchase info) {
                    if (result.isSuccess()) {
                        mOwnedFruits.add(info.getSku());
                    } else {
                        // TODO Error handling!
                    }
                }
            }, mBase64UserId);
    }
}
```

Consuming Products

Once a product is purchased, it can be "consumed." Using consumable objects is useful in games—for example, virtual coins or, in this case, virtual fruit. The following example shows how to "consume" such a virtual fruit that the user has purchased:

```
private void consumeFruit(String sku) {
    mHelper.consumeAsync(mInventory.getPurchase(sku),
                    new IabHelper.OnConsumeFinishedListener() {
        @Override
        public void onConsumeFinished(Purchase purchase, IabResult result)
{
            if(result.isSuccess()) {
                Log.d(TAG, "Purchase successful!");
                mOwnedFruits.remove(purchase.getSku());
            }
        }
    });
}
```

In-app Subscriptions

It's also possible to implement subscriptions as part of the In-app Billing API. Doing so allows users to confirm a recurring charge to their Google Play account. The recurrence is either monthly or yearly (this might change in the future), and the API also supports a first-time free trial for your subscriptions.

Starting the subscription purchase flow works the same way that it does with normal in-app purchases, as shown in the following example:

```
private void subcribeToUnlimitedFruit() {
    if (mHelper.subscriptionsSupported()) {
        mHelper.launchSubscriptionPurchaseFlow(this,
                UNLIMITED_FRUIT_SUBSCRIPTION,
                SUBSCRIBE_UNLIMITED_FRUIT,
                new IabHelper.OnIabPurchaseFinishedListener() {
                    @Override
                    public void onIabPurchaseFinished(IabResult result,
                                                      Purchase info) {
                        if (result.isSuccess() &&
                                UNLIMITED_FRUIT_SUBSCRIPTION.
                                        equals(info.getSku())) {
                            mUnlimitedFruits = true;
                        } else {
                            // TODO Error handling...
                        }
                    }
                });
    }
}
```

How you decide to utilize the In-app Billing API in your application depends on what your application or games do. The preceding example uses fruit, and you treat the fruit as consumables that will be removed from the user's purchased items once the fruit is consumed. If you provide an In-app Billing service for removing ads or upgrading to a Pro version of your applications, then you should not treat the purchases as consumables.

In-app subscriptions aren't supported in all countries, which is why you should always check whether they're available before presenting them to the user. Also, remember that subscriptions involve your commitment to continue to deliver content or services for users who sign up.

Ads in Android Applications

Although selling your application or integrating in-app purchases are ways of monetizing your work, doing so may not always be a viable choice. For example, if you wish to provide the application for free to increase the number of users, you can instead integrate ads that will give you a way to monetize your application while still providing it free-of-charge to your users. Google supports in-app ads through its AdMob services. To use this service, you need to sign up with AdMob at http://www.google.com/ads/admob.

Ironically, by combining ads with an in-app purchase that allows users to get rid of the ads, you can create an additional method for monetizing on your application. In this section, I show how you can integrate ads through the AdMob service provided by Google and also how you can provide the option for removing those ads through an in-app purchase.

To start, you need to download the AdMob SDK for Android, which you can find at `https://developers.google.com/mobile-ads-sdk`. Unzip the archive and copy the file `GoogleAdMobAdsSdk-6.4.1.jar` to the `libs` directory of your project. Next, add the following dependency in your Gradle build script:

```
compile files('libs/GoogleAdMobAdsSdk-6.4.1.jar')
```

You now have the AdMob SDK for Android integrated into your project.

Next, you add the permissions as well as the `AdActivity` to your manifest, as shown here:

```
<uses-permission android:name="android.permission.INTERNET" />
<uses-permission android:name="android.permission.ACCESS_NETWORK_STATE" />

<application
        android:allowBackup="true"
        android:icon="@drawable/ic_launcher"
        android:label="@string/app_name"
        android:theme="@style/AppTheme">
    <activity android:name="com.google.ads.AdActivity"
            android:configChanges="keyboard|keyboardHidden|
                                   orientation|screenLayout|
                                   uiMode|screenSize|
                                   smallestScreenSize"/>
```

The simplest way to integrate ads in your application is by using the class `com.google.ads.AdView`. You can use this class either in your XML layouts or programmatically in Java.

Here is a simple example of using the `AdView` in your XML layout:

```
<LinearLayout xmlns:android="http://schemas.android.com/apk/res/android"
              xmlns:ads="http://schemas.android.com/apk/lib/com.google.
ads"
              xmlns:tools="http://schemas.android.com/tools"
              android:layout_width="match_parent"
              android:layout_height="match_parent"
              tools:context=".AdDemo">
    <com.google.ads.AdView
            android:id="@+id/adView"
            android:layout_width="wrap_content"
            android:layout_height="wrap_content"
            ads:adUnitId="AD_UNIT_ID"
            ads:adSize="SMART_BANNER"
            ads:testDevices="DEVICE_ID_FOR_TESTING"
            ads:loadAdOnCreate="true"/>
</LinearLayout>
```

The first `ads` attribute, `adUnitId`, is your AdMob publisher ID. The `adSize` attribute decides how large your ad will be. A `SMART_BANNER` will adapt itself to the screen size. You can find the full list of supported banner sizes for AdMob SDK at `https://developers.google.com/mobile-ads-sdk/docs/admob/intermediate#android-sizes`. You need to set the `testDevices` attribute to the device ID for your development device. (An example of retrieving the device ID is in the section "Application Licensing" later in this chapter.) Doing so enables you to debug and test the AdMob integration, which otherwise wouldn't be possible.

In the earlier example with the XML layout, the ads are loaded automatically when the `View` is loaded. This may not always be what you want, so when you need more fine-grained control over when ads are loaded, you can use the approach shown in the following method. You can also use this method to refresh the ad manually, which will load a new banner.

```
private void loadAds() {
    AdView adView = (AdView) findViewById(R.id.adView);
    adView.loadAd(new AdRequest());
}
```

Targeting Ads

You can target the ads by giving the `AdRequest` a number of parameters, which you may want to do if you can define the context and user preferences. The following code shows how to define gender, location, birthday and a set of keywords to the `AdRequest`:

```
private void targetAdd(boolean isMale,
                       Location location,
                       Date birthday,
                       Set<String> keywords) {
    AdRequest adRequest = new AdRequest();
    adRequest.setGender(isMale ?
            AdRequest.Gender.MALE : AdRequest.Gender.FEMALE);
    adRequest.setLocation(location);
    adRequest.setBirthday(birthday);
    adRequest.setKeywords(keywords);
    AdView adView = (AdView) findViewById(R.id.adView);
    adView.loadAd(adRequest);
}
```

Another important aspect of targeting ads is determining whether the ads need to comply with the Children's Online Privacy Protection Act (COPPA). You can use this in your application to ensure that all ads displayed are "child safe" according to COPPA.

You can add the following code to indicate that your ads should be displayed according to COPPA. If you want to indicate that the ads should *not* be treated according to COPPA, change the value from 1 to 0.

```
AdMobAdapterExtras adMobAdapterExtras = new AdMobAdapterExtras();
adMobAdapterExtras.addExtra("tag_for_child_directed_treatment", 1);
adRequest.setNetworkExtras(adMobAdapterExtras);
```

Ad Colors

You can also change the overall color scheme of the ads, which is especially useful when you want to adapt the look and feel of the ads to the color scheme of your application.

The following example shows how to set a color scheme for the ads:

```
AdMobAdapterExtras adColor = new AdMobAdapterExtras();
adColor.addExtra("color_bg", "AAAAFF");
adColor.addExtra("color_bg_top", "FFFFFF");
adColor.addExtra("color_border", "FFFFFF");
adColor.addExtra("color_link", "000080");
adColor.addExtra("color_text", "808080");
adColor.addExtra("color_url", "008000");
adRequest.setNetworkExtras(adColor);
```

Use this with care, as a bad color combination can annoy the user and make them abandon your application.

Interstitial Ads

If you think banner ads aren't suitable for your application, you can instead use interstitial ads. These ads allow you to display a full-screen ad in your application that the user can either interact with or dismiss when it times out. Although more intrusive than banner ads, interstitial ads won't affect your own Views in the same way banners do.

The following code illustrates how to load an interstitial ad and display it once it's ready. All you need to do is implement the logic in onDismissScreen() where you move to the next screen in your app or game.

```
private void loadInterstitialAd() {
    mInterstitialAd = new InterstitialAd(this,
                                         MY_INTERSTITIAL_AD_UNIT_ID);
    mInterstitialAd.setAdListener(new AdListener() {
        @Override
        public void onReceiveAd(Ad ad) {
            mInterstitialAd.show();
        }

        @Override
        public void onFailedToReceiveAd(Ad ad,
                                        AdRequest.ErrorCode errorCode) {
        }

        @Override
        public void onPresentScreen(Ad ad) { }

        @Override
        public void onDismissScreen(Ad ad) {
            // TODO User dismissed the ad, show next screen...
        }
```

```
        @Override
        public void onLeaveApplication(Ad ad) { }
    });
    mInterstitialAd.loadAd(new AdRequest());
}
```

Application Licensing

When you sell your application on the Google Play Store, you have a clear way of monetizing on your application. However, because it's possible to extract an APK file from a device, there is a risk that your application will be distributed through channels you haven't approved. The many alternative app stores for Android make it virtually impossible for developers to check all of them.

Once you set up the project and library correctly, you need to add the correct permission to your manifest, as shown next. This allows your application to perform licensing checks.

```
<uses-permission android:name="com.android.vending.CHECK_LICENSE" />
```

Performing a license check is easy:

```
private void checkLicense() {
    String deviceId = Settings.Secure.
            getString(getContentResolver(),
                    Settings.Secure.ANDROID_ID);

    LicenseChecker licenseChecker =
            new LicenseChecker(this,
                    new ServerManagedPolicy(this,
                            new AESObfuscator(SALT,
                                    getPackageName(),
                                    deviceId)),
                    BASE_64_PUBLIC_KEY);
    licenseChecker.checkAccess(mLicenseCheckerCallback);
}
```

The SALT parameter must be a byte array of 20 random bytes. BASE_64_PUBLIC_KEY must be the full licensing key found in your Google Play Developer Console for your application, as shown in Figure 20-2.

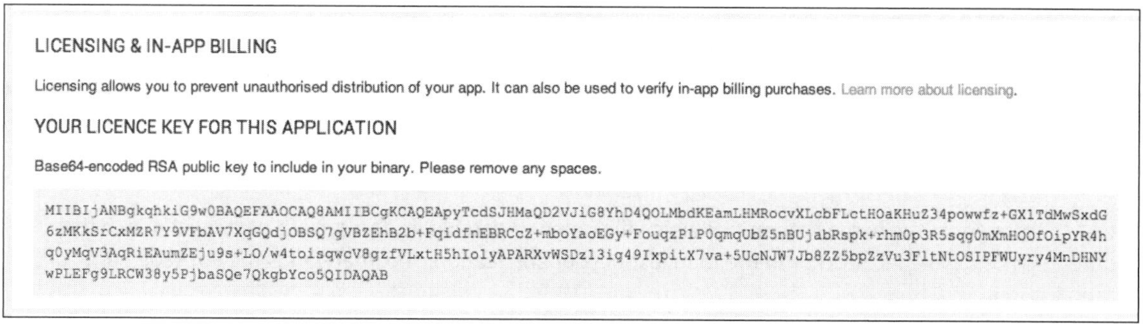

LICENSING & IN-APP BILLING

Licensing allows you to prevent unauthorised distribution of your app. It can also be used to verify in-app billing purchases. Learn more about licensing.

YOUR LICENCE KEY FOR THIS APPLICATION

Base64-encoded RSA public key to include in your binary. Please remove any spaces.

MIIBIjANBgkqhkiG9w0BAQEFAAOCAQ8AMIIBCgKCAQEApyTcdSJHMaQD2VJiG8YhD4QOLMbdKEamLHMRocvXLcbFLctHOaKHuZ34powwfz+GX1TdMwSxdG
6zMKkSrCxMZR7Y9VFbAV7XgGQdjOBSQ7gVBZEhB2b+FqidfnEBRCcZ+mboYaoEGy+FouqzP1P0qmqUbZ5nBUjabRspk+rhm0p3R5sqg0mXmHOOfOipYR4h
q0yMqV3AqRiEAumZEju9s+LO/w4toisqwcV8gzfVLxtH5hIo1yAPARXvWSDz13ig49IxpitX7va+5UcNJW7Jb8ZZ5bpZzVu3F1tNtOSIPFWUyry4MnDHNY
wPLEFg9LRCW38y5PjbaSQe7QkgbYco5QIDAQAB

Figure 20-2 The Base64 encoded public RSA key for the licensing service shown in the Google Play Developer Console

In the callback for the licensing check shown here, you simply display a `Toast` if the user isn't licensed to use this application:

```
class MyLicenseCheckerCallback implements LicenseCheckerCallback {

    @Override
    public void allow(int reason) {
        Log.d(TAG, "License check passed!");
    }

    @Override
    public void dontAllow(int reason) {
        Log.e(TAG, "License check failed - notify user!");
        Toast.makeText(MainActivity.this,
                R.string.licensing_failed_message,
                Toast.LENGTH_LONG).show();

        // TODO Open Google Play Store for this application and quit
    }

    @Override
    public void applicationError(int errorCode) {
        Log.e(TAG, "Application error: " + errorCode);
        finish();
    }
}
```

For each application that uses the licensing service, you have a number of different choices. You can notify the user about a missing license, open Google Play Store for your application, and finish the `Activity`. Another option is to perform a graceful degradation of the enabled features.

APK Expansion Files

When your game (or application) comes with a huge amount of content, the 50MB limit of APK files may not be sufficient. In that case, you can use the APK Expansion Files feature to distribute up to 4GB of additional data. This data will be stored on the shared storage where it will be available to all applications, so if the data is sensitive, you need to encrypt it yourself (refer to Chapter 12 for more on this topic). The exact location of the expansion files is `<shared-storage>/Android/obb/<package-name>`, where `<shared-storage>` is the same path as returned by `Environment.getExternalStorageDirectory()`.

You can have two expansion files, each with a maximum file size of 2GB, and they can contain any kind of data. The first file is named `main`, and the second file, which is optional, is named `patch`. The name of the file uses the following scheme:

```
[main|patch].<expansion-version>.<package-name>.obb
```

The first component of the name determines which file (main or patch) it is. The second part must match the attribute `android:versionCode` in the manifest of your application. The final part is the package name of your application.

Creating Expansion Files

The expansion files can be of any format, but I recommend using the ZIP file format because the Expansion Library provides some helper classes to read files from such an archive. If your expansion file will contain media files that you'll be loading with MediaPlayer or SoundPool, package them without additional compression; that way, you can simply load them with the standard APIs using their offset in the ZIP file.

The following command shows how you can create a ZIP file with your additional content:

```
$ zip -n .mp4;.ogg <expansion-file> <media files>
```

The -n parameter tells the zip command not to compress files with those extensions. <expansion-file> is the filename of your expansion file, and <media files> is a list of all the files you want to include.

Downloading Expansion Files

In most situations, the expansion files are downloaded automatically by the Google Play client and placed in external storage. However, in some situations, the files must be downloaded by your application. This is usually the case when the user has swapped the SD card used for the external storage or deletes the contents of the external storage manually.

In this situation, you need to perform a request using the Application Licensing service (as shown in the earlier section "Application Licensing") that will respond with the URLs for the expansion files. As a result, you must include the License Verification Library, even if your application is free and otherwise wouldn't require the Application Licensing service. Also, because it needs to perform some network operations, your application must declare the android.permission.INTERNET permission.

To simplify the manual download process, a Download Library is included in the Google Play APK Expansion Library package that makes integration of the service easier.

Start by extending the class DownloaderService, as shown here, and add the public key form the licensing service (see previous section):

```
public class MyDownloaderService extends DownloaderService {

    public static final String BASE64_PUBLIC_KEY = "<Base64
LicensingKey>";
    public static final byte[] SALT = new byte[32];

    @Override
    public void onCreate() {
        super.onCreate();
        new Random().nextBytes(SALT);
    }

    @Override
    public String getPublicKey() {
        return BASE64_PUBLIC_KEY;
    }
```

```
    @Override
    public byte[] getSALT() {
        return SALT;
    }

    @Override
    public String getAlarmReceiverClassName() {
        return DownloadAlarmReceiver.class.getName();
    }
}
```

The following is an example of the broadcast receiver that is used for starting the `DownloaderService` in case it is terminated unexpectedly:

```
public class DownloadAlarmReceiver extends BroadcastReceiver {
    private static final String TAG = "DownloadAlarmReceiver";

    public void onReceive(Context context, Intent intent) {
        try {
            DownloaderClientMarshaller.
                startDownloadServiceIfRequired(context,
                                               intent,
                                               MyDownloaderService.
class);
        } catch (PackageManager.NameNotFoundException e) {
            Log.e(TAG, "Cannot find MyDownloaderService.", e);
        }
    }
}
```

Finally, add a method in your main `Activity` that checks whether the correct expansion files have been downloaded. The following is an example of such a method that you can build upon. You should probably extend this method with additional checks of the content, just to be sure the file isn't modified.

```
private void performDownloadIfNeeded() {
    String fileName = Helpers.
            getExpansionAPKFileName(this, true, EXPANSION_FILE_VERSION);
    if (!Helpers.doesFileExist(this, fileName,
            EXPANSION_FILE_SIZE, true)) {
        Intent notifierIntent =
                new Intent(this, MainActivity.class);
        notifierIntent.
                setFlags(Intent.FLAG_ACTIVITY_NEW_TASK |
                        Intent.FLAG_ACTIVITY_CLEAR_TOP);

        PendingIntent pendingIntent =
                PendingIntent.getActivity(this, 0,
                        notifierIntent,
                        PendingIntent.FLAG_UPDATE_CURRENT);
```

```
try {
    DownloaderClientMarshaller.
            startDownloadServiceIfRequired(this,
                    pendingIntent,
                    MyDownloaderService.class);
    } catch (PackageManager.NameNotFoundException e) {
        Log.e(TAG, "Cannot find downloader service.", e);
    }
  }
}
```

This method shows how you can add expansion files to your application on Google Play, how to verify that you have them available, and how to initiate download them when needed. Use the expansion files as the first solution for dealing with content that doesn't fit within the maximum size allowed for APK files.

Summary

In this final chapter, I covered some of the features related to the Google Play Store. The features available for developers presented in this chapter can help you monetize your application as well as deliver additional content that doesn't fit within the 50MB size limit for APK files. You can generate income for your application three ways: You can sell it, add in-app purchases, or integrate ads.

Carefully consider which strategy to use when you decide to monetize your application. Although simply selling your application may seem like the simplest solution, you'll probably gain a larger user base by providing the application for free and offering users the opportunity to buy virtual goods instead. Ads are easy to include but will consume screen space in your application or game. They might also be considered too intrusive by some users. Consider all aspects before deciding on which solution works best for each application because changing your strategy at a later point may be difficult.

Further Resources
Websites

Distributing apps on the Google Play Store: `http://developer.android.com/distribute/index.html`

The Google Play Developer Console: `https://play.google.com/apps/publish`

Resources for Google Play distribution: `http://developer.android.com/google/play/dist.html`

The Google Mobile Ads SDK downloads and documentation: `https://developers.google.com/mobile-ads-sdk`

Google AdMob service: `www.google.com/ads/admob`

Index

Q